Beachside Comprehensive

Beachside Comprehensive

A Case-Study of Secondary Schooling

STEPHEN J. BALL

Lecturer in Education,
University of Sussex

CAMBRIDGE UNIVERSITY PRESS

Cambridge
London   New York   New Rochelle
Melbourne   Sydney

Published by the Press Syndicate of the University of Cambridge
The Pitt Building, Trumpington Street, Cambridge CB2 1RP
32 East 57th Street, New York, NY 10022, USA
296 Beaconsfield Parade, Middle Park, Melbourne 3206, Australia

First published 1981

Photosetting by Thomson Press (I) Ltd., New Delhi
Printed in Great Britain at the University Press, Cambridge

British Library Cataloguing in Publication Data
Ball, Stephen J
Beachside Comprehensive.
1. Comprehensive high schools – England – Case
studies
2. Educational sociology – England – Case studies
I. Title
301.5'6   LA635   80-40458
ISBN 0 521 23238 4 hard covers
ISBN 0 521 29878 4 paperback

To my parents
John and Betty

Contents

List of illustrations   *page* ix

Foreword by Colin Lacey   xi

Preface   xv

Acknowledgements   xxi

1 Comprehensive education: theory and practice   1

2 Banding, identity and experience   22

3 Two case-studies of banded forms   53

4 Adolescents, social life and school life   109

5 Subject-option choice: the selection of knowledge and the
   management of pupils   122

6 Mixed-ability: innovation and debate   163

7 Mixed-ability: implementation and change   193

8 Mixed-ability and banding compared   239

9 Conclusions   280

   Notes   291

   Bibliography   316

   Index   325

Illustrations

1	2TA: first sociomatrix	*page* 55
2	2TA: second sociomatrix	66
3	2CU: first sociomatrix	78
4	2CU: second sociomatrix	91
5	3CU: third sociomatrix	99
6	Distribution of Physics examination marks in 3CU and 3TA	131
7	The chronology of innovation and change	168
8	Comparison of subjects in their attitudes towards and willingness to accept mixed-ability grouping	184
9	The range of attitudes to and interpretations of mixed-ability across two subject-departments	188
10	Variations in the History teachers' use of worksheets	228
11	Change in teaching methods from those used with banded classes	232
12	The allocation of pupils to mixed-ability form groups	242
13	A sociogram of the friendship choices of 3DY boys	255
14	Pro-school and anti-school sub-cultures, and social class differentiation	281

Foreword

COLIN LACEY

In the late 1950s and early 1960s, just before the rapid expansion of sociology in the mid-1960s, the Department of Social Anthropology at Manchester began the experiment of applying social anthropological field work techniques to modern society. The detailed techniques of participant observation and the case-study were applied to the study of village life, small towns, the factory and the school. Max Gluckman, Bill Watson, Ronnie Frankenberg, Tom Lupton, Valdo Pons and others gave rise to a first generation of studies in these areas, and recruited staff and students from both sociology and social anthropology. As research into these areas developed and sociology became a sub-department at first equal to and then much bigger than social anthropology, sociologists were drawn into a close and fruitful association with trained and experienced social anthropologists. The effects were felt in both disciplines. Social anthropologists directed themselves to the study of emerging institutions in African and Middle Eastern society instead of leaving their work at the level of an analysis of traditional society. Manchester sociologists on the other hand pushed much deeper than their contemporaries into understanding social process and the perspectives of actors. Many of the subsequent developments within sociology were reflected in this early burst of development.

Tragically the sub-departments split and the tense hot-house atmosphere of the 1960s degenerated into a period of dispersal and less creative tension. The contribution of the Manchester department passed almost unnoticed into the expanding fields of sociology. It was not lost, however, and has now begun to re-emerge as an important strand in British sociology.

Stephen Ball's study of Beachside Comprehensive is a significant addition to this growing tradition of case-study research in schools. It can be regarded as one of a third generation of studies emerging from the early initiative at Manchester. It is certainly not the first study to be made of a comprehensive school, but it must surely rank as one of the most thorough and strategically important studies.

Its strategic importance lies in two rather different areas. First, comprehensive schools are still new and little understood institutions. Views concerning what they are and what they achieve are often subject to considerable ignorance and prejudice. Recent campaigns in the press have attempted to link disorder, violence and falling educational standards with comprehensive education and at one time it appeared that even our industrial decline was to be blamed on them—despite the fact that very few people working in industry have, as yet, had a comprehensive schooling. At the other extreme, disappointed radicals have criticized comprehensive schools as a corrupt and compromised outcome of the idealistic movement that gave rise to them. In the same vein they are sometimes seen as a more sinister, more efficient way of reproducing the class relations within society than the more naked, class-related system of grammar and secondary modern schools.

It is difficult to argue convincingly against either of the views put forward in these campaigns. Large-scale research on these questions is expensive and rare in this country. It is also extraordinarily difficult to 'measure' the outcome of large, complex, national systems of education in ways that throw any light on these 'theories'. The theories themselves are based on partial understandings of the process of schooling; the protagonists are often far removed from the realities of the classroom. In order to begin to penetrate the questions surrounding comprehensive schooling it is first necessary to appreciate what comprehensive reorganization has meant in the schools themselves and clear away some misapprehensions.

The reform of secondary education and the emergence of comprehensive schooling is sometimes portrayed as a complete and radical reorganization of our system of education. This picture contains a number of inaccuracies. First, more than 10 per cent of the relevant school population attend public or private schools, or schools that have not been reorganized (mostly of the more prestigious variety). So there is still an élite stratum of schools, educating the children of the upper middle class. Secondly, there is no comprehensive *system* as such. Schools have been reorganized in a wide variety of ways. Some are little more than old secondary modern schools with a new label and some encapsulate within one organization the divisions of the former system. Only some consciously embody the ideals of the comprehensive movement in their organization and practice, and even here the variety of interpretation and the degree of implementation are very wide. They also differ with respect to age of entry (11, 12 or 13 years old) and age of leaving (16 or 18 years old). Thirdly, comprehensiveness, in the loose sense that we refer to it today, has been with us for some time. Primary schools, as they emerged after 1944, were every bit as comprehensive as the new developments in secondary education. Seen in this way – as the mere extension of an organizational arrangement through four or five more years of school – the reorganization of secondary education carried no radical message.

At best, the reform of secondary education has given the reformists within education an opportunity to establish *some* new practices in *some* schools. Ball's account examines one such change and this constitutes the second reason for the strategic importance of the study. The change from a broad-ability banding to mixed-ability teaching constitutes for some the realization of a truly comprehensive pedagogy while for their opponents it represents irresponsible radicalism with potentially dangerous outcomes.

Ball found that the broad banding of ability within Beachside Comprehensive school had produced a sub-culture polarization similar to that found in previous studies of secondary modern and grammar schools. Making use of the findings and conceptual frameworks of these earlier studies, Ball is able to 'fine tune' his investigation and point up fascinating differences in the more complex process of sub-culture formation and polarization within the comprehensive school. Careful reading of these chapters reveals much that will be of interest to both teachers and sociologists. In particular the analysis of options and curriculum choices reveals a mechanism that in many respects replaces the streaming of earlier times. Options have apparently inherited the function of finely differentiating pupils beyond the coarse labelling of band.

The change from banding to mixed-ability grouping in the first three years of the school was a reform carried out by the staff and headmaster in opposition to advice from the local authority. Certainly, many outsiders – including some senior administrators within the local authority – regarded this change as radical folly and likely to fail. Ball's description reveals the careful gradualism of the staff in bringing about this change, the democratic and open process of voting for change year by year, and the careful pioneering of change by the English department. But what is most striking is Ball's analysis of the different motives of the staff for supporting the reform. While an influential minority are clear about their educational priorities and the need for greater equality, the majority of staff become convinced by the reform as it begins to solve many discipline problems by abolishing band 2 classes and fundamentally changing the degree of polarization within the school sub-cultures. The careful pragmatism of the majority of the staff coupled with their attachment to a meritocratic ideology is a far remove from the interpretation of mixed-ability teaching as synonymous with radical ideology. It also underlines Ball's concern that education theory has very little relation to what actually goes on in schools.

It is now more than ten years ago that I wrote in the preface to *Hightown Grammar* that one of my concerns in analysing the social process within one school was to throw light on the general problem of the lack of success of working-class children within grammar schools. 'I do so in the belief that to understand this problem within the grammar school is to assist in solving the problem of the working-class pupil within the comprehensive system, which is likely to replace the tripartite system.'

This book takes us much farther along the track. The careful reader will emerge with a deeper understanding of the constraints and possibilities that exist in our schools. It is a protection against futile romantic optimism and an answer to the alarmist or cynical critic. It is a useful and potentially powerful tool in the hands of those who believe that it is only through analysis and understanding that the potential of reformed or innovative social structures will be realized.

February 1980

Preface

This is a detailed study of a single co-educational comprehensive school, referred to under the pseudonym of Beachside Comprehensive. The overall aim of the study is to examine the processes of comprehensive schooling; that is to say, I am concerned with the dynamics of selection, socialization and change within the school as these processes are experienced and dealt with by the pupils and their teachers. The stress is upon the emergent nature of social interaction as well as the playing out of social structural and cultural forces in the school. Several specific aspects of the school are addressed: the impact of selective grouping upon the pupils' experiences of schooling, focussing in particular on the different school careers of the pupils allocated to different ability groups; the introduction of mixed-ability grouping into the school; and the impact of this upon the pupils' experiences of schooling.

In general terms the book takes up the central question of the works by Lacey (1970) and Hargreaves (1967), that is, how one can study the social mechanisms operating within a school and employ such knowledge to explain the disappointing performance of working-class pupils. Social class emerges as a major discriminating factor in the distribution of success and failure within the school examined here. Social class differences are important in terms of allocation to ability groups, the achievement of minor success roles, entry into O-level courses, examination results, early leaving, and entry into the sixth form and A-level courses. However, this study is not concerned simply with the way in which these differences are manifested in terms of rates of achievement or levels of access to high-status courses, but rather with the processes through which they emerge in the school.

The book employs a combination of interactionist and structuralist perspectives to explore and analyse first the definition and social construction of pupils' identities and their school careers, and second the social process of educational innovation. It examines the introduction of mixed-ability grouping as it is experienced and perceived by those involved, as it takes place through time and is part of the social reality of a community of people. However, the book also attempts to situate both the pupils' careers and the innovation process in a context of structural constraints and social determinants. As Sharp and Green (1976) have noted, the understanding of schooling as a process inevitably demands that a combination of perspectives be brought to bear. It involves the problematics of both social psychology and sociology if both the dynamics of interpersonal relationships and the structural relationships of the school are to be examined.

The background of the study

This book belongs to a small school of sociological enquiry into the British education system, that of the intensive study of one institution by participant observation. Though small, this tradition is theoretically and methodologically well-grounded, and reaches back through the Manchester school, and the influence of Max Gluckman, Ron Frankenburg and Tom Lupton, to the British and American era of 'community studies', to the Chicago school and the work of Robert Park, and ultimately to Weber's *verstehen* sociology. I am particularly indebted for the guidance I obtained in writing this book from the previous studies by Lacey (1970) and Hargreaves (1967); but I hope it will do more than merely repeat their work on grammar and secondary modern schools in the new context of comprehensive education. It also has theoretical or methodological links with other work, particularly Sharp and Green's (1976) study of Mapledene Primary School, which provides an interesting parallel to this book, not only in the sense that it is a participant observation study of a single educational institution, but also because it is centrally concerned with the examination of a particular educational ideology, Nash's (1973) book *Classrooms Observed*, which focusses on the influence of teachers' expectations upon the performance of pupils in the classroom; and Keddie's paper 'Classroom knowledge' (1971), in which, in a participant observation study of a comprehensive school Humanities department, she is able to establish a relationship between the teachers' perceptions and categorizations of groups of pupils, the design of the syllabus and the handling of knowledge in classroom practice.

Research in the sociology of education in Britain can be seen to be associated, though usually very indirectly, with changes in educational policy and with innovations in schools. However, for the most part relevant research has tended to lag behind policy changes and so has been aimed at investigating or rationalizing the effects of decisions already made; for instance, we had no detailed sociological studies of grammar or secondary modern schools until the process of comprehensive re-organization was already under way. I hope that this study of streaming and the abolition of streaming in a comprehensive school comes early enough in the debate about streaming to make some practical contribution to it. For although it is true that around 30 per cent of comprehensive schools have mixed-ability grouping in their first-year forms, the case for or against streaming, even in these schools, has not yet been fully debated. In some way, then, this study may contribute to that discussion before the issue becomes purely academic. Ford (1969 : 131) concludes in her study of comprehensive reform that

if one firm policy recommendation can be made on the basis of this study it is that the first step towards the improvement of secondary education is not a blind pursuance of comprehensive reorganization but adequate research into the likely effects of such reorganization. What *is* certain is that we have no grounds for certainty that the continuation of the present policy of comprehensivization will produce any of the supposed results.

Although, as noted above, I share Lacey's concern to explain the disappointing performance of working-class pupils, through the study of the social mechanisms of schooling, it is important for the reader to note that I do not share Lacey's optimism that such study will provide as *powerful* a tool of explanation as he seems to suggest. What is important, I feel, is that such studies should be done in order to explore the limits of possible change within schools, in terms of school organization and curriculum, and to achieve a better understanding of the constraints and determinants which impose and maintain these limits.

Field work

Methodologically, the orientation of this book is interpretative; following Silverman (1970), I am asking the question, What is going on here?, the intention being to reject prescription in favour of analysis. The study seeks in part to describe and understand the social system of the school in terms of the actors' interpretations of the situation. But analytically, the study addresses the task of placing the classroom perceptions and interactions of teachers and pupils within a wider social context and does not rest solely upon the interpretation of teachers' and pupils' utterances.

Inevitably in an exercise of this nature and scale, my portrayal of the school will include a number of distortions. The reality of a social institution as large and varied as a comprehensive school is far too complex and multi-faceted to be susceptible to complete or totally adequate presentation through the relatively crude and inexact conceptual mechanisms of sociology. Much of the analysis is handled through second-order constructs and categories which rigidify, simplify and reify the actual interpretations, perspectives and meanings held by the teachers and pupils. What is offered here is an approximation to reality, an account derived from the experiences of a single researcher, with all the problems of selection, chance and bias that entails; an historical snapshot of an institution in the process of change. It is crucial that the reader recognize that the school described in this study underwent a massive and radical process of change which started before the research reported here was begun, and which continued, and continues, after the research was concluded. Many of the structures and processes explored no longer exist; the changes in organization and sentiment in the school were such that it was a very different institution at the end of my field work from what it was at the beginning. These changes took place in a context of social, ideological and material constraint, and this constantly involved the headmaster and staff in making compromises in the organization of learning in their school which in a less restrictive political and economic period they would not have had to make.

I began my work at Beachside Comprehensive in the autumn term of 1973, starting with a period of general observation and familiarization. At that time the first-year cohort of pupils was divided into ten parallel mixed-ability forms plus two remedial forms, while the second- and third-year cohorts were divided into 'bands' one, two and three, according to ability. My aim, like that of Lacey (1970), was 'to locate a number of strategic areas that would enable me to gain a clear picture of the processes taking place within the school'. This involved a steady focussing down from a general acquaintance with the school to concentrate on specific cohorts of pupils and particular forms, and in some cases particular groups of pupils and teachers.

My participation in the daily life of the school, apart from observing of lessons, etc., was by supply-teaching in the first year of field work plus four periods of timetabled teaching, and three periods of timetabled teaching in the second year of field work. I also accompanied forms on school visits, went on one school trip, invigilated in exams, took registers for absent teachers, played in the staff v. pupils cricket match, and so on. During the first year of the field work I was *in* school for three days each week, during the second year for four days a week, but in the third year my visits were occasional. During the whole period of field work I observed a large number of lessons but I also interviewed pupils and teachers, carried out several small-scale questionnaire studies, sociometric and otherwise, and worked through and analysed school records and registers. I also spent some time in the Beachside community, but this was limited by the fact that I did not live in the immediate vicinity of the school.

It is important to note that the period of field work was concluded early in 1976 and the major part of the writing of this book done between July 1975 and July 1976, that is, before the initiation of 'The Great Education Debate'. In some respects the 'Great Debate' undoubtedly raises issues relevant to comprehensive education which are not dealt with here and would itself have had an impact upon the perceptions and attitudes of Beachside teachers. Towards the very end of the period of field work, the teachers were certainly beginning to introduce issues raised by the William Tyndale affair and the Manchester Comprehensive controversies, but they do not emerge as major issues in this account.

Outline of the book

The book is divided into nine chapters. Chapter 1 introduces the case-study school and examines the national context of the comprehensive debate. Chapters 2, 3, 4 and 5 explore the careers and experiences of schooling of the 'banded' pupils at Beachside. This exploration focusses on two particular forms, one from band 1 and one from band 2. In particular, chapter 4 deals with the intrusion of adolescent cultures into the school lives of the pupils and chapter 5 presents a detailed analysis of the option-allocation procedure at the end of the third year. Chapters 6, 7 and 8 are concerned with the introduction of mixed-ability grouping to replace banding; the process of innovation and debate, the implementation of the change, and a comparison between the experiences of the banded and the mixed-ability pupils. Finally, chapter 9 reviews the major issues raised in the study and returns to consider the relevances of this case-study to the general debate about comprehensive education.

Acknowledgements

This volume is based upon my D.Phil. thesis completed at the University of Sussex. I am greatly indebted to Colin Lacey, my supervisor, for his encouragement and support over a period of five years. I was also constantly helped and encouraged during all the stages of my work by my wife, Trinidad. I would also like to acknowledge the help of Richard Tudor, Barry Cooper, Dennis Marsden and Boris Ford who read and advised me on various chapters and drafts of this study, and of Margaret Ralph who typed many of the original notes from my atrocious handwriting. I must also thank the Headmaster, Staff and pupils of Beachside Comprehensive for their kind and generous co-operation during my field work.

1   Comprehensive education: theory and practice

The research on which this work is based arose from an interest in the practices and processes of comprehensive schooling and a commitment to a particular kind of sociological research: participant observation. This approach to the study of social phenomena necessarily requires the focus of data collection to be a small sector of the social world – in this case, a single comprehensive school, with its unique and specific structure, institutional culture and composition. However, this school, as a comprehensive school, is part of a nation-wide educational movement – comprehensive reorganization – which constitutes the most significant change in the organization of schooling in Britain since the 1944 Education Act. The comprehensive debate continues to be a social and political issue at all levels – national, regional and local; it sways elections, and it generates fierce emotion both among its defenders and its opponents. Thus, before embarking upon an introduction to the school which is the subject of this book, I shall attempt to summarize and analyse the national comprehensive debate, as a context within which the particular social processes evident at Beachside Comprehensive may be situated. I also hope to illustrate through the presentation of the case-study as a whole the way in which the detailed discussion of a single comprehensive school may be used to illuminate the more general issues of comprehensive education.

The comprehensive debate

Comprehensive education remains a highly contentious political issue in Great Britain, but I hope to demonstrate here that much of the political and educational rhetoric which surrounds the notion of comprehensiveness in this country ignores, or is irrelevant to, what actually goes on in schools. Indeed, any examination of the present provision of comprehensive education in Britain can only lead to the conclusion that as a descriptive category the term 'comprehensive school' remains essentially without analytical meaning.

1

The variety of types of 'comprehensive school' is considerable. The comprehensive school survey *Half-way There* by Benn and Simon (1972) clearly demonstrates the variety of forms of organization and structure of comprehensive schools; here I am more concerned with *ideological* variations and their relationship to practices of schooling. Despite the well-documented political struggles between succeeding governments and recalcitrant pro- and anti-comprehensive local authorities, an examination of the literature on comprehensive education soon makes it apparent that there is no agreement either in government policy or in educational theory about the goals and purposes of comprehensive education. There is not even a generally accepted notion of what comprehensive schools are intended to achieve, as there was, as a result of the rhetoric of the 1944 Education Act and the Hadow and Norwood Reports that preceded it, about grammar, secondary modern and technical schools. The notion of three types of child espoused by Norwood and formally recognized in the three corresponding types of secondary school designated in the 1944 Act did establish an ideological and rhetorical framework of accepted, if not agreed, policy concerning what grammar schools, secondary modern schools, and technical schools were all about. No such set of general expectancies about what the schools should be like has accompanied the spread of 'comprehensive education'. This is, in part at least, a reflection of the process of growth of comprehensiveness itself, which has been piecemeal and *ad hoc*, with individual L.E.A.s developing their own unique schemes. But it must also be seen as related to the reluctance, until recently, of the pro-comprehensive Labour Governments to legislate on comprehensivization, much less to lay down any 'policy' about its aims and objectives. Even common-sense accounts, such as may be readily given of the grammar school – for example, that it is 'concerned with giving an academic education to the brighter child' – are not available to cover all the varieties of comprehensive school. Department of Education and Science Circular 10/65, *The Organization of Secondary Education*, was the first explicit statement of government policy on comprehensive education. It did not, however, set out positive objectives for comprehensive schooling; it merely outlined the six main forms of comprehensive reorganization that would be acceptable to the Secretary of State.

This lack of a guiding philosophy was recognized in the report and recommendations of the working-party set up in 1965 by Anthony Crosland, the then Secretary of State, to 'advise him on what research was desirable and possible as a guide to policy in developing comprehensive education'. The working-party suggested first, that the facts about comprehensive schools should be ascertained, that steps should be taken to chart the growth of comprehensiveness and the practical educational problems which it posed, and that a means should be devised to measure how far various forms of comprehensive education attained their declared objectives.   (Monks 1968:v)

The National Foundation for Educational Research (N.F.E.R.) was commissioned to carry out a large-scale investigation, based on the recommendations of this working-party, into comprehensive education and to 'devise a scheme of evaluation'. Even then the first two studies to come out of the N.F.E.R. investigation were descriptive only (Monks 1968 and Monks (ed.) 1970); they worked to the guidelines of the original 1965 working-party report which stated that the objectives of comprehensive schools which distinguished them from other secondary schools could be defined as

1. To eliminate separatism in post-primary education by gathering pupils of the whole ability range in one school so that by their association pupils may benefit each other and that hasty readjustments in grouping and in subjects studied may be made as pupils themselves change and develop.
2. To collect pupils representing a cross-section of society in one school, so that good academic and social standards, an integrated school society and a gradual contribution to an integrated community beyond school may be developed out of this amalgam of varying abilities and social environments.
3. To concentrate teachers, accommodation and equipment so that pupils of all ability groups may be offered a wide variety of educational opportunities, and that scarce resources may be used economically.

                                                    (Monks 1968 :xi)

But this document for the most part concerns itself with educational abstractions, many of which are not open to strict practical interpretation or realistic evaluation. For instance, among aims mentioned are:

provision of individual welfare . . . Continuing equality of opportunity . . . no irrelevant obstacles to self-development . . . Flexibility which . . . encourages individual initiative . . . The achievement of social integration . . . An authority structure . . . which is appropriate to a school within a democratic society.

                                                    (N.F.E.R. 1966 :*passim*)

Very few of the outlines and definitions go further than these educational ideals, and the vacuum created by the absence of formulations that encompass the *practice* of comprehensive education, once the children are in the schools, has only tended to perpetuate the values and attitudes of selective schooling within the new comprehensives. Daunt (1975 :6) says of the working-party statement on comprehensive goals:

There is nothing in all its 1000 odd words, not one sentence, one phrase, one word, which relates specifically to comprehensive education or which could not be construed as totally appropriate to a selective system.

As in the case of many other contributions to the theory of comprehensiveness made at the same time, there are four main themes in this statement: first, structure, that is, putting all children in one school, but always neglecting the continued existence of the private sector in referring to a 'cross-section of society'; second, social integration, the view that a comprehensive school system would ameliorate the effects of class divisions in British society, but once again neglecting the private sector and also the unequal distribution of success in school in terms of examination passes and staying on into the sixth form; third, resources, stressing the hope for advantages of plant facilities and teaching staff that would be economically feasible in the 'big-school', which appeared to be the only size of school considered; and fourth, community, the ties and integrative relationships between a school and its community.

The other major study of comprehensive education carried out at this time, *Half-way There* (Benn and Simon 1969; 2nd edn 1972), was a descriptive survey similar to those being produced by the N.F.E.R. It also made use of a similar definition of the comprehensive school. However, despite the growth in the number of comprehensive schools since 1965, it is still the case that no consensus is emerging; as the National Association of Schoolmasters' (N.A.S.) Report, *The Comprehensive School* (1964), aptly puts it, 'Comprehensive means different things to different people.' This view is put forward by several other writers on comprehensive education; Lawton (1977) and Bellaby (1977) are both critical of the lack of educational theory concerning comprehensive schools. In particular they are critical of the lack of coherent educational debate within the Labour Party. Parkinson (1970 : 126) also makes this point. He says:

The party has not shown a sufficient understanding of the sociological aspects of educational change, and has thought too much in terms of legislative and administrative change.

The 1977 Great Education Debate seemed to indicate that this state of affairs was about to change; the Government Green Paper itself admitted that the period from the end of the Second World War to 1977 was a time when the issues of secondary reorganization and building had 'overshadowed all education debate and education planning'. However, Lawton (1977 : 163) commenting on the Prime Minister's speech at Ruskin College, which heralded the start of the Great Debate, notes that the secret Yellow Paper on which his speech was based betrayed many of the D.E.S. officials' familiar attitudes and prejudices on education, as well as a number of factual errors.

He goes on to add that 'the outstanding need now is still that the purpose of comprehensive schools should be clarified – not the least for the benefits of pupils' parents'.

In the same way that it was naïvely assumed that creation of the tripartite system in 1944 would automatically provide for 'meritocratic' selection and 'parity of esteem', many supporters of comprehensive education assume that calling a school 'comprehensive' and sending all the children from its immediate catchment area to it will eradicate the inequalities and unfairness of the tripartite system. This position fails to take into account either the different, sometimes conflicting, priorities that are held by the various advocates of comprehensive education, or the likelihood of the carry-over of attitudes and practices by teachers, from the grammar and secondary modern schools.

Almost all of the contributions towards the definition of comprehensive education have failed to take into account classroom practice and the internal dynamics of the school. Indeed it would be unrealistic not to recognize that many of the comprehensive schools set up between 1945 and 1965 and after, especially in rural areas, were set up primarily for reasons of economy, rather than from commitment to a comprehensive ideal. It was cheaper to staff, build and equip one all-purpose school than to establish two smaller schools of different types. Also, of course, many schools set up since 1965 have been a reluctant response to the D.E.S. Circular 10/65.

Daunt (1975 : 10), himself the ex-headmaster of a comprehensive school, is one of the few writers on comprehensive education to concern himself with the implementation of a *principle* of comprehensive education. He writes :

I believe that there is such an idea, which I shall call the comprehensive principle, and that it can be clearly identified and expressed.

That principle is that 'the education of all children is held to be of equal worth'. Daunt argues that in the early days of the comprehensive movement in the 1950s the impetus was a negative and institutional opposition to 11 plus selection, and the comprehensive principle really found its beginnings after the first comprehensive schools had already begun to operate. He says :

Teachers in comprehensive schools have discovered that in forming comprehensive schools we have not completed a major act of education reform but started one, have not broken the back of a problem but merely set the scene in which the problem may begin to be tackled.

Three models of comprehensive education

From the mass of literature from the political parties, L.E.A.s, Unions, educationalists and pressure groups, a number of different models of comprehensive schooling can be identified. Marsden (1971) suggests one framework for analysing these models and the categories I use here owe much to his analysis and to that of Hoare (1965). I shall refer to these models or principles as the Meritocratic (equality of opportunity), the Integrative (social engineering), and the Egalitarian. The meritocratic and the egalitarian models may in part be considered as mutually exclusive, the opposite extremes in a continuum of attitude and opinion. As we shall see later, it is possible in some cases to identify these models with actual schools. The integrative model must be regarded as a sub-type not found independently, but often, although not necessarily, in association with one of the other two. Whereas meritocratic and egalitarian principles may be considered in terms of structural differences, the integrative model stresses 'process'.

The principles of the meritocratic school are often couched in terms of 'equality of opportunity', the basis of this notion being that all children will go to the same school and therefore, theoretically at least, will have an equal opportunity to be an educational success. The weak versions of this model are usually simply presented in terms of bland statements about all children going to one school, merely a matter of the catchment area. But the stronger versions state that the comprehensive school must be evaluated in terms of its ability to maximize its pupils' qualifications, whatever may be the consequences in terms of social and societal relationships. This is neatly presented in Julienne Ford's study, *Social Class and the Comprehensive School* (1969 : 32). She says:

It is widely believed that comprehensive reorganisation will go some way towards ameliorating this situation [that working-class areas tend to have smaller proportions of grammar school places than their I.Q. distributions should justify], that the extent of 'wastage of talent' or 'uneducated capacity' will be reduced and that, in fact, comprehensive schooling will provide greater equality of opportunity for those with equal talent.

This democratic ideology of comprehensive education is argued both on economic grounds (Newsom Report 1963 and Robbins Report 1963) and pedagogical grounds (Vaizey and Debeauvais 1961), although in the former case the stress is normally upon the needs of society rather than the pupils themselves.

The view of the school embodied in this model is traditional and orthodox, and the comprehensive school is intended to function in a way that is not essentially different from the selective system, only 'fairer' and more efficient. It is not a rejection of the bipartite system in principle, but on the grounds that the selective system was good in terms of its aims, but that it was not operating adequately. For instance, in the Fabian Pamphlet, *New Look at Comprehensive Schools* (Armstrong and Young 1964 : 1), the point is made that

To achieve genuine equality of opportunity, we require . . . to reorganise the State Secondary Schools on comprehensive lines in order to end the segregation by the 11 plus examination which is now almost universally condemned on educational as well as social grounds.

The model assumes that the schools operate in a cultural vacuum and once given access to the school that the pupils will automatically achieve their 'full potential'. It ignores the factors of class and culture conflict and discontinuity that have been shown to be important in limiting the levels of achievement that children attain.

A typical example of this kind of comprehensive school would be Rhodes Boyson's Highbury Grove, which G. H. Bantock (1975 : 17) described as:

A highly meritocratic institution where the emphasis is on disciplined structured learning and achievement in examination terms. I have visited the school myself on several occasions during Dr Boyson's headmastership. Discipline was firm but cheerful; attention was paid to social matters but the aim of the headmaster was undisguisedly and unashamedly academic in the sense that learning took the first priority.

The meritocratic school is typically streamed and/or heavily set, and is the kind of comprehensive school advocated by the National Association of Schoolmasters:

Incidentally, the term 'comprehensive school' does not necessarily imply as it does in some other countries, [e.g.] the United States, that children of different abilities are placed in the same class. (N.A.S. 1964 : 3)

The integrative school model is based on social engineering, and stresses improved qualities of citizenship and the achievement of a tolerant or socially conscious society, by ensuring that all children from whatever social background go to the same school.

The primary emphasis is on the amelioration or eradication of social class differences through the pupils' experience of social mixing in a common secondary school. This particular view of the comprehensive school has been strongly represented in the Labour Party's thinking about comprehensive education. Anthony Crosland (1956 : 178), stressing the importance of creating *tolerant citizens*, wrote in *The Future of Socialism*:

In these schools it is hoped that class barriers will be broken down, children will mix freely with the 'all sorts' that are supposed to make a world and thus learn the tolerance so essential in their education in and for democracy.

Benn and Simon (1972 : 110) also discuss comprehensive education in these terms, but from a rather different political position, giving more stress to schooling as a mechanism for producing *socially conscious* citizens.

In a society with class and race differences, a school that reflects all sections of a local community will often reflect these differences in the school. The comprehensive school does not offer pupils a chance to hide from society, but the opportunity to learn in the conditions of social reality that prevail in the wider community. Where there are tensions, the opportunity to come to terms with them or to effect improvements through them, [is] just as likely to be realistic, and in the end, lasting, when approached in years to come by men and women who have had a comprehensive, rather than a segregated education.[1]

These ends are not necessarily to be obtained by a radical change in the education that is being offered in school, but rather by the manipulation of social relations by effecting or creating awareness of social differences that exist within society. In as much as the 'tolerance' version of the integrative school, as articulated by Crosland, is coupled with a belief in the maintenance of academic streaming, it conflicts, as we shall see, with the tenets of the egalitarian model. Crosland believed that to abolish streaming would be 'against commonsense', while Harold Wilson referred to comprehensive schools as 'grammar schools for all'.

Thus, as did the previous model, this fails to take into account the curriculum or the organization of the classroom as important factors to be changed in the process of reform.

The third model of comprehensive education, the egalitarian, which although not opposed to either academic excellence or improved social relationships, stresses the importance of changes in educational ethos and the structure of the learning process in school as being necessary to these ends, whereas the first two say nothing *explicit* about changes in the process of schooling. For example, Marsden (1971 : 22–3) argues that if egalitarian education is to be achieved, the

schools must exhibit a whole range of educational innovation and openness in the curriculum and teaching methods and relationships with the outside world which will bring about a new ethos and a new view of the child; only in a cooperative framework which sees children as of equal worth will equality be achieved.

Daunt's (1975 : 10) 'comprehensive principle' would certainly come into this category. Probably the best known example of this kind of school, or coming fairly close to it, would be Countesthorpe College, a school where the instrumental aims are given less importance than the expressive. Bernbaum's (1973) case-study of the school carried out for the Centre for Educational Research and Innovation describes it thus:

The attitude of a 'large number' of the staff towards the academic work of the school is ambiguous. It has already been shown that the largest staff choice for most important innovation (45%) is in the area of greater equality in social relations between staff and children. It has been shown also, that this aspect of the school gives most staff their greatest satisfaction. Moreover, when the teachers were given a list of 12 items by means of which the influence of the school would make itself felt and asked to say whether the item was likely to be 'highly important', 'moderately important', or 'not important', the two items which received the highest number of 'highly important' rulings were:
1. visible improvements in pupils' social adjustment, and
2. visible improvements in the communities' involvement.
Both of these are clearly in the expressive area. Significantly also, visible improvement in pupils' academic achievement was placed 11th out of 12 in the 'highly important' column.

Obviously, examples of the egalitarian comprehensive school are very few and far between. Marsden (1971) argues, in contrast to Daunt, that the egalitarian principles of the early post-war support for comprehensive education (cf. Banks 1955) was couched in terms of this philosophy, but that this was watered down by those who gave their support to an extension of the middle-class grammar school tradition (the meritocratic school). Most of the comprehensives created during the 1960s were probably of the meritocratic type, streamed academically and socially, and competing with grammar schools by entering large numbers of pupils for public examinations. The meritocratic view of the comprehensive school thus replaced the 'three types of child' ideology of the tripartite system with an ideology of equality of opportunity based on the achievement of an 'efficient' education system. Hoare (1965) refers to this line of support for comprehensive education as the 'rationalization' of the system.

I have argued that in the meritocratic and social engineering models of the comprehensive school, the processes going on within the school have been taken as given and go unquestioned. This is also reflected in the 'Black Box' model of the school that was prevalent in research and administration in education during the 1950s and much of the 1960s. Schools were seen to operate around and not through the curriculum and the educational process. Adherents of the meritocratic and social engineering models gave little emphasis to changes in the internal organization of the comprehensive school, assuming that the existence of the school was the only necessary condition for achieving stated aims and ideals. There is in fact considerable carry-over from the forms of school organization that existed in the grammar schools. It is only in the case of the egalitarian school that the processes of teaching and learning themselves are considered as part of what is to be changed, so that the nature, as well as the form, of the educational process becomes problematic.

In presenting this review of comprehensive 'theory', I am not concerned with the pros and cons of the various models as such. Nor am I concerned to evaluate them. What I am concerned to do is first to place Beachside School in an ideological context and, secondly, to demonstrate the lack of attention given to the processes of schooling by many of the contributions cited. Several points do emerge from this review which are open to investigation in the study of a comprehensive school and where appropriate I have taken them up in the text. However, this is not a 'test' of comprehensiveness of the kind done by Ford (1969); this is a study of comprehensive education in action in one school.[2]

These models of comprehensive schooling are derived from different, often rival, ideologies of comprehensive education. And although it has been possible to find examples for the meritocratic and egalitarian models, most comprehensive schools would undoubtedly demonstrate a mixture of these philosophies, if only at the ideological level. This may be evident in a conflict between the stated objectives defined by a headmaster and the actual day-to-day practice of his teachers; alternatively, different ideologies may coexist within different sectors of the same school. But it is clear from the brief review above that attempts to realize a particular principle or philosophy can be linked to different 'types' of comprehensive school and to different forms of internal structure.

The comprehensive ideology of Beachside School

The local authority and comprehensive reorganization
The Local Education Authority of which Beachside is a part was not slow

in putting forward plans for comprehensive reorganization in response to Circular 10/65, although these represented a long-term approach to reorganization rather than a quick switchover to a completely comprehensive secondary sector. However, prior to the circular, the L.E.A. had already set up three comprehensive schools, one dating back as far as 1957, and had plans for two more. In the words of the 1969 Quinquennial Report:

> 'These comprehensive schools had been set up in a period when the comprehensive idea itself was not universally accepted and where they had to compete with firmly based and successful grammar schools.'

Indeed, this competition was to continue until 1975, which 'was the last year that selection for secondary education was carried out and this was only in two small areas of the county' (L.E.A. correspondence). In 1975, there were 45 secondary schools in the L.E.A., 38 comprehensive, 2 grammar and 5 modern; from September 1976, all secondary schools in the county were comprehensive. However, it is also worth noting the conclusion made in the *Report and Recommendations on the Re-organization of Secondary Education*, in which the L.E.A.'s response to Circular 10/65 was presented. It states:

> 'Finally, it would be as well to refer back to the first paragraph of Circular 10/65 and the emphasis it places on the need to 'preserve all that is valuable in grammar school education for those children who now receive it and make it available to more children'. Throughout the discussions with school staffs and Governors, this need had always been in the forefront of our minds.'

The importance of this statement is demonstrated in the L.E.A.'s complete opposition to Beachside's plans for introducing mixed-ability classes for the first time in 1973. The headmaster commented that 'The L.E.A. were absolutely against it and refused to give any money or support', and that 'The L.E.A. insisted that the issue be put before the Governors and although the L.E.A. representative spoke out against it, outlining the dangers, the Governors gave their backing'.

Beachside lacks a formal statement of its philosophy or goals, as do most state schools. Indeed, it is difficult to find any definition of aims or objectives apart from the L.E.A. statement on comprehensive reorganization quoted above – and that of a most generalized kind. It was clear from interviews and discussions with the headmaster and staff at Beachside that all three of the principles of comprehensive education discussed above had their supporters. But these abstract commitments did not always coincide with observed practices and procedures. In an interview conducted during the first year of field work the headmaster offered a view of comprehensive education which clearly fell into the social engineering category.

> 'I still have the idea that an education system can have some impact on a society. Some people say that's a bit naive; on the other hand I look at the impact on people that the public school set-up has.
>
> 'It's social manipulation, it's social engineering but I think in ten years' time then one could examine the structure of the adult society in this country, and see whether, given the fact that the majority of young adults would be products of the comprehensive system, whether the school system can be considered to be one of the reasons for the nature of that society. I think it will be. I do see a much more cohesive society coming out of our comprehensive schools. I think it is already there in this school; there is a great social cohesiveness in this school getting more obvious as the kids get older.'

But in other contexts and to other audiences it was apparent that he also subscribed to the meritocratic view of comprehensive education (see pp. 18 and 187).

In questionnaire responses[3] from the staff at Beachside, by far the largest proportion, 50 per cent, put forward a meritocratic view of comprehensive education as their primary emphasis; this group included almost all – there were two exceptions – of the members of the Mathematics and Modern Languages departments. Among the comments were:

> Comprehensive education is:
> 'an education which provides good opportunities for all.'   (Languages)
> 'an attempt to provide a "fair" system.' (English)
> 'equality of opportunity.'   (History)
> 'equal educational opportunities for all children.'   (Maths)
> 'education which aims to give equal opportunity for each child to fulfill his potential.'   (Maths)

Nineteen per cent of staff put forward an egalitarian view of comprehensive education; Humanities teachers (English, History, Geography) made up two-thirds of this group. Among the comments were:

> Comprehensive education is:
> 'teaching children in an environment in which social distinctions and spuriously assessed academic distinctions are obliterated as far as possible.' (History)
>
> 'the education of all people regardless of ability, intellect, wealth, colour or life style, education in the sense that everyone should be encouraged to

attain as high a degree of development as that person wants and is capable of.' (English)

Nineteen per cent of staff also put forward views of comprehensive education which can be equated with the social engineering model outlined by the headmaster; among the comments were:

Comprehensive education
'offers a widely varying social situation achieved by the integration of all types of child.' (Arts)

'is the breakdown of socio-economic groups, to rid us of distinctions.' (English)

These comments by the Beachside teachers and headmaster may already have begun to create in the mind of the reader a picture of what kind of school it is. But that emerging picture is undoubtedly misleading. It is certainly true that these differences in ideology and commitment among the teachers have some significance for the understanding of the process of innovation, the introduction of mixed-ability teaching, which is dealt with in the second part of the book (chapters 7, 8 and 9). However, Beachside school is not a school marked by strife and dispute amongst its teachers. As is the case in the vast majority of our schools, the everyday talk and interactions between the teachers are not centred upon educational debate and discussion but upon the routine, mundane, and for the most part totally uncontroversial day-to-day running of the school as a social institution. School life is dominated by what is most pressing and most immediate; priorities are constructed on the basis of practical necessity, of survival (Woods 1977). Schools are like that, and in this respect Beachside is not in any way different. But it is a school that is well-regarded; it is seen by many parents, teachers, pupils, local councillors, etc., as a 'good school', a school that does its job well, a school that copes, that satisfies the needs of its pupils. However, this is not an image that is casually borne; the teachers and the headmaster are aware of the necessity of good public relations; they are proud of the school and concerned to maintain its local reputation. In the years covered by this study the school established this reputation on two fronts. On the one hand, the school willingly subjected itself to evaluation according to the traditional criteria of examination success and entries into higher education, as we shall see below. On the other hand, it deliberately adopted innovatory strategies in the grouping of pupils, in the introduction of mixed-ability teaching, and in the development of the curriculum. However, this second aspect of the school's reputation was not

allowed to obscure the more socially acceptable academic achievements of
the Beachside pupils.

The school moved to its present site in 1965 and was reorganized as a
comprehensive two years later, with a roll of 834 boys and girls. The roll
had risen to 1,504 in 1973 when this study was begun, with 79 full-time
staff, and part-time staff who worked an equivalent of 3.8 days a week.[4] It is
well-housed, with all the usual facilities and with the addition of a sixth-
form block, a music block and a large sports hall, although the rapid
growth in pupil numbers required the use of a large number of
prefabricated huts as teaching rooms. There is also a Youth Wing in the
school grounds.

The school serves a seaside community of 17,000 which is sandwiched
between two large and well-known seaside resorts. The Beachside
community itself contains a high proportion of old-age pensioners, being a
popular area for retirement, but there is an industrial estate and a small
holiday trade. However, many Beachside residents work outside the
community in the nearby resort town or, in some cases, London. The
occupations of the parents of the Beachside pupils also included a very high
proportion of self-employed artisans – painters and decorators, plumbers,
electricians, etc. In fact, the employment structure of the community
produces a particularly narrow range of socio-economic backgrounds
among the pupils. This was noted by the headmaster in my first interview
with him.

> 'The intake of pupils, reflecting the community as a whole, does not cover
> the full socio-economic spectrum. It particularly lacks kids from cultured
> backgrounds.'

His comment was borne out in the social class statistics I collected from the
pupils (see table 1.1). Over 50 per cent of the pupils in this sample reported
their parents' occupation either as skilled manual or routine non-manual;
only 7 per cent fall into the extremes of either unskilled manual or
professional and managerial. There is no basis of traditional working-class

Table 1.1. *Social class distribution 1973–4*[5]

I	II	IIIN	IIIM	IV	V	Unclass	Total
41	132	107	358	96	18	(95)	847
4.8%	15.6%	12.6%	42.3%	11.3%	2.1%	11.2%	99.9%

employment in Beachside, nor are there any major social problems in terms of poor housing, poor social services, large transitional populations or high unemployment. Thus it can be said that while it is in no way particularly extraordinary, or untypical of many comprehensive schools, Beachside Comprehensive does provide a context in which the potential for genuine and innovative comprehensive education is high. The school is organized and run with an air of quiet confidence; it welcomes and receives many visitors, and maintains a tradition of public performances, especially in music and drama, of high quality. In the evenings the facilities are used by the Evening Institute, and recently the school has been able to encourage adults to join normal sixth-form A-level courses. Things are always happening in and around the school, and noticeboards are constantly covered with posters announcing discothèques, debates, play and music rehearsals, school trips, and visits, sports events, charity events, and the activities of a wide range of clubs and societies. The school is usually tidy and the grounds well kept; it demonstrates order and orderliness. There is an emphasis on pastoral care and discipline, with a year tutor and a deputy year tutor for each year group plus a senior tutor and senior master with disciplinary responsibilities; the headmaster chooses to expend a considerable proportion of his points allocation in this way.[6] One of the factors that undoubtedly contributes to the vitality of the school in these respects is the relative youth of the staff. In 1973 there were 15 probationary teachers on the staff together with 6 others who were in their first year at the school. The turnover of staff since the comprehensive reorganization had left only 18 staff with more than five years' service at Beachside. In some cases this meant a turnover of whole departments. All the 1971–2 staff from Chemistry, Religious knowledge, Physics, Needlecraft, Home Economics and Human Studies, and all but 2 of Maths and English, the two largest departments, had left by 1975–6. In some schools, a turnover of staff of this kind would signify problems, poor interpersonal relations or stressful working conditions, but this was not so at Beachside; for many of those who left the school during this period, it provided a springboard for promotion, a basis for career development.

This picture of the school must not, however, be taken to indicate that the school was without its problems or that the staff and headmaster were complacent. As we shall see in chapters 2 and 3, there were many forms, especially those from band 2, which presented considerable disciplinary problems to the teachers, and, as we shall see in chapter 7, discipline and 'improvements in social atmosphere' were major factors in the decision to replace the grouping of pupils by bands with mixed-ability classes. Nor

would it be accurate to portray the school as immune to or cut off from
outside influences and effects; the importance of the encroachment of
aspects of teenage cultures into the school in the third, fourth and fifth
years is examined briefly in chapter 4. However, these 'blackspots' in the
school, as one member of staff referred to them, are not represented in the
'preferred view'[7] that is held by most of the staff and which is offered to
outside audiences. Neither do these 'blackspots' adequately represent the
experience of the school for most of its pupils. Despite its emphasis upon
pastoral care, the large proportion of young staff and the time and effort
devoted to extra-curricular and expressive activities, the ethos of the school
is primarily academic. Indeed, as we shall see in chapter 2, the importance
given to academic achievement is not unrelated to the emergence of
disciplinary problems within the system of banding pupils.

Beachside's change from a secondary modern to a comprehensive school
involved 'a considerable change in the nature of the school' (headmaster).
From being a school with only a handful of pupils attempting O-levels, it
quickly became one with a full range of pupil abilities, striving for high
levels of academic excellence and a high rate of examination passes. Benn
and Simon (1972 : 65–6) suggest that this is a pattern typical of new
comprehensives :

Certainly it seems that schools intensify their traditional aspects during the
transitional stage . . . In matters of uniform, speech days and the stress of G.C.E.
academic attainment to the exclusion of other forms of excellence, it is almost as if
comprehensive schools were saying 'we can easily beat selective schools at their
own game'.

It may fairly be argued that Beachside remains strongly in this phase. Once
reorganized as a comprehensive, academic excellence was quickly established as the central tenet of the value system of the school. This academic
orientation, what Lacey (1974) refers to as a 'pressured academic
environment', may be demonstrated by reference to a number of
indicators :

1. Considerable importance is attributed to examination passes and
university attainment by the headmaster and staff (see chapter 5).
Examination passes and particular academic successes, like the two pupils
who obtained Oxbridge places in 1974, were always given major emphasis
in the headmaster's reports to the Governors and his addresses at Speech
Day.

2. *All* pupils entering the fourth year embark upon a full programme of

examination courses at O-level or C.S.E. Mode I or Mode III. There are no non-examination pupils at this stage.

3. There is no limit to the possible number of O-levels that can be taken by one pupil, provided he or she is considered capable. Many take eight or nine O-level subjects in the fourth and fifth year.

4. The sixth form is housed in its own specially designed teaching block and access to A-level courses is carefully monitored.

5. Only two periods per week (out of a total of forty) are devoted to Social Education courses in the fourth and fifth year.

6. There is no integration of subjects; all subjects are timetabled separately.[8]

7. As may be seen from table 1.2, a large proportion of sought-after A-level teaching devolves on the heads of department and the second-in-department teachers.

It is difficult to arrange all categories of teaching in a strict order of prestige, but after A-level, the most sought-after kinds of teaching were O-

Table 1.2. *Analysis of the timetable for the eight academic subject departments with three or more members of staff, 1974–5[a] (average number of periods taught at that level per member of staff). (Percentages refer to the proportion of the timetable taught by each group in each category)*

	Heads of department (8)	Seconds in department (8)	Others (29)	Totals (45)
A-level	7.75 (39.74%)	4.5 (23.08%)	2.0 (34.18%)	100%
Other sixth-form[b]	2.80 (35.04%)	1.2 (15.02%)	1.1 (49.94%)	100%
O-level[b]	8.67 (40.23%)	4.0 (18.55%)	2.45 (41.21%)	100%
C.S.E.	1.00 (5.25%)	4.0 (21.06%)	3.86 (73.67%)	100%
Band 1	0.75 (5.88%)	2.43 (19.06%)	2.64 (74.06%)	100%
Band 2	1.63 (12.66%)	4.14 (32.14%)	1.96 (55.2%)	100%
Band 3 and remedial	1.00 (21.62%)	0.00 –	1.00 (78.38%)	100%
Mixed-ability	6.25 (10.82%)	9.00 (15.59%)	11.72 (73.59%)	100%
	29.85	29.27	26.74[c]	

[a]Maths, English, Chemistry, Physics, Languages, Geography, History, Biology.
[b]Maths and English are not included in the O-level computation as English is taught in mixed-ability classes and Maths is setted.
[c]The totals differ because of the extent of part-time teaching across the departments by specialist teachers and the administrative staff.

level and band 1. In addition to A-level, the majority of other sixth-form and O-level teaching is retained by the heads of departments and their deputies. But the 'others' are responsible for three-quarters of the C.S.E., band 3 and remedial lessons, and over half of the difficult-to-teach band 2 lessons, although it is interesting to note that the departmental deputies are responsible for a third of the band 2 lessons. This is an indication of their disciplinary role with 'problem forms' and is a reflection of the nexus between status and experience which exists for these people at this stage in their professional career. However, compared with a similar analysis of a grammar school timetable by Lacey (1970 : 161), this table does show certain differences in the way that teaching is distributed. For example, 59 per cent of A-level teaching was retained by the grammar school heads of department compared with 39.74 per cent here. The comprehensive heads of department retained 40.23 per cent of the O-level teaching, whereas 41.84 per cent of express stream teaching was retained by the grammar school heads. While the division is less clear-cut and stark than in the grammar school, it is apparent that the teacher-resources within the comprehensive school are allocated differentially according to the pupils' ability. Thus the most experienced teachers spend most of their time teaching the most able pupils. This is a reflection of the fact that the social and psychological rewards offered by the school to its pupils accrue to those who are academically successful and that academic achievement tended to be the single criterion of 'success' in the school. As we shall see, the poor academic performance of the band 2 and band 3 pupils in both internal and public examinations tends to be one of the major aspects of the teachers' poor perception of these forms in general.

However, the 'pressured academic environment' at Beachside is not simply an artefact of the internal organization of the school. As suggested by Benn and Simon (1972; quoted above), the headteachers of many new comprehensives are also concerned to create a public identity for their school in terms of traditional measures of success. It was clear that the headmaster at Beachside felt pressures upon him to achieve the same sort of standards in O-level and A-level results and university places that a grammar school might achieve. It was also apparent that he considered these traditional ways of measuring a school's competence as important in themselves. In one of three interviews he said:

> 'When I came down here there was a situation where we were in competition with the Wallsea Grammar School and high schools for the first year or two during comprehensive reorganization. We all thought that it was very important that we managed to recruit those kids. Clearly

the parents of the able kids who were coming here were very suspicious about it all, wondering whether this school was going to be able to cope with teaching abler children, having grown out of a secondary modern. So one of our early, necessary objectives was their faith.'

And in the 1974 Governors' Report, which was dominated by examination statistics, the headmaster wrote:

'I hope that you may agree that the presentation of this report, more detailed and statistical than usual, is apt at a time when we are bound to be seeking yardsticks to measure what the comprehensive has achieved in its first full cycle.'

But apart from 'those activities, procedures and judgments involved in the acquisition of specific skills' (the instrumental order), there are several other aspects of the school involving 'the promotion of values and their derived norms' (the expressive order) which tend to define it in terms of 'traditional' (educational) values (Bernstein *et al.* 1966). The pupils at Beachside are expected to wear school uniform, although the regulations do allow girls to wear trousers. The school also possesses several other aspects of the ritual and ceremony of traditional grammar school education, including formal assemblies, speech days with visiting dignitary, a separate and privileged sixth form, school detentions, school prizes, the headmaster's report, the ritual of reward in the handing out of examination certificates and sports colours, a school hymn, a school choir, and school concerts and plays. There is no House system, but clearly the school is marked by a number of consensual rituals, 'which function so as to bind together all the members of the school, staff and pupils, as a moral community' (Bernstein *et al.* 1966 : 429). The differentiating rituals which preserve the separations of age and sex and status are also maintained within the school. While retaining many of the expressive rituals of the grammar school tradition, however, Beachside operated with few academic rituals. There was no equivalent to the academic House points system noted by Lacey (1970), nor were form positions calculated for the Christmas and summer examinations, and the awarding of academic prizes at Speech Day was abandoned in 1971.[9]

The organization of knowledge and the nature of pedagogic relationships between teachers and pupils in the school are also important aspects of the ethos of the school, especially insofar as they reflect the social relations of schooling at Beachside. I shall deal with this in greater detail in chapter 7, but here I wish to comment briefly on the social organization of the school's curriculum, following Bernstein's (1971) notions of *classifi-*

cation and *framing*. These terms refer to the organization of and relationship between subjects in the school and the organization of teaching and learning. Classification refers to the degree of boundary maintenance between subjects, and framing to 'the degree of control teacher and pupil possess over the selection, organization, and pacing of the knowledge received in the pedagogical relationship' (Bernstein 1971). In general terms, the organization of the curriculum and pedagogy at Beachside at the time the study began falls clearly within the category of what Bernstein calls a *collection code*: that is, it is represented by strong classification and strong framing. For the most part, teaching methods were traditional and didactic and all curriculum subjects were timetabled and taught separately,[10] the only exceptions being in certain areas of the fourth and fifth year C.S.E. curriculum. As Bernstein (1971 : 52–3) notes:

There is a weaker frame in England between educational knowledge and everyday community knowledge for certain classes of students: the so-called less able.

Many 'less able' pupils in the fourth and fifth years were allocated to internally designed and assessed Mode III C.S.E. courses (see pp. 143–4). These courses involved the pupils in community service activities and learning home care skills (see p. 134). They were designed to cater for those pupils who would have left school without taking examinations, before the raising of the school leaving age.

Summary

At the time the study began, despite the introduction of mixed-ability forms in the first year, Beachside approximated to the ideal type of a 'meritocratic' comprehensive. Anxious to justify itself by its examination achievements, it also maintains a system of organization with uniforms, prefects and detentions, etc., and other forms of consensual and differentiating ritual. The aims of the school as expressed by the headmaster and the staff stress primarily the maximization of the pupils' academic potential.

Nationally, Beachside appears to be a fairly typical established comprehensive, still retaining many features of the grammar schools with which it sees itself competing, but with an impetus for change. As we shall see, however, the extent of this impetus for change is uneven across the school, modifications to the 'traditional' system being more marked in some subject departments than in others. Despite the apparent tempering of the competitive edge of the school, the dominant view of comprehensive education here is in essence to get all children from one area into one school and then to offer them the *opportunity* to be successful. But the point is made by Marsden (1971 :26) that

if we give the new comprehensives the task of competing with selective schools for academic qualifications, the result will be remarkably little change in the selective nature of education. Selection will take place within the school and the working class child's education will still suffer.

Success at Beachside, as mentioned before, is measured in terms of examination passes, the size of the sixth form and the size and type of university entrance; these measures are reflected throughout the school in the evaluation of the social worth of individual pupils. In the classroom, teaching is formal, with the teacher as dispenser and mediator of knowledge; chalk and talk is the most common classroom technique. There is regular homework for all children with a planned timetable for every year group. Marking is competitive and there are twice-yearly examinations, although overall form positions are not used or calculated. And at the end of the third year all children are faced with specialist subject option choices and selection for O-level and C.S.E. courses.

One question to be posed in this book is to what extent the introduction of mixed-ability grouping represents a change in the aims and objectives of the school and its philosophy and ethos, and what is the impact of the mixed-ability innovation on the role of the teacher and on teaching methods. From an outsider's viewpoint and as presented in the statistics of comprehensivization, the move to mixed-ability grouping is usually taken to be indicative of a move to a more progressive and egalitarian form of schooling, in the same way that 'going comprehensive' has been taken to mean the provision of a 'fairer' system of education. But so far there is little evidence from research to suggest that the abolition of a system of overt organizational selection in a school will establish a more egalitarian form of education. It may be that, in the same way that the I.Q. test, the 11 plus and the comprehensive school itself were expected to eradicate the social selectivity of British education and failed, the organizational change to mixed-ability will also prove to be an egalitarian myth.

2 Banding, identity and experience

The account of the Beachside pupils' experiences of comprehensive schooling begins with an examination of the banding system. I intend to look in some detail at this, for three reasons: first, its introduction and consequences are important in the overall process of innovation at Beachside, which lasted several years and which involved changing from a system of grouping pupils by 'fine streaming' to mixed-ability grouping; secondly, it provides a framework of historical, institutional and social factors that are crucial in the understanding of this process of innovation and its outcomes; and thirdly, it provides a basis of comparison for the mixed-ability grouping in terms of differences observed in the school lives of teachers and pupils. In particular, an examination of the banding system is vital in understanding the categories and concepts that teachers work with in making sense of their classroom practice; for example, the ways in which they 'see' their pupils, account for failure and success, and define their subjects, etc. It is also important in understanding the background of rationales, commitments and purposes entertained by the teachers in connection with mixed-ability grouping. This chapter, and the following one, will also serve to explain some of the ideological, material and institutional constraints which limited the interpretation and implement-ation of the mixed-ability innovation by the teachers.

Thus, this chapter will introduce the banding system, demonstrate some of the behavioural differences between band 1 and band 2 forms, and begin to illustrate the different kind of environmental school experience that the banded pupils encountered in their school 'careers'.[1] I shall also deal with the different preconceptions that the teachers have of pupils from band 1 and band 2, particularly the establishment and diffusion of stereotypes of 'band behaviour'. The relationship between banding and friendship choice is also investigated. Where it seems useful I shall make specific references to the two banded forms on which I focussed in some detail during my field work. Many of the quantitative data employed here are drawn from sources available to me in the school, for example, form registers and the detention book.

Banding

The banding system was introduced at Beachside in the first-year intake of 1969 to replace 'fine streaming'.[2] This cohort and each subsequent first year, until 1973, were divided into three broad bands of ability. In the second-year cohort with which we are concerned, there are ten forms in all; band 1 consists of four parallel forms; band 2 also of four parallel forms; and band 3 of two forms, one of which is designated as remedial. The forms are all labelled and referred to by initials taken from the names of their teachers; 2FT being the band 1 form of Miss Foot, 2MA the remedial band 3 form of Mrs Mather, etc. Each form is timetabled separately for academic subjects, with the exception of Mathematics which is 'set' within the bands. There is grouping within the bands between forms for Games and Technical subjects.

The most important consequence of the introduction of the system of banding, as far as the teachers were concerned, was the emergence of problems of discipline and control in band 2 lessons. The headmaster explained in an interview that the replacement of streaming with banding had brought about a considerable increase in misbehaviour and disruption of lessons by pupils.

> 'It took only one year to become aware of the second band mentality in the middle band, with a very low level of participation and involvement in the activities of the school. There even seemed to be more rejection in the middle bands than there was in the middle streams previously.'

The band 2 forms represented for the staff what one teacher described as a 'behavioural and disciplinary blackspot'. There were few teachers taking band 2 forms who did not report to me at one time or another the difficulties of 'order and control' that they had. Thus, in the banding system it is not the pupils at the very 'bottom', the band 3 forms, that present most problems to teachers, as is the case with streaming. Although some band 3 pupils were difficult to control, the teachers suggested that these forms in general were more docile and more easily manageable than band 2 forms.[3] The misbehaviour of the band 3 pupils tended to be defined and dealt with by teachers in terms of emotional problems or maladjustment, rather than as belligerence.[4] Band 2 pupils, on the other hand, were frequently 'in trouble' in lessons or around the school; band 2 forms were often 'kept in'

Table 2.1. *Third-year forms. Detention record 1973–4*

		No. of detentions	No. of pupils in the form	Detentions per pupil
Band 1	3CF	24	31	0.77
	3AG	5	34	0.15
	3WK	0	33	0.00
Band 2	3DI	128	33	3.88
	3FH	76	34	2.24
	3PQ	155	34	4.56
Band 3	3LO (remedial)	38	12	3.17
	3RE	125	10	12.50

by their teachers and particular pupils were 'sent' to the deputy headmaster on many occasions. Some impression of the amount of 'trouble' that the band 2 pupils got into, and the differences between the bands in getting into trouble, can be gained from the analysis of the detention book presented in tables 2.1–2.3,[5] although the record of detentions was only begun after I had been at the school for two terms. Table 2.1 shows the detention record of the cohort prior to the one with which we are primarily concerned, but the pattern of differences between band 1 and band 2 forms is equally marked. As we shall see, the number of detentions recorded per pupil is roughly equivalent to the number received by the case-study cohort in their third year. Third-year forms were normally considered to be the most difficult to control. The differences between the bands are very clear in both years (see tables 2.2 and 2.3), the band 2 forms receiving

Table 2.2. *Second-year forms. Detention record 1973–4*

Band 1	2CU	13	32	0.41
	2FT	2	35	0.06
	2ST	9	33	0.27
	2GD	2	34	0.06
Band 2	2WX	39	33	1.18
	2BH	19	35	0.54
	2TA	108	33	3.88
	2LF	31	35	0.89
Band 3	2UD	8	18	0.44
	2MA (remedial)	2	14	0.14

Table 2.3. *Third-year forms. Detentions recorded 1974–5*

Third year		1st half-term	2nd half-term	3rd half-term	4th half-term	5th half-term	Total	No. of detentions per pupil
Band 1	3CU	6	1	0	2	13	22	0.69
	3FT	0	0	0	4	2	6	0.17
	3ST	1	3	0	5	0	9	0.27
	3GD	3	1	0	0	5	9	0.27
Band 2	3WX	15	42	33	60	35	185	5.61
	3BH	8	35	25	40	17	125	3.57
	3TA	6	35	51	1	17	110	3.33
	3LF	25	32	31	36	27	141	4.03
Band 3	3MA (remedial)	3	0	1	5	4	13	0.93
	3UD	6	39	6	18	49	118	6.56

significantly more detentions than band 1. In the 1973–4 statistics, third-year band 2 forms receive 65 per cent of all third-year detentions, and the second-year band 2 forms receive 85 per cent of all second-year detentions; in the 1974–5 statistics, the band 2 forms receive 76 per cent of all detentions. There is also a clear difference in each case between the ordinary band 3 and the remedial band 3 forms in the number of detentions received. A further indication of differences in being 'in trouble' between bands, at a much less serious level, is in the frequency of rebukes by teachers in lessons. In a small proportion of the lessons I observed I made use of the Flanders interaction-analysis grid.[6] A mark is made on the grid, in the appropriate category, at frequent and regular intervals during the process of a lesson to record the communication events just completed. Even in this small sample of twenty-four lessons, a clear difference between bands emerged in the proportion of the teachers' time spent in 'criticizing or justifying authority'. In band 1 forms, only 1.5 per cent of lesson time was spent in such justification, whereas in band 2 forms it occupied 12.5 per cent of lesson time – a figure which suggests that a great deal more time in band 2 lessons is devoted to the maintenance of discipline.

The selection of two forms

The selection of the two forms on which I based my detailed examination of band 1 and band 2 was made primarily on the basis of convenience and availability. There was a minimum of clash between the timetables of the two forms, so that the same subjects were not always being taught at the same time; and both of the form teachers were very willing to co-operate with me.[7] Both of the banded forms I chose appeared to be generally typical of their band, although every school form is always in some way unique. I have attempted to make clear in my analysis those ways in which these forms were unusual or different from the rest of the band.

Once I had decided upon these forms I began to 'follow' them. I observed as many of their lessons as possible, as regularly as possible; I called into their form rooms at lunch and break-time, and spoke to them in corridors. Generally, I tried to get to know the pupils, and once I had established a rapport I began to interview individuals, and to talk about them to their teachers and the pastoral staff. I was also given access to their school files and records. Later in the year some of the pupils began to keep diaries for me, and during the summer holidays I was able to meet some of them in the town and on the beach. The two forms I chose were 2TA and 2CU.

2CU was the band 1 form of Mrs Culliford and 2TA the band 2 form of Mrs Tanner. From the very beginning of observation these forms appeared very different from each other in their work-performance and their behaviour in lessons. The general conduct of their lessons by the teachers was also very different. Teachers found 2CU generally easy to control, easy 'to teach', co-operative, lively (in the positive sense in which teachers used the word), enthusiastic, and interested. On the other hand, 2TA were described as difficult to control, difficult to teach and to get to work, unco-operative, lively (in the negative sense in which teachers used the word), dull and uninterested. In each case these descriptions were typical of the band as a whole. My observations in other band 1 and band 2 lessons demonstrated a similarity between all the band 1 forms and all the band 2 forms in terms of attitude, behaviour and teacher-pupil relationships.[8]

The lessons of 2CU were usually dominated by the teacher, who was the central focus of activity in the classroom; the form listened quietly when their teachers spoke, responding when required, in an appropriate manner (by putting up their hand and thus acknowledging the teacher's right to call upon them, or not, to make a contribution). In many lessons it was possible to hold 'class discussions', where members of the form and the teacher were able to exchange views or ideas with the attention of the rest of the form. That is to say, activity in 2CU lessons was invariably 'task-oriented', directed towards some end, or involving some endeavour, defined as appropriate by the teacher.

The lessons of 2TA differed from this in many ways; the level of noise was normally higher than in band 1 lessons, except when disciplinary threats were used or in lessons with a 'strict' teacher.[9] The teacher's position as the central focus of activity was a great deal more tenuous and problematic. Individually or in groups, pupils would attempt to diverge from the task-activity of the lesson or actually to challenge the teacher as focus of the lesson. Outbreaks of non-task-oriented behaviour, defined as inappropriate by the teacher, were frequent, and it would typically be necessary for the teacher to re-establish the receptivity of the form as a whole or of particular groups of pupils many times during a lesson. Their lessons were slow getting under way and difficult to organize. This may be seen from the following transcript and notes of a 2TA English lesson:

2TA English with Mrs Bradley: lesson notes

The pupils are arriving singly or in small groups while the teacher waits. The time between the first arrival and the last is over four minutes. While the teacher waits for the last arrivals to sit down, the noise being made by the form is considerable. Corina Newnes is the last to come in.

Teacher 'Where you have been?'

Corina 'Mr Dawson kept me behind.'

Teacher 'What for?'

Corina 'To talk to me.'

Teacher 'Well, this is my lesson now. You should be on time.'

Corina sits down, the teacher addresses the whole class.

Teacher 'All right, let's have some quiet.'

This is shouted over the noise of the class; the teacher is standing at the front of the room with one hand on her hip; she looks displeased. '2TA,' she shouts more loudly; the noise is considerably reduced. 'Peter, I am waiting for you. [To the whole class] I told you last week that I wanted you here on time. It is nearly ten minutes gone now. If it happens next week . . . Peter, I've told you once, what did I just say?'

Peter 'If it happens next week.'

Teacher '*Right*, now stop talking to Sammy and listen to me . . . if it
          happens next week we will stay behind at four o'clock to make up
          the time we've lost.'

Two of the girls at the back are talking and writing on a small book.

Teacher 'Dorothy, bring your books and sit here.' The teacher indicates
          the empty desk at the front, next to one of the boys.

Dorothy 'You moved me last week.'

Teacher 'Well, I'm moving you again, come on.'

Grudgingly, Dorothy gets up, making her chair scrape noisily on the wooden floor, and picks up her books slowly; she goes to the front and stands behind the empty desk.

Dorothy 'Ugh, I'm not sitting next to him.'

She gestures at Wally who is sitting next to the empty desk; several of the

class laugh and the teacher looks angrily around the room; her gaze
returns to Dorothy.
Teacher 'You sit where I tell you.'
Dorothy 'Not next to him.'
She pulls the empty desk away from Wally's until there is a six-inch gap,
and sits down. The teacher seems to be about to say something to her and
then changes her mind; she picks up a book from her desk instead.
Teacher 'We began last week to look at . . .'

Teachers found it almost impossible to organize discussions in 2TA
lessons, and even question and answer sessions tended to deteriorate into
noisy shouted responses. Few members of the form would listen to their
fellows' contributions, and many pupils took such opportunities to talk
amongst themselves or to 'muck about'. In some lessons with young and
inexperienced teachers, 2TA could get completely beyond control. In
extreme cases the pupils would run around the classroom virtually
ignoring the teacher's rebukes or threats or attempts to 'teach'.[10] The
maintenance of quiet and keeping the pupils working involved special
effort in 2TA's lessons.

2TA Biology with Mr Kramer: lesson notes
The pupils are working individually on answering questions written on
the board; the teacher is going round the room to look at books and
answer queries. As he pauses at each bench to look at the pupils' work he
looks round the room to check that all is well; at frequent intervals
during his talk with the pupils his head pops up and down like a gopher
from a hole, to recheck the class.
Teacher 'Wally, get on.'
He looks down, up again.
Teacher 'Jim, your own book. Belinda, you too.'
Down again and up.
Teacher 'Come on, you three, on your own, please.'
Down again and up, and down and up again.
Teacher 'Put that scarf away, Nigel, do I have to separate you three?'
He stares at them for a second or two.
Teacher 'Are you eating, Max?'
The boy nods.
Teacher 'Put it in the bin.'
Max 'Can't I swallow it?'
Teacher 'No, in the bin. Are you eating as well, Peter?'
Peter 'No, sir.'
Teacher 'All right, get on. What's wrong with you, Dorothy?'
Dorothy 'I want you to see my work.'
Teacher 'All right, I will be there in a second. I think you can get on
           without talking, Kathy.'

The lesson continues with this constant barrage of comment and rebuke from the teacher which keeps down the non-task-oriented behaviour to a low level.

These two extracts from observation notes may be contrasted with the notes made from observation of a typical 2CU lesson, in this case Chemistry. Here the teacher's talk is exclusively concerned with the subject matter of the lesson, and there is not a single instance of 'criticizing or justifying authority'.

2CU Chemistry with Mr Baldwin: lesson notes

The lesson begins with twenty minutes of 'administration-talk' from the teacher. Books are returned and he comments on the homework, on writing up experiments, especially the method, and he explains the rationale of the marking. 'So if you got a bad mark for this homework it was not necessarily because the experiment or your conclusion were wrong, but that it was not written up correctly.'

The form is silent and attentive throughout the whole of this time. The teacher now begins some experiments with CO_2 to show its qualities as a fire extinguisher; the form is gathered round the bench at the front but are orderly, without pushing one another or talking. The teacher asks questions as he goes along, hands are raised, he chooses a respondent and the rest of the form listens to the answer given.

Teacher 'Why wouldn't I use water in this case?' He looks up. 'Chris . . .'

The lesson ends with the writing up of what was seen; the bell goes, but the class continues to work as if nothing had happened.

Teacher 'Off you go when you are ready.'

The pupils leave in ones or twos. Several remain for more than five minutes of their break-time to finish writing.

Band identities

It is clear from these transcripts that there are stark differences between the classroom behaviour of the two forms as they were in the second year. But I want to look back now at these forms as they were in the first year, in order to illustrate the changes in the pupils' behaviour between the first and second years. This is necessarily a retrospective view, as I began my study at Beachside in the same year as the new first-year cohort became mixed-ability. In order to study the band system it was therefore necessary to choose second-year forms.

It is important first of all to look at the way in which the pupils are allocated to their bands in the first year. This takes place on the basis of the reports and recommendations of the primary school teachers and headmasters of the four schools that provide Beachside with pupils. Almost all of the pupils who enter the first year at Beachside come from the four 'feeder' primary schools within the community: North Beachside, South Beachside, Iron Road and Sortham. In the cohort with which we are concerned here, the original distribution by school and allocation to bands is as presented in table 2.4 below. There is no significant relationship between primary school of origin and the allocation to bands. The process of negotiation of recommendations and allocation to bands was done by the senior mistress at Beachside. Where the numbers of pupils recommended for band 1 was too large, the primary headmasters were asked to revise their recommendations until an acceptable distribution of pupils in each band was obtained. When they arrived at the secondary school, the pupils went immediately into their banded classes.

> 'The primary school heads sent us lists with their recommendations for band 1, band 2 and band 3; it was up to us to try and fit them into classes. If there were too many in the one band, then we had to go back to the primary heads to ask if all the list was really band 1 material and that way the bands were allocated and then they were broken into classes alphabetically. There was a lot of movement between the classes at the end of the first term, but very little movement between bands.'
>
> (Senior mistress)

Thus Beachside carried out no tests of its own; the primary schools acted as selecting institutions, and Beachside, initially at least, as the passive implementer of selection. Three of the four primary schools did make use of test scores in the decision to recommend pupils for bands, and these were passed on to Beachside on the pupils' record cards, but these test scores were not the sole basis upon which recommendations were made. Teachers' reports were also taken into account.

Table 2.4. *Allocation of pupils to bands according to primary school*

	S. Beachside	N. Beachside	Iron Road	Sortham	Others	Total
Band 1	33	36	37	11	4	121
Band 2	32	16	52	13	4	117
Band 3	17	7	15	4	4	47
Total	82(29%)	59(21%)	104(36%)	28(10%)	12(4%)	285(100%)

Banding and social class

The possibility of biases in teachers' recommendations as a means of allocating pupils to secondary school has been demonstrated in several studies. For instance, both Halsey and Floud (1957) and Douglas (1964) have shown that social class can be an influential factor in teachers' estimates of the abilities of their pupils. The covariance of social class and 'tested ability' in this case is examined below.

The practice adopted by the majority of social researchers has been followed here, in taking the occupation of the father (or head of household) as the principal indicator of pupils' social class background. Although this is not an entirely satisfactory way of measuring social class, the bulk of previous research seems to indicate that, in the majority of cases, the broad classification of occupations into manual and non-manual does correspond to the conventional social categories – middle-class and working-class. For the sake of convenience, I have adopted these social class categories when describing the data of this study.[11]

In discussing the debate on comprehensive education, I made the point that a number of writers had stressed that the comprehensive school would bring about changes in the social class inequalities in education that had been created by the middle-class domination of the grammar school. This position, however, fails to take into account the importance of resources which are distributed differentially by social class (such as emotional support, knowledge of the school system, social skills, and educational skills and qualifications), not to speak of the teachers' conceptualization of pupils and the effects of streaming, which all contribute to the maintenance of these inequalities. It also ignores the fact that pupils are in many schools still selected as they enter, or soon after, on much the same lines as they had been selected previously under the tripartite system; they go into the A stream instead of to a grammar school or into the D stream instead of to a secondary modern.

Beachside was a streamed school until 1969, and was banded at least to some extent until 1975. It was not surprising, then, to find that, as analysis in other schools has shown, there is a significant relationship between banding and social class. If the Registrar General's Classification of Occupations is reduced to a straightforward manual/non-manual social class dichotomy for the occupations of the parents of the pupils, then the distribution of social classes in 2TA and 2CU, the case-study forms, is as shown in table 2.5. There are 20 children from non-manual families in 2CU

Table 2.5. *Distribution of social classes across the case-study forms 2TA and 2CU*

	I	II	IIIN	Total non-manual	IIIM	IV	V	Total manual	Unclass
2CU	5	10	5	20	12	–	–	12	–
2TA	2	3	2	7	15	8	3	26	–

compared with 7 in 2TA, and 12 from manual families in 2CU compared with 26 in 2TA. This is a considerable over-representation of non-manual children in 2CU; a similar over-representation was found in all the band 1 classes across this cohort and in previous banded cohorts.[12] Thus on the basis of reports from junior schools, the tendency is for the children of middle-class non-manual families to be allocated to band 1 forms, whereas children from manual working-class homes are more likely to be allocated to bands 2 or 3.

As discussed in the previous chapter, one of the main platforms of comprehensive reorganization has been that the comprehensive school will provide greater equality of opportunity for those with equal talent. Ford (1969) suggests that the most obvious way of testing whether this is true is 'by the analysis of the interaction of social class and measured intelligence as determinants of academic attainment'. If the impact of social class on educational attainment is greater than can be explained by the covariation of class and I.Q., then the notion of an equality of opportunity must be called into question.

There were no standard I.Q. tests available for the pupils at Beachside,[13] but, as noted above, three of the four 'feeder' primary schools did test their pupils. There was a great variety of tests used, for reading age, reading comprehension, arithmetic and mathematics. Each pupil's record card noted a selection of these test-scores, but only in a few cases were results available for the whole range of tests.

The clearest picture of the interaction between social class, test-scores and band allocation was obtained by comparing pupils who scored at different levels. Taking N.F.E.R. Reading Comprehension and N.F.E.R. Mathematics, the covariation of social class and test-scores within band 1 and band 2 is shown in tables 2.6 and 2.7. By extracting the 100–114 test-score groups the relationship between social class and band allocation may be tested. This suggests a relationship between banding and social class at

Table 2.6. *Banding allocation and social class, using the* N.F.E.R. *Reading Comprehension Test*

Test-score	Band 1		Band 2	
	Working-class	Middle-class	Working-class	Middle-class
115 and over	3	7	1	0
100–114	10	12	16	2
1–99	5	1	24	5
	18	20	41	7

Table 2.7. *Banding allocation and social class, using the* N.F.E.R. *Mathematics Test*

Test-score	Band 1		Band 2	
	Working-class	Middle-class	Working-class	Middle-class
115 and over	5	8	0	0
100–114	15	13	15	3
1–99	1	0	25	1
	21	21	40	4

N.F.E.R. *Reading Comprehension Test*
(scores 100–114)

	Working-class	Middle-class
Band 1	10	12
Band 2	16	2

$\chi^2 = 8.2$ d.f. $= 1$ $p < 0.01$.   C $= 0.41$.

N.F.E.R. *Mathematics Test* (scores 100–114)

	Working-class	Middle-class
Band 1	15	13
Band 2	15	3

$\chi^2 = 4.28$ d.f. $= 1$ $p < 0.05$.   C $= 0.29$.

levels of similar ability. Taking the Mathematics tests-scores, there is also a significant relationship. Altogether, the evidence of these test-scores concerning selection for banding was far from conclusive; the result is to some extent dependent upon which test is used. It is clear, however, that social class is significant, and that ability measured by test-score does not totally explain the allocation to bands. This falls into line with the findings of Ford (1969) and others that selection on the basis of streaming in the comprehensive school, like selection under the tripartite system, tends to underline social class differentials in educational opportunity. However, my work with these results also suggests that, to some extent at least, findings concerning the relationships between test-performance and social class must be regarded as an artefact of the nature of the tests employed, and thus the researcher must be careful what he makes of them.

Movement between bands

The separation of the pupils into bands was considered necessary and efficient, and 'the only way to teach' – that is, until banding was replaced by mixed-ability. Even then, as we shall see,[14] some staff continued to feel that the creation of homogeneous teaching groups was the only way of teaching suited to their particular subject, and the only way to do justice to the pupils of different abilities. Within the banding system, by definition, band 2 pupils were considered to be unsuited to the 'academic' teaching of band 1 lessons. Band 1 teaching was directed at the 'faster ones', those who were quite likely 'to go on to O-level'. It was thought that, when grouped with other pupils of similar ability, the band 2 pupil would be able to profit from a 'slower pace' and work of a 'less academic' nature. But, given the problems of identifying and categorizing pupils of different abilities, one important consideration in any system of streaming by ability is the extent of reallocation or movement between groups. After two completed years, the total number of band-changes in the 2CU/2TA cohort was 40. Most of the changes took place at the beginning of the second term in the first year on the basis of the results of the Christmas examinations. However, closer examination reveals that few of these changes involved pupils moving into band 1 (see table 2.8). Of the total of 40 pupils who moved band, 31 of these moved into band 2, 15 were demoted from band 1 and 16 were promoted from band 3. Only 7 pupils were promoted into band 1. As only 9 pupils moved out of band 2, there was an overall increase in size of 16 per cent, excluding pupils who entered or left the school over this period.

One History teacher commented that 'The band 2 forms are a disaster; they can just become a dumping ground for all the problem children in the

Table 2.8. *Summary of movement of pupils between bands after two completed years in the secondary school*

	In	Out	Overall change
Band 1	7	15	− 8
Band 2	31	9	+ 22
Band 3	2	16	− 14
	40	40	

school.' As only 8 per cent of band 2 pupils were reallocated, this represents a discovered error of placement smaller than the 10 per cent error found in the 11 plus exam.[15] While the discovered error of placement in band 1 turns out to be 12 per cent, the movement from band 2 into band 1 represents a reallocation of only 5 per cent overall. It is certainly possible that the 'purging' of band 1, at the end of the first term, of those pupils who had not performed as expected, may have contributed further to the inferior-status identities of pupils in band 2. The pupils who were joining these forms had already been found to be 'failures', and pupils who had been successful in band 2 were promoted out. These changes would also tend to reinforce the low academic status of the band 2 forms as a whole, in the eyes of their teachers. As Woods (1976:144) notes, 'tidying up the "misplacements" illustrates how the wedge is even more firmly driven between two types of pupil'.

After that first term, movement between bands was much less frequent. Promotion to band 1 was especially rare, as can be seen from the figures above. Even those few pupils who were put forward by their form teacher or their year tutor as good prospects for promotion to band 1 were often hindered by differences between the bands in the standard and amount of syllabus work that had been covered. For instance, it was suggested that Corina Newnes, a member of 2TA, was capable of working in a band 1 form. She had originally been 'misplaced' in a band 3 form and then reallocated to band 2. But by the time that the move to band 1 was put forward, in the middle of the second year, the Maths department considered that her Maths was too far behind that which would be required, and vetoed the idea.[16]

After the first term, the increasing differences of syllabus and curriculum which develop between the bands mean that band 2 or band 3 pupils would have to perform exceptionally well, if not brilliantly, to overcome the limitations placed upon them by the organization of the syllabus – unless, that is, other criteria altogether are brought into play.[17] But apart from movement between bands, there is a lot more movement between forms within the bands. Most of this, and some of the inter-band movement, takes place on social rather than academic grounds. Indeed, social or disciplinary arguments could be used both for and against moving pupils. For instance, two boys in 2CU, Talston and Patten (see pp. 88–90), were not demoted because of the possible 'social con-sequences', while other pupils were 'separated' or 'given a fresh start'. At the end of the second year, as we shall see (p. 77), three girls from 2TA were 'split up' and assigned to other band 2 forms. Also, at the beginning of the second year, one boy was moved out of 2TA into 2LF; one boy, Max Vassart, was moved into 2TA from 2BH; and during the course of the year one boy, Timothy Kinney, was removed from the form for six weeks (see p. 61). In all of these cases, the moves were used as sanctions against disruptive behaviour, although occasionally the impetus for movement came from the pupils themselves or from their parents (see p. 66).

Banding and band stereotypes

The fact that the pupils came to the secondary school pre-selected, sorted out into bands, may have been important in making the allocation 'real' to the Beachside teachers. As the band allocation of the pupils was a 'given', a label imposed from outside prior to any contact with the pupils, the teachers were 'taking', and deriving assumptions on the basis of, that label, rather than 'making' their own evaluation of the relative abilities of individual pupils.[18] Each band-label carries its own particular status within the school and the staff hold preconceived and institutionalized notions about the typical 'band 2 child', the 'remedial child', etc. To a great extent these typifications are based on what the teacher knows about the bands in terms of their status identity. From the teacher's point of view the behaviour of band 2 forms is 'deviant', contravening their expectations of appropriate classroom behaviour. These labels are consistent and embed-ded aspects of the system of meanings shared by all the teachers, and are not dependent upon the identification of particular forms or pupils. Once established, the typification 'band 2 form' or 'band 2 pupil' merely awaits the arrival of each new cohort in the school. I am not suggesting that the 'label' of being band 2 in itself creates a 'deviant' identity and is the cause of the 'deviant' acts described previously. But the label of being band 2 imposes certain limitations upon the sort of social identity that may be negotiated by the band 2 pupil. When persons are subjected to a process of categorization, they are subject also to the imputation of various social identities by virtue of their membership of that category. In this case, it is an identity that involves a status-evaluation and allocation to an inferior position in the status-hierarchy of the school. Band 2 forms, as we shall see, are considered to be 'not up to much academically' and most teachers find them 'unrewarding' to teach. Certainly, by the beginning of the second year in the careers of the case-study forms, it is a label that denotes a behavioural stereotype. The teachers hold stereotypical images of band identity (which I shall refer to as the 'bandness' of pupils). That is, they tend to jump from a single cue or a small number of cues in actual, suspected or alleged behaviour, to a general picture of the 'kind of person with whom one is dealing'.

In one sense, stereotyping may be understood quite straightforwardly in terms of the demands of a complex interaction situation. The classroom involves one individual interacting in various ways with 35 other individuals, and stereotyping may be necessary for the teacher to be able to order his expectations of, and thus predict the actions of, the pupils.[19] The reality of everyday life commonly involves stereotyping in terms of which others are 'dealt with'. That is, people apprehend others through patterns built up from previous experiences. But in regard to individual pupils in the banded classroom, stereotyping by the teacher may also be considered as a reaction that is based upon a selective perception or incorrect assessment of pupils, derived from preconceived notions of band behaviour. In their attempts to make sense of, and derive meaning from, social situations, people tend to organize data about other people in their environment. They tend to do so by making interpretations and inferences from what they 'know' and what they can see in front of them. Once such interpretations and inferences are made, further information is sought to confirm and strengthen them, and contradictory information tends to be overlooked.

The normal way of discussing pupils among the staff was in terms of singular and unitary characteristics, a categorical identification that tended to become a pejorative label. Thus, with regard to projects:

> 'the band 1 child, who is intelligent, loves doing projects but the lower-band child will just copy chunks out of a book and cover about four sides.'
>
> (English teacher)

The band 1 child is 'intelligent' and by implication here the band 2 child is not. Yet the discrimination between band 1 and band 2 in the original allocation of pupils makes no such distinction; these differentiating perceptions are socially constructed. The original sum-variable basis of allocation to bands, recommendations made by the primary school indicating pupils of more or less ability, is here transformed into a zero-sum perception: band 1 pupils have ability; band 2 pupils do not. Cohen (1972 : 12) makes the point that

Society labels rule breakers as belonging to certain deviant groups and, once the person is thus typecast, his acts are interpreted in terms of the status to which he has been assigned.

In this way the band stereotypes were an important aspect of the shared meanings of the staff in their perceptions of and interactions with pupils. As Cohen indicates, 'the deviant or delinquent is always portrayed as a certain type'. As labels, the stereotypes of band identity provide a framework within which the pupil must negotiate his social identity in the school. Thus the band to which he is allocated is an important constraint upon the range of possible social identities available to him. For example, 'brilliant pupil' is an identity that is not normally available to the 'band 2 pupil' because of the sorts of notions that accompany that label. However, as we have seen, there is still the possibility that *some* pupils may negotiate identities that supersede these constraints, at least in the early stages of their band career.

The framework of identities which derive from the band-labels can be seen in the following composite band-profiles, constructed from teachers' descriptions. These are the stereotypical notions that the teachers hold about the bands. As such they are also situational-expectations, that is, expectations about 'what this form is going to be like'. These stereotypes are constraints which the teacher brings into the classroom and with which the pupil has to deal.

The band 1 child
'Has academic potential . . . will do O-levels . . . and a good number will stay on to the sixth form . . . likes doing projects . . . knows what the teacher wants . . . is bright, alert and enthusiastic . . . can concentrate . . . produces neat work . . . is interested . . . wants to get on . . . is grammar school material . . . you can have discussions with . . . friendly . . . rewarding . . . has common sense.'

The band 2 child
'Is not interested in school work . . . difficult to control . . . rowdy and lazy . . . has little self control . . . is immature . . . loses and forgets books

with monotonous regularity . . . cannot take part in discussions . . . is moody . . . of low standard . . . technical inability . . . lacks concentration . . . is poorly behaved . . . not up to much academically.'

The band 3 child
'Is unfortunate . . . is low ability . . . maladjusted . . . anti-school . . . lacks a mature view of education . . . mentally retarded . . . emotionally unstable and . . . a waste of time.'

It is apparent that by the beginning of the second year the majority of the teachers 'see', that is make sense of, the classroom in terms of these preconceived notions. They act as a 'filter' upon the teacher's perceptions of the pupils. And yet they derive from a fairly arbitrary line of demarcation between pupils; the importance of these stereotypes is perhaps best seen in terms of the borderline child who would be differently perceived in each band according to the point at which the allocation line is drawn. Keddie (1971:139) also makes the point that 'what a teacher knows about pupils derives from the organisational device of banding or streaming'.

Maddock (1977 : 575) takes this even further. From a study of the relationship between streaming and pupils' identities in an Australian High School, he concludes that

Teachers conventionally typify pupils by locating them somewhere along the academic/non-academic continuum. On the basis of an assumed hierarchy of pupils, ordered according to their ability to handle 'academic work', various forms of knowledge, or various approaches to what is supposed to be a common body of knowledge are presented to pupils or, more precisely, to groups or categories of pupils . . . High School streams, with a differentiated distribution of school knowledge, have given rise to sub-worlds within the total reality of the school. Within these sub-worlds, the pupils tend to identify themselves, and are identified by others, as academic or non-academic types.

I want to emphasize that I am not arguing that the method of grouping pupils absolutely determines their level of academic achievement or their behaviour. Clearly, one view of the banding is that it merely mirrors the real differences between pupils in terms of ability and behaviour and thus reproduces and describes an empirical reality. From this perspective the processes described here can be said to represent the inevitable playing out of those differences. Inasmuch as the differences between pupils are related to processes of categorization at work in the primary school, it should not be unexpected that teachers in the secondary school also find these typifications of relevance to them.[20]

But the fact remains that the estimated potential of the 2TA pupils based

on the reports from their junior schools, which led to their being allocated
to band 2, was such as to label them 'failures' in a system that had not given
them the opportunity to show their worth (despite the rhetoric of equality
of opportunity). This system required them to respect it and to accept from
it values which stressed the importance of hard work, enthusiasm, good
behaviour and academic striving – even though, by assigning them to
band 2, the system had assumed and accepted that they would be lacking in
these qualities. Whereas it was suggested to the children that they were
placed in band 2 so that they could be given work more suited to their
abilities, what actually happened (in an institution whose staff were
working towards the achievement of fairly specific educational attainments
that these children were not expected to be able to obtain or even to attempt)
was that the teachers simply expected them to be pupils of low, second-rate
ability. As one Human Studies teacher put it, 'Band 2 lessons are essentially
dull for both teacher and pupils.' For these children, their secondary school
careers had begun with a decision which meant that they were to strive for
rewards in a race from which they had already been disqualified. But despite
this they were to try their hardest to run as fast as the winners, and expect to
be punished if they did not keep to the rules.[21]

The teachers' own descriptions of the early behaviour of 2TA show that
the form did not appear initially to conform to the stereotypes applied to
them. During their first term at the school, known then as 1TA, the form
was described to me, by the teachers most closely involved with them, their
form teacher and year tutor, in these terms:

> 'The promise was there, they were keen and enthusiastic school boys and
> girls, running to lessons; worried about work. But towards the end of the
> first year some of the girls were beginning to put their eyes on boys higher
> up the school.'
>
> (Year tutor)

> 'They were delightful, for the first six months they were one of the forms
> that everyone talked about as being lively and enthusiastic. Then the rot
> set in and they began to assert themselves as individuals and they began to
> lose their form identity.'
>
> (Form teacher)

By the second and third terms 1TA had already begun to demonstrate an
unwillingness to accept the authority of their teachers and to indulge in
behaviour, both inside and outside school, that involved them more and
more frequently in being punished or reprimanded. Their reputation as a
'problem' form began to develop from this time on.

Banding, behaviour and attitudes

Some measure of the beginnings of anti-school behaviour by members of the form can be gained from remarks in their personal files. These comments are presented chronologically; the first was recorded in the middle of the second term in the first year, and they cover the period up to the end of the first term in the second year. Both boys and girls are involved.

> 'Stealing from shops.'
> 'Rude to staff, mother asked to visit school.'
> 'Mother worried about boy friends, anxious that she be kept off the streets.'
> 'Cheeky and unco-operative in lessons.'
> 'On report.'
> 'Rudeness and bad behaviour.'
> 'Nuisance in assembly.'
> 'Spitting.'
> 'Swearing at member of staff.'

Comments like these are notably absent from the files of band 1 forms. In 1CU only one boy received any such remarks[22] on his file over the same period. During the second and third years the number of such comments increased in frequency and distribution in the files of band 2 and 3 forms. But other data available on the first year of these forms are scarce; no detention records were kept at this time and the school did not maintain very comprehensive written records of its pupils.

The declining standard of behaviour of the band 2 forms described by the teachers during the first year continued into the second year. Some of the pupils in 2TA were now very frequently 'in trouble', both informally in face to face conflict with teachers and formally in detention. Sometimes the whole form was kept in on 'informal' detentions, as a result of misbehaviour or disobedience in lessons, rudeness to teachers or failure to do work. The example presented below is a typical classroom incident.

> *Second-year Maths (setted group) : lesson notes*
> The group contains eleven pupils from 2TA. There is a lot of talking; the teacher issues a continuous stream of individual rebukes.
> *Teacher* 'When we do something together you've got to listen.'
> She is explaining how to do multiplication with a slide rule. Corina is turned completely round talking to the girls behind her. The teacher stops and waits.
> *Teacher* 'We are waiting for the same old people.'

The teacher begins talking and then stops.

Teacher 'We are not carrying on until you are all absolutely quiet – we are still waiting for those people who keep us waiting every lesson. Corina stop talking.'

She is still turned with her back to the teacher.

Teacher 'Corina!' [shouts]

Corina still does not turn round or stop talking.

Teacher 'All right, get outside – do as I tell you.'

The teacher is red and ruffled, but Corina gets up and walks out, slamming the door behind her. Minutes pass. Corina is outside the door with her nose pressed against the glass; she opens the door and walks away.

Teacher 'Corina – Michael, close the door please.'

A few minutes and Corina lets it open again. The teacher writes some calculations on the board, then goes outside to speak to Corina. (She was eventually sent to the year tutor and later transferred out of this Maths group.)

A further illustration of the progressive change in the school behaviour of the band 2 pupils, and the emergence of differences between them and the band 1 pupils, is their record of attendance over the first and second years (see tables 2.9 and 2.10). The average number of absences per pupil in band 1 is always at a lower level than in band 2, but the difference between them increases from 1.44 per pupil in the first term to 3.1 in the second and 2.53 in the third. The band 3 absences are presented separately in table 2.10 to show the difference in pattern between the remedial and non-remedial form. As far as the other bands are concerned, by the end of the second year the average number of absences in band 2 is nearly twice that of band 1, the difference being 6.31 per pupil. The level of absences in band 1 has increased very little from the first year.[23] Taking the two case-study forms independently over this period, the figures are as shown in table 2.11. The 1TA pupils begin in the first two terms of the first year with a better attendance record than 1CU. But as with the general trend, the number of

Table 2.9. *First year: average number of sessions absent per pupil in each term*

	Term 1	Term 2	Term 3
Band 1	6.23	7.54	7.29
Band 2	7.67	10.55	9.82
Band 3	10.24	11.71	10.91

Table 2.10. *Second year: average number of sessions absent per pupil in each term*

	Term 1	Term 2	Term 3
Band 1	7.23	11.21[a]	7.86
Band 2	12.33	12.83	14.17
Band 3 2MA (remedial)	19.75	17.29	22.56
2UD	10.64	16.95	16.22

[a]The sharp increase in band 1 in this term is accounted for by a flu epidemic that hit the school and made a considerable impact on attendances for four weeks.

Table 2.11. *Case-study forms: average number of sessions absent per pupil in each term*

	Term 1	Term 2	Term 3
ICU	7.53	9.45	8.10
1TA	6.66	7.70	9.47
	Term 4	Term 5	Term 6
2CU	8.13	11.64	9.15
2TA	12.59	13.22	12.64

sessions of absence per term per pupil increases steadily term by term, although here the differences between the forms are less great than across the whole cohort. These indicators generally suggest that the adaptation of the 2TA pupils to the pressures of secondary schooling was different from that of the pupils of 2CU. This is 'visible' in terms of their behaviour in lessons, but it is also manifest in their attitude towards the school generally, towards their teachers and towards schoolwork, and in the extent of their involvement and participation in extra-curricular school activities and clubs, sports teams, societies and choirs, etc. I asked the pupils in both forms to write down for me all the clubs or teams they belonged to, and the extra-curricular activities they did at school. Only 5 members of 2TA said that they took part in any such school activity, and only 2 said they were connected with any club or organization outside school. In 2CU, on the other hand, 21 people were involved in extra-curricular activities, and 7 in clubs outside school. 2TA pupils mentioned a total of 10 activities and clubs altogether, while 2CU pupils could muster 43.

Because participation of this kind is not obligatory, the pupil involved is seen as being committed to the school in the widest sense (see headmaster's comments, p. 169). It is interesting to note that information regarding involvement in school activities and the holding of posts of responsibility is requested and normally included in headmaster's reports for university application. (Out-of-school activities can thus be seen to have a selective function.) Furthermore, King (1973) notes that the experience of joining school clubs is expected by teachers to result in the generation of lasting interests and the modification of behaviour in approved directions.

It was clear that the interests and attitudes of many of the 2TA pupils were developing in quite another way. Indeed, the increase in disruptive behaviour in the classroom seemed to be accompanied by a general disenchantment with school and all activities associated with it. A teacher who had been responsible for the first-year football team explained that one of the boys in 2TA, Donald Gaskell, 'used to be the best footballer in the first year, but now he's no longer interested and he's lost his figure'. The keenness and enthusiasm reported from 1TA had almost completely disappeared in the second year. I asked the pupils in the two second-year forms to write down whether on the whole they liked or disliked school. 48 per cent (17) of the pupils in 2TA said they disliked school on the whole, while 52 per cent (18) liked it, but only 13 per cent (4) of the pupils in 2CU expressed dislike, and 87 per cent (18) said they liked school.

The work-habits of the pupils of the two forms were also different. I asked them how long they usually spent in doing their homework each evening. The pupils in 2CU were willing to spend three times as long on their homework as 2TA pupils.[24] The average time per pupil for 2TA was 16 minutes, while that for 2CU was 47 minutes.[25] In 2TA 13 pupils reported that they did no homework, but only one pupil in 2CU said this.[26] Homework is supposed to be set for two subjects each week-night and three subjects on Fridays, and this work *was* set as it was due in most of the lessons I observed. However, some 2TA pupils were regularly 'in trouble' for not handing in their homework, and many others did it at school, quickly at lunch time or during pastoral periods in the mornings. For most of them it was a meaningless chore to be dispensed with as quickly as possible rather than something to be done carefully to ensure a good mark. Their unwillingness to do homework was symptomatic of their lack of interest in schoolwork and their reluctance to do any. However, the differences between the forms with respect to doing homework should not be taken to mean that the pupils of 2CU were wholeheartedly in favour of it and would always have done work at home if it were not specifically 'set'. One of the boys in 2CU who was most successful academically[27] frequently urged me 'to do something about getting homework abolished' and 'put it in my book'. Few of 2CU would probably have done homework if it were not insisted upon, but almost all did it because it was. On the occasions that extra, non-compulsory discovery-tasks were suggested by teachers, these were done by only a minority of the form.[28]

The doing of homework and doing it well represents further confirmation of the identification of the 2CU pupils with the school's values, stressing the importance of academic achievement, and thus the reinforcement of their self-image and status as pupils who are successful at school. Homework was a different sort of activity for the pupils from the different bands. The real difference between these forms in 'doing' homework was that most of the pupils in 2CU took time and trouble to do it 'well' and get as good a mark as possible, whereas most of the pupils in 2TA did homework in as little time as possible, with the least trouble, with little concern about the mark.

Academic performance

One of the major dimensions of the band stereotypes presented above is clearly concerned with the teachers' perceptions of the *'level' of academic performance* of which the pupils from different bands are capable. The marks obtained in homework and other assessable work is an indication of this 'level' to the teacher, and further indicates the sort of importance which the pupils attach to 'doing well'. At the end of each school year all forms have internal examinations, and although the first-, second- and third-band forms are set different examinations based upon work done during the year, it is useful to compare the results. While not strictly comparable in a quantitative sense, a qualitative comparison of the 'levels' of performance attained by 2CU and 2TA does provide an illustration once again of the differences between them. The level of marks obtained is a measure of the degree of 'academic excellence' achieved by the forms. As may be seen, at the extremes of very good and very bad marks the differences between them are dramatic indeed. For all subjects, except Maths (which was 'setted') and English (the department did not set a formal examination), the distribution of marks for the two classes was as follows:

%	2TA	2CU
above 70	1	36
60–9	4	60
50–9	23	30
40–9	47	51
30–9	58	34
below 30	77	9

On the basis of these seven subjects, 2TA pupils only obtained 28 marks above half-marks (out of a total of 251 marks) compared with 126 marks above half-marks by 2CU pupils (out of a total of 219 marks).

Banding and differentiation

In every respect, in examinations, classwork and homework, 2CU performed at an academic level more acceptable to their teachers; so that not only was their behaviour in lessons well-perceived by staff but academically they were able to 'deliver the goods' as well in a far more satisfactory way. This is explained by an English teacher.

> 'They can both [band 1 and 2] attempt the same tasks but the quality of discussion is very different. The responses of the first band are more what a teacher, as an academic, would recognize as relevant. They know what the teacher wants and are able to give it to him.'

For the teacher of the band 1 form, the problems in the classroom are related to the teaching process, the organization and preparation of material, the coverage of the syllabus, and the preparation for tests and examinations; the major concern is normally with the maintenance of standards.[29] The great majority of the teachers' 'talk' and interaction with pupils in the classroom is concerned with subject material or work-tasks. In the case of the band 2 lessons, however, the teacher's major concerns in the classroom are problems of order and control. In some cases the 'order and control' problems in band 2 lessons are so great that work is virtually abandoned. 'Band 2 kids are often neglected and their lessons are the least prepared of the week', a year tutor said.

It is understandable that teachers should devote less care and energy to the preparation of lessons in which a great deal of time is spent maintaining or trying to maintain order and control, and in which little time goes to those tasks that the teachers consider valuable and worthwhile. Large numbers of pupils in the band 2 lessons expressed a considerable lack of interest in their school-work, made efforts not to have to do any work, and

frequently tried deliberately to divert lessons away from work-activity
This may be interpreted as the outcome of the interaction between the
expectations that teachers have of band 2 pupils, based on stereotypes, and
the pupils' response to these expectations.[30] Several studies of stereotyping
have shown that definitions of the situation that are held by actors who are
reacting to 'deviant' behaviour, definitions which are themselves to a great
extent shaped by stereotyped beliefs, can have so overwhelming an impact
that the 'deviating' individual may find himself unable to sustain any
alternative definition of himself. Schur (1971 : 51) argues that stereotyping

at the level of direct personal interaction significantly influences the expectations of
others, causing serious problems of response and 'identity' management for
deviators.

One Beachside year tutor commented in a similar vein that 'some teachers
don't expect much from second-band forms, they accept anything for the
standard of work'. The band 2 pupils are confronted by teachers who hold
very negative perceptions of their intelligence and ability and likely
attainment – 'they are not up to much academically'. These perceptions
have both attitudinal and practical consequences for the pupils' experiences
of learning. That is, lack of enthusiasm for band 2 teaching is transmitted
both in the teachers' attitude to the pupils and in their classroom
management techniques, their organization of learning and their mediation
of the syllabus. In these ways, the stereotypical notions of band-identity
inherent in the teachers' perceptions of the pupils actually contribute to the
increasing differences between band 1 and 2 pupils during the first and
second years. Several of the teachers certainly attributed the changing
attitudes and behaviour of the band 2 forms to the pupils' increasing
awareness of inferior status.

> 'In the first year they started off fresh and the same, but by the end of the
> first year they began to realize that being in band 2 or band 3 is not quite
> the same. And in the second year they click and in the third they switch
> off; it's tragic.'
>
> (Assistant year tutor)

> 'I had a band 2 form in the first and second year, they were tremendously
> self-motivated, really great kids, there was none of this 'we're at the
> bottom sod it' in the first year, it really came out in the third.'
>
> (Art teacher)

It is apparent that in the second year the teachers of band 1 and band 2
forms have well-established and very different expectations of them.

Indeed, the social processes at work here appear to be essentially similar to the processes identified by Lacey (1970) and Hargreaves (1967) as *differentiation* – that is, the separation and ranking of pupils by the teachers. As Lacey suggests, this separation and ranking takes place along a number of dimensions or scales, but two appear to be most important, the academic scale and the behaviour scale. The academic scale relates to those qualities of achievement and performance in schoolwork which are consistently a part of the teachers' perception and evaluation of pupils; it includes things like numeracy and literacy skills, answering questions in lessons, and the neat presentation of book work. The behaviour scale 'would include considerations as varied as general classroom behaviour and attitudes; politeness; attention; helpfulness; the time spent in school societies and sports' (Lacey 1970:57).

In Hargreaves' terms the pupils are 'categorized' by their teachers and this begins from the moment that they enter the first year and join their banded forms. But beyond seeing them in terms of the allocated status of band 1, band 2 or band 3, the teachers are continually rating pupils in terms of the criteria listed by Lacey. Further consideration of this aspect of the process of differentiation is taken up in more detail in subsequent chapters. But the evaluation and separation of pupils by the teachers is only one part of the overall process of differentiation. The second aspect of the model, which Lacey suggests 'describes the passage of pupils through' the school, is *polarization*, the formation of sub-cultural groups. This

takes place within the student body, partly as a result of differentiation, but influenced by external factors . . . It is a process of sub-culture formation in which the school-dominated, normative culture is opposed by an alternative culture which I refer to as the anti-group culture.

(Lacey 1970 : 57)

Clearly, the changing patterns of behaviour of the band 2 pupils over the first two years may be interpreted as representing the emergence of the anti-school sub-culture to which Lacey refers. It is certainly the case that the behaviour of band 2 pupils in their lessons, as we have seen, presents a challenge to the normative school culture, whereas the behaviour of band 1 pupils normally does not. The situation facing the band 2 pupils is that they are perceived by their teachers as academically inferior to the band 1 pupils. This is inherent in the banding system. The band 2 pupils have low status and thus it is not in their interest to maintain a commitment to the school's values. The returns to them in terms of satisfaction are extremely limited; as we have seen, very few band 2 pupils achieve levels of performance in examinations that are considered to be acceptable by their teachers; neither do their teachers find band 2 lessons very rewarding to teach. (However, as will become clear in the following chapter, there are pupils who are successful in band 2 and who remain committed to the normative culture of the school.) By the beginning of the second year, the existence of anti-school groups within the band 2 forms was clearly marked and the greater part of the disruption of band 2 lessons could be traced to these pupils. In Cohen's terms the emergence of these anti-school sub-cultural groups represents the adjustment of these pupils to the status problems with which they are confronted. He notes:

One solution is for individuals who share such problems to gravitate toward one another and jointly establish new norms, new criteria of status which define as meritorious the characteristics they *do* possess, the kinds of conduct of which they *are* capable.

(Cohen 1955:66)

The sub-cultural polarization within the banded forms which emerges through the different value-orientations of pro- and anti-school pupils will be taken up in more detail in the following chapter. The final section of this chapter will examine the relationship between banding and the distribution of friendship choices across the bands.

Choosing friends

The description and analysis of the banded forms has concentrated so far upon the formal aspects of lessons and classroom behaviour. But the classroom as a social setting is made up of two worlds. One is the formal context of teacher-pupil interaction, of schoolwork and discipline, and the other is the informal context of social relationships among the pupils, of friendships and social groups. From the analysis of the distribution of friendship choices and the friendship groupings[31] of the banded forms it emerges that not only are the bands separate and distinct in the minds of the teachers, as two different types of pupils with different behaviour patterns and work capabilities, but the pupils also separate themselves out and hold stereotypical views of one another on the basis of their bands. The reality of this separation is borne out by the distribution of nominated choices of close friends. From the sociometric questionnaires that each of the second-year forms completed for me, it was possible to plot the distribution of friendship choices between forms and between bands. Taking only those choices made outside the form group, the distribution by band is as shown

Table 2.12. *Distribution of friendship choices between pupils of different forms by band, amended for band size*

	Choice to:		
Choices from	Band 1	Band 2	Band 3
Band 1	67	21	3
Band 2	19	55	42
Band 3	6	30	24

in table 2.12. The preference of band 2 pupils for band 3 rather than band 1 pupils is clear here; so too is the low level of choice between band 1 and band 3. In real terms, the vast majority of choices are made within bands. This can be explained in terms either of the constraints of the school organization, or of the normative requirements of the informal social structure among the pupils.

It is evident, then, that the way in which the pupils are formally grouped largely determines the patterns of pupil peer-groups by imposing constraints both on the nature and the range of contacts between pupils. Thus, pupils tend to choose for their friends those people with whom they have most contact and whom they know best. Overall, 78 per cent of the school friends nominated by pupils in this cohort came from within the same form. This is in line with the findings of Julienne Ford (1969), Lacey (1970), Hargreaves (1967) and Murdock and Phelps (1973), although none of these studies reported such a high percentage of 'within-form' choices. However, the preference of pupils for friends from the same band *can* also be related to the development of pro- and anti-school groups. 'It can be assumed that a person chooses for his friends those whom he respects and likes and those who he perceives to be like himself in some significant respects' (Lacey 1970 : 78). As we shall see later, when the friendship structures of the case-study forms are examined, friendship groups are held together by common values and develop norms which limit the acceptable behaviour of group members and control entry into the group by defining the criteria of membership. Other groups and other pupils come to be seen in terms of how similar they are to other members of the group or how different they are from them. The problem with the previous argument, that the general level of distribution of friendship choices is affected by the limitations of contact between pupils, is that it does not explain why some other choices are made across the boundaries of the bands. The latter argument, however, does.

A few of the friendship ties that were made between bands were left over from junior school, but it often turned out that some secondary factor lay behind the maintenance of the tie, such as propinquity. Pupils who lived in the same street would have the opportunity to meet outside school and to travel to and from school together. However, when I examined the friendship-group structures of 2TA and 2CU in terms of propinquity, only two of the six best-friend pairs lived close to one another (within a mile). The one significant basis of cross-cutting ties which I did discover was the friendship choices made between members of the various boys' sports teams in the second year. I am not suggesting that the tendency to choose outside form groups is actually encouraged by team membership, but that this is a basis of cross-cutting choice. Team membership and interest in sport are both opportunities to interact and the bases of shared interests. There were no other friendship networks of this kind extending across bands in the year-cohort. *All* other friendship choices made across bands were either reciprocating friendship pairs or unreciprocated choices made by individual pupils.

Separation between bands, however, is not simply reflected in the low level of friendship choice between them, but also in the negative and antipathetic attitudes that they entertain towards each other. These are some of the comments made by 2TA and 2CU pupils in interviews with me.

Kathleen Hopkins (2CU)	'I wouldn't want to be in a second band, I would try to get out if I was in one – they are thick.'
Dorothy Haines (2TA)	'They are not so friendly – they think they are better than us because they are in a higher band.'
Eddy (2CU)	'I don't like the people, they are a bit thick – simple.'
Belinda Hammet (2TA)	'They are stuck up – because they think they are so brainy.'
Smaldon (2CU)	'They are rough . . . tough kids in band 2.'
Kathy Forest (2TA)	'They're snobby, I don't like people in band 1.'
Fawcett (2CU)	'It's not easy to talk to them, they talk in a simpler way – they're only interested in football!'
Acre (2TA)	'They let you know they are in band 1 and how clever they are.'

Groome (2TA)   'Snobs – mainly it's the girls isn't it, in there,
                                  are poofy boys and they don't want to do
                                  nufink, they just stick around in class.'

Only two pupils in 2TA made favourable or neutral comments about
band 1 pupils, and only six in 2CU made favourable or neutral comments
about band 2 pupils.

Felton (2CU)   'I've got friends in band 2, I come to school
                                  with one and play with one sometimes.'

The existence of this mutual hostility can be seen in terms of Newcomb's
(1947) findings, that barriers to communication are likely to lead to the
formation of stereotypes, especially where differences in status are
involved.

From this analysis, it is apparent that the *polarization* described by Lacey
(1970) in the streamed Hightown Grammar is also an aspect of the process
of relationships between the banded pupils in Beachside Comprehensive.
This certainly suggests that the 'integrative function' so frequently
attributed to the comprehensive school is not being achieved here. The
negative implications of this segregation and mutual hostility become even
clearer when the social class structure of the bands is taken into account.[32]

Summary

This chapter has considered one banded year-cohort as a whole, as well as
introducing two case-study forms. I have argued that *post factum* evidence
indicates that 2TA, the band 2 form, has *become* different from the band 1
form, since the beginning of the first year and, further, that this can be
related to the status-differentials that exist between the bands and to the
assumptions that teachers make about the abilities and capabilities of the
pupils in different bands. In particular I have indicated the importance of
band stereotypes in the teachers' perceptions of, and behaviour towards,
different forms. These stereotypes are an important component of the
shared system of meanings of the Beachside staff, through which forms and
pupils can be discussed and compared. I have also suggested that the social
processes and social structures identified within this year-cohort are to a
considerable extent represented by the concepts *polarization* and *differentiation*. As the two case-study forms are examined in more detail in the
following chapter, the relevance of those concepts will become still more
apparent.

3   Two case-studies of banded forms

The crudity of the stereotypes of 'bandness' which were presented in the previous chapter becomes clear when we examine the social structures of the case-study forms, and the changes in these structures over a period of time. This chapter will illustrate the attitudes and perspectives and 'lines of adaptation' of the pro- and anti-school pupils, and relate the evolution and development of the anti-school sub-culture to the problems of 'failure' faced by many of the band 2 pupils at Beachside.

The data relating to these questions were obtained from the administration of a number of sociometric tests to the two case-study forms, in combination with 'naturalistic' observation, stretching over a period of seven school terms.

Sociometry is a means of presenting simply and graphically the . . . structure of relations existing at a given time among members of a given group. The major lines of communication, or the pattern of attraction and rejection in its full scope, are made readily comprehensible at a glance.

(Jennings 1948 : 11)

The combination of observation and sociometry provides a methodology which avoids the danger of creating an abstraction that reflects the nature and vagaries of the sociometric method rather than the realities of the classroom. A considerable amount of observation had been completed before the sociometric questionnaires were collected and analysed, avoiding in this way the danger of their having any predetermining influence upon observation. Gronlund (1959 : 25) makes this point:

Many of the limitations of the sociometric test arise from sole dependence on sociometric data as a means of studying group status and structure. Thus, these limitations can be eliminated or minimized by supplementing sociometric results with other sources of information.

One indication of the appropriateness and sensitivity of the techniques used here is the stability of the social structures over time. This seems to

53

suggest that, rather than being the product of momentary whim or the variations in data-collection procedures, the choices made by the pupils in the sociometric questionnaires accurately reflect the structure of friendship relationships in the form. Adolescent friendships appear to be volatile in the short term, with people falling out with one another and making up again,[1] but many school friendships, once established during the first year of secondary school or earlier, are maintained over several years, as long as the pupils stay together in the same form. However, it is important to recognize that despite the tendency towards stability the social structure of the forms represented in the sociomatrices is not fixed. The complex network of friendship choices is changing over time.

The questionnaires used to elicit friendship choices included a series of differently worded sociometric questions, but the sociomatrices presented below make use of responses to questions concerning 'close friend' choices and 'best friend' choices.

The social structure of 2TA

The friendship structure of 2TA and the changes in this structure over time are presented below in a series of sociomatrices (figures 1 and 2). From the first of these (figure 1, constructed in the spring term), it may be seen that the form consists of seven single-sex friendship cliques or pairs and two social isolates. The membership of these groups is as follows.

Group A (7 girls)

	Father's occupation	End-of-year exam position	Detentions received	Socio-economic group
Christine Downes	Lorry driver	Absent	7	IIIM
Daphne Galt	Salesman	31	3	IIIN
Belinda Hammett	Plumber	25	8	IIIM
Pamela Jarvis	Office worker	12	0	IIIN
Felicity Johnson	G.P.O. engineer	1	6	IIIM
Dorothy Haines	Double glazer	17	5	IIIM
Kathy Forrest	Machine operator	Left	1	IV

These girls were often involved in 'disruption' of lessons and were frequently rebuked for talking or 'mucking around' and for insolent behaviour. Included in this group and group B are most of the girls in 2TA who were most often 'in trouble'. Out of 98 school detentions received by members of 2TA during the whole of the second year, 41 (43 per cent) were received by the nine girls in groups A and B (27 per cent of the class).

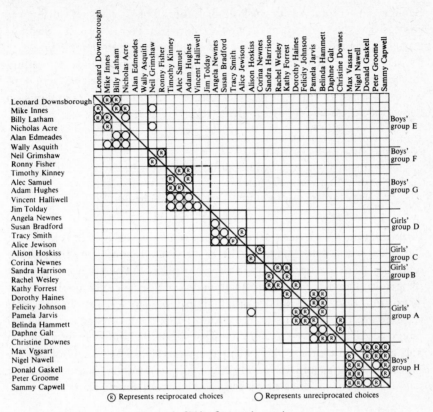

Figure 1. 2TA: first sociomatrix

Among the offences committed by the girls and cited in the detention book were:

- leaving school at lunch time
- disturbance in the library
- smoking
- disobedience
- misconduct in class
- failure to attend class detention
- disruptive behaviour
- defiance.

The numbers of individual detentions received are given in the table above. Christine, Felicity, Belinda and Dorothy, who received most of the detentions, were usually at the centre of disturbances in the classroom, with

Belinda most often cast in the role of leader. This is reflected in the five choices that she received in the first sociomatrix. Her popularity was not, however, carried over into the second questionnaire.[2] In the third term of the second year Belinda was twice reported to the year tutor for calling teachers names and being rude. He asked her mother to visit the school to discuss the matter and sent round a note to collect teachers' comments on her work in lessons. The comments received were:

- dislikes staff
- poor presentation
- Belinda is a very disturbing influence on the class
- lives in a permanent dream
- tends to be an exhibitionist, can be very disruptive
- a nuisance in class.

In an interview with her I asked if there were any teachers in school that she liked, and she said, 'I hate all the teachers in the whole school . . . They're horrible, it's a rubbishy prison.' The other members of the group, Pamela, Kathy and Daphne, were normally not instigators of disruption, and were not as often 'in trouble' in lessons. Pamela and Daphne are the two girls in the group from homes in the non-manual category. All the girls were 'up' on the latest fashions and were interested in pop music and clothes; they spent most of their time at school talking about these things and about boy friends. None of them belonged to any school clubs or societies or played in any school sports teams.

Group B (2 girls)

	Father's occupation	End-of-year exam position	Detentions received	Socio-economic group
Sandra Harrison	Fork-lift truck driver	27	5	IIIM
Rachel Wesley	Warehouseman	11	6	IV

This pair is linked to the larger group by the choices made between them and Kathy. While Kathy is the 'best' and inseparable friend of Dorothy and much involved in the activities of the former group, she is much closer in temperament and behaviour to these two girls. They were generally quieter and more attentive in lessons than the girls in group A, although Sandra did sometimes misbehave and get 'in trouble'. Neither reported doing any homework, and neither belonged to any school clubs or societies; when not at school Sandra liked best going out with her boyfriend and Rachel liked going to parties and discothèques.

Group C (2 girls)

	Father's occupation	End-of-year exam position	Detentions received	Socio-economic group
Alison Hoskiss	Shop-owner	23	0	II
Corina Newnes	Consultant engineer	14	5	I

These two form an isolate pair who had a major shared interest in horses and riding; they both visited a local stable every day to work or ride. Alison was not popular with the other girls in the form; she was quiet in lessons, usually getting on with her work and not joining in with disruptive behaviour. Corina's sister Angela is also in the form, although they have different friends and different interests. In the lessons I observed Corina's behaviour varied considerably; in some lessons she worked hard and was well-behaved, yet in others she was individually disruptive, disobedient and difficult to control, as we have already seen. But she did her homework regularly and was a member of the Gym Club and the Dance Club; she also played hockey and competed in athletics for the school, the only girl in the form to participate in these types of pro-school-oriented activities. Yet at the same time, she clearly professed her dislike for school and for teachers. Nonetheless, there are important differences between these two girls and the girls of group A, both in terms of attitude and behaviour, although both this pair and Sandra and Rachel *were* peripheral and aspirant members of group A.

While it is not absolutely clear from the sociomatrix, groups A, B and C do constitute a bounded friendship area. In Furlong's (1976) terms, the group may be regarded as the boundary of a number of *interaction sets*, which change in membership during the course of the school day. It was apparent from my observations of the form that these girls spent a lot of time together at school – in lessons, at break and dinner time, and so forth. And as we shall see later, individual changes in the choices made by these girls are best understood in the context of the larger friendship network.

Group D (4 girls)

	Father's occupation	End-of-year exam position	Detentions received	Socio-economic group
Angela Newnes	Consultant engineer	23	2	I
Susan Bradford	Building worker	29	2	V
Tracy Smith	Porter	24	2	IV
Alice Jewison	Carpenter	30	3	IIIM

These four girls always sat together in lessons. They were normally very quiet but not very hard-working; they were all low-achievers. They were almost 'invisible' during lessons, rarely speaking to, or being spoken to by, teachers. Angela had moved from the third-band form 2UD with her sister at the beginning of the second year, and her friendship choices in the first sociometric questionnaire were still to her friends in that form, although she was a full interactional member of this group. Apart from choosing Angela, Susan also chose her friends outside the form at this time. She came to the school soon after the beginning of the second year and although she made her initial friendships via Angela, she also chose into 2UD in the first sociometric questionnaire. None of the group is involved in extra-curricular school activities of any kind. One member of the group, Tracy, is particularly unpopular with the boys. She received ten rejection choices from them and was often insulted and called names.

Group E (6 boys)

	Father's occupation	End-of-year exam position	Detentions received	Socio-economic group
Leonard Downs-borough	Docker	7	0	IV
Billy Latham	Labourer	9	2	V
Mike Innes	Accountant	8	1	II
Nicholas Acre	Roundsman	14	1	IV
Alan Edmeades	Tool-setter	21	1	IIIM
Wally Asquith	Electrician	4	1	IIIM

All the boys in this group were quiet and attentive in lessons, and hard-working. They tended to be well-perceived by their teachers and were not often in trouble. More than any other members of the form they were involved in the formal interactional process of their lessons, answering teachers' questions, making contributions and generally participating in the lesson.

In a sentence-completion test, when asked what teachers were like, they wrote:

> Teachers are . . . alright I suppose
> . . . nice sometimes
> . . . fairly good
> . . . some are good
> . . . very friendly.
> And when teachers tell me my work is bad
> I . . . try to do better

    . . . try to do it again
    . . . am ashamed
    . . . try to do better
    . . . re-do the work.
A good lesson is one in which
    . . . we do a bit of work and learn something
    . . . I sit down and work
    . . . I get on with the teacher and do my work.

The pro-school attitudes of the group are clear from these comments. What was also clear, by the end of the third year, was the domination by this group of the top examination positions in the form (see p. 103). For those boys from this group and the other pro-school groups, who were in the middle or bottom levels of achievement in the second year, their pro-school orientation paid off. Edmeades and Acre considerably improved their academic results. The remaining members, Asquith, Downsborough and Latham, also improved and consolidated their performance. The boys from group F, Grimshaw and Fisher, also improved.

Group F (2 boys)

	Father's occupation	End-of-year exam position	Detentions received	Socio-economic group
Neil Grimshaw	Shopkeeper	16	0	II
Ronny Fisher	Motor mechanic	22	0	IIIM

These two boys exchanged best-friend choices, and Neil was chosen also by Innes and Acre. They are in many ways similar to the boys of group E above, especially in their positive attitude to work, and often sat with or near them in lessons. Neil was always particularly keen to answer questions in lessons and tended to dominate the teacher's attention if allowed to do so. In some lessons, especially history and geography, he showed the kind of enthusiasm only normally associated with first years, straining to answer questions and participating with unsolicited contributions of his own. He was a gregarious boy, but intolerant of the gibes or laughter of his form-mates.

History, term one, second year : lesson notes
The teacher's 'talk' to the form is interrupted by their noise for the third time. He stops talking and waits, saying nothing. The noise from the form continues. Neil Grimshaw, from his place at the front, turns round and yells 'shut up' at them.

It is hardly likely that Neil was especially frightened of the consequences of the continuous noise. He was listening to the teacher anyway, but was exasperated by the behaviour of his form-mates and their interruption of his favourite lesson.

Ronny, his best friend and constant companion at this time, is an interesting comparison with the gregarious Neil. He made no contributions at all to lessons. This was not because of lack of interest or motivation, but because he rarely spoke at all – he was shy to the point of being withdrawn. It was reported to me that during his last year in primary school he had never once spoken to his form teacher, and on only one occasion during the whole period of my observation did he actually initiate a conversation with me. Neither of these boys was among the academically most successful in the form during the second year – although, as we shall see, they improved their exam position considerably in the third year – but both were well-perceived by teachers. Neither received any school detentions in the second year. One way, however, in which they differed from other pupils in 2TA was in the involvement of their parents in their school careers and aspirations. Neil's father visited the school on several occasions to discuss his son's progress, and was particularly anxious that Neil should do German as a second language. In the normal course of events, band 2 forms do not take a second language, so Mr Grimshaw had to persuade the school to make a special arrangement for Neil to join a band 1 set especially for German. He also arranged for Neil to have private German lessons at home. The father also made a point of visiting the school at the time that option choices were being made at the end of Neil's third year. He was able to ensure that Neil was admitted to the German C.S.E. course and into Science courses. In Ronny's case it was his mother who visited the school. She was particularly concerned about his shyness and unwillingness to talk. Through the school she was able to arrange for him to see the L.E.A. schools' psychologist and a speech therapist, and she participated in exercises at home to encourage him to talk.

Group G (3 boys)

	Father's occupation	End-of-year exam position	Detentions received	Socio-economic group
Alec Samuel	Office manager	5	0	II
Adam Hughes	Plumber	3	5	IIIM
Timothy Kinney	G.P.O. engineer	19	0	IIIM

All three boys in this group were quiet and attentive in class, and all three were in the Scouts. Alec and Adam could almost be described as over-quiet, but not to the extent that Ronny was.[3] Timothy participated more in lessons, but teachers found it difficult to get contributions from the other two. However, Timothy was moved out of the form for a time during the second year for a period of six weeks. 'He was very upset when he was moved and was almost in tears', his form teacher said. 'But we may let him come back at the end of the term.' He was moved because of the part he seemed to be playing in provoking his friends to misbehave, getting them into trouble without being involved himself.[4]

Group H (5 boys)

	Father's occupation	End-of-year exam position	Detentions received	Socio-economic group
Max Vassart	Motor mechanic	6	14	IIIM
Donald Gaskell	Factory worker	26	5	IV
Peter Groome	Crane driver	28	6	IIIM
Sammy Capwell	Docker	18	0	IV
Nigel Nawell	Carpenter	20	1	IIIM

These five boys formed a close-knit friendship group; they were together in lessons, around the school and out of school. They were all working-class boys with, except for Sammy, little interest in schoolwork; they were often involved in trouble in lessons and frequently received school detentions for 'classroom offences' of various kinds. Their combined total of school detentions in the second year was 26. Their recorded offences included:

- caught on the building site
- misconduct in class
- missing English department detention
- climbing out of windows
- disruptive behaviour in Biology lessons.

The group sat together in lessons, usually in a row and usually at the back.

From lesson notes

English: Max Vassart moved for talking and interrupting the lesson.

History: Max, Donald, Peter, Sammy and Nigel are rebuked for the third time for 'mucking about'.

History: Teacher shouts at Peter and Donald for opening the fire door at the back of the room.

French: Peter and Nigel are out of their places during the lesson. Are rebuked by the teacher.

Only Max was a high-achiever and then not consistently. Sammy had once been considered as being 'worthy' of a move into band 1 at the end of the first year, but did not want to go and had deliberately done work badly to make sure he was not moved.

> 'He will not be convinced that he will not have to go up a band if he does well. When he was told that his work was good enough for him to go up, his work fell off disastrously and it took us some time to realize that it was because he did not want to go up. He's back to getting all A's again now but still won't accept that he doesn't have to go up a band if he doesn't want to.'
>
> (Form teacher)

Sammy gives the same account:

> 'I had a chance in the first year to go up to band 1 because Mrs Tanner came to me and said that I had a chance to go up, but I didn't want to and my work slipped since then. I didn't want to leave 1TA. My work slipped because I thought they might make me go up.'

Max Vassart moved into the form soon after the beginning of the second year. He had been taken out of the form he was in because he had been causing trouble in lessons with another boy; he became almost immediately an integral member of this group. Despite his high position in the end-of-year examinations, he did not appear to work hard or to participate frequently in lessons or to do homework when he could help it. In the end-of-third-year examinations his position fell to sixteenth. He received the highest individual total of school detentions in the form – fourteen in all.

When asked about their favourite subjects, Don chose Games because 'you don't do much', Peter chose Games and English because 'I like the teachers', Max chose music 'because we don't do any work', and Sammy chose music because 'we muck about'. Peter was the only member of the group who reported that he did any homework. They also wrote:

> When lessons are boring . . . I muck about
> . . . I go around mucking about
> . . . I don't listen to the teachers.
> [Sammy and Donald did not reply]

And they did not have a high opinion of teachers:

> Teachers are . . . wankers
> . . . rotten

>   ... stupid
>   ... bastards.
>   [Sammy did not reply]
> When teachers tell me my work is bad
> I ... don't care
>   ... go red [Sammy]
>   ... argue with them
>   ... don't listen
>   ... don't take no notice.
> Teachers in this school think of me as
>   ... capable [Sammy]
>   ... a pest
>   ... a little prat
>   ... hopeless.

From these examples Sammy may be seen to be rather different from his friends in the group.

Donald wanted to join the Navy when he left school. Peter wanted to be a footballer and Max wanted to be a long-distance lorry driver. Only Peter was involved in any school clubs or societies; he played football for the second-year 'B' team.

Two social isolates and rejectees: Vince Halliwell and Jim Tolday

Vince's father was a production-line worker. Vince was an aspirant member of friendship group G; he made choices to all three boys and chose Adam as 'best friend'. He had been part of this group during the first year, but having a friend outside the form had made him unpopular and he now received no friendship choices. Indeed, Adam and Samuel gave him rejection choices. He often made attempts to 'curry favour' with the group and taunting Jim Tolday was one of the ways that he often used.

Jim was often the butt of insults and taunts as well as physical abuse from his classmates. He received fifteen rejection choices and no friendship choices from the form. He may be described as what Northway (1944) calls a 'socially ineffective isolate'. He was keen to join in with the form but did not know how to do so: his attempts to overcome his isolation were naïve and useless, usually ending in further abuse and rejection. He was a large and ungainly boy with an unusual manner that did not make it easy for him to make friends. He chose the boys in friendship group G in the sociometric test and included Vince in his choices. He always tried hard to associate himself with them, but only during the time that Timothy Kinney was out of the form did they in any way accept him, and he was able to sit with them in lessons. Kinney was in the forefront of his taunters, although he was picked on by everyone in the form, including the girls, as is shown by the two following incidents:

French: lesson notes
Belinda has taken Jim's pencil case from his desk and passes it to Pamela while he gets up to recover it. Dorothy has taken his French book, Pamela has given his pencil case to Felicity, and he is chasing around the girls to find who has what. While he is running around, Belinda has taken his briefcase and hidden it behind the lockers at the back of the room. He is getting desperate and has gone to complain to the teacher who has just arrived.

Diary notes 4 April 1974
While walking back to the staffroom at 4 o'clock Jim Tolday ran past me being chased by Peter Groome, Nigel Nawell, Donald Gaskell and Max Vassart. They were kicking at him and pushing him trying to make him drop his briefcase and they were shouting, 'Come on get him, get him.'

Jim's parents were frequently in contact with the school and were visited many times by the year tutor and a psychologist from the schools' psychological service. But despite the support of these various agencies and his parents, little progress was made in terms of his social adjustment. His father, who worked as a self-employed electrician, brought him to school every day and picked him up at 4 o'clock. In lessons Jim participated more than most. The history teacher said of him: 'Verbally he can be brilliant, but he's not good on paper.' He came tenth in the end-of-year examinations. Neither he nor Vince received any school detentions during the year.

The boundaries of the friendship groups in 2TA were not only evident from sociometric responses, but were 'visible' to the observer in the daily interaction of the pupils. Apart from 'going around together' at break and lunch time, the groups were most obviously and straightforwardly demarcated in the seating arrangements of lessons. Normally the boys of group H occupied desks at the back of the form. In contrast, the pro-school boys of groups E and F were normally seated fairly close to the teacher's desk. The seating distribution tended overall to reflect Waller's (1961 : 161) comment:

In large classes where students are left free to choose their own positions, the author has found a certain distribution to recur. In the front row is a plentiful sprinkling of over-dependent types, mixed perhaps with a number of extremely zealous students. In the back row are persons in rebellion against authority . . . in rebellion against being in the class.

From this examination of the first sociomatrix it is apparent that the friendship groupings of pupils in 2TA represent some clear-cut differences in value-orientation and attitudes. The form may be divided into several distinct areas of friendship which are distinguished by their attitudes to teachers, to schoolwork and to school in general. Taken individually, however, sociomatrices present a snapshot of social relations which may be untypical or subject to constant change. Obviously, if the friendship structure is constantly in a state of flux, then it would be quite invalid to draw conclusions about a particular structure isolated at a particular point in time. It would be very difficult, for instance, to argue that the structure is related to pressures and processes inherent in the organization of forms and in the nature of teacher-pupil relationships.

However, it may be seen from the second questionnaire (see figure 2), completed towards the end of the summer term – that is, at the end of the form's second year – that there was no major reorganization of the friendship groupings, only some marginal changes in the choices made by individuals. The most dramatic change of all occurred in the A/B/C network grouping, the focus of which changed. In this questionnaire Daphne Galt received the highest number of choices, six in all, but neither she nor Christine Downes made any other choices this time except to each other. Although a quiet girl, Daphne was totally uninterested in school, and she came bottom (thirty-first) in the end-of-year examinations. However, she was interested in boyfriends and clothes and was very popular with boys higher up the school. Whenever I saw her outside school, she was dressed in the latest fashions and looked considerably older than she actually was. This social sophistication seemed to be the basis of her popularity with the other girls. The exchange of choices among the other girls in the core-group consolidated them as a clique: these were the four most badly behaved girls in the form. Indeed, the group was to be 'broken up' at the end of the second year in order to 'purge' the form of some of its difficult pupils. The fact that Kathy Forrest had left the school by this time also broke the link that she had maintained between group A and Rachel and Sandra. Sandra had become progressively more unpopular during the year and received no choices from the form in the second questionnaire, even from Rachel, who had been her best friend. Rachel now exchanged friendship choices with Corina. Corina no longer chose Alison, leaving Alison as a neglectee[5] – she was only chosen by Sandra. Alison had also

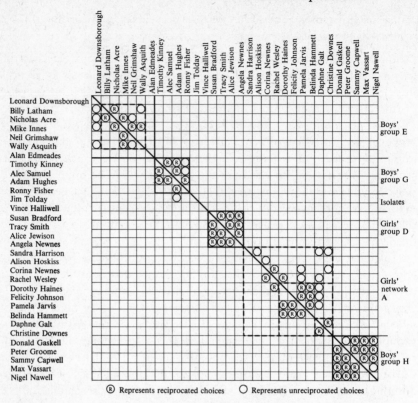

Figure 2. 2TA: second sociomatrix

become more unpopular with the other girls, and her mother complained to the school that they had been bullying her. She was always quiet in lessons and rarely involved in disruption. Unlike the other girls in the group, she was well-perceived by teachers and she came second in the end-of-year exams. Her attitudes to work and lack of identification with the anti-school girls was reflected in her unpopularity and the bullying to which she was subjected. Yet she shared the interests of the anti-school girls in fashion, pop music and boyfriends. Indeed, the pop-media culture, especially in terms of clothes, hair-styles, shoes, pop-group allegiance, knowledge of dances, etc., was important for all the girls in 2TA, irrespective of their attitude to school. Alison, for instance, always wore a large 'Bay City Rollers' badge on the front of her school cardigan. Furthermore, the group A girls were clearly the focus in the form for participation and popularity, in terms of these values. As a result, such girls as Alison, and to some extent Rachel and Corina, were confronted with, on the one hand, the pressure from home 'to do well at school', to behave well and work hard and so forth, and, on the other hand, the pressure to seek approval in the eyes of the group A girls. Thus, although she aspired to membership of this group, on the basis of mutual interest in the pop-media culture, Alison was disqualified on the basis of her attitude to school and her behaviour towards teachers in lessons. These problems of equating popularity and academic success in 2TA are illustrated in the sociometric structure of the form, and may account for the low status and fringe position of Alison, Rachel, Corina, and also to some extent Felicity, in relation to group A. Felicity, Alison and Rachel, all of whom came in the top ten positions in the end-of-year exams, were all sociometrically 'low status'.

	First questionnaire	Second questionnaire
Felicity received	2 choices	2 choices
Alison received	2 choices	1 choice
Rachel received	2 choices	2 choices

Changes in the rest of the form were much less drastic. *Group D* changed only inasmuch as it became fully reciprocating. Susan and Angela no longer chose outside the form. But *group E* also underwent a change of focus. Mike Innes had become very much the key figure in the group. His new exchange of choices with Neil Grimshaw and Wally Asquith, together with his continued choice of Nicholas Acre, now makes these four the core of the group. Neil Grimshaw's defection to this group and his developing friendship with Mike Innes were mostly based upon their shared attitudes towards school-work. They both participated a lot in lessons and had begun to sit together, almost always at the front of the form near to the teacher. Ronny, who had been Neil Grimshaw's best friend, also changed his friendship allegiance to align himself with the quiet boys of *group G*, who were similar to him in temperament and classroom behaviour. He chose Adam Hughes, who reciprocated the choice. He also received choices from Alec Samuel and Timothy Kinney. The other choices in this group remained the same. As for the rejectees, Jim Tolday, although he still chose Adam, had given up his fruitless pursuit of the other members of this group. He now chose outside the form to boys in higher years whom he had met by joining the sea cadets. Vince had also given up making unreciprocated choices to this group. The choices made by the boys in *group H* were repeated exactly as in the first sociomatrix.

The changes that have taken place overall in the friendship structure of the form have been marginal. With the exception of Ronny and Neil, that is, the changes have taken place within the framework of existing groups or friendship networks. Certainly, there has been no movement between groups of different types. But the realignments that have taken place represent a move towards an even closer congruence between group structure and differences in behaviour and in orientation to the normative culture of the school. What emerges from the analysis of the informal social structure of 2TA is the existence of persistent pro- and anti-school sub-cultures. Despite the fact that they were regarded almost universally by their teachers as a 'problem form', and different from band 1 forms, this detailed examination of the form reveals that within 2TA there exist clear differences between pupils in terms of behaviour and attitude to school. The sort of comparison of indices that were made between the band 1 and band 2 forms in chapter 2 can also be made within 2TA between the different groups of pupils; that is, in terms of classroom behaviour, detentions received, attitudes to school, levels of academic achievement, etc. Taking the groups together, three different types of groups are apparent. First, those pupils who are members of the pro-school sub-culture, the boys of groups E, F and G, who are positively oriented to the school and their teachers; second, those pupils who are ambivalent to school, the girls of group D (and Alison perhaps); and third, those pupils who represent the anti-school sub-culture, the girls of the group A friendship network and the boys of group H, who are negatively oriented to the school and to their teachers. The anti-school pupils obtain prestige from their peers for cheeking the teacher and not doing homework, for smoking, bullying, and acts of vandalism against school property; the sub-culture takes its norms from the larger culture but turns them upside down (Cohen 1955 : 131). The pro-school pupils continue to be committed to the school and its normative culture, compete amongst themselves to answer questions in lessons, do their homework and adhere closely to school uniform, etc. In other words, they seek prestige from the rewards dispensed by the teacher.

However, Lacey (1970 : 86) makes the important point in his study that 'The existence of the two opposed sub-cultures does not mean that every pupil can be neatly classified as an adherent of one or other'. Thus, neither Alison nor the girls of group D can be 'neatly classified' as pro- or anti-school. The girls of group D were not disruptive or difficult to control in lessons, but neither did they participate or work hard. They tended to sit quietly or talk amongst themselves, offering neither threat nor support to their teachers. They are, to an extent, anti-school in their attitudes but not in their behaviour.

The separation out of these groups is not merely a matter of heuristic convenience, but also represents the normal boundaries of interaction between pupils, and their own perceptual classification of the classroom. The members of the different groups tended to regard one another with suspicion and hostility. It was evident from my observations that there was a considerable amount of interaction between the anti-school boys of group H and the anti-school girls of groups A, B and C, but only essential and unavoidable contact between these groups and the other boys and girls in the form. Sometimes, indeed, the girls from group A 'went out' with the boys from group H as boyfriend and girlfriend. On one occasion Belinda told me that she 'went to Sandra's party with Nigel, and Daphne went with Max'. In general, the girls approved of these boys.

> Interview notes
> Belinda   'Max, he's nice and funny, and Nigel, he's nice.'
> Kathy   'And Donald and Peter, they're modern.'
> S. Ball   'Who is the most popular boy?'
> Corina   'Philip and David.'
> Kathy   'They're not really popular, they're modern.'
> Daphne   'The rest of the boys are weeds.'

They did not approve of the pro-school boys; they were 'weeds', were not 'modern', and did not wear the latest fashions or haircuts. They were not 'a laugh'; they were too serious and too involved in doing schoolwork. As noted previously, this process of the separation out of groups among the pupils themselves is what Lacey (1970) terms polarization. The insularity of the groups is illustrated in the distribution of friendship choices from the

Table 3.1. *Friendship choices between groups: 2TA*

	1	2	3	4
1 Girls' groups in network A	31(26)[a]	–	–	–
2 Boys' group H	–	17(18)	–	–
3 Girls' group D	–	–	7(12)	–
4 Boys' groups E/G	1[b]	–	–	30(26)

[a] Choices from the second questionnaire are given in brackets.
[b] This was Mike Innes's choice for Christine Downes.

sociometric questionnaire shown in table 3.1. Taking the groups together in this way, there is only one friendship choice in the first questionnaire made between groups that are of different orientation – that is, Mike Innes's choice for Christine Downes. There are no inter-group choices of this kind made in the second questionnaire.

One aspect of the behavioural differences between the groups which can be demonstrated quantitatively is time spent on homework. The members of the different groups gave distinctly different responses. None of the anti-school girls reported doing any homework at home in the evening, although three of them did say that they did their homework at school. The group of ambivalent girls reported more than three times as much time as did the anti-school boys of group H, and the pro-school boys had an average considerably higher than any of the other groups. There are only one or two individual cases of overlap between groups. The groups also differed considerably in the number of detentions they received during the second year. The pattern of detentions received again coincides with the sub-cultural orientations of the different groups.

There are also overall differences between the groups in regard to

Table 3.2. *Average reported time spent per night on homework for the friendship groups in 2TA*

		Minutes
Group network A	anti-school	0
Group H		6
Group D and Alison	ambivalent	22
Groups E/F/G	pro-school	40

Table 3.3. *Number of detentions received by the members of the friendship groups in 2TA*

		Detentions received	
		total	No. per pupil
Group network A	anti-school	72	5.54
Group H			
Group D and Alison	ambivalent	9	1.8
Groups E/F/G	pro-school	11	0.92

Table 3.4. *Covariation of examination achievement and friendship-group membership in 2TA*

		Examination positions			Average position per group
		top third	mid third	bottom third	
Group network A	anti-school	1	4	3	17.25
Group H		1	2	2	
Group D	ambivalent	0	0	4	26.5
Alison		1	–	–	2.0
Groups E/F/G	pro-school	7	4	2	11.1

$\chi^2 = 4.66$ d.f. $= 1$ p < 0.05 c $= 0.36$.

academic achievement, measured in terms of the end-of-year examination results, as shown in table 3.4. In the top ten places in the examinations there are only two pupils from the anti-school groups; in the bottom eleven places there are five pupils from the anti-school groups and all four of the girls of group D. Taking only the pro-school and anti-school groups and a top-half/bottom-half split in the examination positions (to overcome the problem of small expected frequencies), the relationship between group orientation and attainment is statistically significant.

These last two tables, showing detentions and examination achievement, demonstrate very crudely the positive relationship that exists between academic performance and 'behaviour'. Generally, the pro-school pupils did well in terms of academic performance in the school exams and received few detentions. These indices also lend support to the earlier material which indicated normative sub-cultural differences between the different friendship areas in the form. As we have seen, a sub-cultural polarization is taking place as these pupils move through the school: the pro-school values, 'which orientate the individual towards academic achievement and a characteristically middle class value complex emphasising the importance of "good behaviour"' (Lacey 1970:85), are taken up most strongly by those pupils who are academically 'successful' in the form (although there are anomalies, as we have seen), and anti-school values, based around a negative polarity of the dominant school culture, are taken up most strongly among the least 'successful' pupils. As noted in the previous chapter, the explanation of the emergence of these sub-cultural differences rests upon the assumption (also used by Lacey (1970) and Hargreaves (1967)) that there is a relationship between status and 'behaviour'. In simple terms, the reasoning behind this assumption is that the pupils who receive status-rewards from the school system will tend to behave well and thus reinforce the system, whereas the pupils who do not receive status-rewards or who are allocated to low status by the school system will be predisposed to reject the values of the school as a source of status and seek for alternatives. The corollary of this, as noted by Lacey (1970:82), is that:

Teachers well disposed towards a well behaved boy tend to encourage, praise and even raise marks for trying hard.

Teachers ill disposed towards a badly behaved boy tend to criticise, punish and reduce marks as a further method of punishment.

Anti-school pupils clearly 'disrupt teachers' expectations and violate their norms of appropriate social, moral and intellectual pupil behaviour' (Keddie 1971:134). Their lack of success in terms of the instrumental culture of the school (that relating to the acquisition of specific skills) tends to alienate them from, and bring them into conflict with, the expressive culture – that complex of behaviour and activities in the school which has to do with conduct, character and manners (Bernstein *et al.* 1966:429). Indeed, the teachers' views of pupils tend to include judgements both of the instrumental order and the expressive.

A further illustration of the relationship between performance and behaviour, in terms of the teachers' perception and evaluation of pupils, can be given by means of a repertorial grid test. This test elicits a system of personal constructs through which the teacher perceives and understands, and thus anticipates interaction with, the pupils in the form.[6]

When all of the constructs obtained from any one teacher are scored for each of the pupils in a form, on a four-point scale, the most favourable end scoring one point, the unfavourable end scoring four points, the pupils can be listed in order according to the total scores they received, those who scored lowest being the most favourably perceived by their teachers. The lists shown in table 3.5 begin from the lowest score. There are several interesting points of difference between the lists with regard to the actual constructs elicited from the teachers. The first and most obvious is the length of the two lists; there are only five bi-polar constructs obtained from the English teacher but nine from the Geography teacher. It seems likely, therefore, that the Geography teacher's list contains constructs having different ranges of convenience – there are more or less people or situations to which they might be applied. Kelly's theory of personal constructs

Table 3.5. *Rank orders of pupils according to construct-scores from 2TA's English teacher and Geography teacher*

English		Geography	
Rank-order by construct-scores	Exam position	Rank-order by construct-scores	Exam position
1 Mike Innes	8	1 Nicholas Acre	14
2 Kathy Forrest	left	2 Billy Latham	9
3 Alison Hoskiss	2	3 Mike Innes	8
4 Jim Tolday	10	4 Leonard Downsborough	7
5 Adam Hughes	3	5 Adam Hughes	3
6 Nicholas Acre	14	6 Neil Grimshaw	16
7 Leonard Downsborough	7	7 Sammy Capwell	18
8 Neil Grimshaw	16	8 Alec Samuel	5
9 Daphne Galt	31	9 Alison Hoskiss	2
10 Billy Latham	9	10 Rachel Wesley	11
11 Felicity Johnson	1	11 Ronny Fisher	22
12 Wally Asquith	4	12 Kathy Forrest	left
13 Alec Samuel	5	13 Wally Asquith	4
14 Alice Jewison	30	14 Felicity Johnson	1
15 Tracy Smith	24	15 Vince Halliwell	15
16 Pamela Jarvis	12	16 Pamela Jarvis	12
17 Angela Newnes	23	17 Alan Edmeades	21
18 Susan Bradford	29	18 Jim Tolday	10
19 Dorothy Haines	17	19 Timothy Kinney	19
20 Vince Halliwell	15	20 Christine Downes	absent
21 Ronny Fisher	22	21 Max Vassart	6
22 Alan Edmeades	21	22 Tracy Smith	24
23 Sandra Harrison	27	23 Daphne Galt	31
24 Corina Newnes	14	24 Angela Newnes	23
25 Belinda Hammett	25	25 Corina Newnes	14
26 Timothy Kinney	19	26 Susan Bradford	29
27 Christine Downes	absent	27 Alice Jewison	30
28 Sammy Capwell	18	28 Dorothy Haines	17
29 Rachel Wesley	11	29 Peter Groome	28
30 Peter Groome	28	30 Nigel Nawell	20
31 Donald Gaskell	26	31 Donald Gaskell	26
32 Max Vassart	6	32 Belinda Hammett	25
33 Nigel Nawell	20	33 Sandra Harrison	27

English constructs	Geography constructs
anti-school–pro-school	immature–mature
lazy–hard-working	difficult–responsive
does not try–always tries	erratic – consistent
no concentration–always concentrates	demanding–self-sufficient
mature–immature	lazy–hard-working
	uninterested–eager to please
	mucks about – serious
	lacks school ability – has school ability
	quiet – talkative

postulates that 'more superordinate constructs will have more implications and a wider range of convenience than their subordinate constructs' (Bannister 1970 : 57). In particular, the analysis of rank-positions presented below suggests that 'behaviour' and 'ability' constructs are superordinate (that is, they have greater general applicability than other constructs and include all other constructs as elements within their context) and perhaps pre-emptive (that is, excluding the possibility of elaborative construing) in teachers' perceptions of their pupils. However, it must be remembered that construct systems are obtained by means of 'third-party talk' (Hargreaves 1977 : 281) and their truth to the relationship of teacher and pupil in the classroom should not be exaggerated. These constructs are not here related to or situated in specific interactive contexts. They must be regarded as only an approximation to the teacher's perceptions of his pupils as those perceptions are re-formed and modified in a continuous process.

Nonetheless, the comparison of the rank-lists based on these construct systems is revealing. Seven of the top eleven positions in the English teacher's rank-order of perceptions are occupied by pupils in the top eleven examination positions; the Geography teacher also has seven. Seven pupils also appear in the top eleven positions in both teachers' lists. They are:

	Overall exam position	Rank positions:	
		English	Geography
Mike Innes	8	1	3
Alison Hoskiss	2	3	9
Adam Hughes	3	5	5
Nicholas Acre	14	6	1
Leonard Downsborough	7	7	4
Neil Grimshaw	16	8	6
Billy Latham	10	9	2

Four boys from the pro-school group E are included here, and Acre and Grimshaw are included despite mediocre examination performances. Clearly, they are similar to the other boys on the list as regards their pro-schoolness in terms of attitudes and behaviour.

As regards the bottom positions, six pupils are included in the bottom eleven in both lists. They are:

| | Overall exam position | Rank positions: | |
		English	Geography
Sandra Harrison	27	23	33
Corina Newnes	14	24	25
Belinda Hammett	25	25	32
Peter Groome	28	30	29
Donald Gaskell	26	31	31
Nigel Nawell	20	33	30

Included here are three girls from the large anti-school friendship network and three of the boys from the anti-school group H. They are all, except Corina, low-achievers, and all presented control problems to their teachers in lessons. The overall cross-tabulation of rank-order positions from the perception scores with group membership is shown in table 3.6. The association between the two sets of grid positions was tested by the use of Spearman's coefficient of rank-correlation and found to be significant at the 0.001 level ($r_s = 0.61$). There is also a high level of correlation between each of the rankings elicited from the teachers and the pupil's examination positions, in both cases significant at the 0.001 level ($r_s = 0.65$).

Two points emerge clearly from the consideration of the relationship between academic achievement, behaviour and the teachers' perception of pupils. First, the most favourably-perceived pupils in the form tend to be those who are pro-school and academically successful. Those pupils who are affiliated to the anti-school groups but are well-perceived tend to be less well-integrated or of low status in these groups; they diverge from the prevailing norms of their groups. Second, behaviour appears to be the more important criterion of differentiation among the pupils. The ·positions of Kathy and Daphne, Max Vassart and the four girls from group D reflect this. The girls in group D all come within the lowest achievement group. They are 23rd, 24th, 29th and 30th respectively in the

Table 3.6. *Cross-tabulation of construct rank-order positions and friendship-group membership*

Group network	Rank-order positions	Well-perceived 1–11	12–22	Poorly-perceived 22–33
Group H	anti-school	3(2)[a]	2(5)	10(8)
Group D and Alison	ambivalent	1(1)	5(1)	1(3)
Groups E/F/G	pro-school	7(8)	5(5)	1(–)

[a]The numbers in parenthesis are drawn from the Geography teacher's rankings.

examinations at the end of the second year. Alice, Tracy and Susan were 27th, 19th and 26th respectively in the end-of-year examinations, but as noted earlier, they are not badly behaved in lessons or difficult to control. A similar analysis applied in the case of Jimmy Patten in 2CU, who is a consistently poor academic performer, but quiet and well-behaved in lessons (see pp. 88–90). He is more favourably-perceived by his teachers than are badly behaved pupils who are considerably better than Jimmy academically. In the same way, although Max Vassart came 6th in the end-of-year examinations, he occupies the 32nd and 21st positions in the rank-orders of perception. He was frequently 'in trouble', as we have seen, and was frequently an initiator of disruption in lessons. Thus, his relatively high level of academic achievement is completely overshadowed in his teachers' perceptions of him by his behaviour in lessons and his attitude to school.

There is obviously much interplay between behaviour and achievement in the teachers' 'ranking and separation' of pupils. For instance, it is unlikely that the pupil who never brings a pen and is always late and then talks for most of the lesson will attain an acceptable level of work. Furthermore, the norms of the anti-group may actually prohibit overt co-operation with staff or the doing of schoolwork when it is at all possible to avoid it. Also, talking and 'mucking around' makes it difficult for the pupil to give much attention to the process of the lesson, and such behaviour may actually disrupt the lesson or push the teacher into using teaching techniques which make learning more difficult – for example, not giving explanations because 'class teaching' as such becomes impossible. Altogether, the relationship between behaviour and performance must be seen as self-reinforcing in terms of teachers' perceptions, motivation and classroom climate. Those pupils who embrace membership of the anti-school sub-culture because of lack of success in schoolwork become committed to a behaviour pattern which virtually eliminates the possibility of being successful in the future.

3TA in the third year

While I did not continue with close observation of the band 2 form in the third year, I shall be referring to them again in the final section of this chapter, and in chapter 5 with regard to the option choice and allocation procedures at the end of the third year. I did keep in contact with the progress of the form through their teachers and through discussions with the pupils themselves. The following comments were made by their teachers towards the end of the third year when I asked, 'How are 3TA getting on in your subject?'

English 'I had them this morning, perhaps that's why I'm feeling so depressed now.'

Biology 'They're really hard work . . . They manage to give the impression of chaos, but it's only one or two really, like Max Vassart, who make it so hard. Their work is really quite good.'

Year tutor 'History was a fiasco. The new supply teacher, he started teaching and Peter Groome started throwing a ball around the room.'

Geography 'It's like sitting on a keg of dynamite, too tense, I cannot do the sort of lesson I want to.'

French 'You know, they still are the only form that won't come in the way I want them to at the beginning of the lesson. The other forms come in and sit down quietly or wait until I tell them to come in; but *they* come in noisy and shouting and bang the door and scrape the chairs. I tell them everytime but they're terrible.'

Physics 'Together they're awful, I hate them, but I tell them *that* and I say that on their own I like them all. I even like Vassart and Groome on their own, it's when they're together that they get out of control.'

Form teacher 'What can I say, they're 3TA.'

For the most part, the remainder of this chapter concentrates upon the band 1 case-study form, CU, tracing the development of the social structure of the form through its second and third years.

Several factors led me to decide to concentrate on the development of 3CU. First, 2TA underwent a considerable reorganization at the end of the second year. As noted above (p. 36), four girls were moved into other band 2 forms as a result of problems in the form during the second year; one boy, Michael Innes, was promoted into band 1; the Newnes sisters left the school; and six new pupils were moved into the form. Also, the form was allocated a new form teacher. I anticipated that these changes of personnel would have a considerable impact upon the structure of friendships in the form and would entail the collection of a great many fresh data.[7] Secondly, concomitant with the first point, I was becoming heavily engaged in observing and collecting other data from the second year of the mixed-ability cohort, and it was impossible to maintain an adequate level of data collection across four case-study forms. Thirdly, the future development of the band 1 form seemed to be more problematic from the end of the second year. I was especially interested in the extent to which the polarization and differentiation within the form would increase. In 2TA, the social structure of the form was already starkly polarized. I thought it likely that polarization and differentiation would increase in 3CU as the point of decision for O-level and C.S.E. courses came closer and academic achievement became more crucial in terms of future planning.

The social structure of 2CU

As we shall see, the social structure of 2CU was already well established at the point at which the pupils' careers were taken up. Overall, the structure was more stable over time than that of 2TA, although individual movements did take place.[8] The form completed three sociometric questionnaires over a period of four terms during their second and third years. The first and second questionnaire were administered at the same time as those given to 2TA, in the spring and summer terms of the second year; the third was administered in the spring term of the third year to coincide with the third-year-option examinations.[9] The first sociomatrix (figure 3) shows the basic structure of friendship groups and cliques in the form. The first obvious point to note is that once again, as in 2TA and the other banded forms which completed the questionnaires, there is an almost total absence of cross-sex choices; only two are made here. Furthermore,

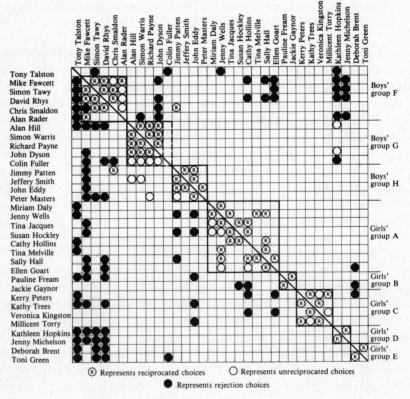

Figure 3. 2CU: first sociomatrix

the concentration of reciprocated choices close to the diagonal central line in the sociomatrix indicates, as in 2TA, the insularity of each of the friendship-group areas.[10] Rejection choices are also recorded on this sociomatrix, taken from answers to questions about the 'people you can't get on with'. As may be seen, they are concentrated on a few members of the form and are made to the same persons by both boys and girls. These 'rejectees' and also the single sociometric 'isolate' will be dealt with in the discussion below.

Friendship choice in 2CU

Compared with 2TA, the social class composition of this form is more evenly balanced, although middle-class pupils are considerably over-represented in proportion to the composition of the school as a whole (62.5 per cent in 2CU as against 33 per cent in the school as a whole). Social class is an important factor in the distribution of friendship choices in the form. The relationship between social class and friendship choice shown in table 3.7 is statistically significant, $x^2 = 9.29$ d.f. $= 1$ p < 0.01. C $= 0.29$. Only 27 per cent of the choices made by middle-class members are made to working-class members and only 45 per cent of choices made by working-class members are made to middle-class members. However, the manifestation of this insular tendency could simply be a function of the size of the respective social class groups in the form. Therefore Procter and Loomis's (1951) Index of In-group Preference was calculated[11] to take into account the different sizes of the groups; the values obtained are shown in table 3.8. The index values are greater than unity for three of the four sub-groups, which confirms the general tendency towards social class in-group preference. The out-group preference for working-class girls can probably be accounted for in terms of the popularity-system among the girls, which is evident in the friendship structure discussed below. But the values for the

Table 3.7. *Distribution of friendship choices between social classes: 2CU*

Choices from:	Choices to:	
	Middle-class	Working-class
Middle-class	50	18
Working-class	14	19

Table 3.8. *Index of In-group Preference values for social class in 2CU: first sociomatrix (taken separately by sex)*

	Boys		Girls	
	Middle-class	Working-class	Middle-class	Working-class
Index of In-group Preference values	1.25	5.00	2.17	0.81

Table 3.9. *Index of In-group Preference values for levels of academic achievement in 2CU: first sociomatrix (taken separately by sex)*

	Boys		Girls	
	Top-half positions	Bottom-half positions	Top-half positions	Bottom-half positions
Index of In-group Preference values	0.8	0.91	0.6	1.11

other sub-groups indicates what Ford (1969 : 103) refers to as 'consciousness of kind' in friendship choice. However, in my observations of and discussions with members of the form there was no evidence of social class being an explicit construct of differentiation. That is, the pupils did not appear to be making judgements about members of the form in terms of social or economic status *per se*.[12] Nevertheless, the tendency to choose friends from the same social class background is clear enough. However, as there is also a relationship between friendship choice and level of achievement it could be argued that this is a more immediate basis of friendship choice in the pupils' social-phenomenal world – that 'friends' are chosen primarily because of similarities in terms of ability and interest in schoolwork. An analysis of choices made between achievement groups, however, demonstrates that level of achievement is only a basis of choice among the middle-class girls. The values obtained by using the Index of In-group Preference again, taking pupils in the top half and bottom half of the end-of-year examination, are shown in table 3.9. The values are less than unity except in the case of the girls in the bottom half of the rank-order of examination positions.[13]

Friendship groups

As with 2TA, each of the groups and cliques within the form will be briefly examined in turn, taking the girls' groups first.

Group A (8 girls)

	Father's occupation	Exam position	No. of detentions received	Social class
Miriam Daly	Business consultant	3	–	II
Jenny Wells	Office worker	18	–	IIIN
Tina Jacques	Toolsetter	20	–	IIIM
Sally Hall	Valuer	13	–	II
Ellen Goart	Accountant	4	–	II
Susan Hockley	Accountant	11	–	II
Cathy Hollins	Shop assistant	10	–	IIIM
Tina Melville	Art dealer	14	–	II

The girls in this group were all hard-working, with positive attitudes to schoolwork (and as can be seen from their end-of-term examinations, average position 11.7, they were all fairly successful). They were all conscientious and attentive in lessons, always gave in their homework and never got into trouble; they were well-perceived by the staff and involved in extra-curricular school activities. They averaged 41 minutes homework per night. Miriam was involved in the school hockey and netball teams and had her school colours. She was named nine times in a Guess-Who-Test[14] as 'most popular girl' in the class. Sally was an athlete and competed for the school and for a club. Jenny and Tina were in the school music club and played instruments, and Ellen took part in the school's drama activities. Schoolwork, and the teachers' acceptance and appraisal of that work, were important and significant aspects of the school lives of these girls. Ellen and Sue differed somewhat from the rest of the group in that they were less concerned with modern fashions and trends; they usually dressed more casually and nearer to the 'student' than the pupil. This orientation was also reflected in their choice of 'favourite pop-groups'; they did not pick any of the groups that were currently popular and mentioned by other pupils: Mud, Slade, Alvin Stardust, David Cassidy and David Essex. Ellen chose Bob Dylan and the Rolling Stones, and Sue chose Black Sabbath and Deep Purple. Murdock and Phelps (1973) categorized these groups as 'underground/progressive' rather than the 'mainstream white pop' that was popular with most other pupils. The boys of group F often called these two girls 'The Freaks'. I asked pupils in both 2TA and 2CU to name their favourite pop-groups but there was no differentiation between the forms. Ellen and Sue's choices were deviant across both forms.

Friendship-pairing B

	Father's occupation	Exam position	No. of detentions received	Social class
Pauline Fream	Doctor	2	–	I
Jackie Gaynor	Plumber	17	–	IIIM

These were two quiet, hard-working girls who were not involved in the larger friendship area. Their friendship in the form appeared to be maintained for lack of anything better; neither of them was popular with the rest of the girls but they were both highly motivated in their schoolwork. They reported a norm of 45 and 50 minutes per night spent in doing homework. Both girls were unpopular in the form, and they received no other friendship choices. Pauline was disliked by the rest of the girls because of her boastfulness, especially about her boyfriends, and Jackie was regarded by the others as 'immature'.

Friendship area C (4 girls)

	Father's occupation	Exam position	No. of detentions received	Social class
Kerry Peters	Office manager	15	–	II
Kethy Trees	College lecturer	21	–	II
Veronica Kingston	Office manager	8	–	II
Millicent Torry	Clerk	(left before exams)	–	IIIN

This was another loose-knit group of four girls, less obviously hard-working and less successful overall than the previous groups. The girls were all middle-class. They were quiet in lessons and much less involved in lesson activity than any of the other girls. Veronica was the most vocal in lessons, but her contributions were still very few. Kathy had come into 2CU from a second-band form and was in the process of establishing herself in the form both socially and academically; she achieved 21st place in the examinations at the end of the year, and improved her position further in the third-year-option examinations. She had in fact been promoted from 1TA at the end of the first year. She had been popular in 1TA and was elected as form captain in the first term. Sandra Harrison had been her particular friend and they still occasionally ate lunch together, but they did not choose each other in any of the sociometric questionnaires. Even in the first year Kathy had been aware of the pressures existing in her form against working hard and doing well in schoolwork. She had been pleased to move into 2CU. She said:

> 'It's much nicer, they are much more friendly; it was horrible in the other form. They weren't nice people. I had friends but I used to get higher marks and they called me a "creep" and things. They seemed much older in this form when I came in.'

In the sentence-completion test (which the form did after Millicent had left), the girls in this group wrote:

When lessons are boring
I . . . doodle on my exercise book.
   . . . muck about and write on different things.
   . . . write pop stars' names on my book.

It is interesting to contrast this 'passive' disengagement from the boring lesson with the more active response of the anti-school pupils in band 2. The group reported an average of 75 minutes homework per night, considerably above the form average of 47 minutes per night.

Friendship-pairing D

Kathleen Hopkins and Jenny Michelson were both from social class II; their fathers were a Gas Board Executive and a Teacher, respectively. They both stated 'boys' as their major out-of-school activity, and were among the least enthusiastic and involved members of the form as regards schoolwork during the second year. Their attitude to work was passive. They were occasionally in trouble for not doing homework, but their work was usually done eventually, though it was not of a high standard. Kathleen came 27th in the end-of-year examinations and Jenny 25th. Jenny chose needlework as her favourite subject; Kathleen chose games. They both reported doing 30 minutes homework per night, and neither received any school detentions during the second year.

These two girls did not typically represent the 'educative drive' of the middle-class pupil but rather an ambivalence to schoolwork. Their choice of careers was, however, more in line with their family background; Jenny wanted to be a medical secretary and Kathleen a pharmacist. And their examination performance had improved considerably by the end of the third year (see p. 105). Alan Hill from the friendship group G often sat with these girls in lessons, and both he and Dyson made cross-sex friendship choices to Kathleen, but she did not reciprocate.

Friendship-pairing E

Deborah Brent and Toni Green were both quiet and hard-working girls of working-class parents. Deborah's father was a lorry driver and Toni's a dock worker. Here again we have a reversal of the typical social class and education relationship in so far as both of the girls, particularly Toni, were under a great deal of pressure from their fathers to do well at school. They were not very successful in the end-of-term examinations, – Toni was 19th and Deborah 23rd – but in the third-year-option examinations Toni improved to 11th and Deborah to 20th. Toni's father insisted that she should play a musical instrument and that she should practise for an hour each evening. She wanted to be a games teacher or a secretary when she left school; she was very interested in athletics. Deborah wanted to be a window-dresser when she left school. She reported spending $1\frac{1}{4}$ to $1\frac{1}{2}$ hours per night on homework, and Tina $1\frac{1}{2}$ to 2 hours. Neither received any detentions during the second year.

Group F (5 boys)

	Father's occupation	Exam position	No. of detentions received	Social class
Mike Fawcett	Divorced. Mother buyer for a large store	24	3	II
Simon Tawy	G.P.O. engineer	12	–	IIIM
David Rhys	Certified accountant	16	1	II
Chris Smaldon	Installs greenhouse heating-systems	26	–	IIIM
Alan Rader	Pharmacist	28	–	II

The boys in this group are on the whole medium- to low-achievers and the central clique particularly was often noisy in lessons and more frequently rebuked by teachers than was normal for the rest of the form;[15] they were usually in trouble for 'silly' things such as making paper aeroplanes and pushing each other, 'fooling around'. Rhys received one school detention during the year, for breaking a window, and Tawy was put on report for a while, but these two did noticeably better in the end-of-year examinations than the rest of the group.[16] The average examination position for the group was 22nd and they reported an average of only 26 minutes spent on homework each night, compared with the class average of 47 minutes. Only Smaldon reported any involvement in after-school act- ivities – playing football – although he was never picked for any of the teams. The members of the core-clique were united by their interest in model boats and model-building, and both Fawcett and Tawy expressed their intention of joining the Navy after leaving school. Fawcett was an active member of the Nautical Training Corps and played in their band, but he refused to take part in any musical activities at school. He explained:

> 'If you miss a band practice at N.T.C. then that is O.K., it's your decision, they don't say anything. But at school, if you miss a rehearsal for the orchestra, then they are after you to find out why.'

He felt that the school treated him as a child but in the N.T.C. he was treated as an adult. He expressed his general attitude to school as 'lessons are boring. We don't like just sitting there, we like to talk.' The group generally showed little interest in schoolwork and were often in trouble with teachers for not completing homework. The group, again especially the core-clique, had poor relations with the rest of the form, who tended to regard them as 'loud and vulgar and stupid', and this triad received 35 rejection choices between them. They were fond of insulting and annoying the other members of the form, particularly the girls, by giving them nicknames. The members of this group were also poorly-perceived by staff. Something of this may be gathered from an incident which occurred when the three came to fetch me from the staffroom for an interview I had arranged with them. They arrived early and were waiting outside the small stockroom near to the staffroom where I often used to talk to children and record interviews. Before I arrived, as I was told afterwards, they had been pushing each other and getting in the way of people coming into the staffroom area. As I arrived from lunch one of the teachers came out of the staffroom. 'Are these three waiting for you?' he asked me. I assented. 'Well, they have been a bloody nuisance'. He turned to the boys:

> 'I could hear your stupid cackling laugh in the staffroom, Fawcett. You've been behaving like five-year-olds and getting in everyone's way. I'm fed up with you and your antics and I'm going to come down on you hard, do you understand?'

The teacher was shouting; Fawcett unfortunately was smiling.

> 'And you can take that bloody stupid grin off your face before I knock it off. You think you're special case in this school. Well, I can tell you that you're not.'

He glared at them for a few seconds, and then turned away and stalked into the staffroom. Later, in the staffroom, when I had finished the interview he came up to me.

'I'm sorry about that, but they really annoyed me with their mucking about there. That Fawcett's getting a damn sight too big for his boots and is going to come to a very sticky end if he doesn't watch it.'

In their attitude to school, and their behaviour in some lessons and out of lesson time, this core-clique from group F displayed some embryonic features of being 'anti-school'.

Group G (5 boys)

	Father's occupation	Exam position	No. of detentions received	Social class
Alan Hill	Painter	20		IIIM
John Dyson	Electrician	23	–	IIIM
Simon Warris	Kitchen porter	5	–	V
Richard Payne	Mother works on factory shop-floor	7	–	IV
Colin Fuller	Industrial buyer	28	–	II

Fuller was new to the school at the beginning of the second year but by the time of the first sociometric questionnaire he was already a participating member of the group, both in the classroom and outside it, and he subsequently became fully integrated. The boys in the core of the group – Hill, Warris, Payne and Dyson – are all from working-class families. Fuller, the aspirant, however, is middle-class. These boys were rarely in trouble with their teachers and were well-perceived. Their average position in the end-of-year examinations was 17.2. The boys were popular with their classmates and were on good terms with the girls in the form; they also tended to get on well with the teachers. Payne was regarded by the form as their spokesman and organizer; whenever they were involved in form group-activities, he would negotiate with the teachers. When, for instance, the form decided to run an all-day rounders match to raise money for charity,[17] it was Payne who approached the sports staff for permission and to ask to borrow equipment. It was also Payne who then approached the form's subject teachers for permission to miss lessons; he also came to see me to ask me to spend part of the day with them as a supervisor. He was reported ten times as 'the most popular boy in the form' in the Guess-Who-Test. The group was also considerably involved in extra-curricular activities. Payne played rugby and ran cross-country for the school; Warris was captain of the second-year basketball team; Hill was a regular member of the second-year football team; and Dyson also played football for the school.

Some affirmation of the positive attitude of these boys to school and schoolwork can be gained from their questionnaire responses. For instance, in sentence-completion tests they wrote:

> Teachers are . . . on the whole quite good people.
> . . . alright if it is a good subject.
> . . . alright except for [he named two].
> . . . not bad.
> . . . not too bad.
> When teachers tell me my work is bad
> I . . . try to do better.
> . . . listen and try to correct it.
> . . . try to improve.
> . . . agree.
> . . . hurl abuse under my breath [Warris].

These two groups, F and G, represent an interesting reversal of the usual direction of association between social class and involvement in school. The boys in group G, from working-class backgrounds, were far more involved in school activities, had a more positive attitude towards school, and tended to be better behaved than the boys in group F, who were mainly from middle-class backgrounds. The group G boys are clearly pro-school in their attitudes and behaviour, whereas the group F boys are an incipient anti-school group. However, both Tawy and Rhys came under pressure from their parents when it seemed as though their schoolwork was deteriorating as a result of their increasing misbehaviour in lessons. Both sets of parents were successful in bringing their 'resources'[18] to bear when the academic future of their sons seemed to be threatened (see pp. 153–7). This demonstrates both the independence of the informal social system of the classroom from forces that are external to it, but it also shows the likelihood that this informal system will yield to such external pressure when it is directly applied.

Group H (4 boys)

	Father's occupation	Exam position	No. of detentions received	Social class
Jimmy Patten	Sales representative	32	–	II
Jeffery Smith	Doctor	9	–	I
John Eddy	Teacher	6	–	I
Peter Masters	Office clerk	1	–	II

This was an all-middle-class group and three of the members were also among the most academically successful in the class. In the Guess-Who-

Test Masters was mentioned six times as 'good-natured' and sixteen times as 'hard-working'. It is interesting that the boy who came top in the examinations was in the same friendship group, and in fact made a friendship choice to, the boy who came bottom in the examinations. The other two boys, Smith and Eddy, who were both in the top ten exam positions, also chose Patten. The key to their friendship seems to lie in a similarity of temperament above and beyond the academic success of Smith, Eddy and Masters. They are all quiet and hard-working and were never in trouble or even rebuked in lessons. Masters and Eddy were somewhat isolated from the rest of the form, and Masters particularly had the reputation for 'brains' in the form. He was first or second in six of the end-of-year examinations, and in Maths, his favourite lesson, he had usually to be set work of his own to get on with because he was so far ahead of the rest of the form.

Maths: lesson notes

The teacher is giving back books after a homework had been marked.
Teacher 'I'm going to go over the questions in the homework because only one person managed to get them all right.'
'Peter Masters' – half a dozen voices sound from the form.
Teacher 'Yes, it was Peter. [To him:] I'll set you some work to be getting on with.'

Even though Jimmy Patten was consistently the 'weakest' academically in the form, all suggestions of demotion to band 2 had been rejected. He was quiet and polite, tried hard at his work, and was never a cause of disciplinary problems to staff. Despite his poor academic performance, the year tutor felt that to expose him to a band 2 environment would have created problems for him. He was chosen thirteen times as 'poor at work' in the Guess-Who-Test. His end of year report comments may be contrasted with those received by Talston (see below).

Isolate Tony Talston

The remaining member of the form is Tony Talston. Talston was a rejectee; he did not receive a single friendship choice from any member of the form, and did not himself make any choices to other members of the form. He received fifteen rejection choices, seven from boys and eight from girls. He was disliked by most of the form and feared by several. In a Guess-Who-Test he was named twenty-two times as 'a bully' and twenty times as 'badly behaved'. It must be stressed that Talston was a highly untypical band 1 pupil, not only in 2CU but overall in band 1; he was unique in his attitudes and behaviour. It is revealing to contrast his 'isolate' status with that of Jim Tolday in 2TA. Whereas Tolday was an unwilling isolate, wanting to make friends but handicapped by his lack of social skills, Talston pursued a deliberate policy of isolation. Never in any of the sociometric questionnaires did he make any friendship choices to other pupils in 2CU, nor was he consistently friendly to members of the form. One important reason for this was that he did not want to have what he regarded as low-status friends. He said of 2CU, 'They're just a load of kids in here. My mates are in the fifth year'. His behaviour was aggressive and violent in lessons and outside; he appeared to enjoy insulting and upsetting members of the form whenever possible. He actually 'beat up' two of the boys in the form after school and it was only with great reluctance that they were persuaded to report these incidents to the year tutor. Talston's friends were boys much older than him in the fourth and fifth years of the school; he spent break and lunch time with them at school and was part of their gang outside the school. He was several times 'in trouble' with the police and once appeared in court. This gang was his normative reference-group, acting as a source of attitudes and values, and he deliberately built his 'image' around his membership of the gang. In lessons he was often cheeky, off-hand, and rude to teachers, and did little work and no homework when he could help it. But the incidents which got him into serious trouble usually happened in the company of his older friends. In the period covered by the school detention records reported earlier, 2CU as a whole had received 20 school detentions. This is the highest number of detentions received by any of the band 1 forms. The totals for the other forms over the same period were:

3/2FT	2
3/2ST	13
3/2GD	6

However, 16 out of the 20 detentions received by 3/2CU were received by Tony Talston. In his school file he was twice reported for fighting during the first year, and once for smoking on the field. During the first term of the second year he was reported for running away from a teacher and for bullying, when the parents of other pupils complained about him to the school. He regarded school as 'a laugh' and when I asked him on one occasion whether he intended to leave as soon as he could, he replied, 'I don't want to leave. School days are the happiest days of your life, aren't they?'

Talston's father was a carpenter, and Talston intended to work with his brother as a shopfitter when he left school. When I asked him why he never bothered with school work, he explained: 'School exams don't seem much point when you can earn 80 to 100 quid a week doing that.' In the examinations at the end of the second year, he came 31st out of 32.

Extract from Patten's end-of-year report
English Steady but slow progress.
Maths Should not be put off by his low exam mark.
French Insufficient efforts to overcome his difficulties.
Chemistry Very quiet; his written work pulls him down.
Physics Class work often unfinished.
History Works well but disappointing exam.
Woodwork Tried hard.
Metalwork Quietly does his best.

Comments on Tony Talston's end-of-year report
English Little evidence of effort.
French Must use his ability and make greater efforts.
History Rarely makes the effort to exploit his ability.
Music Not much interest or effort.
P.E. Very poor standard of work. The most disappointing boy in the
       year.
Geography Too often has a don't care attitude.
Physics Sloppy work.
Biology Tony is too concerned with himself to worry about his poor work.
Spanish Too often wastes his time in truculence.

The combination of 'bad behaviour' and 'poor performance' produces harsh condemnation from Talston's teachers. This report differs considerably in tone from that of Jimmy Patten. While Patten was bottom in the examinations, he was never badly behaved. This demonstrates once again the importance of the interaction between academic attainment and behaviour in the teachers' view of and assessment of pupils.

It was clear that Talston failed to meet the usual criteria of performance and behaviour for the band 1 pupil. It was suggested more than once by members of staff that he should be demoted to band 2, but this was always rejected by the year tutors for fear he would create even greater problems for staff in band 2, especially if he was in 'association' with other 'problem-pupils'. As it was, most of the experienced staff found him controllable in 2CU, as a minority of one.

The changing structure of friendships

As in the analysis of 2TA, I want now to note the changes in the social structure of friendships over time in 2CU. In this section a second sociomatrix is presented, and data referring to the end-of-year examination results and teachers' perceptions of the pupils of 2CU are introduced into the analysis.

Second questionnaire

The pupils of 2CU completed a second sociometric questionnaire at the end of their second year (see figure 4). Comparing this with the previous one, it is apparent that there had been no radical redistribution of friendship choices. The same friendship groupings remained and I continued to observe them in the school. The changes that *had* taken place over the period between the questionnaires were in the status and position of

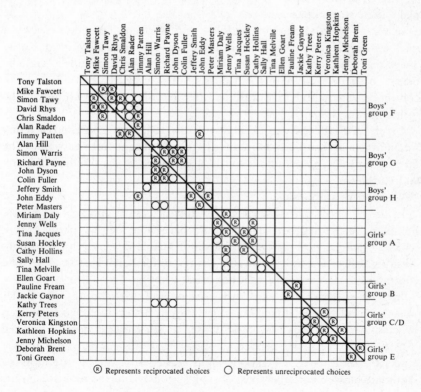

Figure 4. 2CU: second sociomatrix

particular individuals. However, the organization of the friendship groups in the form must be regarded as still 'in process'. The changes in group membership and the personnel of the form represented in the second sociomatrix are summarized below.

In *group A* (predominantly middle-class, hard-working and participative), Ellen Goart now only received one friendship choice (from Sally Hall). She had grown steadily more unpopular with the other girls in the group. Her eccentricity and 'progressive' tastes made her a deviant in terms of the interests and attitudes of the rest of the group. This was especially true of her growing interests in Art and Music, which led her into friendship with sixth-form girls. Tina Melville and Sally Hall, both friends of Ellen, also lost sociometric status and were less a part of the larger group.

In *group B* (quiet and hard-working), Pauline Fream and Jackie Gaynor now became an isolated friendship pair. They did not make or receive choices from the rest of the form. Their ardent pro-schoolness tended to make them unpopular.

In *group C* (less successful, middle-class) Millicent Torry left school in mid-term, and Kerry Peters was to leave school at the end of term. Kathy Trees made her only friendship choice to the boys in group G, and she began to spend time with them outside of school (see p. 100). But she continued to sit with Kerry until the latter left. She was now chosen by the girls in group D.

Group D (disaffected middle-class and low-achievers) consisted of Jenny Michelson and Kathleen Hopkins. Before Millicent left the school the interaction between groups C and D was limited by her dislike of Jenny and Kathleen.

Group E was unchanged.

In *group F* (boys of mixed social class and incipiently anti-school) Jimmy Patten moved from group H to become a peripheral member of this group, which contained boys of a similar level of academic achievement to him. Although there was no observable change in his behaviour in lessons he continued to be quiet and well behaved.

In *group G* (working-class, hard-working and pro-school) Colin Fuller was now a fully-fledged member of the group; he received two friendship choices. Alan Hill was no longer chosen at all. He thus became a social isolate in the form. He tended to spend more time with other pupils, especially older girls, at school. This, together with his attempts to ingratiate himself with members of staff, seriously affected his status in the form.

Group H (hard-working, pro-school) was unchanged, except for the defection of Jimmy Patten to group F.

Overall, during the period of the second year the structure of the form was relatively stable. There were few changes in group membership in the period between the collection of data for the two sociomatrices. Of these changes, only Jimmy Patten's defection from the pro-school group H to the incipient anti-school group actually enhanced the existing polarized structure of the form. However, the effects of the continuing processes of polarization and differentiation were more evident during the third year. Other factors, such as personality differences, pupils leaving the school, and the divergence of out-of-school interests, had a greater impact over this period. In particular during the third year the pupils' increasing involvement in the cultures of adolescence and the pop media impinged on the friendship structure.

At the end of the second year, in comparison with 2TA, the polarization of this band 1 form was much less clear-cut, and the extremes of attitude and behaviour much less divergent. It is apparent that the band 1 context imposes its own constraints upon the range of identities available to the pupil, in that the dominant normative culture of the form reinforces that of the school, and there are social pressures within the form which limit extremes of behaviour. Talston, whose normative reference group was an anti-school gang in the fifth year, was an exception to this. But even Talston committed the bulk of his 'offences' – bullying, smoking, fighting, vandalism, etc. – out of lesson time. Disciplinary problems in 2CU lessons were problems of 'misbehaviour' rather than 'disruption', in contrast to 2TA. In 2CU the pupils actually contributed to the maintenance of orderly working conditions in lessons. The pressures of the peer-group are towards conformity to the expectations of teachers. Nonetheless, as we have already seen, the pressures of academic competition do lead to the emergence of anti-schoolness, even in this band 1 form.

Table 3.10. *Index of In-group Preference values for social class in 2CU: second sociomatrix (taken separately by sex)*

Boys		Girls	
Middle-class	Working-class	Middle-class	Working-class
3.75	0.92	2.17	1.43

In the case of the second sociomatrix, the results of the Index of In-group Preference statistic still indicate social class as a basis for friendship choice among the pupils as shown in table 3.10. The middle-class boys are now the only sub-groups where there is no in-group preference, although the values for the working-class boys and middle-class girls have both moved closer to unity. In the case of similar achievement, in-group preference exists in two of the four sub-groups – that is, among boys in the bottom half of the rank-order of examination positions and girls in the top half (see table 3.11).

Once again, taking the two second-year sociomatrices into account, there are two distinct polarities within the friendship structure of the form. In 2CU, one is between the pro-school boys and the incipient anti-school boys, and the other is between the girls as a whole and the boys as a whole. There is only one reciprocated choice between the groups represented in different parts of the first sociomatrix and only two, generated by Patten's movement between groups, in the second (see table 3.12).

Table 3.11. *Index of In-group Preference values for level of academic achievement in 2CU: second sociomatrix (taken separately by sex)*

Boys		Girls	
Top-half positions	Bottom-half positions	Top-half positions	Bottom-half positions
0.86	1.27	1.67	0.73

Table 3.12. *Friendship choices between the three sections of the sociomatrix: 2CU*

	Girls	Pro-school boys	Incipient anti-school group[a]
Girls	40(37)[b]	– (3)	– (–)
Pro-school boys	2(1)	22(21)	1(2)
Incipient anti-school group	– (–)	1(1)	15(18)

[a] Including Tony Talston.
[b] Choices from the second questionnaire are in round brackets.

Table 3.13. *Negative rejection choices between the three sections of the first sociomatrix: 2CU[a]*

	Girls	Pro-school boys	Incipient anti-school group[b]
Girls	9	9	32
Pro-school boys	1	–	16
Incipient anti-school group	17	6	7[c]

[a]The rejection questions were not used in the second administration of the sociometric questionnaire.
[b]Including Tony Talston.
[c]Five of these to Tony Talston.

Added to this lack of positive choice between the groups, there is a large number of negative choices, as shown on the first sociomatrix, made to and from the incipient anti-school boys, to and from the rest of the boys *and* girls in the form (see table 3.13). This is an indication of the degree of animosity that existed between these groups.

Teachers' perceptions
A further dimension may be added to the consideration of the structure of the form by the examination of the teachers' perceptions of the pupils. Some indications of this should already be apparent from the incidents described and some of the accounts of the groups that have been given. But in order to obtain a reliable basis for the teachers' view of the pupils in the form I made use once again of the repertorial grid tests in the same way as with 2TA. Four teachers completed the tests in connection with 2CU and, as with other forms, I have selected for detailed examination the ranking of one Arts subject teacher and one Science subject teacher. Table 3.14 shows the two rank-orders constructed from the repertorial grid scores for 2CU, one produced by a Science teacher, the other by an English teacher. In comparing the actual constructs elicited from these teachers, it is interesting to note that the Science teacher, who has comparatively to spend more time giving instructions and explanations to the form, has a construct that puts 'quiet' as a desirable quality and 'noisy' as not. For the English teacher the similar 'lively-quiet' construct takes on a different meaning. Where in English the success of a lesson often depends very much on a lot of contributions from the pupils, being 'lively' (rather than 'noisy')

Table 3.14. *Rank-order of teachers' perceptions: English and Science*

English	Overall class exam position	Science	Overall class exam position
1 Cathy Hollins	10	1 Pauline Fream	2
2 Miriam Daly	3	2 Jeffery Smith	9
3 Peter Masters	1	3 Mirian Daly	3
4 Susan Hockley	11	4 Peter Masters	1
5 Richard Payne	7	5 John Eddy	6
6 Simon Warris	5	6 Jackie Gaynor	17
7 Pauline Fream	2	7 Ellen Goart	4
8 Ellen Goart	4	8 Richard Payne	7
9 Jackie Gaynor	17	9 Sally Hall	13
10 John Eddy	6	10 Kathy Trees	21
11 Chris Smaldon	28	11 Kathleen Hopkins	27
12 John Dyson	24	12 Cathy Hollins	10
13 Kathleen Hopkins	27	13 Tina Melville	14
14 Kerry Peters	15	14 Chris Smaldon	28
15 Jenny Michelson	25	15 Jenny Michelson	25
16 Tina Jacques	20	16 Simon Warris	5
17 Deborah Brent	23	17 Susan Hockley	11
18 Kathy Trees	21	18 Kerry Peters	15
19 Sally Hall	13	19 Tina Jacques	20
20 David Rhys	16	20 Jenny Wells	18
21 Veronica Kingston	8	21 Veronica Kingston	8
22 Alan Rader	30	22 Toni Green	19
23 Jenny Wells	18	23 Jimmy Patten	32
24 Toni Green	19	24 John Dyson	24
25 Mike Fawcett	25	25 Alan Rader	30
26 Alan Hill	21	26 Deborah Brent	23
27 Jimmy Patten	32	27 Simon Tawy	12
28 Tony Talston	31	28 Colin Fuller	29
29 Tina Melville	14	29 Alan Hill	21
30 Jeffery Smith	9	30 Mike Fawcett	25
31 Colin Fuller	29	31 Tony Talston	31
32 Simon Tawy	12	32 David Rhys	16

English constructs:	Science constructs:
Integrated–isolated	Bright–slow
Pro-school–anti-school	Useful contributor–does not contribute
Work-centred–disruptive	Quiet–noisy
Lively–quiet	Interested–uninterested
Works hard–lazy	Works hard–lazy
Sharp–slow	Attentive–disruptive
Mature–normal	Mature–immature

becomes a virtue rather than a vice. Both teachers have an 'intelligence' category, 'bright–slow' and 'sharp–slow' respectively; both have a 'hard work–laziness' construct; and both a 'maturity' construct and a 'disruptive' construct.

Comparing the two lists, nine of the English teacher's top eleven positions in the rank-order of perceptions are occupied by pupils from the top eleven positions in the end-of-year examinations. The Science teacher has seven. Seven pupils appear in the top eleven positions of both teachers' lists. They are:

	Overall exam position	Rank positions	
		Science	English
Peter Masters	1	4	3
Pauline Fream	2	1	7
Miriam Daly	3	3	2
Ellen Goart	4	7	8
John Eddy	6	5	10
Richard Payne	7	8	5
Jackie Gaynor	17	6	9

The pupil who came fifth in the end-of-year examinations, Warris, was placed sixth in the English teacher's rank-order, but sixteenth in the Science teacher's.

It is important to note that Jackie Gaynor is included by both teachers, although she did not do particularly well in the end-of-year examinations. She appears ninth and sixth in the respective lists. This gives an indication of the way in which these construct lists give a more sophisticated guide to the classroom *persona* of the pupil than a simple list of attainments or examination positions. The construct-elicitation system provides a composite of the criteria of work-performance assessment and behavioural assessment. Thus, Jackie, although not a high-achiever in terms of examination success, is in many other ways very close to the 'ideal pupil'.[19] She is quiet and attentive in lessons, but makes contributions when they are called for; polite and helpful to the teacher and a respecter of his authority, she always wears school uniform, comes to lessons on time and is well-prepared; she is interested and hard-working; always gives in homework and on time; does not talk when she should not; never needs to be rebuked; but is friendly and reasonably capable academically. In other words, she is highly educable. In a similar way, Jimmy Patten, although bottom in the exams and usually struggling academically with most of his subjects (he did not get a mark above 50 per cent in any of the exams in fact), comes 27th and 23rd on the respective construct lists. While not the most hard-working of pupils and rarely making any contribution to lessons, he is quiet, attentive, obedient, polite and friendly. This follows the trend of association noted previously.

In the bottom positions of the lists – the place, that is, of the least favourably perceived pupils – the English teacher has five pupils who come in the bottom 11 positions in the examinations, and the Science teacher has seven. Both have Tony Talston in this group, 28th and 31st respectively. In the English list Tawy and Fawcett are in the bottom group but not Rhys; in the Science list Tawy, Fawcett and Rhys, who is last, are all in the bottom group.

The association between the two sets of grid-positions was tested by the use of Spearman's coefficient of rank-correlation and found to be significant at the 0.001 level ($r_s = 0.60$). This test was also used as a measure of association between the grid-positions and the rank-positions of the pupils in the second-year examinations. The association was found to be significant at the 0.001 level in both cases (the Science grid $r_s = 0.68$ and the English grid $r_s = 0.53$).[20] This, then, confirms the interrelationship that exists between the teachers' overall perception of pupils and their level of achieved ability.

The third year

As noted earlier, as the two banded case-study forms entered their third year, I continued to follow the careers of both, but I devoted more time and energy to plotting the progress of 3CU.

3CU filled in a third sociometric questionnaire (see figure 5) in March, in the second term of their third year, and once again the analysis revealed only marginal changes in the social structure of the form. These changes were almost entirely limited to the girls' groups. Essentially, they consisted of a split in group A, with Sue and Ellen ('the Freaks') and Tina becoming separated from the rest, and the creation of a loose amalgamated friendship network among groups B, C, and D. This loose-knit structure emerged partly as the result of two girls from group C leaving the school and was partly a function of the changes in attitudes and interests taking place among the girls. There were only two other changes in the friendship pattern worthy of note. The first was the arrival of a new girl, Sarah Simmons, who received no choices in this questionnaire, but who, as a dedicated and hard-working scholar, soon began to make an impact in academic work, although, as with Peter Masters, her inflexible concern

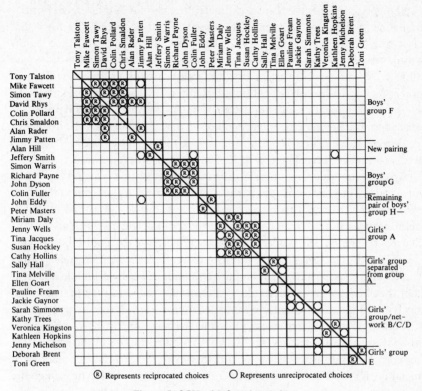

Figure 5. 3CU: third sociomatrix

with schoolwork did not make her popular in the form. The second change was the total separation of Hill from friendship group G and his replacement in the group by Fuller; Hill became an isolate.

These realignments in the form, while having a minimal effect on its structure, did have an impact on the distribution of friendship choice on the basis of social class and academic achievement. The Index of In-group

Table 3.15. *Index of In-group Preference values for social class in 3CU: third sociomatrix (taken separately by sex)*

Boys		Girls	
Working-class	Middle-class	Working-class	Middle-class
1.5	2.29	1.38	1.5

Preference scores for the third sociomatrix are shown in table 3.15. For the first time in the three sociomatrices there is in-group preference for social class in all four sub-groups. As in the previous sociomatrix, there is in-group preference by achievement in two of the sub-groups only (see table 3.16), but even in these two the values obtained are very close to unity. As we shall see in the following chapter, there are pressures affecting the social organization of friendships in the form other than the pressures of academic achievement. In particular, during the third year, the impact of adolescent sub-cultures is of importance and, as noted by Lacey (1970), this tends to modify the effects of polarization and differentiation.

Apart from the sociometric questionnaires, data collected by other means also illustrated changes in the social structure of the form in the third year. Indeed, material from diaries kept by some of the pupils in 3CU[21] demonstrated both a lack of subtlety in the sociometric instruments and the degree to which the collection of sociometric data could be socially constrained. The sociometric questionnaires failed to pick up the casual friendships that existed between pupils outside school, and made it appear that they had no such contact. In addition, they failed to pick up the cross-sex friendships that were also established at this time. Perhaps the notion of 'friendships' is too narrow and ill-defined to account for these other kinds of adolescent relationships (see Ward 1976). The entries in the diaries that several of the pupils wrote for me did, however, refer to these contacts. For instance, Kathy Trees's friendship choices to Warris and Payne, which did appear in the previous questionnaire, began to make sense.

> 7 February. Rich [Payne] and Jack [Dyson] came down this morning and we played cards for a while and Jack managed to break the handle of my bedroom door.
> 2 February. I met Jack, Colin [Fuller], Simon [Warris] down at the Beach Green. Rich could not come again we went to the amusement arcade and then mucked about on the beach.

Table 3.16. *Index of In-group Preference values for level of academic achievement in 3CU: third sociomatrix (taken separately by sex)*

	Boys		Girls	
	Top-half positions	Bottom-half positions	Top-half positions	Bottom-half positions
	0.57	1.09	0.42	1.06

There are several other references in Kathy's diary to meetings with the boys from group G, although always in group situations, and with other girls 'close' to Kathy in the sociomatrix. Typically:

> 1 March. I went to Wallsea with Kathleen and Deborah, we walked around for ages and then went to the market. Kath and I bought a record and I bought mum and dad an anniversary present.

The other point that emerged from these diaries and from talks with the pupils was the increase in the number of unsupervised social activities. As noted by Lacey (1970 : 121), there is a 'developing of roles and disjunction between the world of the school and the adolescent peer group' as the pupil moves through the school. Unsupervised peer-group activity both increases as the pupils become older and becomes more independent of the social worlds of home and school.

But changes in the form during the third year were not only evident in the structure of friendships and the distribution of academic success. The development of anti-school behaviour also affected 3CU during this time. This is illustrated by the comments below, which were made by 3CU's Economics teacher. Her view of the form is typical of many of their teachers during the third year. After a disastrous start to the year which culminated in the year tutor being brought in to 'talk to' the form, the Economics teacher said this:

> 'I'm more pleased with 3CU now they are making better progress and doing better work. The girls particularly are doing very good work. But they are still noisy. They don't seem to be able to work in silence . . . the boys are generally weak, though I'm sure it's their attitude and not their ability which affects their progress.'

Most of the problems in 3CU's lessons stemmed, in fact, from Talston and the boys of group F, especially Fawcett, as in the following case.

3CU Chemistry: lesson notes

There is an administrative delay to the start of the lesson; detentions are given to those pupils who failed to do their homework. The whole form is threatened with being kept in at lunch time, but Talston deliberately keeps up a constant barrage of loud talk.

The form is in groups to do an experiment which involves trays of water. Rhys, Tawy and Talston are going round the room to other groups' experiments and deliberately disrupting them by spilling water and pushing apparatus over.

Most of the form are doing the set work of observation tasks listed on the board, but Tawy, Rhys, and Fawcett and Talston are all playing with a tray of water, splashing each other and creating a large puddle on the floor.

Apart from the attention focussed on Talston, Fawcett and the others as a result of incidents like this, some of 3CU's subject teachers were also criticized by the form tutor and the year tutor for their failure to exert 'proper classroom control'. Indeed, one of the points that may be drawn from the incidents of disruption and misbehaviour evident in some of 3CU's lessons is the difference in the way in which 'control problems' were construed, between band 1 and band 2. Throughout the school the blame for disciplinary problems would be assigned primarily either to the pupils *or* the teacher, in relation to notions of 'bandness' (discussed in chapter 2). On the assumption that everyone should be able to control band 1 forms, discipline problems with these forms were normally attributed to the teacher's ineptitude or inexperience or both. In the case of band 2 forms, 'blame' invariably rested with the pupils. Thus, while problems experienced with band 2 forms would not necessarily impair a teacher's status in the staffroom, problems experienced with band 1 forms would be damaging. Consequently, new teachers were most anxious to be successful with their band 1 forms; failure with band 2 was less important. Indeed, young staff were expected to have problems in band 2 lessons.

Third-year-option examinations

At Easter in their third year all pupils take examinations. The results of these examinations are intended as a final guide and indicator, both for the pupils and for their teachers, as to which subjects they should take as options in the fourth year (see chapter 5). But in addition to their intended purposes, these results provide a further opportunity to examine the relationships between achievement and peer-group membership in 3TA and 3CU. The overall rank-order of examination positions for the two forms was as follows:

3TA	3CU
1 Wally Asquith	1 Peter Masters
2 Adam Hughes	2 Pauline Fream
3 Leonard Downsborough	3 Sarah Simmons[a]
4 Billy Latham	4 Miriam Daly
5 Rachel Wesley	5 John Eddy
6 Nicholas Acre	6 Jenny Michelson
7 Ronny Fisher / Alison Hoskiss	Simon Warris
	8 Kathy Trees

9	Alec Samuel	9	Richard Payne
10	Pamela Jarvis	10	David Rhys
	Sammy Capwell	11	Toni Green
12	Neil Grimshaw	12	Kathleen Hopkins
13	Erica Findon[a]	13	Jeffery Smith
14	Alan Edmeades	14	Sally Hall
15	Ann Symes[a]	15	Ellen Goart
16	Max Vassart	16	Susan Hockley
17	Jim Tolday	17	Alan Hill
	June Harris[a]	18	Colin Fuller
19	Tracy Smith	19	Veronica Kingston
20	Dorothy Haines	20	Deborah Brent
21	Donald Gaskell	21	Alan Rader
22	Cynthia Aldiss[a]	22	Simon Tawy
23	Peter Groome	23	Jackie Gaynor
24	Nigel Nawell	24	John Dyson
25	Christine Downes	25	Tina Jacques
26	Susan Bradford	26	Cathy Hollins
27	Alice Jewison	27	Jenny Wells
28	Daphne Galt	28	Chris Smaldon
29	Judith Nichols[a]	29	Mike Fawcett
		30	Tina Melville
		31	Jimmy Patten

[a]New to the form since the second year.[22]

In the first 11 positions of 3TA there are six boys from the pro-school groups E and G. All the boys from these two groups and their periphery are now in the top half of the form, except for Jim Tolday who is 17th. As noted earlier, Ronny Fisher has improved from 22nd to 7th, and Neil Grimshaw from 21st to 14th. Of the anti-school pupils, Max Vassart, who had come 6th in the second-year exams, is now 16th, but Sammy Capwell shares 10th position with Pamela Jarvis, and Rachel Wesley is 5th. The tendency of association between attitude and behaviour, in terms of group membership and academic success as measured by examinations results, is even clearer now than it was in the second year. This is shown in table 3.17. A similar pattern is evident is 3CU, with David Rhys as the only pupil from the incipient anti-group in the top twenty positions (see table 3.18). Furthermore, if these examination positions are cross-tabulated with social class in 3CU, it may be seen that there is a much closer association between the social class background of the pupils and their formal academic achievement than was true in the second year. Working-class pupils now occupy seven out of the bottom eleven places. The positions of 'failure' and low status within the band 1 form are being taken over by the working-

Table 3.17. *3TA : group membership and academic achievement*

		Exam positions		
		Top third	Middle third	Bottom third
Girls' group A network Boys' group H	anti-school	3	2	5
Girls' group D Alison	ambivalent	1	1	2
Other 'new' girls Boys' groups E and G	pro-school	7	6	2
		11[a]	9	9

[a]There was a joint 10th position.

Table 3.18. *3 CU : group membership and academic achievement*

		Exam positions		
		Top third	Middle third	Bottom third
		1–10	11–20	21–32
Girls' group A		1	3	4
B/C/D		4	2	1
F	pro-school	–	2	–
Boys' group G		2	1	–
H		2	2	–
Boys' group F		1	–	5
	incipient anti-school			
Tony Talston		–	–	1

class pupils (see table 3.19). Within these categories, the movement of places is also different for the middle- and working-class pupils. The trend towards a closer association between social class and examination success is clear from table 3.20. Some of the individual changes in position from the second-year examinations are also worth considering. For instance, four girls who had occupied low positions in the previous examinations, made considerable improvement in the option exams. Three of the girls are middle-class. Toni Green is the exception, but she received a considerable amount of 'pushing' from her parents (see p. 84). Jenny and Kathleen had been friends consistently during the period of study, but all four girls have

Table 3.19. *3CU : social class and academic achievement*

| | Exam positions | | |
	Top third	Middle third	Bottom third
Middle-class	8	7	5
Working-class	2	3	7

Table 3.20. *3CU: social class and academic achievement. Changes in examination attainment between second year and third year*

| | Middle-class | | Working-class | |
	No.	%	No.	%
Pupils whose positions improved	7	35	3	25
Pupils whose positions declined	8	40	7	58
Pupils whose positions remained unchanged	5	25	2	17
	20	100	12	100

occupied sociometrically low-status positions, receiving few friendship choices. The great similarity between them is in temperament and demeanour in lessons; they are all quiet and well-behaved, but none of them makes much contribution to answering or discussions. I asked the girls to account for their improved performance but none of them was able to offer an explanation. The form teacher, however, did have one; she described Kathy and Toni as girls who 'worried' about their work, and Jenny and Kathleen as highly competitive with one another in their work.

	Social class	Previous position	New position
Jenny Michelson	M/C	25	6
Kathy Trees	M/C	21	8
Toni Green	W/C	19	11
Kathleen Hopkins	M/C	27	12

	Position in second year	Position in third year	Change
Miriam Daly	3	4	− 1
Ellen Goart	4	15	− 11
Cathy Hollins	10	26	− 26
Susan Hockley	11	16	− 5
Sally Hall	13	14	− 1
Tina Melville	14	30	− 16
Jenny Wells	18	27	− 9
Tina Jacques	20	25	− 5

She also suggested that Kathy had been settling down since moving into 3CU from band 2.

Among the girls, there were further notable changes in examination attainment which affected group A, a high-achieving group in the second year. Every one of the girls in the group declined from the position she had held in the second year. The average examination position for the group declined from 11.63 to 19.63. All these girls tended to lose interest in work during the year and became particularly concerned with social life activities, especially 'boyfriends'. They were competitive in this and spent a great deal of time discussing boys. They were always very concerned with who was going out with whom, and sometimes competing for the same boys, which resulted several times in arguments and tears. The boys they were interested in and went out with were usually older than themselves, sometimes out of school with jobs. They were more socially sophisticated in this than, for instance, the four girls mentioned above whose examination performance had improved so much. Boyfriends became the prime concern of the girls in group A, and work was relegated to a place of little importance. In contrast, while Kathy, Kathleen and Toni from the group of successful girls all acquired steady boyfriends during the third year, in each case these boyfriends were also from the third year. Kathy's boyfriend was Richard Payne and Kathleen's was Alan Hill. A point made by Murdock and Phelps (1973 : 61) is certainly relevant here:

Girls are likely to have experienced the onset of menstruation somewhere about the age of 13, and, consequently, during their third year they will be coming to terms with their awakening consciousness of themselves as physically mature and sexually desirable. But it is exactly this awareness that is suppressed by the social organisation and official culture of the school, as the regulations attaching to school uniforms demonstrate.

While the girls of group A certainly did not become anti-school, they did move away from a socially narrow definition of themselves in terms of the

	Position in second year	Position in third year	Change
Alan Hill	27	17	+ 10
Colin Fuller	29	18	+ 11

values of the school. Their attachment to a school *persona* was weakened considerably more than in the case of any of the other pro-school pupils in 3CU in the third year. They had begun to establish a more broadly based sense of self and in particular had developed a greater interest in social relationships. Most of the other pro-school pupils in 3CU continued to maintain a socially narrower definition of themselves in terms of the values of the school.[23] (Variations within the pro-school sub-culture and the problems posed for pro-school pupils by the non-academic orientation of the adolescent sub-culture are explored in chapter 4.)

There are also some notable changes from previous examination performances among the boys. For instance, Alan Hill and Colin Fuller, both of whom were involved with the pro-school friendship group G, have improved their positions. They now occupy positions much closer to the high-achievement levels of Warris and Payne – for them, a pro-school orientation is paying off. The average examination position of group G has improved from 16.6 to 14.6. In contrast, in group F, the incipient anti-school group, two of the core members have declined notably. This reinforces the poor achievement-profile of the group as a whole; the average examination position has declined from 23.0 to 23.5.

	Position in second year	Position in third year	Change
Simon Tawy	12	21	− 9
Mike Fawcett	24	29	− 5

Summary

In the social structures of the two case-study forms the processes of polarization and differentiation have made their mark. This is evident in the total distribution of friendship choices and in changes in clique member-ship, as well as in changes in the relative distribution of academic success. While in CU none of the members of the form is totally free from the academic pressures of the band 1 context, the deviant roles of the incipient anti-school group, and of Talston, are clear. The lowest achievement-positions in both forms are occupied almost exclusively by anti-school pupils or by pro-school pupils who have developed social involvements outside school which tend to compete with school work for their commitment. But the other crucial factor of relevance in understanding the changing and evolving distribution of academic achievement in 3CU in particular is social class. As in the grammar school, so in the selective context of band 1, working-class pupils tend to percolate downwards in the processes of academic and behavioural differentiation.

4 Adolescents, social life and school life

Until recently sociologists have given little attention to the interpretation of the social life and school life of school pupils. Studies of 'youth culture', of the work experiences of school leavers, of juvenile delinquency and of pupils' experiences of schooling have been carried out separately by researchers identified with different sociological specialisms. Certainly, we know little as yet about the ways in which pupils, especially those aged between fourteen and sixteen, make sense of school as part of their whole life-world. In the context of the raising of the school-leaving age and the extremely high levels of unemployment among school leavers in the late 1970s, this is an especially important area of investigation. I hope in this chapter to explore some interrelationships which exist between pupils' experiences of social development out of school and the demands made on them within school. In doing so, the chapter extends the analysis of the school careers of the banded pupils at Beachside from the second and third into the fourth and fifth years, with the aim of demonstrating the increased complexity of pupils' adaptations to, and involvements in, school during this time. As Lacey (1970 : 71) notes:

The development of the adolescent sub-culture in the fourth, fifth and sixth forms can be expected to modify the process of polarization which is so markedly a feature of the third year.

It would be an artificial exercise to attempt to discuss shifts in the pupils' attitudes to school and changes in their informal social relations in isolation from their involvement in adolescent culture. Even by the third year, it was clear that many of the pupils in both case-study forms and their peers were engaged in an 'adolescent culture'.[1] The academic achievement of pupils in 3CU can, for instance, be related to the impact of adolescent social activities. I shall begin here with an attempt to outline the most notable changes in the social lives of pupils in the two case-study forms from their second to their third years.

The second year

From questionnaires and interviews I attempted to build up a picture of how the pupils in 2CU and 2TA normally spent their time out of school – what sorts of things they normally did in the evenings and at weekends, where they went and with whom they spent their time. What was immediately apparent from these data collected in the second year was a general similarity between the pupils from the two case-study forms in terms of their social lives out of school. Four particular points emerged from these data.

First, the pupils' social horizons were narrow and generally home-centred. There was little evidence that pupils very often left the immediate neighbourhood of their homes, and they spent a great deal of time actually at home when not at school.

Second, there was very little participation in casual adolescent social life activities, such as going regularly to clubs or discothèques or cafés, and so on, or taking part in activities organized by adults. This may in part be a reflection of the sociology of Beachside itself; the provision of casual social life activities for teenagers in the Beachside community, apart from the occasional discothèques run in the local halls, and by the factory social clubs on the industrial estate for the families of employees, was almost nil. There were the usual voluntary youth organizations – the scouts and guides, and the Army Training Corps and the Nautical Training Corps for both girls and boys – but the provision of youth clubs and other non-statutory youth facilities was particularly sparse. This comment from Jenny Wells (2CU) typifies the situation:

> 'I don't go out in the evenings, there is nothing to do in Beachside. Sometimes I go to Wallsea for the cinema but my mother thinks I'm too young to go to Pierton.'

The local cinema had been turned into a bingo hall, and the school Youth Wing admitted members only after their first term in the third year. In the questionnaire responses to 'Can you give a short description of what you did last night between the time that you arrived home and the time you went to bed?' only one pupil in either of the two forms mentioned attendance at a youth club, and there was no mention of youth-club activities in any other response by any of the pupils elsewhere in questionnaires or in interviews carried out during the second year.[2]

Third, there is a cut-off between group social life inside school and social life outside. Time spent with school friends outside school time is limited, and friendship groups that are close-knit in the classroom do not normally come together as a group outside school. The out-of-school friendship interaction of these pupils is considerably limited by propinquity and is thus fragmented. Pupils meet and interact mostly with neighbourhood friends of different ages, and with brothers and sisters, not necessarily the same people who are 'close' or 'best friends' at school.

Finally, the pupils spent a considerable amount of time out of school watching television. From the 31 replies to 'Can you give a short description of what you did last night between the time that you arrived home and the time you went to bed?' from 2CU, 22 mentioned watching television during the previous evening, and from 2TA 19 out of 27 replies mentioned watching television. Taking together all the pupils who mentioned 'watching television', 41 in all, only 5 mentioned any other non-essential activities.

These four points are illustrated in the following extracts from questionnaire responses and interviews. The most striking point is the 'home-centredness' of these pupils; friends and social activities outside the home were rarely mentioned.

> 'Watch TV and had my tea. Then I went round my friend's house until 7.30, then she came to my house until 9.00. We watched TV and talked.'
>
> (Sandra Harrison, 2TA)
>
> 'Last night I went to my uncle's to help him with odd jobs and then when I came back I watched the film on TV till 11.00 then I went to bed.'
>
> (Adam Hughes, 2TA)
>
> 'I watched TV and then I had my dinner. Then I went up the rec [recreation ground] then I came home and went to bed.'
>
> (Felicity Johnson, 2TA)
>
> 'I came home and had my tea. I watched the telly for a short while and then went out. I rode down to the beach and went swimming. I got home at 9.30 then I watched the telly until 10.00 and then I went to bed.'
>
> (Colin Fuller, 2CU)
>
> 'I got home at 5.30, had my tea and took my sister to her ballet school. I took the dog out for a walk on the beach, then collected my sister, watched Top of the Pops and Dad's Army, did my homework, and watched telly until 10.30. Went to bed.'
>
> (Miriam Daly, 2CU)

The one point of difference which did emerge between the two case-study forms was that ten pupils in 2CU mentioned spending time doing homework during the previous evening, whereas only two from 2TA did so. One point of sex-difference also emerged: several girls from both forms mentioned doing domestic chores, but none of the boys. In all, only three respondents, all from 2CU, mentioned any shared social life activities[3] during the previous evening; one girl was involved in a local drama group, another 'went down the pub', and one boy went to a youth club in Wallsea.

Despite the weaknesses and unsystematic nature of the questionnaire method used here,[4] if it is taken in combination with informal interviews it is possible to construct a schematic account of the social life of these second-year pupils. As will be seen, important changes take place between the time these data were collected, when the pupils were between $12\frac{1}{2}$ and $13\frac{1}{2}$ years old, and their third year of school.

The third year

The 'home-centredness' of the pupils noted in the second year was less evident in the third. The number of unsupervised activities with their peers increased, and their social horizons also broadened, both in terms of types of activities, references to 'pop-concerts', etc., and in terms of time spent away from Beachside itself. Wallsea (the nearest seaside town) was now commonly mentioned in the diaries pupils kept for me, and Pierton (a large seaside resort twelve miles from Beachside) was also occasionally mentioned.[5]

John Dyson's diary
1 May. Went to Dursiton [small town nearby, very similar to Beachside] Sports Centre and played squash.
2 May. In the afternoon I went to the pictures in Wallsea to see 'The Man with the Golden Gun' with Simon.
7 May. In the afternoon I went into Wallsea with Simon. We went on the pier and I won 30p, then we saw two films 'Blazing Saddles' and 'Now for Something Completely Different'.
8 May. At 8pm I went to Graham Sarker's party [a boy in another band 1 class] with Rich and Simon and got home about 11 pm slightly drunk!

Kathy Trees's diary
10 April. Jill phoned and we went to Wallsea. I bought a record and we went bowling.
22 April. In the evening I phoned Jill and asked her if she would like to see 'Cockney Rebel' [a pop group] with me. So Jill, Simon, Rich and me went to the Tower booking office [in Pierton] but when we got there it was closed. So on Monday Rich is phoning and booking seven seats.

Miriam Daly's diary
3 February. I am going to a disco in Beachside tonight, with loads of other people I know, it should be good.

8 February. I went to see 'Blazing Saddles' in Wallsea on Sunday. It was really funny. 16 of us went and we had the whole back three rows of the cinema.

Increasingly during the third year the pupils were developing areas of behaviour that took them outside the immediate supervision of parents and teachers. This often involved more active and direct participation in pop-culture activities, such as going to concerts and discothèques, and buying records, etc., but 'boyfriends' and 'girlfriends' were also becoming more important and more frequently mentioned. This was also true of activities that included physical involvement in a group, such as visiting friends, going out at night – to the cinema, to cafés and pubs, to parties – hanging around in the streets or on the beach, and doing shopping. The various aspects of the adolescent cultures in which most pupils were becoming engaged provided systems of values which competed with or conflicted with the 'official' adult culture represented by the school. For instance, Murdock and Phelps (1973 : 71) contrast the values transmitted by the pop-media with those sponsored by the school:

Values sponsored by the school	*Values transmitted by the pop media*
Work/production	Play/consumption
Preparing for the future	Living in the present
Mind/intellect	Body and emotion/feeling
Self control	Physical and emotional expression

These alternative value-systems and styles of social life dominated the leisure time of many pupils, but the extent of commitment to them and the use to which they were put differed among pupils. For many of the pro-school pupils, involvement in the adolescent sub-culture required a considerable diversion of time and energy from schoolwork, but for the anti-school pupils it also provided 'an inversion of the related values of . . . academic achievement and conformity to rules' (Sugarman 1967 : 151). For example, it is interesting to note that, although the girls in 3CU were always fashionably dressed and much concerned with fasion and pop music, their style of dress did differ from that of many of the girls in the second-band forms. The clothes worn by band 2 and 3 girls tended much more to be at the extreme of the latest fashions, the colours brighter, and the heels higher – that is, less in line with the school uniform regulations. Many band 2 girls wore large silver badges portraying their favourite pop stars, and during the period of great popularity of the Bay City Rollers many band 2 girls wore tartan scarves on their wrists. I did not observe any band 1 girls wearing either of these items of allegiance. In their case, overt support for pop groups was usually limited to the occasional picture on the front of an exercise book. Murdock and Phelps (1973 : 71) make the point that, although 'the pop-media provide a potential source of oppositional meanings and expressions, it does not necessarily follow that all pupils will make use of this potential'. For most band 1 pupils, schoolwork continued to impinge considerably upon their out-of-school time in the form of homework and revision for exams.

Cathy Hollins's diary
3 February. I'm going to see a film tomorrow evening, I can't go tonight because we've got our cookery exam tomorrow so I've got to revise.

Kathleen Hopkins's diary
10 February. Cathy phoned and came round at 7.30 we played my new L.P. and tried to revise.

For the anti-school band 2 pupils and some band 1 pupils, the influence of school is less pervasive, and they attach less importance to it. There are no mentions of revising for exams in the diary entries recorded by band 2 pupils.[6]

Belinda Hammett's diary
16 February. I went to see my Gran in the morning and in the afternoon I watched telly. At six o'clock I listened to the Top 20 on the radio in the bath. Then I watched the film on television and went to bed.
17 February. At school we had our exams, first we had music and then French and Physics, we had a Maths lesson but we've got the exam tomorrow. Daphne came round in the evening to listen to my records.[7]

There are certain aspects of the social life of pupils at Beachside which differ from the accounts of the role of the adolescent subculture offered by Lacey (1970) and Hargreaves (1967). There are three particular points of difference between their accounts and the findings from Beachside. First, there is much earlier involvement of the comprehensive school pupils in the world of teenage groups and 'pop media'. Second, at Beachside there is a much greater encroachment of group-life and 'pop media' on to the world of the school. This is apparent not only in the talk of the pupils but also in their dress and behaviour. The barriers between the world of school and the world of adolescence are much less strictly maintained at Beachside than they were at Hightown or Lumley, and the pupils bring into the school more of the interests and experiences of their adolescent sub-cultures. Third, as a co-educational setting, the immediacy of cross-sexual relationships makes the presentation of self in terms of knowledge of and participation in the current trends and fashions of the pop media culture more important *within* the school. Although it is obviously not possible categorically to separate out the impact of co-education from other factors of difference between Beachside and Hightown and Lumley, such as the social composition of the school or changes in the pop media themselves towards the involvement of younger age-groups, it is evident that in the third year the management of the self in terms of the trends of the pop media does come to contribute to the relative popularity and status of pupils. Even those pupils who appear to deviate least from the pro-school academic values are still looking to their peers for social rewards as well as to the adult community.[8]

Lacey (1970 : 87–8) noted that 'a boy who exhibits extremes of pro-school or anti-school behaviour in an inflexible way will not be popular'. Pupils like Peter Masters and Sarah Simmons, who are rigidly committed to pro-school values of hard work and conformity to rules, are not popular in 3CU and have low sociometric status, whereas Miriam Daly, for instance, who is able to combine her high level of academic achievement with an involvement in the fashions and trends of the pop media and with having boyfriends, is very popular in the form. She was named nine times as 'the most popular girl' in the Guess-Who-Test. The overall pattern of social relations in 3CU is constrained by forces not unlike those described by Coleman (1961). One aspect of the impact of adolescent sub-cultures on the informal structure of the form is in terms of the rewards and punishments that are distributed to the members of the form by their peers. These range from popularity, respect, and acceptance on the one hand, to isolation, ridicule, and exclusion on the other. Coleman (1961 : 39) notes that

Although 'being smart' or 'intelligent' have something to do with membership in the leading crowd, it is by no means the most important . . . from girls the most frequent response was 'having a good personality' and among various attributes, 'good looks' comes second and the matter of 'having good clothes' is important.

Certainly, in the third year these factors have an important influence upon the popularity of both boys and girls. However, this is not the case all the way through the secondary school. The evolution of the social structure of the form group is one concomitant aspect of the increasing importance of independent social life activities and the adolescent sub-cultures. The values of popularity evident in the first year, particularly in regard to girls, have undergone a considerable change by the third year. Where 'being smart' may have been adequate in the early years, social sophistication and good personality are well-established as criteria for popularity by the third year, and for those girls who stay on into the sixth form there is yet another shift in values in store.

The fourth and fifth years

Looking back over the first three years of secondary schooling at Beachside, represented in the experience of the two case-study forms, a clear picture emerges of two polarized pupil sub-cultures. In general terms, there is a band 1 pro-school sub-culture which is dominated by values which are positively oriented to the school and to the teachers, and a band 2 and 3 anti-school sub-culture which is dominated by values which are negatively oriented to the school and to the teachers. This, then, is a model essentially similar to those identified by Hargreaves (1967 : 162) and Lacey (1970). But it is important to mention that, as Hargreaves notes, 'to posit the existence of such sub-cultures is to propose a model or "ideal type" of the school's cultural structure'.

In fact, this general model must be qualified to take into account both the extent of cultural polarization within forms in each band as well as between bands, and the number of pupils who do not adhere clearly to either set of values, who have been described as ambivalent. As I have attempted to show in the previous chapter, this polarization and differentiation of sub-cultures is a *process*. It is clear that the bifurcated structure becomes more rigid and more complex over time and also becomes more correlated with academic achievement, but these sub-cultural groups are clearly identifiable at least as early as the second year at Beachside.

However, in this process of evolution in the social life and related cultural affiliations of the pupils, the period during the third year is particularly important as a time of considerable social development for almost all pupils. In particular, it is a time of transition from a clearly home-centred and school-based social life to one that is to a much greater extent independent of both.[9] The impact of this social development on the *school lives* of the pupils is not, however, the same for all. The peer-group cultures to which children belong may, as Bronfenbrenner (1971) suggests, be 'deviant' for all, but in this context they only appeared to become *alternative* cultures for some. Many of the pro-school pupils who were clearly identified by their teachers as 'good pupils' also participated in the trends and tastes of the pop media culture and played in neighbourhood street gangs. However, it was those pupils who were identified as anti-school by their teachers who increasingly tended to adapt or revert to these systems of commitment as *alternatives* to the culture of the school, their 'anti-schoolness' becoming less school-based and less a manifestation of negative polarity – that is to say, those pupils were no longer dependent upon a reversal of school norms and values as a source of alternative status and opposition. The difference between these anti-school pupils and the pro-school pupils lies in the 'use' made of their environmental cultures within the school, and the degree of insulation between them and the school culture – that is, the extent to which they were 'brought into' the formal school contexts where they would normally have been defined by teachers as irrelevant.[10] In moving on to examine the social organization of pupils in the fourth and fifth years at Beachside, it is apparent that for some anti-school pupils their involvement in a social life independent of the world of school becomes crucially important in the way in which they order, interpret and handle their experience of schooling.[11]

Out of school, many of these adolescents had jobs, went to pubs and to dances, and were able to make their own decisions or to participate in the decision-making of the social group. They participated in or aspired to much of an 'adult working-class culture'. However, the values of physical prowess, self-determinance and collective behaviour to which they adhered clashed fundamentally with the value-system of the school–academic prowess, long-term goals, subordination, and individual effort in competition with others. That is not to suggest that the pupils who aspired to adult working-class culture did not also *have* long-term goals. The real difference between them and the pro-school pupils lay in their rejection of the school as a means of achieving these goals. Indeed, this would not be irrational, given the lack of success they had thus far experienced at school and the improbability of their achieving future success in school, at least in any way that would objectively change their immediate prospects of employment. These pupils had rejected the long-term goals *of the school*.

Some part at least of these pupils' alternative views of themselves, outside their ascribed role as pupil (alternatives which are available to all), derives from the new status attributed to teenagers by the commercial system in recognition of their economic independence and greater social freedom. This contributes to the creation of a conception of self for the pupil which is very different from the child-based conception of the pupil of earlier generations. The school is stressing conformity, uniformity, and the acceptance of the role of complaint pupil (passed down through the paternalistic system: 'teacher knows best'), while outside the normative influence of the teacher-centred school culture, the pressures on the pupils stress an individual freedom of choice and social sophistication that is incompatible with this traditional pupil role. For the pupils who belong to anti-school groups their greater economic and social autonomy outside school takes them out of the cultural world of schooling, and, to use Coleman's (1961) term, they are 'released' into the delinquescent[12] working-class culture of the 'corner boy'. However, the constraints of finishing a compulsory school career maintain these pupils on the periphery of this life-world, especially in that they lack some of the fundamental role-relationships of such a culture, most particularly work-relationships. What appears to be happening here is a complicated set of interactions and accommodations between the media-relayed teenage leisure culture, the dominant adult culture, and the subordinate situated working-class culture.[13]

Conventionally, the sociologists of education have tended to take over the teachers' view of the disruptive anti-school pupil and, with a few recent exceptions, have failed to take into account the pupils' own systems of relevance. Ian Birksted (1976 : 74), an anthropologist, provides one of the few views of education from the other side, from the pupils' point of view.

Adolescents whom I did participant observation with inside and outside of school during their fourth and fifth year at a comprehensive, did not see school as an organisational principle of their lives. They evaluated the usefulness to them of exams in terms of their occupation plans for the future. This evaluation governed their perception of the usefulness of school and their performance at school. Thus school achievement and performance can be seen as strategies decided upon by pupils in terms of their perceptions of ends and means. A group of boys who were seen as hostile by the teachers and who would be classified by sociologists as one of the under-achieving cliques 'that the school most needs to teach', can only be thus labelled by ignoring the logic and meaning of their decisions, strategies and tactics. What school-staff call failure, and colluding educational sociologists call under-achievement, is an externally imposed one-dimensional judgement applied across the board, which does not take into account the reality of each adolescent's plans and personal and socio-cultural meanings.

As in Birksted's study, the anti-school pupils at Beachside who were normally viewed as failures by their teachers, can alternatively be seen as rationally weighing up the value of school in terms of returns to their immediate goals and life plans, accepting those parts of the experience of schooling that they saw as valuable and rejecting the rest.[14] It is only logically reasonable to label these pupils *en bloc* as school failures, if one views them as striving after rewards that the school has to offer. Anti-school pupils at Beachside, by the time they entered their fourth and fifth years, had ceased to be participants in any real sense in the socio-cultural world of schooling. It was apparent that they had come to see school as an alien institution, whose teachers denied them status-rewards, and that access to environmental or latent cultures provided status-alternatives and forms of satisfaction not available to them within the competitive and achievement-oriented school culture. One implication of this must be that the expressive culture of the school, as well as its organization, is a major factor contributing to the generation of extreme forms of antipathy for, and disaffection from, school. In the fourth and fifth years all the pupils exercise a greater degree of social autonomy and are more involved in adolescent social activities than in the first three years at school. Most of them are beginning to participate as equals in certain areas of adult social life. As I have suggested, their status outside school is changing. For some, this involves a further separation from the culture of the school and the values of their teachers. However, those pupils who continue to accept these values also change status within the school; the greater social maturity attributed to them by the staff often brings them into a closer involvement with the 'world of school'. This usually means greater participation in extra-curricular activities and more informal contacts with the staff. At Beachside this meant participation in drama productions and music, as well as 'social community' activities, fêtes, collecting money for charities, school holidays and trips, school parties and dances, etc. Thus, although the standards set by their adolescent peer-group and the cultures of adolescence become more important for pro-school pupils, so do the standards set by the school and the expectations held by their teachers. In the eyes of the anti-school pupils, the pro-school pupil is low in status and social maturity. In the eyes of their teachers the pro-school pupils are high in status and social maturity, and it is the anti-school pupils who are viewed as immature and socially naïve. The pro-school pupils are often those who are destined for the sixth form, and their school-based social life in the fourth and fifth years can be seen to be an anticipatory socialization. Once in the sixth form, relationships between pupils and staff become even more informal.

Both Lacey (1970) and Hargreaves (1967) suggest that the latter years of compulsory schooling are likely to witness an increase in the complexity of pupil sub-cultures, especially with regard to the impact of external adolescent, working-class and pop media cultures. But both continue to regard the pro- and anti- sub-cultures that they describe as existing in these latter years as in themselves unitary groups. While both qualify their model of pupil relationships to the extent that some pupils cannot be neatly classified into either sub-cultural extreme,[15] neither suggests that these opposing sub-cultures may themselves become sub-divided and that informal groupings may become differentiated and polarized *within* these aggregate classifications of pro- and anti-school. However, it seems too simplistic to view the outcome of the countervailing pressures of school life and social life in terms of the continuation of merely a bifurcated pro- and anti-school system of polarized sub-cultures. Rather, these pressures of peer groups v. teacher and academic pursuits v. leisure pursuits give rise to a further proliferation of adaptation-strategies *within* the pro- and anti-school divisions. I shall attempt to describe a fourfold classification of such strategies below, but it may be that even this model does not do justice to the pupils' social world. Certainly, for instance, it would be possible to introduce pop media and pop-cult phenomena as further complicating and cross-cutting factors – for example, rock-and-roll, punk-rock, soul, etc.[16]

But even excluding these factors there is a further breakdown of attitudes and friendship allegiance within the pro- and anti-school cultures at Beachside which reflect different kinds of commitments to and rejections of the normative order of the school. These different kinds of commitment and rejection may be classified as follows, in terms of their approximation to the components of the typology of pupils' informal social systems suggested by Lambert *et al.* (1973).[17]

Pro-school

1. Supportive of the formal system. These pupils share normatively in a conception of school as 'education'. This would be similar to Etzioni's 'moral involvement' (1961 : 66).

2. Manipulative of the formal system. These pupils use features of the formal social system to their own ends. They have a utilitarian view of school and are concerned mainly with a concrete return on the investment of their time and energy, in terms of getting 'exam passes' and 'qualifications'.[18] This would be similar to Etzioni's 'calculative involvement' (1961 : 66). These pupils' attachment to the school is weak compared with that of the previous group. As indicated by Etzioni, calculative involvement designates an orientation of low intensity, which can be engendered in either positive or negative attitudes towards those in power.

Anti-school

1. Passive. These pupils ignore aspects of the formal structure of schooling, as well as the teachers' authority in particular areas. They maintain a considerable degree of insularity between their private world and the demands of their teachers without resorting to active intransigence.

2. Rejecting. These pupils reject the goals and the authority of the school. This line of adaptation is represented, for instance, by the anti-school pupils in 3TA. It would be similar to Etzioni's 'alienative involvement' (1961 : 65).

These 'lines of adaptation', and there may be others, may be used to describe the attitudes and behaviour of individual pupils or of particular social groups or friendship groups. Once again, however, it should be said that not every individual can be neatly fitted into one or other of the categories. There are some pupils who display patterns of behaviour appropriate to more than one category. But this must be expected, for, as Lacey (1970) points out, extreme deviance in either a pro- or an anti-school direction leads to unpopularity. Without the reinforcement of a strong peer-group most pupils were *flexible* in both attitude and behaviour. In general terms, however, few pupils at this stage in their school careers see their commitment to school totally in terms of a normative identification with the school culture. Many more tend to view school calculatively, as a provider of negotiable qualifications, and some reject both the values of the school culture and its products.

The changes in values that take place within the pupils' social worlds are concomitant with the changes in the social organization of friendship discussed in the previous chapter. But the changes in pupils' attitudes and behaviour over this time cannot be explained entirely in terms of greater participation in life-worlds outside school. Factors related to the pupils' continuing experience of school are still of major importance. One of these factors, the processes of option choice and allocation which take place at the end of the third year, is examined in the following chapter. This allocation of pupils to different options is of crucial importance in the comprehensive school, for it is the point of formal structural differentiation in the school careers of comprehensive pupils. It is, as we shall see, as fundamental to their future life-chances as was the 11 plus examination in the tripartite system.

5 Subject-option choice: the selection of knowledge and the management of pupils

The examinations taken by all pupils at Easter in their third year are a precursor to their 'choice' of and allocation to subject 'options' for the fourth year. The pupils take these option courses throughout the fourth and fifth years, and unless they leave school early, will take external examinations at O-level or C.S.E. at the end of the fifth year.[1]

The option allocation process is a crucial point in the school careers of pupils. Decisions made at this time by them, and their teachers and parents, clearly have implications for their future lives which reach far beyond the limits of schooling. It is also a process which has been almost completely neglected in the sociology of education. Cicourel and Kitsuse's (1963) study in the U.S.A. and Peter Woods's (1976) recent work in a British secondary modern school are the only examples to date. Most of the other analyses which *have* been done have been concerned with the reasons for pupils' subject 'choices', or differences between boys and girls in the 'choices' which they make. This sort of approach totally neglects the importance of the making of 'choices' as a process in which both pupils *and* their teachers are involved.

These comments from the D.E.S. (1975:11) Survey paper, 'Curricular differences for boys and girls', are typical of the misconceived 'free-choice' view of the option process.

Choice may be influenced by likes and dislikes, by career aspirations, by the influence of friends or by the advice and guidance of members of staff.

At Beachside in the 'Third Year Options' handbook issued by the school to all third-year pupils, as a guide to their option choices, it is stated that:

At Beachside you all have the chance to do O-level or C.S.E. exams at the end of the fifth year.

The policy of the school as presented to the pupils and their parents is that any pupil should be able to take the subject he wants at the level he wants.

122

In fact, however, there are important constraints upon the choice that pupils have both in terms of subjects and of whether to do O-level or C.S.E. courses. Three of the most important limitations upon freedom of choice are the arrangement of the option-sheet into 'lines' from which choices must be made, the size of teaching-groups in certain courses, and the negotiation of a set of options that are acceptable to the pupils, to their teachers and, in some cases, to their parents.

Line	Curriculum 1975–6. (The figures in round brackets indicate the number of teaching-groups available.)
A	Creative Design O/C.S.E. (2), Biology O (2), British Constitution O (1), Geography O (2), Geology C.S.E. (1), Human Studies C.S.E. (1),[a] Social Science C.S.E. (2)
B	Chemistry O (1), Chemistry C.S.E. (1), Classics in Translation O/C.S.E. (1), Geography O (1), Geography C.S.E. (2), History O (1), History C.S.E. (1), Home Studies C.S.E. (3),[a] Music C.S.E. (1), Physics (N) O (1), Physics C.S.E. (1)
C	Chemistry O (1), Drama O/C.S.E. (1), Economics O (1), Economics C.S.E. (1), Home Economics O/C.S.E. (1), Home Economics C.S.E. (2), Human Studies C.S.E. (1), Music O (1), Technical Studies O (2), Technical Studies C.S.E. (2)
D	Astronomy O/C.S.E. (1), Biology C.S.E. (2), French O (2), French C.S.E. (2), Modern Applications of the Sciences (1),[a] Needlecraft O (1), Needlecraft C.S.E. (1), Rural Science C.S.E. (1), Technical Drawing O (1), Technical Drawing O/C.S.E. (2)
E	Design Drawing O (1), Design Drawing C.S.E. (1), Geography C.S.E. (2), Geology O (1), History O (2), History C.S.E. (2), Latin O (1), Modern Applications of the Sciences (1),[a] Needlecraft O (1), Needlecraft C.S.E. (1), Sociology O (1)
F	Chemistry C.S.E. (1), European Studies C.S.E. (2), German O (1), German C.S.E. (1), Home Studies (3),[a] Physics O (1), Physics C.S.E. (1), Religious Studies O (1), Religious Studies O/C.S.E. (1), Religious Studies C.S.E. (1), Spanish O/C.S.E. (1)

[a] Mode III C.S.E. courses.

The first two of these constraints are primarily practical and stem from administrative expedience. The option-sheet is arranged into six choice-lines – groups of subjects from which one only must be chosen. This arrangement, which is derived from the exigencies of timetabling, means that some combinations of choices are logistically impossible. In my discussions with pupils about option choice the arbitrariness of some of their choices was clearly apparent. Many times when they were explaining why they chose a particular subject, it turned out that after having made their fourth or fifth choice, History, or Design Drawing, or Physics, or whatever, was chosen just to complete the six choices. These final choices were made because:

'There was nothing else in that line I liked.'

'I don't like Geography, but it's the only one I could do.'

'I'm having to do Art now, but I'm not interested in that.'

'And History, I took it because there was nothing else in that line.'

'On the rest of the line there were all horrible subjects, so I chose that one.'

'Music? There wasn't anything on that line I liked.'

'I didn't like the others of the line.'

'Well, Sociology, there was nothing else in that line, nothing else that I like, so I had to do that.'[2]

The band 2 pupils particularly tended to run out of 'positive reasons' for choosing subjects. This is in part a reflection of the greater number of subjects that the band 2 pupils are no longer interested in, or actively dislike, or are totally unsuccessful in, by the end of the third year. For many of them this is a further aspect of their general disaffection from the processes of schooling. Woods (1976) suggests that for many low-stream pupils the option-choice process is a non-event. Indeed, all but five of the pupils in 3TA, the band 2 class, talked about making these sorts of non-positive choice.

The second administrative constraint that impinges upon the choice of subjects is the size of teaching-groups in the option courses. Some subjects become over-subscribed and some under-subscribed, so that it becomes necessary to encourage pupils to change their choices because too many people have chosen a particular option. This sort of administrative need is often neglected as a 'taken for granted' in studies of processes of allocation, as it is 'taken for granted' in the school, even though it represents a clear move away from the principle of freedom of choice noted earlier.

The problems of over-subscription are related to factors such as the staff's inability to cope with the numbers involved, the limitations of resources, and legal constraints. An example of the first of these occurred in Creative Design. Because of a combination of the limitations of equipment and space, a maximum of 100 was set on the number of pupils who could do Creative Design in the fourth year, but 110 pupils had chosen it. The year tutor consulted the Creative Design department, and the head of department reiterated the 100 maximum. It was therefore necessary to reduce the 110 choices made to 100. The head of Creative Design wrote:

> On your original list of 98 people we indicated 23 people who we thought could be dropped from the Creative Design group on the basis of clearly demonstrated lack of interest and application. (This you remember was in

the event of our losing one teaching area from the department so
reducing our maximum to 75.) If you still have this list you could choose
10 people from it.

The responsibility for these final changes now lay with the year tutor and
his assistant, and they 'selected' ten likely candidates for moving to other
options on the Creative Design line.

I was present at one of the 'talks' with these pupils in the year tutor's
office.

> The pupil, Alan Williams of 3WX, a band 2 form, came in; the year tutor
> and his Assistant were both present.
>
> *AYT* 'It's about your options, Alan; there are a couple of problems.' [He
> had also made two choices in one line.]
>
> The boy nodded and waited.
>
> *AYT* 'You see, we have too many people in C.S.E. Creative Design,
> there just isn't enough space. We wondered if you would like to
> move to another subject in that line that you might like.'
>
> The boy nodded hesitantly.
>
> *AYT* 'There is Biology.'
>
> *AW* 'I don't want to do that.'
>
> *AYT* 'What about Social Science?'
>
> *AW* 'All right.'
>
> *AYT* 'Do you know what it is?'
>
> *AW* 'It's something to do with gardening.'
>
> *AYT* 'That's Rural Science; this is called a science but it's about people,
> it's about . . .'
>
> *YT* 'It deals with people, with how the country runs, the law and courts
> and the population and the Third World.'
>
> *AYT* 'There's Geography, you could do that [the AYT's own subject],
> or the Biology.'
>
> *AW* 'I don't want to do that.'
>
> *AYT* 'Well, we've put you down provisionally for Social Science and I'll
> have a word with Mr Leach.'

An example of the second problem of over-subscription was that a
maximum of 20 girls could do Needlecraft because of the limited number of
available sewing machines. Similar constraints applied to Technical
Drawing and Art equipment and Scientific equipment. Examples of the
third problem were a legal limit on the number of pupils who could be
present in the metalwork work-shop and cookery rooms at any time. In
each case of over-subscription it was necessary for some pupils to be
redirected into other under-subscribed courses.

The negotiation of appropriate choices

Apart from the demands of administrative expediency, the other constraints on the pupils' selection of options arise from the problem of
negotiating a set of options which match the teachers' perceptions of the
pupils' level of ability, behaviour and motivation. This process of
negotiation will be discussed in some detail.[3]

From the outset, some original choices made by pupils – that is, those
choices made on the option-sheets that the pupils were first given to take
home – turned out to be unacceptable to the members of staff responsible
for teaching the courses they had chosen.

After the option forms were collected in, the senior master collated the
choices into course-subject lists, making a list of all pupils opting for C.S.E.
Geography and O-level Geography, O-level French and C.S.E. French,
etc., etc. These lists were then presented to the members of staff responsible
for the course, who were expected to scrutinize the lists and return them to
the senior master with a tick for acceptance, or a cross for rejection, or a
question mark, together with an explanatory comment, against each pupil's
name.

The question marks normally referred to those pupils whom the teacher
considered should perhaps be doing O-level instead of C.S.E., or vice
versa, or who was considered a borderline case in some other way. The
head of History said:

> 'In History we do not say to people that you cannot do History. We may
> suggest that people do C.S.E. instead of O-level, and a handful are
> advised to do O-level rather than C.S.E. because they have chosen it as a
> soft option or followed a group, when they were obviously capable of O-
> level.'

It is up to the senior master or the teacher concerned to counsel pupils on
changing their choice, if the original choice is unacceptable. For example:

> 'I put down for History O-level but Mr Plummer, he advised me that I'm
> not so good in essay questions, so he said, it would be better to do C.S.E.'
>   (Chris Smaldon, 3CU)
> 'German O-level – I can't do that, it had to be C.S.E., because they didn't
> think I was up to doing O.'   (Tina Melville, 3CU)

Apart from those pupils who were directed from O-level to C.S.E., some
were rejected outright from a subject as 'unsuitable', 'not O-level material',
'has made no progress in this subject', or 'cannot cope'.[4]

Two types of pupil appeared to be most often rejected from subjects outright – those whom the teacher considered to lack any ability in the subject concerned, and those who had gained a reputation for being 'problems' in the first three years. For example, fifty-five pupils opted for C.S.E. Domestic Science, all but two of whom were from band 2 and band 3 forms. Nine of these pupils were rejected by the head of Domestic Science, five of whom were known to me as being regarded as 'problem' pupils. For one boy, who had the distinction of having the record for the highest number of school detentions received by any individual, the comment was 'not Domestic Science ever'. Another boy known as a 'troublemaker' (he had hit a member of staff some time before) was described as of 'unsuitable temperament'. Another was 'not suitable', and two girls also regarded as 'problems' received the comments 'has sloppy attitude' and 'unsuitable temperament'.

However, comments of this kind were often regarded by the senior master as unreasonable grounds for rejection and eventually only two of the nine, the two boys mentioned first, were transferred to other subjects – in both cases to the Human Studies option, a Mode III C.S.E. The senior master argued that 'You can't turn them down for C.S.E. in a school like this, but they do. And I ask, where do they go then?' In some subjects an embargo was operated against bands or forms as a whole. In the case of Physics O-level and Mode I C.S.E., the rule was made on the choice-sheet that 'all UD have to go to Mr Temple', that is, all those pupils opting from the non-remedial band 3 form 3UD were redirected to the Mode III Modern Applications of the Sciences option.

The number of times that any pupil may be rejected is of course limited, for every pupil must end up with a full timetable. In practice two or three rejections tended to be the maximum.

> 'They make the original decision and the subject teachers go through and say yes or no. But they've got to go somewhere.'
>
> (Senior master)

In practice the rejection-power of courses also varied. The O-level teacher had a considerable power of rejection, because the academic argument was very persuasive: 'not O-level material', 'cannot cope', 'better C.S.E.'. But the C.S.E. course teacher had much less power of rejection:

> 'If they are not capable of doing C.S.E. they shouldn't be in this school.'
>
> (Senior master)

However, it was possible for pupils rejected from the traditional C.S.E.s to be guided into the 'new' Mode III C.S.E. subjects that are run under the auspices of the Human Studies department. This applied in the case of the two boys from Domestic Science.

The experience of this kind of reallocation or redirection following rejection was common among the band 2 pupils I interviewed.

> 'I had to change from Design Drawing, I wasn't recommended to do it.'
>
> (Dorothy Haines, 3TA)
>
> 'I had to change Biology (because I am not allowed to do O-level) I had to change it altogether I'm having to do Art now.'
>
> (Wally Asquith, 3TA)
>
> 'I'm not doing Needlecraft now, I think it's Geography. She wouldn't take me on. She doesn't hardly know me, either.'
>
> (Peter Groome, 3TA)

I am not suggesting that at this stage in their school career some pupils are not objectively incapable of O-level course work, but rather that the process of selection for O-level or C.S.E. was not compatible with what was the professed ideology of free choice of subjects and examination-level open to pupils. Furthermore, many of the staff involved in the option-choice process appeared to operate with a notion of what was *appropriate* for certain pupils, and this was related to the 'appropriateness' of a particular kind and level of course for pupils from each band. This notion can be expressed roughly as O-level for band 1, traditional Mode I C.S.E.s for band 2, and new Mode III C.S.E.s for band 3.[5]

This notion of 'appropriateness' is an extrapolation of the banded educational identities that have been created during the first three years, especially the expectations of academic performance that are a part of these identities.[6] The teachers felt that the O-level courses were beyond the capabilities of the band 2 and band 3 pupils; that was why they were in band 2 and 3. This notion of appropriateness was transmitted to the pupils through the option-choice and allocation processes.

> 'I chose French O-level but I can't do that now. I've got to do C.S.E. Well, because nine of us are doing French C.S.E., because it [O-level] is for the first bands.'
>
> (Dorothy Haines, 3TA)

Another aspect of the teachers' thinking about 'appropriateness' is that, as the senior master explained:

> 'Most O-levels are for the academic pupils, for those from band 1 who have the necessary background.'

This point of 'necessary background' derives from differences between bands in terms of the subject material that is 'covered' up to the time the choice is made. Partly by design, partly by necessity – because of the problems of discipline and control – the coverage of syllabus material in band 2 and band 3 forms is slower or different in the first three years. These differences, from the teacher's point of view, often made the choice of an O-level course by band 2 and 3 pupils impossible, 'because they haven't the necessary background'. Taking this into account across a number of subjects, the allocation to bands in the first year also involves the allocation to different curricular routes.[7]

Even in the case of Maths, although it is not an option, in the sense that every pupil must take some sort of Maths course in the fourth and fifth year, there is still a process of allocation to be done – to O-level, C.S.E. Mode I or Modern Applications of Maths, C.S.E. Mode III (which is for the band 3 pupil and makes Maths 'relevant', applying simple mathematics to house purchase, insurance, interest payments, etc.). In effect, allocation to Maths courses in the fourth year is made soon after the pupils enter the school. The head of the mathematics department explained:

> 'Because of the greater intensity of the O-level syllabus the decision about who takes O-level is in effect made at the end of the second year under the banded system. The others just can't be pushed at that pace.'

Top sets in Maths follow a School Mathematics Project (S.M.P.) number-book syllabus which leads on to the O-level course. Other sets follow an S.M.P. letter-book syllabus which does not prepare for O-level. This setting within bands for Maths even allowed for the development of a hybrid group which the staff of the Maths department commonly referred to as 'the grammar school stream'.

This early selection through curriculum differentiation also has its effect in other non-academic subjects. Even in Music, band 1 and band 2

> '. . . don't cover the same ground. Major scales go well with the first band; people don't usually try them with band 2.'
>
> (Music teacher)

Furthermore, in all subjects except Chemistry and Physics, the actual options examinations taken in band 1 at Easter in the third year were different from those taken in band 2. Typically, the head of French explained that in his subject they 'have to be different' because 'the "gap" is far too large at that stage'.

Thus, in some subjects where the 'demands' of the O-level syllabus percolate down into the first three years, certain topics or 'basics' have come to be defined as 'needing to be covered' before O-level can be attempted. Given the low level of movement into band 1 from the other bands, there is in fact a system of selection operating from the beginning of the first year. This is of a sponsorship-type early selection for subject elitism, followed by careful training and initiation. French, for instance, is reduced form being a subject taken in the first year by the whole year-group to being a subject taken by a single group studying for O-levels in their fourth and fifth years. In the Summer examinations of 1974, the French department entered 33 candidates for O-level and obtained an 88 per cent pass rate.

Further illustration of the option-allocation process at work may be found in a detailed examination of Physics and Chemistry. As noted above, unlike the other departments Physics and Chemistry had actually given band 1 and band 2 forms the same examinations at the end of the third year, so results are directly comparable. They were given the same examination to provide an objective basis from which the teachers would be able to respond to option-choices. A rule was made that a mark of 50 per cent or over was required in these examinations to be accepted to do O-level.

One of the Physics staff explained that:

> 'The Physics exams for band 1 and band 2 are the same. It is the only way to decide which course they could follow in the fourth and fifth year. It gives the band 2 pupils the chance to get into the course which will stretch them to their full potential. But it may also mean that some do very badly which can be very deflating.'

When I compared the Physics examination results of 3CU and 3TA I found that the top ten pupils in 3TA had achieved higher marks than the bottom eleven pupils in 3CU. There was a considerable overlap, that is, in the distribution of marks between the two forms. All of the top ten pupils in 3TA achieved marks above 50 per cent. The distribution of marks in the two forms is shown diagramatically in figure 6. The top ten pupils in 3TA and their marks are listed below but only three of these pupils actually opted for O-level Physics.

Physics examination marks

Leonard Downsborough	78%–opted for and accepted for O-level Physics.
Alec Samuel	$71\frac{1}{2}$%–opted for and accepted for O-level Physics.
Billy Latham	71%–did not opt.
Adam Hughes	$64\frac{1}{2}$%–opted for and accepted for C.S.E. Physics.
Wally Asquith	$63\frac{1}{2}$%–opted for and accepted for O-level Physics.
Alan Edmeades	59%–did not opt.
Rachel Wesley	59%–did not opt.
Sue Harnes	59%–did not opt.
Nicholas Acre	$58\frac{1}{2}$%–did not opt.
Pauline Jarvis	$55\frac{1}{2}$%–did not opt.

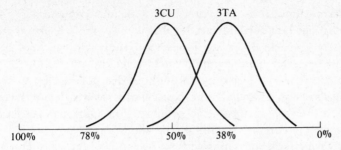

Figure 6. Distribution of Physics examination marks in 3CU and 3TA

Three pupils, Adam Hughes and two others who obtained less than 50 per cent in the examination, chose C.S.E. Physics and were accepted. Although Hughes's mark of $64\frac{1}{2}$ per cent was considerably above the acceptable pass-mark for entry into O-level, it was not suggested to him that he might choose the O-level course. Ten pupils from 3CU opted for and were accepted for O-level Physics; of these, six obtained marks lower than Hughes's. This pattern of choice and acceptance is a reflection both of the counselling procedures within the school and of parental knowledge of and involvement in their children's option-choices (see p. 155).

A similar distribution of marks and pattern of choices was found in the case of Chemistry. Overall, sixteen pupils in 3TA achieved marks higher than the bottom mark of 35 per cent in 3CU and six pupils in 3TA achieved marks over 50 per cent, as listed below.

Chemistry examination marks

Wally Asquith	65%–opted for and accepted for O-level Chemistry.
Billy Latham	65%–did not opt.
Adam Hughes	56%–did not opt.
Alec Samuel	52%–opted for and accepted for O-level Chemistry.
Alison Hoskiss	52%–did not opt.
Alan Edmeades	50%–opted for and accepted for C.S.E. Chemistry.

The examination marks obtained by Asquith and Latham would have placed them in joint 10th position in 3CU. Once again, three pupils from 3TA opted for O-level, but in this case Downsborough, who achieved 45 per cent in the examination, was rejected. Samuel and Asquith were accepted. In addition, Edmeades and Tolday, who achieved less than 50 per cent, opted for and were accepted for C.S.E. Chemistry. Once again, there are several pupils who would have been accepted to do O-level if they had opted, but who did not do so.

Using this system of comparable examination marks, Physics and

Chemistry account for 23 per cent of all O-level acceptances in 3TA (see p. 141). It may be inferred from this that without the 'objective' guidance of comparable marks other factors enter into the course-teachers' decisions to accept or reject band 2 pupils for O-level courses. Also, the option procedures at Beachside assume throughout that pupils' choices are made on the basis of equal familial resources,[8] but this is patently not the case (see p. 155). Moreover, in theory, according to the Options Handbook and 'talks' given at Parents' Evenings, the allocation of options is intended primarily to provide the pupils with a satisfaction of future-oriented needs, in the attainment of examination passes for employment or further education or the sixth form:

> 'We are always stressing to them that, you are doing this course to get qualifications so that you can go and get a good job.'
>
> (Department head)

The allocation of options is also intended to allow pupils to do the subjects they like and enjoy. But the teachers also have 'interests' in the option-allocation procedure and in which pupils are allocated to their courses, especially in the case of O-levels. The percentage of passes obtained by a department is an important gauge of the status of that department. Most teachers considered pass-rates as a significant reflection of the success of their departments.

> 'There are constraints upon us to get good results. There are demands from society we are expected to get good O and A level results, and, for ourselves as subject specialists, we want to maintain the level of achievement in our subject.'
>
> (Head of Maths)

Woods (1976 : 45) also notes the importance attributed to the achievement of good examination results as 'a public relations exercise', and he goes further to conclude that:

It appears therefore that teacher mediation does not operate in the interests of the individual pupil, but is predicated rather on considerations of status, career, and professionalization, rendered particularly acute by the external influence of parental pressure.

This happened to the Geography department for two consecutive years, as may be seen from table 5.1 below. In 1974, more candidates were entered for Geography O-level than for any other subject except English (which is compulsory in the fourth and fifth year) and obtained a relatively low pass-rate. Again, in 1975, Geography entered a large number of pupils for the O-level examinations and had the lowest pass-rate of any subject except Art.

The results were poor enough to warrant the concern of the headmaster and a change in departmental policy in regard to accepting pupils and entering them for O-level:

> 'All the department must have been called into him at least three times. We were all called in there, individual ones talked to individually. The previous head of department was talked to, I was talked to, to see why the results were so bad . . . Now this year, come the mocks, we absolutely cut out all the border-lines and when we saw the C.S.E. results, it justified everything we had done then. It was no good saying to the kids, "Well, we think you might if you carry on for a year." No, we said, "You'll do C.S.E. and that is it and you'll get something," and they have, and the results are considerably better – so the O-level results should be.'[9]

(Head of Geography)

The entries and pass-rates at O-level over all the 'main' academic subjects (those taken by all pupils in the first three years) in 1974 and 1975 are shown in table 5.1. The considerations of percentage passes and the nature of the teaching-group serve to reinforce the maintenance of 'appropriateness' as a working basis for the acceptance and rejection of pupils. This is particularly clear with regard to the band 3 pupils for whom it is the 'new' Mode III C.S.E.s that are most 'appropriate':[10]

> 'There are three sink subjects, Creative Arts and Crafts, Human Studies and Modern Applications of Science, which are eight periods each a week, which attract the remedials; they only skim the material, which is

Table 5.1. *Entries and pass-rates at O-level of the 'main' curriculum subjects in 1974 and 1975*

	1974			1975		
	Entered	Passed	%	Entered	Passed	%
Music	15	13	86	8	5	54
Art	17	12	70	25	6	24
French	33	29	88	25	20	80
History	65	44	68	68	41	60
Biology	43	28	65	43	26	61
Religious Knowledge	51	29	57	44	14	32
Physics	49	21	43	54	23	43
Chemistry	20	10	50	35	26	74
Geography	91	32	35	80	22	28
Home Economics	28	–	–	28	15	54
English (Language)	100	43	43	144	70	49
Maths	82	43	52	66	37	56

all they can manage really; they are now open to other pupils but most of them are remedials.'

(Head of Human Studies)

These courses cater mostly for those pupils who would have left school before taking examinations prior to the raising of the school-leaving age.

'The course in Human Studies and the more recently introduced Design and Technical Studies are both devised to meet the needs of the new group of fourth-formers for relevant but solid work.'

(Headmaster's Report to the Governors)

'Before the ROSLA the Human Studies Department used to be a place for the "rotters", but then you see only a handful stayed on after the fourth year to take the exam, so it was not much of a problem.'

(Head of Human Studies)

Pupils from band 3 and some from band 2, either choosing these subjects initially or after being rejected from other subjects, do in effect 'sink' into the Human Studies department. They are offered courses which are perceived by the staff as 'appropriate' to their abilities – 'It's all they can manage' (Geography teacher).

Although these 'new' subjects are examinable by C.S.E. Mode III, they are regarded by staff as different in kind from the other C.S.E.s in traditional subjects, and this difference is reinforced by the 'appropriate-ness' of the pupils who take the courses.

Maths department meeting

T1 'Do they have a choice of question . . .?'

T2 '. . . a choice in Modern Applications! they're so thick they need a choice.'

Discussion is about the form that the exam paper will take and about revision.

T1 'It's worth going over it with them.'

T2 'Yes, close to the exam.'

T3 'Just before they go in if you don't want them to forget.'

The band positions of the pupils who were entered for 'new' subject examinations in the fifth form in 1975 quite clearly reflect the subjects' 'appropriateness'. There were four 'new' subjects in that year: Workshop Crafts and Design, Creative Arts and Crafts, Human Studies (Citizenship), and Chemistry for Living. There were 34 pupils doing at least two of these, 23 from band 3, 10 from band 2, and only 1 from band 1. In 1975 the Human Studies course was in fact considerably over-subscribed. This can be accounted for to some extent, in that all the new subjects offered in the fourth and fifth years, which had not been included in the first three years of the curriculum, tended to attract a lot of choices, especially from band 2 and band 3 pupils who had not been successful in their main subjects in the first three years. The senior master recognized this.

'They all tend to gravitate to something new, so there were 65 who wanted to do Human Studies, which was originally designed for slow-learners.'

This often emerged also in my discussions with fourth- and fifth-formers about their subject-choices. One girl typically explained:

'I thought it would give me a clean start, something new that I had never done before that I might be able to get on with.'

But the over-subscription also brought into play the notion of 'appropriateness'. Although anyone could choose it, for many band 2 pupils Human Studies was seen as 'inappropriate'; they were 'capable of something better'.

'It was massively over-subscribed. We had to gently persuade the more academic kids to do something else.'

(Senior master)

'Something else' for band 2 pupils means either a traditional C.S.E. or a practical C.S.E. subject like Technical Studies or Design Drawing. The movement of choices, the gentle persuasion to change, involves the senior master or other staff in counselling the pupils – that is, in raising or lowering the academic horizons, and thus the occupational horizons, of those pupils who have made the 'inappropriate' choice.

'I tell them I would like to be director of Harwell or to swim the channel but I know that I would sink before I got half-way across.'

(Senior master)

In effect, these pupils are 'cooled out'.[11]

Many of the pupils interviewed about their options had been given accounts of themselves, and they couched their aspirations in these terms.

'Mrs Cogan says that I'm just not capable of doing O-level.'

(Boy, band 2)

'Rural Science, I'm not going to do that any more, it's just thicko's. It's meant to be for digging and I thought it was about plants.'

(John Dyson, 3CU)

The counselling procedure which deals with the over-aspiring (and under-aspiring) pupil often makes reference to his record of performance.[12] The examinations which take place immediately before the options are the final piece in an accumulation of evidence with which he is confronted, and he may be exposed to his own failure, despite the opportunities he was given.[13]

The senior master has the initial task of reorienting the pupil's aspirations and establishing the criteria for acceptance of alternative choices which are more 'appropriate'. But this procedure may be short-circuited either if the pupil himself is adamant in wanting to take a particular course or, more likely, if he calls in his parents to reinforce his choice. Redirection, persuasion and counselling still take place within the framework of total freedom of choice by the pupil.

> 'Ultimately, we follow the policy of the school; it's up to the kids what they decide to do. I had one parent up about this last week.'
>
> (Head of History)

Most pupils who are redirected, however, do not ask their parents to intervene (see pp. 153–7).

Despite the need to redirect some, most pupils do make appropriate choices in the first place. They have, during the first three years of secondary school, internalized the notions of their relative capabilities presented to them by the staff. Band 2 pupils come to see band 1 forms in terms like this:

> 'The work is harder up there [in band 1].'
> 'I'm not bright enough, the work's just right for me in band 2, you know, not too hard and not too easy.'

Band 1 means:

> 'That you are a lot brainier and quicker at work.'
> 'They do it faster.'

Almost every pupil interviewed from 3TA was able to account for his relatively inferior academic status in these terms. Woods (1976 : 135–6) notes of the low-stream pupils in his study that

years of interactions, tests and examinations have taught them their place. By the time of the third year, these processes have completed the shifting and groups have worked out their modus vivendi.

In the terms of a functionalist analysis of education systems, Hopper (1971 b) argues that a process of selection is not simply choosing some and not others for high-status futures; the choices must be justified to and accepted by the pupils. Those who have not been selected must be persuaded by experience to accept their positions of inferior status, and their ambitions must be reduced to a level compatible with the potentials of that inferior status. This is what Hopper calls 'status training'. From this perspective the band 2 career may be seen as a 'cooling-out' route and the band 1 career as the 'warming-up' route through the school.

This 'cooling-out', however, is not without its problems. The staff find that band 2 and 3 pupils tend to lose motivation in the third year, which can make keeping control in band 2 lessons even more difficult than is usual. This is part of what Hopper refers to as the 'warming-up – cooling-out dilemma'; that is the problem of the loss of interest and commitment of those who have been cooled out, especially when they are expected to remain in the system for a long period after the original selection choice, which in this case is allocation to band 2. Hopper (1971b : 305) argues that 'throughout the system . . . a need exists for the simultaneous provision of warming-up and cooling-out experiences', to minimize the disruption that stems from lack of interest and commitment. A possible solution to this lack of motivation and its attendant problems in band 2 was put forward by the headmaster in a meeting of heads of departments.

> 'Anxiety has already been expressed this term about the third year; you get a very heavy fall away in motivation. What are the ways that we might get around this capitulation? This is academically depressing and also has its effects upon the morale of the school. It did not happen in the early years of banding but perhaps now we are seeing the effects of reinforced failure, perhaps the anticipation also of subjects to be dropped. I have been giving consideration to the possibility of awarding an end-of-year certificate for any subjects satisfactorily completed during the first three years.'

Although this suggestion was not accepted by the heads of departments, they certainly expressed an awareness of the 'problems' the headmaster spoke of.

> 'I think these kids know that they are being treated second best.'
>
> (Head of Technical Studies)
> 'It's a question of working hard in a band 2 class. I think Heads of Departments must be sure in their own minds that what is going on in these forms is what they want to go on.'
>
> (Third-year tutor)

In referring to Hopper's (1971 b) analysis I do not wish to put the present account of cooling-out into a functionalist framework, but merely to note the similarities of the processes described here to the functions identified by Hopper. I am not suggesting that I am able to establish a functional relationship between these processes and the occupational structure or the objectively differentiated structure of the upper school.[14]

What emerges in consideration of the notion of the 'appropriateness' of particular kinds of pupils for particular kinds of courses, with the matching of abilities and capabilities, is a differentiation not unlike that made in the Norwood Report[15] an embodied in the classical form of the tripartite system – that is, the variety of capacity. The notion is that there are three types of pupil who require three different types of curriculum: the academic, the practical, and the general. Particularly in the case of the last of these, there is a great similarity between the courses offered in the Human Studies department and the recommendations of the Norwood Report. The report states:

In the third type of curriculum a balanced training of mind and body and a correlated approach to humanities [Human Studies], Natural Science [Modern Applications of Science] and the Arts [Creative Arts and Crafts] would provide an equipment varied enough to enable pupils to take up the work of life.[16]

The same kind of status differentiation which existed between the grammar, secondary modern and technical schools, which was based on the access they gave to occupational position and into higher education, also differentiates the status of the fourth- and fifth-year curriculum subjects.

Subject status

While the 'appropriateness' of pupils for different 'kinds' of subjects or courses is closely related to the status of that subject, as we have seen, the high-status academic subjects of a 'pure' variety are not normally available to the band 2 or band 3 pupil. Conversely, the pupils who take the subjects also reinforce the status of the subject, so that a subject may be of high status, not only because it is academically 'pure', but also because it is only taken by band 1 pupils. It thus becomes attractive for the staff and there is a demand for it to be taught. Thus, differentiation plays a part both in creating and in reflecting a system of status of knowledge. But basically the hierarchy of status of subjects is that which derives from the traditional access-routes they provide into the sixth form, and thus to university.[17]

Those subjects with the highest exchange-value, as passports into further or higher education or into high-status positions in the occupation market, are of highest status, while the Mode III examined, 'new' C.S.E.s have little negotiable value even in the lowest reaches of the occupation market. When I asked the head of Human Studies whether C.S.E. Mode III passes were in practice negotiable in the labour market, he said:

'I don't think they are. The employers see through them for what they are, but they are C.S.E.s although up till now in the history of the Human Studies department no one has got above a grade 3 though that record may be broken this year.'

This was reinforced by the school Careers Master.

Stephen Ball 'What sort of status have new C.S.E.s got with employers?'
Careers Master 'I don't think they've got an awful lot really. Employers are very behind the times in all this, and therefore while we try to think of the whole person, they are thinking in very narrow qualification, by and large they split people down into three classes, the people who are capable of A-levels and degrees, then below that the people who are capable of O-level jobs, and then the others who are just the others. They haven't refined that. If they were to refine it then these C.S.E.s would become important, but they haven't; they're very crude in their interviewing techniques and even the ones who use exams use old fashioned intelligence tests.'

'The only advantage is in certain cases it enables a boy to say I've got four C.S.E.s and if the employer is the type who is happy at that then that's fine, but there are other employers who will say, What in?'

'There is a lot of suspicion with anything that's got a long name, anything that's not a traditional school subject because to them qualifications mean success in school subjects, and so of course something that goes right across subject barriers they have no idea.'

The Local Careers Officer – whose role it is to liaise between the school leavers and prospective employers – also stressed the differential status accredited to the various examinations by employers. He said:

'It's taken 10 years for even C.S.E. Grade 1 to be accepted by employers. Large organizations will recognize them but the local employers are still very suspicious . . . For craft apprentices they want grade 3s, but even then they still want to be offered English, Maths and History. The others [Mode III C.S.E.s and non-traditional subjects] don't really carry any weight with employers. With these new fangled C.S.E.s their response is usually, "My God, what's this, we want the 3 Rs", they don't know what Modern Applications of Science, or Environmental Science is all about really . . . There's no feedback on course content and that devalues the worth of the qualification . . . they *are* much more worried about the low level of arithmetic and spelling.'

In conventional terms, the traditional O-level subjects – Maths, English, the Languages, Sciences, History, Geography, etc. – are all high-status, with high exchange-value in the education and occupation markets. These are now joined by one or two newer subjects like Sociology, Economics and Geology, which, although they lack a tradition of high status, are accepted for university entrance. These high-status subjects have an academic orientation in common; they are concerned with theoretical knowledge. They are subjects for the brighter, the academic, the band 1 pupil. Martin Shipman (1971 : 102) makes the ironic point that:

While the universities have acted to inhibit innovation in the education of their potential intake, they have been sharing in promoting new curriculum for those who will go into employment or further education straight from school.

Next in status come the other O-levels, the practical subjects, which are not purely academic. These subjects do not count towards university entrance but still may be negotiable for further education – as 'other' O-levels for Colleges of Further Education and Technology, or as basic qualifications for vocational training courses – and can also be valuable assets in the occupation market. Included here are Home Economics, Needlecraft, Technical Studies, Design Drawing, Metalwork and Technical Drawing. These are subjects operating with a lower level of theoretical sophistication, but maintained at a high level of performance.

In the case of C.S.E.s, a pass at other than Grade 1 will not for the most part suffice as a qualification for higher education, although lower grades are accepted as a guide for the prospective employer in certain subjects. But it is also necessary to differentiate between the status of the traditional C.S.E. subjects and the 'new' Mode III C.S.E.s. The new C.S.E.s are probably of lowest status, even in the case of job applications, for where qualifications are asked for, the employer is usually looking for passes in Maths and English or the more practical-vocational subjects. Human Studies, Home Studies and Modern Applications of the Sciences are concerned with knowledge of everyday life, with enactive knowledge. The nominal line which divides school knowledge from the world of everyday life is here almost indistinguishable.[18]

In effect the curriculum is 'stratified', to use Michael Young's (1971 b) term, in the value that is placed on certain parts of it, both from within the school and from the outside. This stratification operates primarily in terms of the access that the different courses give to positions of prestige in the wider society.[19] But the curriculum is also stratified in the sense that there is a restriction of access to certain knowledge-areas. As a result, once the options are finalized and pupils are allocated, there is a notable distinction between band 1, and band 2 and 3 pupils. As Esland (1971 : 96) points out 'the distinction is likely to be one between a curriculum where enactive or concrete knowledge is predominant, and a curriculum based on theoretical provinces of meaning'. The band 1 and band 2 and 3 pupils move into separate curricular areas which institutionalize the differences that have existed in the curricular presentation during the first three years.[20] This separation emerged clearly from the original choices made by 3CU and 3TA pupils and then later in the final allocation of those pupils to courses. The choices are presented below.

Option allocation

As demonstrated by the previous discussion of the processes of redirection and rejection of option-choices, the choices made are by no means the end point of the option-allocation procedure. The final allocation to fourth-year courses shows notable differences from these original choices. Table 5.2 compares the choices made with the actual allocation to courses for the pupils of 3TA and 3CU. Eventually, out of a total of 186 courses, the 3TA pupils were only allowed to take 22 O-level courses (that is, 0.71

Tables 5.2–5.4. *Option choices made by pupils in 3CU and 3TA, with the actual courses to which they were allocated at the end of the option procedure*
Table 5.2. *Comparing level of course*

	3CU				3TA			
	O-level	O/C.S.E.	C.S.E.	Total	O-level	O/C.S.E.	C.S.E.	Total
Chosen	81%(165)	10%(20)	9%(19)	100%(204)	15%(27)	15%(28)	70%(131)	100%(186)
Allocated	71%(145)	14%(29)	15%(30)	100%(204)	11%(22)	18%(33)	71%(131)	100%(186)

Table 5.3. *Comparing 'minority' and 'main' subjects*[a]

	3CU			3TA		
	Minority	Main	Totals	Minority	Main	Totals
Chosen	24%(48)	76%(156)	100%(204)	46%(86)	54%(100)	100%(186)
Allocated	13%(39)	81%(165)	100%(204)	28%(53)	72%(133)	100%(186)

[a]Main subjects are those subjects which are a part of the curriculum in the first, second and third years. Minority subjects are those subjects being offered for the first time in the fourth and fifth years.

per pupil compared with 4.27 per pupil for 3CU). It is important to note, however, that the redirection of O-level choices is not limited to the band 2 pupils. There were 11 O-level choices made by band 1 pupils which were redirected into C.S.E., and a further 9 which were redirected into O/C.S.E. courses. This 'over-aspiration' by band 1 pupils is a further aspect of the warming-up/cooling-out dilemma. Moreover, the notion of 'appropriateness' and the counselling procedures for the lowering of aspirations are not limited to the band 2 and band 3 pupils. As we have seen, there are band 1 pupils who are poorly-perceived by their teachers and who perform poorly in comparison with their classmates, although table 5.2 does tend to exaggerate the extent of redirection among band 1 pupils (see p. 144). In table 5.3 it can be seen that both forms finally take more 'main' curriculum subjects than originally chosen but, even so, the 3TA pupils still end up taking a higher proportion of minority courses (1.7 per pupil compared with 1.13 in 3CU). The much larger proportion of choices made for 'minority' subjects by the band 2 pupils reinforces the point made earlier about the attraction of a 'fresh start' in the fourth year. In table 5.4 it can be seen that the pressures of change operate to increase the differences between the two forms. Pupils from 3TA end by taking more practical subjects than they chose originally (2.77 per pupil), and the 3CU pupils end by taking fewer (0.76 per pupil). Thus, 3TA pupils have been directed away from the 'academic' towards the practical, while the reverse has happened for the 3CU pupils.

Only one pupil in 3CU chose any of the 'new' subjects, whereas 34 were chosen by 3TA pupils – 17 per cent of all choices made. This is made up of 2 per cent of the choices from boys and 15 per cent from the girls. Hollingshead (1961) noted a similar differentiation of curriculum choice among the pupils of Elmtown High School.[21]

There were also academic subject choice-differences between the forms:

Table 5.4. *Comparing 'practical' and 'academic' subjects*[a]

	3CU			3TA		
	Practical	Academic	Totals	Practical	Academic	Totals
Chosen	19%(38)	81%(166)	100%(204)	37%(68)	63%(118)	100%(186)
Allocated	13%(26)	87%(178)	100%(204)	46%(86)	54%(100)	100%(186)

[a]Practical subjects include Metalwork, Woodwork, Design Drawing, Domestic Science, Needlework and Art.

3CU	3TA
Number of Science courses chosen: 53 (26% of all choices)	Number of Science courses chosen: 19 (10.2% of all choices)
Number of Language courses chosen: 27 (13% of all choices)	Number of Language courses chosen: 11 (6% of all choices)
Number of girls' choices made for Science: 20 (10% of all choices)	Number of girls' choices made for Science: 1 (0.5% of all choices)
Number of boys' choices made for Science: 33 (16% of all choices)	Number of boys' choices made for Science: 18 (9.7% of all choices)

In 3CU 13 per cent of choices were made for Language courses, but only 6 per cent in 3TA; 26 per cent of choices were made for Science courses in 3CU, but only 11 per cent in 3TA.

Once again this differentiation between the two forms can be related to differences in subject-status. For instance, King (1974 : 92) makes the point that, 'The specialized study of Science provides access to forms of explanation that imply the mastery of nature and some control of the destiny of men.' The band 2 pupils only chose or gained access to these high-status courses in very small numbers.[22]

However, the *overall* extent of the redirection of pupils is not fully apparent from the tables above. It becomes much clearer when the number of 'rejections' from courses are examined across the whole year-group.

The total numbers of 'rejections' from courses at each level is shown in table 5.5. The variation in the number of 'rejections' between the bands is

Table 5.5. *Number of rejections from examination courses per band*

	O-levels[a] (20 courses)	O/C.S.E. (6 courses)	Traditional C.S.E.s (20 courses)	'New' Mode III C.S.E.s (6 courses)
Band 1	38	6	43[b]	15
Band 2	72	13	100[c]	68
Band 3	3	3	12	11

[a]These figures include all but two O-level options (Physics and Biology) for which I did not have the necessary data.
[b]11 of these pupils were specifically recommended for the O-level in the same subject.
[c]3 of these pupils were specifically recommended for the O-level in the same subject.

Table 5.6. *Rejections from O-level courses as a percentage of all choices made for O-levels*

	O-levels[a]	Total made
Band 1	5.6%(38)	679
Band 2	32.14%(72)	224
Band 3	100.00%(3)	3

[a]These figures include all but two O-level options (Physics and Biology) for which I did not have the necessary data.

Table 5.7. *Distribution of 'new' courses allotted across the bands*

	Band 1	Band 2	Band 3
Human Studies 1	2	11	14
Modern Applications of Science	–	9	13
Human Studies 2	3	11	15
Home Studies	3	34	20
	8(6% of all 'new' choices)	65(48% of all 'new' choices)	62 (46% of all 'new' choices)

of course a reflection of the number of choices made for each type of course; clearly, the number of 'rejections' received by band 2 pupils from O-level courses must be viewed in terms of a proportion of all such choices made. This is shown in table 5.6. From these figures it is evident that the patterns of allocation of the pupils from the two case-study forms was repeated in the other forms in this year-group. This results in band 1 pupils being heavily over-represented in the O-level courses, and the band 3 pupils especially being over-represented in the Mode III 'new' courses. The total choices by each band for the 'new' subjects are shown in table 5.7.

Options and life-chances

The pattern of allocation to options outlined above was also repeated in previous year-cohorts in the school. The data presented below concern some of these previous cohorts.

The point was made earlier that the allocation to option-courses would be important in terms of the future life-chances of the pupils. In the immediate sense, within the school, this means access to the sixth form and to A-level courses. Passes at A-level would thence provide the sixth-form leaver with access to higher education or training for high-status occupations. These access-points would not normally be available to those pupils leaving at the end of the fifth-year courses, even those with good O-level passes. This is clearly shown in the initial job destinations of fifth- and sixth-form leavers from Summer 1974 (see tables 5.8 and 5.11).

Table 5.8. *Fifth-form leavers' initial job destinations or places obtained in Further Education, 1974 (presented by band and sex)*[23]

	Number of O-levels passed	Number of C.S.E.s Grades 2–5
BOYS		
Band 1		
Apprentice Technician, R.A.F.	7	2
Seaman, R.N.	–	6
Packer	1	2
Police Cadet	3	2
College of Further Education, Civil Engineering	7	2
Naval Cadet	3	3
Band 2		
Bank Clerk	–	7
Apprentice Plasterer	–	8
Warehouseman	–	3
Trainee Butcher	–	8
Bank Clerk	–	6
Packer	–	–
Apprentice Electrician	–	4
Nautical College	–	6
Trainee Machinist	–	8
Apprentice Butcher	–	8
Aerial Rigger	–	5
Assistant Photographer	–	7
Junior Engineer Fitter	–	7
Junior Engineer Fitter	–	8
Army Infantryman	–	3
Apprentice Joiner	–	8
Apprentice Linesman	–	5
Trainee Machine Operator	–	5
Trainee Assembler	–	3

Table 5.8 (*contd.*)	Number of O-levels passed	Number of C.S.E.s Grade 2–5
Animal Attendant	–	–
Apprentice Motor Mechanic	–	6
Trainee Welder	–	5
Car Mechanic	–	8
Musician	–	4
Apprentice Electrician	–	5
College of Further Education, A-levels	2	5
Commercial College	–	8
Band 3		
Sorter	–	–
Sales Assistant	–	5
Electrician, R.N.	–	6
Paint Sprayer	–	5
Shop Assistant	–	4
Car Body Repairer	–	2
Trainee Machinist	–	2
Labourer	–	–
Infantryman Army	–	2
Apprentice Carpenter	–	5
Apprentice Signalman, Army	–	7
College of Further Education, Catering	–	3
GIRLS		
Band 1		
Typist	–	4
Trainee Clerk	3	2
Key Check Operator	1	3
Apprentice Hairdresser	–	3
Punch Card Operator	–	2
Compositor Operator	2	3
Assembler	–	1
Junior Typist	1	3
Junior Librarian	–	4
College of Further Education, Secretarial Course	1	7
College of Further Education, Catering	4	4
College of Further Education, Secretarial Course	–	4
College of Further Education	4	3
Bank Clerk	4	2
College of Further Education, Secretarial/Languages	3	3

College of Further Education,
   Catering — 3
Council Office Clerk 1 4
Council Office Clerk 3 4
Factory Process Worker — 5
Medical Secretary 9 —
Bank Clerk — 5
Drama School 3 1

Band 2
Bank Clerk 1 7
Bank Clerk — 6
College of Further Education,
   Secretarial Course — 6
Bank Cashier (trained) — 6
Trained Clerk — 7
Bank Clerk — 5
Bank Cashier — 5
Shop Cashier — 3
Junior Bank Clerk — 8
G.P.O. Telephonist — 4
Office Junior — 7
Junior Bank Clerk — 5
Darkroom Assistant 1 5
Bank Clerk — 6
Bank Clerk — 8
Bank Clerk — 4
Hairdresser — 4

Band 3
Punch Card Operator — 7
Trainee machinist — 6
Junior Bank Clerk — 5
Packer — —
Nursery Hand — 3
Key Check Operator — 4
Punch Card Operator — —
Apprentice Hairdresser — 5
Punch Card Operator — 2
Trainee Machinist — 5
Trainee Clerk — 5
Order Processer — 4
Trainee Book-Binder — 3
Junior Clerk — 2
Assembler — 4
Trainee Cook — 7
Sales Assistant — 3
Filing Clerk — 4
Dental Nurse — 5
Junior Clerk — 4
Office Worker — 5[24]

For the fifth-year-examination leavers or those who left before taking examinations, the school is a jumping-off point only into the local job-market. What Lacey (1970) refers to as the 'professionalizing' and 'finishing school' functions of the school are not available to the pupils who leave at this stage.[25]

Each traceable destination for one whole leaving-cohort is noted above in table 5.8. There is a reason for this. A. H. Halsey concluded from the Oxford study of social mobility (1974 : 5) that 'the overall correlation between education and occupation is clear enough but it is just as important to notice the patchiness or varying closeness of relation in the different sectors of the occupational structure'. He also made the point that 'a disaggregated description is required for accurate appraisal of the bond between education and occupation'. Patchiness and variation in fit is evident in the area examined here, but so too is the relationship between certification and occupational entry when the data are examined in their disaggregated form.

The tabular presentation of these first job positions and Further Education places is given in table 5.9. Apart from overall differences between the bands in the attainment of manual and non-manual occupations and going on to Further Education, it is evident that more particular differences exist. Some of the important distinctions are blurred by the presentation of the data simply in terms of a manual/non-manual dichotomy. It would appear that non-manual jobs are well-represented in bands 2 and 3, and, indeed, that band 3 pupils were more successful in

Table 5.9. *Distribution of first job destinations and Further Education places, by band and sex*

	Total	H.M. Forces	Non-manual jobs	Manual jobs	Further Education
Band 1					
Girls	22(100%)	0	12(54%)	3(14%)	7(32%)
Boys	6(100%)	3(50%)	1(16.67%)	1(16.6%)	1(16.67%)
Band 2					
Girls	17(100%)	0	13(76%)	3(18%)	1(6%)
Boys	28(100%)	2(7%)	3(11%)	20(71%)	2(7%)
Band 3					
Girls	21(100%)	0	13(62%)	8(38%)	0
Boys	12(100%)	3(25%)	2(17%)	6(50%)	1(8%)

Table 5.10. *Distribution of secretarial, clerical and office machine operator jobs obtained by girls*

	Percentage of all leavers	Secretary/typist	Clerk	Office Machine operator
Band 1	32	3	1	3
Band 2	6	–	1	–
Band 3	48	–	6	4

obtaining non-manual jobs than were band 2 pupils. Overall, 36 per cent of band 2 pupils come into this category compared with 45 per cent of band 3. However, the distribution of manual and non-manual jobs is decisively influenced by the number of girls who obtained secretarial or clerical jobs (see table 5.10). There is also a further differentiation between the bands that must be taken into account, especially between bands 2 and 3, in terms of the particular kinds of jobs obtained by the pupils from the different bands. This lies in the difference between job and career development and social status. For instance, among the boys, apprenticeship is an important differentiating factor. Eight boys (30 per cent) from band 2 took up apprenticeships, compared with only two (17 per cent) from band 3. Among the girls, the job of Bank Clerk separates the bands in a similar way. Ten girls (59 per cent) from band 2 obtained jobs as Bank Clerks, while only one girl (5 per cent) from band 3 obtained such a job. The non-manual jobs among the band 3 girls include a considerable proportion of office machine operators, as we have seen.

However, it is also apparent from these lists that the relationship between examination attainment and occupational placement does not occur mechanically, although it is the case that the average number of C.S.E. and G.C.E. examination passes obtained by the boys in band 2 going into other manual jobs is smaller (5.47), compared with those going into apprenticeships (6.5), and those going into non-manual jobs or college (6.71). Furthermore, among the girls from band 2 the only three girls to get less than five C.S.E.s may be clearly differentiated from the others in terms of first job-destinations; they became a hairdresser, shop cashier and G.P.O. telephonist respectively.

Nevertheless, within the other bands such clear-cut relationships do not emerge, and comparing individual cases it is possible to find anomalies. For instance, among the girls of band 3 there is a Punch Card Operator with seven C.S.E.s and another with none at all. As suggested previously, there are certain basic or traditionally high-status subjects that carry more weight with employers, and it is passes in these subjects, not necessarily the total number of passes obtained by individual pupils, that seem to be important in finding jobs. To quote Halsey (1974 : 6) again, 'Education places people at more or less advantageous entry points to a working career. Within that framework the relation between qualifications, jobs and income may be a fairly loose one.'

What is striking from this very small sample is that, at least in band 2 and band 3, the *type* of subject taken at C.S.E., which is related to band, appears to be a more important factor in pupils obtaining jobs than the *number* of examinations passed. While differences in kind in the pupils' first job-destinations are obviously, at least in part, a function of the pupils' aspirations, they are also certainly related to the way in which employers make decisions about whom to employ. As yet, researchers have failed to give much attention to employers' decision-making for this level of appointment.

The vast majority of these fifth-form leavers, whether entering their first job or going on to further education, remained in the local area, taking up jobs with local firms or going to the College of Further Education in the adjacent seaside town. It was only those pupils who joined the Armed Forces who were immediately 'released' from the local job-market. Access to the national occupation-market or to higher education, university or polytechnic, is rarely achieved in the period immediately after the end of schooling, except for those pupils who stay on into the sixth form and do A-levels. This can be seen in table 5.11, in the list of destinations of sixth-form leavers, Summer 1974.[26] This list contrasts in many respects with that of the fifth-form leavers. Eighteen pupils (32 per cent) went on to degree-courses in higher education, while a further eight pupils (15 per cent) entered other forms of higher or further education. Several traditionally high-status occupations were also achieved, including the Civil Service, the law, surveying, electronic engineering, management, stockbroking and teaching at a preparatory school.

In effect, then, the selection decisions for fourth-year options, subsequent examination attainment at O-level and C.S.E. at the end of the fifth year, and later entry into the occupational hierarchy or higher or further education, are all critically influenced by the allocation to bands at the beginning of the first year. This allocation is, in turn, based upon educational identities created in the primary school.

Given the relationship between banding and social class shown earlier,[27] the differentiation of access to high-status knowledge areas with high

Table 5.11. *Job and Further and Higher Education destinations for sixth-form leavers, Summer 1974*

Boys
College of Further Education
Trainee Electronic Engineer, National Electronic Company
O.N.C. Business Studies, Insurance Company
Business Studies degree, Aston University
Computer Studies degree, East Anglia University, R. N. Sponsorship
Chemical Company
Civil Service
Marketing Department, International Car Company
College of Design, Foundation Studies
Estate Management degree, South Bank Polytechnic
Equestrian
B. Ed., Bretton Hall College
Retail Trade
Trainee management, Higher Education, 1975
Biochemistry degree, Liverpool University
Intending to enter Civil Service
Dartmouth College, Royal Navy
Physics Degree, Oxford University
Engineering Company
Law degree, Birmingham Polytechnic
Housemaster, Prep. school—Higher Education, 1975
Catering, College of Further Education
Steel Stockholding Firm
Quantity Surveying, London firm
Humanities degree, Huddersfield Polytechnic
Temporary job pending parents' move to new area
Bank
Business Studies degree, Brighton Polytechnic
Trainee electronics engineer
Foundation Studies, College of Design
B. Ed., Loughborough College
Working in electrician's firm
Post Office Engineer
Maths/Physics degree, Warwick University
Marine Biology degree, Bangor University

Girls
Secretary, South Bank Polytechnic
B. Ed., Coventry College
H.N.D. Catering, Portsmouth Polytechnic
Housemother, Children's home
Window-dresser
Languages course, London
Biology degree, Manchester University
Bank
Law degree

Table 5.11 (*contd.*)

Birmingham University, 1975
Intends Polytechnic English degree, 1975
Dental Nurse
Local Newspaper
Inland Revenue
Multi-lingual Secretary, Chemical Company
Legal Executive
Banking, then B.Ed., Didsbury College, 1975[28]

negotiable value is crucially related to socio-economic status. This form of early selection and the subsequent 'warming-up' of the band 1, predominantly middle-class, pupils, and the 'cooling-out' of the band 2 and 3, predominantly working-class, pupils, fits what is described by Hopper (1971b) as an elitist sponsorship selection ideology. Over and above real differences in measurable intelligence that may exist between pupils from band 1 and band 2, the system operating here is selecting at 11 for O-levels and future careers. Woods (1976) found an exactly similar state of affairs in his secondary modern study.[29]

It is evident, then, that despite the notions of equality of opportunity that have been attached to the reorganization to comprehensive education, the internal organization of the schools may still allow the maintenance of a system of early selection and separate provision of curriculum, that is essentially similar to that of tripartitism and sponsorship. When they occur within one school rather than between schools, selection processes may not be so obviously apparent. But while the internal organization and the philosophies of individual comprehensive schools remain unquestioned, then the distribution of success and failure through schooling seems unlikely to change significantly.

In particular it is apparent here that the hierarchical organization of knowledge through banding in the first three years of the school is related to the 'future life-chances' of the pupils and entry into the occupation-market. Option-allocation is a point at which school careers become firmly differentiated and at which the informal differences between pupils in terms of social reputation and their experiences of the curriculum lower down the school are formalized into separate curricular routes and examination destinations. It is here that the stratified nature of the occupation-structure is directly reflected in the 'ability' stratification within the school.[30]

Both the differential status of the knowledge areas in the curriculum and the access to the sixth form that certain courses provide are aspects of the selection of pupils for further and higher education and the occupation-market. The selection process and negotiation of meanings that go to make up the option-allocation procedure are part of the structural relationships within the school which label pupils with different statuses and educational identities. Halsey (1974) makes the point that 'What one is taught may be of importance to one's future position in society, but what one is taught depends very largely on who one is, i.e. one's social class antecedents'. This is clearly relevant here in the way in which the teachers monitor and control entry into certain subjects and examination courses.[31] But it has a further relevance which becomes even clearer in the examination of the role of parents in the option-allocation process.

The role of parents

Both from the interviews with the pupils and discussions with the teachers about the option-process, it was apparent that the parents of the 3CU pupils had played a rather different role in their children's choice of and access to options from that of the parents of 3TA pupils. In many cases, the 3CU parents had been the final arbiters of their children's choices, and in some instances had insisted on a particular combination of subjects against the child's own wishes. Twenty of the 3CU pupils interviewed referred to their parents in describing how they had made their choices. Only four pupils, all boys in 3TA, mentioned their parents being involved in their choice of subjects.

> 'They helped me choose some of them.'   (Ronny Fisher)
> 'I wrote them down on the option sheet and I gave them to them and they said whether they wanted me to do it.'   (Wally Asquith)
> 'They wanted me to do some O-levels.'   (Alan Edmeades)
> 'My mum encouraged me to do Social Science, I heard what it was all about and I quite like it. And I like technical stuff. I prefer that to a language and my dad encouraged me.'   (Neil Grimshaw)

Two pupils in this form described their parents' failure to concern themselves with their choices.

> 'No . . . she had a look but she did not really mind what I did. They don't make me do anything I don't want to.'   (Christine Downes)
> 'I took the sheet home once and then I asked her to help me and she said "Yeah, sure later", and then just forgot all about it and I just chose them at school, what I thought would be best.'   (Peter Groome)

Woods (1976) identifies five types of parental influence: compulsion; strong guidance; mutual resolution; reassurance; and little or none. Some of these types may be recognized from the comments made by the 3TA pupils quoted above. But for some pupils their parents were not simply involved in helping to make choices; they were actually able to intervene on the schoolside of the allocation procedure. Some parents, by contacting the school directly, were able to change decisions made by the staff in response to pupils' choices and thus sometimes to overcome the notions of 'appropriateness' attached to their child, deriving from a band-identity or a reputation. The year tutor explained that

> 'Ten pupils have gone into subjects against the advice of staff. Two into Art who were moved when their mothers complained. One boy in Mr Upland's form [band 3] whose father came up, and the rest into Physics and Geography.'

Heads of departments usually gave way to parental pressure. The head of History explained that

> 'Ultimately, we follow the policy of the school; it's up to the kids what they decide to do. I had one parent up about this last week.'

But 'ultimately' is a key word here, for it is normally only when the parents actually make a point of visiting or contacting the school that pupils who had been rejected from courses they originally chose were reinstated. Presented below are the outlines of some cases of parental intervention.

Case 1. Paul Patterson: Band 3 low-achiever. Father: Estate Agent
Paul's father became worried about the sort of options to which his son had been allocated, mostly Mode III C.S.E.s. He was also worried about the stories of 'difficult' forms he had heard from his son and his son's friends. Mr Patterson himself had been to a private school and was concerned that his son should 'succeed' at school. He was not impressed with Modern Applications of Science and Chemistry for Living and wanted Paul to take traditional curriculum subjects, particularly French. In fact, the band 3 form had dropped French at the end of the second year and when Mr Patterson rang the year tutor he was told that French was impossible. As a result, he began to make arrangements to send Paul to a private school in Wallsea where he could do traditional subjects and he made an appointment with Paul's form teacher, Mr Upland, to discuss with him what other subjects his son should do in the new school. As a result of this meeting the form teacher agreed to speak to the head of Languages about the French. He managed to secure for Paul a half-term trial period doing C.S.E. French in the fourth year and Mr Patterson dropped his plans to send his son to another school.

Case 2. Selina Nielsen: Band 1 3ST. Father: Senior Clerk

Selina opted for O-level Biology, but the Biology staff felt that C.S.E. would be more 'realistic' and she was redirected to the C.S.E. course. However, Selina's parents wanted her to do the O-level course because of her enthusiasm for the subject. They visited the school together and spoke to the year tutor and the head of the Biology Department. As a result, it was arranged that Selina would take the O-level on a 'trial basis'.

Case 3. Norman Mendel: Band 2 3LF. Mother widowed: Teacher

Norman's mother specifically wanted him to do Chemistry and German at O-level, but he was turned down for both these courses. The choice of these subjects was linked to a specific career-aspiration and when Norman was redirected, his mother visited the school. As a result, he was allowed to do both courses even though his Chemistry teacher felt that 'he will not stand a chance at O-level'.

Case 4. Neil Grimshaw: Band 2 2TA. Father: Shopkeeper

As noted earlier (see p. 60), Neil's father came to the school during the option-allocation period and made representations to the year tutor to ensure that Neil was able to go into the German and Physics option groups. He was admitted to German C.S.E. and was thus the only band 2 pupil to be doing a second language; he also became the only band 2 pupil doing Nuffield Physics.

As these cases indicate, the direct intervention of parents in the option process was effective in reinstating pupils in courses to which they would normally have been denied access. The parental insistence that their child should be allowed to do a course was thus one way in which 'routes' through the school could be changed. This re-emphasizes the discrepancy between the 'freedom of choice' ideology of the option process and the selection and stratification of knowledge that takes place in practice. But it is important also to reiterate that the extent of involvement differs between parents of pupils in 3CU and 3TA. Indeed, this pattern of differences in the involvement of parents of band 1 and band 2 pupils is apparent across the whole year-group. This is illustrated in the number of visits to the school made by parents to discuss options with the third-year tutor. There were 31 visits made by parents of pupils in band 1 forms, 18 by parents of band 2 pupils (8 of these were the parents of pupils in one form, 3HL, which was taught by the year tutor), and 3 by the parents of band 3 pupils.

All these instances highlight both the nature of the allocation process and the different rates of involvement of the parents of band 1, predominantly middle-class, pupils, and band 2, predominantly working-class, pupils. As Morrison and MacIntyre (1971 : 202) suggest:

Middle-class parents, more career oriented in their thinking, are more likely to appreciate the importance of this decision, to seek from teachers the information they want and to challenge teachers' opinions or even schools' timetabling arrangements.

And Lacey (1970 : 77) makes the point that:

Parents' ability to interfere . . . on their children's behalf is related to their ability to present the problem in terms of the school's ideology, and it is linked to social class.

This differential pattern of involvement of parents has been documented in several other studies. Halsey, Floud and Martin (1956), Jackson and Marsden (1962), J. W. B. Douglas (1964), and more recently Lacey (1970) have all drawn attention to the importance of a family's 'resources' in supporting their children in school. To many working-class parents 'school is an alien though desirable agency, where professionals practise their considerable expertise behind well-defined boundaries' (Woods 1976 : 142).

As we have seen here, there are several factors which contribute to parents' ability to intervene on their child's behalf. They need some knowledge of the organization of the school, especially of the structure of responsibilities. They also require some knowledge of the relative status of different subjects and courses, and need to have the skills necessary to manipulate the symbolic system of the school. An understanding of these points makes it possible for some parents to reorient their children into examination courses which provide qualifications of high status and high negotiable value.

Although some parents had the necessary skills to intervene and to deal with the school as an organization, it was apparent that many pupils and their parents dealt with this most important choice-point in an extremely haphazard manner. Burgess (1973 : 112) has made a simple but important comment about the option-choice systems of large comprehensive schools. They give the pupils

greatly increased choices within the schools, between courses, subjects and examinations. The wealth of opportunity here can be almost bewildering.

At Beachside, despite option 'talks', the pupils' understanding of some of the subjects from which they had to choose was extremely vague. For their parents too the mysteries of Chemistry for Living, Social Science or

Human Studies often operated as a barrier to their being able to take a useful part in their child's choice of subjects.

Parents are not usually part of the contemporary educational community. Their children's experiences of education deviate, often drastically, from their own. Very often the only insight into their children's experience that is available to them is indirectly, through the children themselves. Teachers do not appear to spend a great deal of time in explaining to parents the pedagogical rationale of their methods or their curriculum, or why the pupils are 'grouped' in a particular way.[32] Parents are not usually involved in a school's decision-making nor are they in the mainstream of changes in educational culture. The major basis of parents' knowledge of education is most often their own schooling, which is to a great extent being made irrelevant by the pace of change in all aspects of education over the past ten years. Without 'inside' knowledge, it is often difficult to apply support and guidance, and this is especially true in regard to the increasing range of curriculum choices in the large comprehensive and the proliferation of examinations of different types.

If the school is considered as an arena, in which parents and children as teams compete for scarce rewards, then many pupils are seriously handicapped by the lack of knowledge and expertise, and of interest, of their parents.[33] There is thus, for many pupils, a continually compounding interrelationship between differentiation experiences at school and lack of relevant support from home.

Banding, examinations and the sixth form

We have already examined in some detail in this chapter the initial job destinations of the fifth-form leavers in the 1973/4 fifth-form cohort. It now only remains to review the examination-attainments of these pupils, the extent of early leaving, and the access into the sixth form for those who did not terminate their schooling at this point.

At the end of their fifth year, most pupils are involved in taking O-levels and C.S.E. examinations, which for the majority mark the end of their secondary-school careers. However, examination successes are also important at Beachside both in the teachers' evaluation of their practice and in the maintenance of an objective basis for the separation and ranking of pupils into bands. In this section I want to examine the differences between the bands in terms of examination entries and passes, and explore the relationship between banding, examination success and entry into the sixth form.

Table 5.12. *Banding and social class: fifth-year cohort 1973–4 (80 per cent sample)*

Social class	I	II	IIIN	IIIM	IV	V	Unclass.	Total
Band								
1	6	25	14	28	10	1	20	104
2	1	7	8	32	18	4	9	79
3	0	2	2	23	6	1	10	44
Total	7	34	24	83	34	6	39	227

(Using a simple manual/non-manual dichotomy, there is a significant relationship between band and social class. $X^2 = 20.24$ d.f. $= 2$ p $> .001$.)

As applies in the case-study cohort discussed previously, one of the social divisions created by the system of banding is the considerable over-representation of middle-class pupils in band 1 and over-representation of working-class pupils in band 2. This distribution is also clear in the data presented in table 5.12 from the fifth-year cohort of 1973–4, although it should be borne in mind that the forms are no longer teaching-groups but now only pastoral units. These social class differences should be considered in relation to other differences between the bands – for example, the figures on early leaving and examination passes which represent the outcomes of different educational experiences of secondary schooling.

Obviously, the raising of the school leaving age has meant that there are quite a number of pupils who stay on into the fifth year at Beachside, who previously would have left at the age of fifteen. But the ROSLA legislation does allow two dates for leaving, Easter and Summer, so that some pupils, if they are old enough, can still leave before taking examinations (see table 5.13). 84 per cent of all the early leavers came from bands 2 and 3, and 67

Table 5.13. *Easter leavers: cohort 1973–4 (by band and sex)*

	Boys	Girls
Band 1	0	7
Band 2	10	12
Band 3	5	11
	15	30

Table 5.14. *Passes in and entries for O-level examinations by band: cohort 1974–5*

	Band 1	Band 2	Band 3
No. of pupils entered for O-levels	105	57	3
Average no. of entries per pupil	5.55	2.58	1.71
Passes per pupil entered	3.12	0.68	0.57
Percentage pass-rates	56.29%	26.53%	33.33%

per cent of all leavers were girls. This may reflect either the lesser vocational importance of examination qualifications to girls or perhaps the lesser importance given by parents to girls 'staying on'.

The examination results of the fifth-year pupils from the 1974–5 cohort are presented in table 5.14. Even though far fewer band 2 and band 3 pupils are actually entered for O-level examinations, their pass-rates are still much lower than those of band 1 pupils. Only 11.59 per cent of the total of all O-level passes was obtained by pupils outside band 1.[34] These figures provide an overall pass-rate of 49.9 per cent, compared with the national figure of 59.1 per cent, although, given the differences in composition between the Beachside entries and national entries, any conclusions to be drawn from this comparison must be made very carefully.[35]

A similar pattern of distribution to that of O-levels exists for C.S.E. Grade 1 passes (see table 5.15).[36] However, as might be expected, the pattern of results for grades 2–5 C.S.E. is different (see table 5.16). Overall, the band 2 and 3 pupils were markedly unsuccessful in public examinations compared with band 1 pupils. This pattern was found in each of the years of results examined. Few pupils from bands 2 and 3 obtained the examination passes necessary for entry into further or higher education

Table 5.15. *Passes at C.S.E. Grade 1 by band: cohort 1974–5*

C.S.E. Grade 1	Band 1	Band 2	Band 3
Total no. of passes	79	43	4
Passes per pupil in band	0.75	0.4	0.11
No. of pupils in each band	(105)	(108)	(36)

Table 5.16. *Passes at C.S.E. Grades 2–5 by band: cohort 1974–5*

C.S.E. Grades 2–5	Band 1	Band 2	Band 3
Total no.	258	531	170
No. of passes per pupil in band	2.46	4.92	4.72

or into 'careers'. However, some did 'stay on' into the sixth form. But although entry into the sixth form was 'open',[37] there was a further separation of and allocation of pupils to courses of different worth and status within the sixth form. The sixth form is 'open' in that no academic qualifications are required to enter it at Beachside, although there were sometimes 'queries' about individual pupils on 'social grounds', which meant that certain pupils were taken 'on probation'. There were also questions of 'suitability', and pupils who intended to do vocational courses, such as catering or specialized language training, were sometimes encouraged to go to the College of Further Education in Wallsea. However, access to A-level courses within the sixth form is not open. Entry into these courses depends on having at least a pass at O-level, usually not lower than Grade B, although this is subject to consultation. Once again there is a clear-cut stratification of knowledge, in the sense that procedures exist to limit access of pupils to certain types of courses; a mechanism which reinforces their intrinsic high status.

As a result of the 'open sixth form' policy a large proportion of those pupils in the first year of the sixth form each year are either repeating O-level courses and intending to leave after the one year, or hoping to go on subsequently to two years of A-level courses (see table 5.17).[38] Thus a large proportion of the girls in the lower sixth, 66 per cent, are not on A-level courses. The A-level differentiation is also related to banding, as shown in

Table 5.17. *Entry to A-level courses for boys and girls: lower sixth 1974–5*

	Boys[a]	Percentage	Girls	Percentage	Total	Percentage
Taking A-levels	38	76	13	34	51	58
Not taking A-levels	12	24	25	66	37	42
Totals	50	100	38	100	88	100

[a]One boy left after a few weeks and is not included here.

Table 5.18. *Entry to A-level courses by band: lower sixth 1974–5*

	Band 1	Percentage	Band 2	Percentage	Band 3	Percentage
Taking A-levels	40	58	4	23	0	–
Not taking A-levels	29	42	13	77	2	
Totals	69	100	17	100	2	

table 5.18. Only 4 pupils from the total of 17 from band 2 and 3 are taking A-level courses. Neave (1975 : 227) in his recent survey of the impact of comprehensive reorganization on University entry makes the point that 'The open sixth form is replacing the elite "tradition" that grew up with the academic sixth of the modern grammar school after 1944.' This overlooks the fact, however, that many pupils in open sixth forms may not be taking A-level courses. It is A-levels which provide access to higher education and the 'elite' professions, not sixth-form membership *per se*.

Neave also makes the point that

To what extent the opening up of the sixth form changes its social class composition is not clear at the present time, but recent enquiries have shown that a far higher proportion of sixth formers in comprehensive schools come from working-class homes than was the case in grammar schools (1975 : 222–3).

He gives figures of 34 per cent for the grammar school and 51 per cent for the comprehensive. This figure is almost identical to that at Beachside; in this cohort exactly 50 per cent of those pupils who could be classified were working-class. But there are also differences between working-class and middle-class pupils in terms of taking A-level and non-A-level courses (see table 5.19). Although this sixth-form cohort is composed of an exactly equal proportion of middle-class and working-class pupils, only

Table 5.19. *Social class and entry into A-level courses: lower sixth 1974–5*

	Middle-class		Working-class		Unclassified	
Taking A-levels	28	74%	17	45%	6	50%
Not taking A-levels	10	26%	21	55%	6	50%
Totals	38	100%	38	100%	12	100%

(The relationship between taking A-levels and social class background is statistically significant. $\chi^2 = 6.59$ d.f. $= 1$ p > 0.01.)

38 per cent of those pupils taking A-levels are working-class compared with 68 per cent of those who are not. Thus, the differentiation of knowledge and separation of learning environments, evident lower down the school, continues within the sixth form. Once again, this involves the separation of routes of schooling, and access to different positions of entry into the occupational hierarchy. The differences between pupils taking A-levels and those not taking A-levels are evident in terms of band, sex, and social class. Thus, although Neave (1975) is able to demonstrate that working-class pupils increasingly stay on in the 'open' sixth form in comprehensive schools, this does not in itself imply an increased opportunity for working-class pupils to go to university. The important point of differentiation *within* the sixth form between A-level and non-A-level courses must be taken into account.

It is possible to argue from the examination results presented above that, inasmuch as the pupils 'lived up' to their banding positions, the banding system represents a fairly accurate and efficient procedure for separating out the academically more able, and predicting which pupils will be 'successful' and which will 'fail'. I do not wish to argue that academic ability is irrelevant to the successes and failures of individual pupils. However, I have tried to demonstrate in the earlier chapters the several ways in which the allocation to band 2 in itself imposes limitations upon the possibilities of success for individual pupils, particularly inasmuch as the allocation to the different bands involves an allocation to different moral careers or experiential routes through the school.

Furthermore, I have tried to demonstrate the ways in which these experiential differences are related to and derived from the different levels of expectation that teachers hold for the pupils from different bands and the distribution of status in the school; and the way in which these differences have practical implications for the allocation of pupils to courses of different negotiable value in the fourth and fifth years. Thus, it may be that the band 2 route through the school is an inadequate preparation for success, both educationally and psychologically.

6　Mixed-ability: innovation and debate

In the various chapters of this study so far I have sought to present an account of the processes at work in the banded classrooms of Beachside Comprehensive and to trace the progress of children through the banded system of the school from the first year into the fifth and sixth years. But in the academic year 1973–4 the new first-year intake into the school was not allocated to bands; instead the pupils were divided into ten forms of mixed ability and two small remedial forms.

This chapter is concerned with the process of and debate about the mixed-ability innovation as it involved the teachers. This involves a change in the level of analysis; for the most part this chapter deals with the innovation at the level of the whole school, rather than at the level of the classroom or of pupil-teacher interaction. It concentrates on the teachers as decision-makers and innovators. This change of level also involves the explicit use of a conceptual framework derived from the 'action frame of reference'. Following Silverman (1970:222–3), this approach is to be used as an alternative to the traditional 'systems' type analysis of organizational change. Silverman says:

The action approach, while it involves some metatheoretical assumptions, can most usefully be seen as a method of analysis rather than a theory. It offers a frame of reference from which can be devised a series of related questions about the notion of social life in any organization. Only empirical studies can provide the answers to these questions but the material which they accumulate can be referred back to a consistent analytical structure.

The innovation here is not to be considered as an objective structural entity that can be understood aside from the different meanings and significances it has for the different teachers involved. Therefore, 'mixed-ability' is not to be taken as a given, based in a shared understanding, but as a term, covering different kinds of possible orientation and forms of relationships, that remains to be defined by the experiences and practices of those

involved in it. Innovation is taken to be a cultural phenomenon, as defined
by Esland (1972 : 103):

Essentially, the term 'innovation' refers to an idea or practice which is perceived by
a group of people to be a significant departure from existing practice. Moreover it
is a social process. It takes place through time and is part of the social reality of a
community of people. Although the innovative idea is in individual consciousness,
it nevertheless remains a product of social interaction. Furthermore, it can only be
sustained through social interaction.

The topic of the analysis, then, is the innovation as an interaction
process, rather than as a statement of intent by the organization's
superordinate members. Indeed, as we shall see, there are no formally
stated or commonly accepted goals or objectives assigned to the innovation
against which the outcomes of the change could be measured. The
aspirations for the innovation held by the staff were informal and not
universal. The innovation should not, then, be seen in terms of a system-
product analysis of change. However, there were clear and universal 'anti-
goals', or sets of unacceptable consequences, which constrained the
possibilities of change. Although neither the teachers nor the headmaster
considered the innovation to be the concern of the parents, they were
certainly aware of the 'community' expectations for the school (see
pp. 186–7). The school was expected to continue to provide high levels
of examination passes. Thus, although there were no extrinsic criteria for
success attached to the introduction of mixed-ability, there were criteria for
failure.[1]

Before embarking on the details of the Beachside innovation, it will
perhaps be useful to compare it in general terms with two other
sociologically-oriented case-studies of organizational change in schools. I
hope that these comparisons will serve to highlight some of the particular
features of the innovation at Beachside. The two are Gross, Giaquinta and
Bernstein's (1971) study of a Cambire experimental school, and Smith and
Keith's (1971) study of Kensington High School, both from the United
States.

The study by Gross, Giaquinta and Bernstein is of a school-based
innovation which was introduced by the school's management. The study
presents an account of the attempt to make radical changes in teaching-style
away from teacher-directed learning. The change was proposed by the
management, but approved by the staff of the school, and there was a
considerable extra provision of resources both in terms of staff and
materials. However, the attempts to change the teachers' classroom style
failed and there was a considerable loss of morale among the staff.

From this brief synopsis, it is possible to draw out three fundamental points at which Beachside's innovation differed from that of Cambire. First, the introduction of the change at Beachside was made on the basis of a democratic vote of staff; the impetus for the change arose from within the school and indeed the Local Authority was opposed to its introduction and attempted to stop it. There was no outside agent of change involved. Second, at the formal level, the change was a reorganization of the grouping of pupils entering the first year. It was not explicitly concerned with changes in the teachers' behaviour although such changes were inevitably implied and assumed by most of the staff. It was also expected, as we shall see, that the reorganization of forms would bring about a change in the behaviour of pupils. Third, few extra resources were available. The Local Authority was unwilling to provide extra money for the school and the change took place against a background of general reduction in education expenditure, although the headmaster made use of the facility to 'carry over' up to 10 per cent of the annual capitation grant in order to provide some extra funding.

Gross, Giaquinta and Bernstein's analysis of the innovation at Cambire places responsibility for the failure of the change on the management for failing to recognize and overcome the various problems encountered by the staff in implementing it. This cannot be said of Beachside. The Beachside innovation was primarily a change in structure, and the evaluation of its failure or success by the actors lay in the teachers' perceptions of its effect upon the kinds of interaction that took place between the pupils and themselves. The evaluation of the change is thus not simply to be understood in terms of the successful achievement of agreed objectives. Indeed, there was no formal written 'mandate' for the innovation.[2] The mandate, if such it was, rested in the informal expectations that the teachers held in regard to the role of mixed-ability grouping in improving control-relationships or making Beachside more like a 'true comprehensive school'.

The second study, that by Smith and Keith (1971) of Kensington High School, is concerned with the introduction of a programme of team-teaching, individualized instruction and multi-age grouping. These changes were intended to orientate pupils' development towards 'a self-directed, internally motivated and productive competence'.

In the words of the authors of this study 'a number of events took place that demanded additional labels. These include mandate, institutional plan and facade'. These labels were defined as follows. The 'institutional plan' was the principal's (the headmaster's) conception of changes in teaching methods, presented as a formal document. No such expression of outlines or principles was ever a part of the innovation-process at Beachside. The 'mandate' was defined as the formal change or directive given by the school superintendent and characterized by its long-term goals. Again, no such formal expression of goals was made at Beachside. Finally, the 'facade' refers to the image that the school presents to its several publics – in the case of Kensington High School the discontinuity which existed between the formal definition of the innovation and its facade 'led to the special "public face" which centred on intentions, "what we are trying to do", and on special atypical concrete instances that illustrated these intentions'. However, since the public image of the Beachside innovation is not dealt with here, the concept of 'facade' is not directly relevant.[3]

I must repeat that the absence of explicitly and formally stated objectives must not be taken to suggest that the actors in the innovation did not attribute objectives to it. It is clear that in their interpretation and understanding of the innovation, in terms of its anticipated consequences, the teachers informally attributed to it several identifiable sets of objectives.

The most strongly represented of these was the hope expressed by many staff that the introduction of mixed-ability groups would bring about a general improvement in 'social atmosphere' and in pupil-teacher re-lationships. But, in addition, the headmaster clearly saw the introduction of mixed-ability as a further move towards his conception of a 'true' comprehensive school. And a small number of staff, several members of the English department among them, saw it as the beginning of a move towards a more egalitarian form of schooling.[4]

It is important to bear in mind that there was also a small group of teachers who were opposed to mixed-ability and who therefore did not attribute important positive objectives to it, although they were aware of possible advantages. According to Smith and Keith, the innovation at Kensington was a saga of 'uncertainty and unintended consequences'. But their analysis is concerned primarily with innovation-strategies and innovative organization rather than with the substance of change – that is, with change itself rather than with what is being changed. The prime concern of the present analysis is with the substance of change, situated as it is within a more widely ranging account of comprehensive education in one school. However, it is a secondary aim here to make a more general contribution to the understanding of change in educational institutions.[5]

As views of innovation, the studies by Gross, Giaquinta and Bernstein, Smith and Keith, and others of a similar kind, all appear to involve a common conception of the nature of innovations. They all view innovation from an outsider's perspective, and thus change comes to be seen as a non-negotiable reality. It is presented as fixed, specific and immutable, and as such is normally subjected to a systems model of analysis in terms of input-throughput-output: the achievement of specific goals and measurable or clearly definable outcomes.

This account of an internally-generated change is derived primarily from the interpretations of it made by the actors involved in 'changing'. From this perspective, the nature of the change appears to be much less of an immutable or fixed reality.[6]

The process of innovation at Beachside extended over a period of several years. The changes involved were introduced gradually and important decisions were taken year by year. To account for the outcomes of the innovation it will be necessary to present and discuss this process in some detail, particularly the issues raised and the arguments put forward in favour of or against the innovation.

Thus, in the remainder of this chapter I intend to examine the natural history of the innovation from its conception to its implementation; the emergence of perspectives of meaning attributed to the innovation by different groups among the teaching staff; some possible explanations for the existence of these perspectives; and some of the social and organizational constraints upon the ways in which teachers defined their role and made sense of the innovation in terms of their interaction with pupils in the new lesson-context. The following chapter is concerned with a detailed examination of the implementation of the innovation.

The natural history of the innovation

As noted earlier, innovations viewed from the outside are often seen simply in terms of cause and effect, or problem-stimulus and product-change. However, in terms of understanding the processes of schooling and the ways in which a change in the school's organization may affect the interaction between pupils and teacher, it is important to know what meanings are attached by the actors to the changes, both in their initial interpretation and subsequent practical 'handling' of them.

An essential analytical difficulty involved in trying to evaluate attempts at planned change is to establish how the phenomena to be changed came to be designated as needing changing. The reconstruction of the history of the innovation at Beachside and the monitoring of the continuing debate, presented below, are intended to discover where the impetus for the innovation came from, and where support for it and opposition to it lay.

	1967	Beachside becomes comprehensive; fine streaming.
	1968	English Department goes over to banding.
		Period of 'gathering a team' begins.
	1969	8 form entry; 3 bands.
	1969-72	Consolidation of banding and consideration of mixed-ability begin.
	Summer 1972	Vote of staff; only two against experiment of mixed-ability in the first year, after a year of preparation.
	Sept. 1972	English department goes over to mixed-ability in the fourth and fifth years.
	1972-3	Preparation year.
Year 1 of the innova- tion	Sept. 1973	12 form entry: 10 mixed-ability, 2 remedial.
	Dec. 1973	Staff meeting to ratify experiment and extend mixed-ability in the second year. Voting: 60 for, 10 against continuing mixed-ability in the first year; 45 for, 25 against extending this into the second year.
		Maths and French will be allowed to set.
Year 2 of the innova- tion	Sept. 1974	Social Economics goes mixed-ability in the fourth and fifth year.
		First and second year mixed-ability.
	Dec. 1974	Staff meeting to ratify second year experiment and extend mixed-ability into the third year. Voting: 70 for, 5 against.
		Science will be allowed to set in the third year.
Year 3 of the innova- tion	Sept. 1975	Mixed-ability in first, second and third year. Maths abandons setting in the second year.

Where relevant, teachers' comments of evaluation quoted in
the text are labelled according to their timing in the process
of innovation and implementation, and their context of
collection.

Figure 7. The chronology of innovation and change

The chronology of the innovation will be made clearer by a table of events (see figure 7). Where relevant, teachers' comments of evaluation quoted in the text are labelled according to their timing in the process of innovation and implementation, and their context of collection.

The inception of the idea of mixed-ability grouping is impossible to isolate exactly. From discussions with members of the staff and the headmaster, it appears to have been related to a growth of opinion among those younger staff who arrived after the school became comprehensive. But the role of the headmaster as opinion leader was crucial in giving the original drive to the innovation. He explained.

> 'I had always been interested in un-streaming. I was in my previous school ten years ago. It was one of the things I had had in my mind that I wanted to do, but I did not want to do it straight away, it was necessary first of all to gain parental confidence. It would have been an outrageous move at the time.'

The time to which he refers is 1968, when he took over the school as headmaster. It had only recently become a comprehensive and was still in competition with local grammar schools for the cream of the catchment intake. The forms were still in fact organized by fine streaming, but with the lead coming from the headmaster and with a ground-swell of support from the new staff, a banding system was introduced in 1969.

> 'Funnily enough, it was the old staff from the secondary modern who had been around for donkeys years who were by far and away the most suspicious about moving away from the fine streaming. And that was another important factor at that time, for they still made up by far the majority of the staff – about two-thirds – and the other third were young graduates; *they* were the ones who were anxious and willing to go ahead and open up the ability range.'
>
> (Headmaster)

The positive consequences of the change to banding were quickly apparent in the improved performance of many pupils.

> 'One immediate effect was that you got one hundred kids who thought that they were in the top stream and they started performing like top streamers.'
>
> (Headmaster)

However, despite what seemed to be the initial success of the system of bands, this type of organization of forms was found also to have drawbacks.

> 'It only took one year to become aware of the second-band mentality of the second-band forms, with a very low level of participation and involvement in the school. There even seemed to be more rejection in the middle band than there was in the middle streams previously.'
>
> (Headmaster)

As the headmaster saw it, this came about because

> 'The energies of the staff were most strongly directed to the top-band forms. They seemed to consider that the second-band forms were not worth bothering about to the same extent. They had low expectations of these forms and there was a lowering of the level of effort produced by the kids.'

The problems that emerged from the banding system enabled the headmaster to press on to consider the possibility of introducing mixed-ability, with the continuing support of many of the staff.

> 'We did not stop there; we went straight on to start to investigate what the situation was regarding mixed-ability nationally. We had a very good group of people and we were all very like-minded, I think.'

As one of the members of the staff who arrived at the school at this time saw it:

> 'I think there was pressure from the staff who came; I know when I came for an interview I asked about mixed-ability, and I know a lot of the other people also asked about it. I think there was a sort of ground-swell, and the headmaster was in favour of it and the deputy-head who was here then. So I think it was a two-way process; there was a lot of pressure and there were meetings of heads of departments and they took soundings of who seemed to be in favour and finally it was voted on.'
>
> (Year tutor)

Another teacher described this ground-swell as coming from a group of teachers who saw mixed-ability as a move towards a more 'truly comprehensive school' and who were not happy with the banding which they regarded as another form of streaming.

To some extent, the appointments policy during the period immediately after the introduction of banding may be seen as the headmaster 'gathering a team'. For instance, when the head of the English department left in 1971, the headmaster explained that 'One was looking for somebody who was a progressive sort of fellow.' It is clear that the headmaster came to be identified as the 'sponsor' of the innovation. This role was attributed to him as the 'saga' of the innovation became institutionalized.[7]

> 'The headmaster wanted it and appointed people who were sympathetic to it and who he thought would support him . . . and he manipulated things so it happened.'
>
> (Head of the English department)

'I think it was the enthusiasm of the headmaster really, he led us into it. There wasn't, as far as I was aware, a great spontaneous demand welling up but when it was put to us we felt it logical to try it.'

(Head of the Geography department)

'It was a desire of the staff, the desire . . . willingness of the headmaster. He pushed the school, he bent over backwards so the staff would want it too. And it was a reaction against the second-band thing.'

(Head of the Music department)

'I think there were certain people who were keen on it, certainly the headmaster, I think there were certain department heads who were keen on it, particularly the head of English. I think it came from the personalities in the school. I think the headmaster has kept a fairly open mind on it, he will only go for something that works.'

(Head of the French department)

The decision to introduce mixed-ability was actually taken by stages, as can be seen from the chronology (see figure 7), with an open ballot of all the staff on each occasion.[8] Although the headmaster was always insistent that the decision should not be influenced by his opinions, it was always clear where his sympathies lay and what he hoped the outcome of the vote would be. This in itself may have played an important part in the decision of many of the staff to vote in favour of mixed-ability. He chaired all the meetings and formulated the motions to be voted on.

The first vote introduced mixed-ability as an experiment in the first year for one year. It was intended that the experiment would be examined after a period of operation before further votes were taken confirm (or reject) its continuance with future first-year cohorts and to extend it (or not) into the second year. This process of confirmation and extension was then repeated for the second and third years. In fact, however, because of the problems of forward-planning, the second and third votes were taken in December on each occasion, thus allowing only three months of operation of the scheme in each year on which to base decisions. No formal evaluation-procedures were employed and decisions were made primarily on the basis of the evidence of individual teachers' experiences in the classroom. Votes on the original decision, and indeed all the subsequent votes to maintain and extend mixed-ability through the first three years of the school, were carried by large majorities, as may be seen on the chronology.

So far, it has only been possible to account for the *commitment* of the headmaster and a small number of the rest of the staff. How was it that so many of the teachers were willing to accept the change to mixed-ability grouping, against the noted reluctance of educational systems to accept innovations?

The debate

The debate about mixed-ability among the staff became a central interest in my examination of the process of the innovation. As it proceeded, three major different interpretations of the innovation emerged. That is, there were three different *perspectives*, which we shall see later have consequences in the teaching of mixed-ability, and which are closely related to different subject sub-cultures.

In each of the staff meetings at which the votes for mixed-ability were taken, the two major issues of discipline and academic standards were raised. Almost all the teachers seemed to feel some degree of dissatisfaction with the banding, particularly with the band 2 forms. The continuing problem of control in these forms created stressful working conditions and produced a learning-environment that lacked much intellectual stimulation for either teacher or pupils. This was particularly acute for new and inexperienced teachers. It was this situation which drew support for the proposed introduction of mixed-ability from many teachers who might not normally have given their support to such a plan. As we have seen in the previous chapters, many teachers found band 2 pupils disruptive and unco-operative, and the high level of support for mixed-ability must be seen, in part, as a response to this. The innovation was accepted by many teachers in the hope that the disciplinary problems created by the second-band forms would disappear. It seemed to me that to a large extent the mixed-ability innovation was interpreted by teachers as a solution to *their* problems.

I asked members of staff in interviews: 'Why did you feel that there was a need for this particular innovation?' The majority of their replies were concerned with what were termed the 'social' benefits of mixed-ability – that is, the eradication of the disciplinary problems of the second-band forms.[9] For example:

> '. . . to rid ourselves of the very few disciplinary black spots.'
> 'It was necessary from the disciplinary point of view.'
> '. . . socially.'
> '. . . for disciplinary reasons.'
> 'As a year tutor, my reasons for voting were not educational but social. I had the same kids being referred to me week after week from the banded system and I had very little I could do with them, and I voted for mixed-

ability to solve my own problems. It would give me elbow room; I can move them around and break up the problem groups and hopefully get some of the kids off the path to a sticky end.'

All of these comments were recorded in interviews conducted during the first year of the innovation. The teachers who responded in this way felt that this eradication would be achieved either simply by the redistribution of the 'problem' children across the whole year so that there would not be whole forms dominated by 'disruptive elements':

> 'It's a dilution, really. You don't get 35 kids who don't like school all in one form. It spreads the butter very thin.'
>
> (English teacher, Year 1)

or by putting an end to the effects of labelling by bands:

> 'Well, the idea seems to be that everyone is equal, and to separate people on an academic basis or level is bad and gives the children inferiority complexes. "We are in band two or three" – and they give up because they don't think anything is expected of them.'
>
> (Physics teacher, Year 1)

The emphasis in each case is on the eradication of the discipline problems found in teaching second-band forms. These problems are the problems of the teacher, of being unable to teach because of the difficulty – or even the impossibility – of asserting control over the pupils.

Against these arguments for the social advantages of mixed-ability – that is, of creating more harmonious teaching environments – there were arguments which stressed the academic disadvantages. Some teachers saw the introduction of mixed-ability as being the death knell of academic excellence in the comprehensive school. Almost all the arguments, formal and informal, for and against the innovation, were concerned with these two major issues – the possible improvement in behaviour and the possible fall in standards – although, as we shall see, there is a third strand of argument which was propounded by a small number of teachers. However, the majority of arguments in favour of the mixed-ability system were in terms of the 'behaviour' dimension of the teachers' view of the classroom, 'the social advantages'. Conversely, almost all of the arguments against the introduction of mixed-ability and for retaining the banded system stemmed from the 'work' dimension of the teachers' view of the classroom, and were concerned with the possible loss of academic excellence.

So although the introduction of mixed-ability forms might mean the solution of the problems and dissatisfactions created by banding, it was felt that the mixed-ability groups were perhaps not without drawbacks. The 'fate' of the 'brighter child' was most often quoted by the opponents.

> 'I'm concerned about the problems of the more able children.'
>
> (French teacher, Year 1)
>
> 'I'm not sure about mixed-ability; I have a soft spot for the bright ones too, and wonder whether they get a fair crack of the whip. I suppose I am of an age when I still think the grammar school important, that if it was good enough for me it would be good enough for them.'
>
> (Remedial teacher, Year 1)
>
> 'I felt that there might be a lowering of the higher academic standards due to the less pressure being exerted on the brighter children.'
>
> (Science teacher, Year 2)
>
> 'I think in our department we are going to have to think very carefully about whether mixed-ability is working and doing justice to the kids – whether the brighter ones are going to get their exams.'
>
> (Maths teacher, Year 1)
>
> 'It does worry me to some extent that the brighter ones are still being held back, I know that this is to be catered for in other ways, but it does worry me when I see them switching-off and being bored.'
>
> (Geography teacher, Year 2)
>
> 'I'm not convinced that the most able child gains from it; I have no evidence for that and I shall want to see improved exam results but I don't think the "high flyers" get enough out of it.'
>
> (Technical Studies teacher, Year 3)

In response to this climate of concern for the progress of the 'brighter child' (see also p. 235), the headmaster created a post of special responsibility in the school 'for the most able child'. This post was given to a senior member of the Science department, an ex-grammar-school teacher, who was one of the strongest opponents of mixed-ability.

Only a very few members of staff put forward the third viewpoint, which was to stress the role of mixed-ability as being part of what 'a comprehensive school is all about', and to argue that it should be introduced in order to move towards a more open and fairer form of schooling for all pupils. They tended to be the most active proponents of mixed-ability.

> 'In the comprehensive school the comprehensive ideal should be carried through and certainly where mixed-ability first-year groups exist they are a particularly appropriate way of beginning life at Beachside.'
>
> (Drama teacher)
>
> 'To me comprehensive means mixed-ability and if it does not, then this is

not the sort of school that I would want to be concerned with.'

(Head of English department)

These different views of the mixed-ability innovation represent the different interpretations given to it by the teachers – that is, the system of meanings through which the teachers incorporated it into their existing view of education and made sense of it. Different meanings may be attached to the notion of mixed-ability which may lead to totally different forms of implementation. Therefore the implementation can only be explained when the meanings which the (typical) actor attributes to it have been understood.

The clusters of such meanings that centre around each point of argument I shall refer to as perspectives, which Becker (1961 : 33–4) defines as

a coordinated set of ideas and actions a person uses in dealing with some problematic situation, to refer to a person's ordinary way of thinking about and feeling about and action in such a situation.

Group perspectives are 'perspectives held collectively by a group of people'. In this case, the problematic situation is the suggested introduction of mixed-ability grouping and the possibility of having to teach mixed-ability forms. But in contrast with Becker's study of medical students, among whom perspectives were 'characteristic of almost the entire student body, the exceptions being easily identified isolates and deviants', the perspectives referred to here were not held in common by all the staff; there were competing perspectives held by different groups of teachers.

From the data collected from the arguments and debates surrounding the mixed-ability issue in the school, three quite clear and separate 'co-ordinated views and plans of action' emerged. The first I have called the *academic perspective*, which was concerned with 'standards' and academic excellence, and where the focus was upon the 'brighter' child, and the importance of the subject. This may be seen as an expression of a fear of the loss of subject orientation and 'academic' teaching in the school. Many of the opponents of mixed-ability considered that their subject would be damaged if taught to mixed-ability forms, and that examination attainments would inevitably suffer as a result. In particular, it was felt that the progress and attainment of the 'brighter child' would be affected by mixed-ability teaching where it would be difficult to 'stretch' these pupils academically.

The second, the *disciplinary perspective*, was held by those teachers who considered the control of pupils in the classroom as a major 'problem' which mixed-ability would solve. This related to their concern with the classroom 'atmosphere', and being able to get on with teaching in a harmonious environment rather than in a confrontation situation, such as occurred, as we have seen, in many band 2 classrooms.

The third, the *idealist perspective*, held by only a few members of staff, viewed mixed-ability forms as an important part of being in a comprehensive school, offering an equality of opportunity to the pupils, which was not available under the banding system.[10]

The major bastion of the idealist perspective was the English department, and several of its members were active proponents of this view. Indeed, the role of the English department in the process of innovation and change overall is particularly interesting, fulfilling in many respects the stereotypical radical role that is so often attributed to English teachers generally.[11] The department represented the single largest 'idealist' group. For instance, the head of department described the function of mixed-ability in these terms:

> 'It's to keep all their options open for as long as possible, not judging them too early. Most of the judging that goes on is concerned with verbal ability and fluency and I don't think that necessarily has all that much to do with intelligence or endowed ability.'

And describing the ethos of the whole school much later, after mixed-ability was established in the first three years, he explained:

> 'I think it's moving towards being a comprehensive school. I think it's got a long way to go. I think the basic idea of each kid having himself as his own taskmaster and setting his own standards according to his own ability, I think the school is very much short of that. I think we are still living in the era when it was banded and the school is still dominated by banded thinking and exams and competition between pupils. And I think most kids, when you talk to them, and most staff, think that kids have to measure each other against other kids and think in terms of whether they are better at Geography than somebody else, or better at English than somebody else, and I suppose the main motivation for work and study in this school is examinations, external O-levels and A-levels. That seems to be the basic driving force of the school – it seems a pity. I don't know whether all schools, by their very nature, must inevitably be like that. The ideals of the school, that kids should find the work itself interesting and should be striving to improve on their own standards and so on – I think the school's a long way off that yet.'

The English department operated both with banding and with mixed-ability in the year before each was adopted by the rest of the school. As the headmaster explained:

'The English department has had a seminal role in this . . . it was the English department who pioneered the actual mixed-ability; it's very important in innovation to show people that it can be done.'

In the year before mixed-ability was introduced throughout the school in the first-year cohort, the English department introduced it in the fourth and fifth years, amalgamating the O-level and C.S.E. groups which had previously been taught separately. (In only one other area in the school was there any mixed-ability teaching in the fourth and fifth year. The staff responsible for Social Economics O-level and Commerce C.S.E., who both expressed an idealist perspective, amalgamated their groups and taught them in two mixed-ability groups.)

The head of History also couched his support for mixed-ability in terms of an idealist perspective:

'We see educational objectives rather than social and academic, things like attitude to work and the development of the personality. We felt these are best achieved in mixed-ability. We find it a better situation for doing the job; we want it in the third year and even beyond, but we have only talked about that. It's even better for the brighter kids, catering for all levels, although more remedial extraction might be useful.'

(Year 2, staff meeting)

Inter-department opposition

The emergence of the two major perspectives, the academic and the disciplinary, may be linked further to an unwillingness on the part of the members of two of the departments, Maths and Modern Languages, to accept mixed-ability grouping in their subjects beyond the first year. The extension of these perspectives beyond the mixed-ability issues reveals other attitudinal and ideological differences between the teachers who were for and against it. The political nature of the general debate and discussion of the innovation tended to uncover the existence of conflict among the staff about fundamental issues regarding the nature of the comprehensive school and their roles in it.

Furthermore, the different perspectives can be seen to be reflected, in general terms, in the opposition between different subject sub-cultures. The perspective held by the members of the Mathematics and Languages departments in their opposition to mixed-ability in their subjects was that essentially they saw the introduction of mixed-ability as a threat to the traditional values of their subjects at that time.[12] *However, these perspectives represent the differences in the prime orientation of groups of teachers within the whole staff, and they were not in every case exclusively held.* Thus the academicist and idealist teachers were also concerned with the problems of discipline; the idealist teachers were also concerned with the academic achievement of their pupils; and many of the teachers identified with the disciplinary perspective were not unsympathetic to the egalitarian possibilities of mixed-ability. But in each case this does not represent their prime orientation towards the innovation.

That the innovation was viewed in terms of these opposing sets of meanings attributed to it suggest a differential effort within the school both in furthering the process of innovation, and, as we shall see in chapter 7, in the implementation of change in the classroom.

When it came to a vote to extend mixed-ability into the second year in 1973, both the Mathematics and Languages departments made it clear that they would not consider allowing their subjects to be taught in mixed-ability groups beyond the first year.[13] The motion finally agreed on and voted on by the staff specifically excluded Maths and Languages, and arrangements were made to 'set' these subjects in the second and later the third year. As the form-groups were mixed-ability, 'setting' in Maths and Languages in fact allowed a finer grouping of abilities than had been the case under the banded system. Where Maths had previously been 'set' within each band, in the mixed-ability context it was 'set' across the whole year-group. However, the teachers in these two departments were well aware of the generally improved social atmosphere which was attributed to mixed-ability grouping and from which they also benefited.

> 'Mixed-ability would have been impossible in the second year, although I am glad that there will be mixed-ability in the other subjects because the social atmosphere is definitely improved.'
>
> (Maths teacher, Year 2)

The improved social atmosphere certainly reinforced their willingness to vote in favour of the extension of mixed-ability for the rest of the school, if their own departments were exempted. Thus by allowing these departments to set, the headmaster, and the staff in favour of mixed-ability in their own subjects, ensured that the vote would be carried. However, this should not be taken to mean that *all* the teachers in *all* the other departments were in favour of mixed-ability in their subjects, nor that all the members of the Maths and Languages departments were willing to vote for mixed-ability for the rest of the curriculum, nor that every single member of the Languages and Maths departments was against mixed-ability in his own subject. This was certainly not so. In the voting which took place during Year 1 of innovation, there were 25 staff – that is, 30 per cent – who voted against the motion to extend mixed-ability whilst exempting Languages and Mathematics.

Nevertheless, the members of the Maths and Languages departments were aware of differences between their views of their subject and those of other departments in the school. The head of Maths explained:

> 'I think if you look at our aims and the aims of the school you could find that they are very different. We are teaching a skill and the subject is very important; I think of our department as a mini-university. I am concerned to design a course that is relevant to the kids and that the teachers teach it in an interesting way.'[14]

The arguments put forward by the teachers who saw their subjects in this way were closely related to the issue of academic excellence and obtaining a high level of success in passing examinations, which might have reflected upon the school's reputation. The case of academic excellence was put most forcefully by the Classics master, who asserted that parents operated a league table of local schools based upon the numbers of examinations being passed at O-level and A-level, and that Beachside's reputation would be seriously affected by the introduction of mixed-ability.

The subject sub-culture traditions in Maths and Languages maintained a view of these subjects among the staff in these departments – a view often reinforced by other staff – that the 'deep structure' of their subjects made it very difficult or impossible to teach them to mixed-ability groups without a radical reduction in the level of academic work normally expected of the 'brighter' pupil. The head of Languages explained:

> 'I think it's got to be a building-up subject; it's the most building-up subject of all, possibly more so than Mathematics . . . Now in the country as a whole only one or two people have done mixed-ability teaching but it usually comes down to doing some sort of group-work, worksheets and self-correcting worksheets which I think are a nonsense . . . I think that French in itself is not interesting after a certain point, it's interesting to be able to count up to 20 in French, to say "Je m'appelle Louise", that sort of thing, but you can't say the sorts of things you want to in English Therefore, I think class teaching, where you're standing in the front of the class, reading a piece from a text or talking, is what makes the thing work.'

Because of the demands made by the nature of the subject, the head of Languages felt that mixed-ability French was really impossible.

> 'You see, children who can't write it very well, and can't read it very well, then they can't pronounce it either, they have poor oral discrimi-

nation . . . I suppose some people would work out their Mode III O-level as we have our Mode III C.S.E. – in fact some people would be happy with a French Studies curriculum, but that's not French to my way of thinking. If you were going to do that you would really lower the already not very good language-ability of English people.

'I can't see how it could be changed; I can't envisage how one would change the sort of thing one is trying to achieve; I could imagine one could produce masses and masses of different graded worksheets on certain sorts of topics, the thematic approach. But so much is linear; the tenses are the problem, they're a big problem; children have a poor conception of what a tense is in English, and this is a big stumbling block. I can't conceive how it would change. It's changed a bit over the years; recently there's been more emphasis on the oral and listening and understanding.'

This stance of 'academicism' in the face of mixed-ability innovation in the case of both Languages and Mathematics teachers is common in the literature of de-streaming. Warnes (1975 : 97) is very critical of Language departments on these grounds, but his view is certainly a minority one among language teachers:

Foreign languages have become a sort of reserved occupation where the brightest and the best strive for standards of excellence far beyond the reach of most of their peers. The problem in most subjects is to tailor the work to fit the child; in French it is the reverse. A process of elimination hastens to consign the unchosen to Art and Woodwork rooms, leaving the way clear for the unimpeded progress of the gifted to O-level and beyond. The Language Department becomes the embattled stronghold of unashamed academicism, the rightful guardian of those standards now threatened by this gadarene rush to mediocrity; the last refuge of the gentleman scholar.

There are many similar descriptions of the subject traditions of Mathematics, such as these comments from Woodrow (1973 : 48):

The resistance of many Mathematics teachers to mixed-ability grouping lies in the history of Mathematics teaching, in that it is traditionally a goal-oriented subject which is easily and 'accurately' (even momentarily) assessed. This 'modus operandi' emphasizes the gradation between pupils and makes ability grouping a natural structure. Indeed a philosophy which is goal-oriented is to some extent contradictory to the philosophy underlying mixed-ability grouping.[15]

The various staff meetings at which mixed-ability was discussed and the votes were taken provoked some conflict between staff who held different perspectives.[16] This was particularly acute between the 'academics' and the 'idealists'. But one important characteristic of the innovation process was the possibility of allowing for the resolution of these conflicting educational philosophies, a possibility which stemmed from the level of generality of the innovation and the absence of an 'institutional plan'. The introduction of mixed-ability was a 'black-box' change; that is, the innovation introduced mixed-ability grouping rather than mixed-ability teaching. As noted earlier, the content and organization of classroom methods were left to be resolved at the departmental level or by individual teachers. The organizational reference and level of commitment for the individual participating members could either be the whole school, or their department, or it could lie in their own personal classroom management practices. This flexibility within the innovation allowed for a considerable range of 'adaptations', within as well as between departments, in the actual practice of mixed-ability teaching, although the extent of flexibility was different for each department. This will be taken up again in the discussion of the implementation stage in the following chapter.

When it came to the vote to extend mixed-ability grouping into the third year (December 1974), the Science departments also stressed the difficulties that they were anticipating with a further year of mixed-ability. As a result the motion that was passed extended to Science the right to 'set' in the third year, in addition to Mathematics[17] and Languages. All three of these dissenting departments put forward the argument that there was something in the nature of the subject that made it impossible to teach it to mixed-ability forms beyond a certain level of conceptual difficulty, without concessions being made which would drastically affect the academic rigour of the subject. These were concessions that the departmental heads and many other departmental members were unwilling to consider making.[18] Some teachers simply felt that:

> 'There are a number of subjects that would be damaged by de-streaming.'
> (Craft teacher in the second staff meeting)

But more refined arguments suggested that at some point the range of levels in the pupils' conceptual development became too great to consider teaching them in heterogeneous groups. These arguments were applied in Science in particular.

> 'I've always been in favour of mixed-ability but in the third year, it is impossible; in the third year conceptual abilities diverge.'
> (Science teacher, Year 2, staff meeting)
> 'Mixed-ability is working socially, but I don't see how we can carry it on in the third year, if we are going to teach it properly and get through the material necessary as a foundation for O-level. By the time we get into the

second term of the third year, the kids are so strung out in their level of achievement I don't see how we can keep them together.'

(Head of Science, Year 2 staff meeting)

The assumption underlying these comments, and the teachers' anticipation of the problems of teaching mixed-ability classes, is that whereas the 'brighter' band 1 child is able to move beyond the 'basics' into the structure of the subject, the grasp of these basics is supposed to be the limit of the ability of band 2 and 3 pupils.

This sort of argument was also used in French:

'Oral work and linear development make mixed-ability impossible after the first year.'

(French teacher, Year 1)

'Even teaching French to a band 1 class is not very easy with a spread of ability that includes Miriam Daly at one end and Tony Talston at the other; they are at entirely different levels. That is why I am absolutely against mixed-ability.'

(French teacher, Year 1)

The opposition to mixed-ability from these departments can be seen as deriving in part from the professional self-image of the members as subject specialists, but more particularly from the problems and difficulties involved in teaching these subjects in an 'acceptable' way to mixed-ability groups. This stems from a view that the children must be matched and selected to suit the subject rather than the other way round.[19]

As with Mathematics and Languages, the Science teachers' attitude to mixed-ability presents a view of science teaching current within a subject sub-culture. Like the other dissenting subjects, the teaching of science is made up of a set of symbolic constraints and demands that provide for certain 'necessary' concepts to be covered by certain stages in the school careers of certain pupils. The demands and constraints of teaching science in mixed-ability groups have to be reconciled with this view of good practice. The common view of 'good science' in schools has undergone several changes and will probably continue to change. But the professional and specialist allegiance of the Science teachers to their subject and its demands must be understood at any point in time in terms of the currently predominant paradigm view.[20]

In some schools the paradigm has shifted, at least in the dimension of 'how to teach' science.[21] But little change has yet taken place along the dimension of 'what to teach',[22] at least in the first three years of secondary school. In other subjects in the curriculum, changes have taken place in the 'what to teach' dimension – modern Maths, for example, and S.M.P. – but not so much in the 'how to teach' dimension. In some cases, shifts in both dimensions have taken or are taking place, especially in English and Geography.

Bailey (1976 : 24–5) makes the point that

Part of the puzzle here is to know why certain subjects are alike in some respects that make them more suitable for mixed-ability grouping, whilst being distinctly unlike another group of subjects held to be suitable for such grouping.

He goes on to suggest that there is nothing about the intrinsic nature of Science, Mathematics and Languages which makes mixed-ability teaching inappropriate, but that it is their value in providing access to social status and wealth that does so – that is, the appropriateness of mixed-ability grouping in a particular subject is socially constructed. This is closely related to the argument being put forward here.[23]

The difference in overall perspective and opinion about the innovation between the subject departments is most correctly represented as a continuum, extending from strong support (English department) to strong opposition (Modern Languages department), each position on the continuum representing differences in attitude to the subject and the innovation, and in the degree of willingness by the teachers to accept the innovation in their own subjects (see figure 8).

It is always necessary to take care when generalizing upon the basis of a single study. However, the differences noted here between subjects in terms of (what could be referred to as) the traditionalism or radicalism of their teachers' attitudes to education are reflected in other studies of subject cultures. Certainly, studies both of experienced teachers and teachers in training have indicated the importance of subject sub-cultures as a differentiating factor between those teachers holding radical views and those holding traditional views on educational issues. McLeish (1970: 182), in a large sample of College of Education students and lecturers, found that

The most remarkable differences in attitude of any in the total sample appear to be between subject specialists. These are certainly more significant than the differences due to political or religious affiliation. Similar differences to those found in the students on entry to their course are found between college lecturers specializing in these main subjects.

Lacey (1977 : 63–4), describing the findings of a study of Post-Graduate Certificate of Education (P.G.C.E.) students in five universities, suggests that

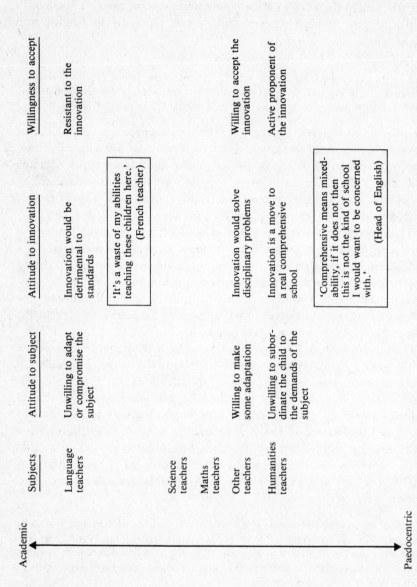

Figure 8. Comparison of subjects in their attitudes towards and willingness to accept mixed-ability grouping

The subject sub-culture appears therefore to be a pervasive phenomenon, affecting a student-teacher's behaviour in school and university, as well as [his] choice of friends and [his] attitude towards education. It would seem there is a case for considering the process of becoming a teacher as a multi-stranded process in which subject sub-cultures insulate the various strands from one another.

These subject sub-cultures are obviously related to wider subject-perspectives, 'the particular symbolizations and meanings which have been institutionally oriented towards particular questions about the universe' (Esland 1971 : 99). But the concept of subject sub-cultures is less concerned with subject content *per se* and the explanatory methodology and epistemology of disciplines than with the organization and selection of subject-knowledge for teaching purposes and the maintenance of collectively-approved subject pedagogies.

However, having established the existence of the three perspectives, the academic, the idealist, and the disciplinary, and having begun to relate them to the differences between departments and subject sub-cultures, it is important to qualify what is a generalization of attitudes by pointing out differences within the perspectives and within subject departments, as well as similarities across subject departments and across perspectives.

First, it is clear that few teachers in the school differentiated between mixed-ability teaching and mixed-ability grouping in their thinking about the innovation. That is, little of the discussion about the advantages and disadvantages of the innovation was carried out in reference to teaching methods. As we shall see later (see p. 194), even the departmental reports to the headmaster did not concern themselves in detail with how the mixed-ability lessons would be taught. Clearly the absence of such a distinction in the teachers' view of the innovation may be related to the importance of improvements in 'social atmosphere' and behaviour which were seen to be linked simply to the way in which the pupils were grouped and not to the way in which they were taught.[24]

But the absence of this distinction between mixed-ability grouping and mixed-ability teaching must also be recognized as being related to the importance given to the individual teacher's right to determine for himself how best to teach mixed-ability. It was clearly linked to the notion in the school that different teachers have different styles and that it would therefore be unproductive, as well as undesirable, to prescribe specific ways of teaching mixed-ability. At no time was the innovation taken to necessitate a reduction in the degree of teaching isolation,[25] or restricted-autonomy, which had existed for teachers in the school until that time.

'The point is that when we teach mixed-ability everyone's got a different approach so the person might say, "Here's the book, you work at your own pace." You get someone who goes through it with the class as a whole and then you get someone who'll say, "I want you to stop here, discuss a particular concept, and then go on." So we can't have a common policy . . . I mean it's all right in a text book with some fellows at the university saying that is how it should be done. When it actually comes down to the nitty gritty of being there with 36 kids, things are very different. I would never try to say, "Hey everybody, this is the right way," no, I wouldn't.'

(Head of Geography, Year 3, interview)

I use the term restricted-autonomy here to describe a situation where staff were teaching in relative isolation; that is, there was no team-teaching or visiting between lessons, and for the most part teachers were left to evolve their own particular styles and methods.[26] However, it was a situation where the range of possible styles and methods was in fact restricted. It was clear that the individual teachers considered themselves to be under pressure from three sources, all of which engendered limitations on practice in the classroom. The first of these was his own subject sub-culture; that is, the range of possible styles and methods available to the subject-teacher is defined by what counts as 'good practice' within his subject-culture. The second was his colleagues in the school; that is, the culture of the school as a whole, particularly through the collegiate structure, defined for the individual teacher 'acceptable practice' in terms of classroom style and control relationships. This quite clearly operated in the case of teachers who found control a problem but also existed more generally in regard to styles and methods of teaching. This was in itself related to those 'goals' which the school defines as valuable. As we have seen, at Beachside academic achievement, especially in terms of examination passes, is given particular importance and value. What emerges is a commonly-held conception of appropriate practice in the classroom, 'modal role behaviour'.

Finally, external constraints also operated against certain aspects of mixed-ability teaching in all subjects in the curriculum. The importance of preparation for external examination, for instance, can percolate down the years, and very probably has a pervasive influence from the time that the pupil enters secondary education. The Beloe Report (1960 : 21) makes this clear.

The examination system dictates the curriculum and cannot do otherwise. It confines experiments, limits the free choice of subjects, hampers treatment of subjects, encourages wrong values in the curriculum.

Several members of staff explicitly referred to examinations as a perceived constraint upon the possibilities of change in their teaching methods.

> 'There are constraints upon us to get good results. There are demands from society, we are expected to get good O and A-level results, and, for ourselves as subject specialists, we want to maintain the level of achievement in our subject.'[27]
>
> (Head of Maths, Year 2, interview)

In recognizing the constraints that the teachers perceived to be limiting their actions, to the extent in some subjects of not being able to accept mixed-ability beyond a certain level, and dictating in most subjects certain forms of pedagogy and syllabus (as we shall see later), it is necessary to bear in mind the general expectations that society at large has of its teachers. This is particularly relevant in the light of the growing importance of 'accountability' and the reaction to the use of progressive methods in schools.

Many of the teachers at Beachside expressed a clear awareness of the constraints imposed upon them by the expectations of the public.

> 'The thing [mixed-ability] on the public side has got to be justified ... You can't say, Well, we are turning out kids who are more socially adjusted – they are probably not anyway – but if we could say that, it's intangible, whereas the tangible proof that you've got comprehensives that work is this examination business, isn't it? I mean it was like that in Tameside, quoting exam figures. Manchester were in favour of grammar schools and said they had had terrible results from the comprehensives. How must you justify the school to the public? This is it.'
>
> (History teacher, Year 3, interview)[28]

The headmaster clearly felt that the constraints exerted upon the school, especially by parents, would make full commitment to the aims and objectives of the idealist perspective impossible. The extension of mixed-ability in all subjects through the first five years and a move away from the competitive ethos of academic excellence was inconceivable.

> 'We cannot take up the possibilities of mixed-ability at this stage because we would be doing a disservice to the kids and have their parents in uproar because they are not doing exams, we can't do that locally until the system of 16 plus examinations changes nationally.'[29]
>
> (Headmaster, Year 2)

Although much of the debate so far has been portrayed particularly in terms of differences between subject-departments, it must also be taken

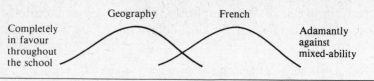

Range of attitudes to and interpretations of mixed-ability

Figure 9. The range of attitudes to and interpretations of mixed-ability across two subject-departments

into account that there were also differences of opinion and attitude towards the innovation within departments. Although each department tended to present a single dominant attitude to the innovation, usually, but not always, best-represented by the head of department, not all the departments maintained a complete consensus.

The range of attitudes to and interpretations of the innovation within departments is best understood in terms of a modal position and a distribution around it. This may be represented diagramatically (see figure 9). Although there might be a considerable difference between the Geography department as a whole and the French department as a whole, an examination of the orientations of individual members of these departments demonstrated a wide spread of attitudes within each department and a degree of overlap between them.

In the Geography department, for example, one member commented:

> 'Purely from the academic Geography viewpoint, I felt probably we should lose something of the cutting edge of the highest ability range. I thought that the sum total was an improvement in understanding all around.'
>
> (Year 3, interview)

But generally the support for mixed-ability within the department was unequivocal.

> 'In Geography we felt that this was an opportunity to look at what we were trying to do. Some of us were a little dissatisfied with the sort of Geography being taught in the school.'
>
> (Year 3, interview)
>
> 'I think that in Geography the mixed-ability has been very successful this year. We are very pleased with it.'
>
> (Year 2, staff meeting)

Similarly, in the Languages department, despite a general opposition to mixed-ability, one teacher expressed doubts about setting in the second and third years.

'I don't like the idea of splitting them up and ending with a bottom group because of the level of work that is set for them . . . It doesn't fool them for a minute and they come to realize that the Modern Languages department has discarded them, and in the third year there will be disciplinary problems in this bottom group.'

(Year 2, interview)

One further point of qualification on the general classification of perspectives is the variation of philosophies within the idealist perspective. Elliot (1976 : 4) proposes that:

Mixed-ability teaching takes place when a teacher tries to regulate his treatment of individual differences by the principle of equality.

He goes on to suggest that the nature of the 'problems' thrown up by mixed-ability teaching – that is, what are perceived as 'problems' by actors – will reflect the teachers' commitment to different views of equality.

It is apparent that at Beachside, the genuine form of mixed-ability teaching proposed by Elliot is not attained. It would appear from evidence presented so far that mixed-ability grouping was adopted at Beachside without a general commitment to mixed-ability teaching. But leaving that aside for the moment, it is interesting to note the relationship of the 'problems' anticipated and experienced by the Beachside teachers to the typology of equality that Elliot (1976 : 5) has suggested.

Throughout the mixed-ability debate, the major 'problem' perceived by the staff, even among those within the idealist perspective, remained that of 'what to do about the most able pupil'. According to Elliot, this kind of concern stems from a principle of 'equality of opportunity for social goods' which is 'that human beings have an equal right to opportunities of achieving certain social goods'. This particular principle, and the view of equality it encompasses, Elliot argues, can be separated from two other principles of equality – the principle of 'equality of respect for individuals as endowed with the capacity of self-awareness and autonomy', 'that human beings have a right to equality of respect by virtue of their common humanity', and the principle of 'equality of opportunity for self-development', 'that human beings have an equal right to opportunities for self-development'. This third principle can be recognized in the views of mixed-ability held by the head of English, but was not widespread even among the idealist teachers.

As Elliot indicated, the problem of 'what to do about the most able' is most acute in high-status subject-areas and in the age-groups closest to public examinations. It is certainly the case at Beachside that the Maths, Languages and Science subjects, traditionally high-status areas, were most concerned with the problem of the most able in relation to mixed-ability, and the most reluctant to extend mixed-ability beyond the first or second years. And overall, except in English and Social Economics, it was considered impossible to go further with mixed-ability once the public examination syllabus had been formally begun in the fourth year.

The problem of the most able was fundamental to much of the opposition to mixed-ability and also concerned most of those teachers who were in favour of it. The concern of the anti-mixed-ability teachers, identified with the academic perspective and the 'brighter' pupils, has been dealt with previously (see p. 174). The following selection of quotations recorded between year 1 and year 3 of the innovation indicate a similar and continuing concern by some of the pro-mixed-ability teachers.[30]

> 'In theory, I think it's good; in practice, I think it is harmful to the brighter kids. I think that most secondary-school teachers are not trained to teach mixed-ability groups. And to continue chalk and talk methods in mixed-ability groups is disastrous.'
>
> (Social Studies teacher, Year 2, interview)
>
> 'It's a bit awkward when the bright kids have finished their work and the slower ones are still plodding; they don't want to do extra work. I usually ask them to do something related to what they have finished – an illustration or a poem.'
>
> (English teacher, Year 1, interview)
>
> 'I feel that the brighter kids don't do so well in these classes; they aren't stretched enough. Working with the workcards means that they finish the card and then do no more and get bored.'
>
> (Craft teacher, Year 3, interview)
>
> 'There is the problem of trying to stretch the two or three bright ones and the problems with the ones at the bottom who can hardly write.'
>
> (Physics teacher, Year 2, interview)
>
> 'We've had no grammar-school stream or top stream this year in the first year, so the very bright kids have not been pushed as far as they were last year, but I don't think that this has been damaging.'
>
> (Maths teacher, Year 1, interview)
>
> 'But how do you push the bright?'
>
> (Biology teacher, Year 1, interview)

As noted above, even among the *idealist* supporters of mixed-ability, the head of English was the only clear exponent of an alternative to the 'equality of opportunity for social goods' philosophy; his view would be closest to the 'equality of opportunity for self-development':

'The teachers teaching English, many of us in the department are ideologically opposed to the competitive ethos of the school and work positively against it. I think the general attitude in the school overlaps into all departments as far as the kids are concerned and what we offer (in English) are certain practical advantages for kids so that in effect they don't have to make harsh decisions early on but they are fully aware that they are going to, and at the beginning of the fourth year in a mixed-ability class you can see the kids who know full well that they are going to do O-level and those who know full well that they are going to do C.S.E. and don't have a strong sense of individual value in the group. The kids who know they are going to do C.S.E. know that the others are better than they are and believe that the school thinks they are better and altogether more worthy. However hard you try, you can't work against the whole ethos of the school like that. Only this is an answer to the idea of what I think a comprehensive school is and the way I think it should be going. I think these are the areas of being comprehensive I'm most bothered about.'

(Year 1, interview)

But even the head of English took the trouble to collect and analyse the O-level and C.S.E. results obtained by the pupils taught in mixed-ability English groups, to compare them with the achievements of previous cohorts which had been taught separately. He used these figures to support his argument in favour of mixed-ability in staff meetings (see p. 266).

Summary

I have attempted to demonstrate here the lack of consensus that existed *within* the change to mixed-ability grouping in Beachside Comprehensive – that is, by an analysis of the process of the innovation from the point of view of the actors' definitions and meanings, to demonstrate the negotiable nature of the reality of the innovation. It should be clear from this, in terms of the origins and processes of the Beachside innovation, that few of the teachers were concerned with the sorts of generalized expectations attributed to the introduction of mixed-ability grouping by educational prophets and pundits. Indeed, I hope that this chapter may have illustrated the misconceptions that are created when importing externally-generated meanings to explain or evaluate an internally-generated change.[31]

In the following chapter I intend to extend this analysis of the innovation to its implementation – that is, to the relationship between the categories and concepts through which mixed-ability teaching is understood by the teacher, and the way in which the world of practice, the classroom, is organized.

It may be anticipated that the nature of the changes in classroom practice that are introduced to accommodate mixed-ability groups will be defined by the systems of constraint and expectation which represent 'good practice' within the school, by the expectations of outcome attributed by the teachers to the public audiences of the school,[32] and also by the 'proximal frames'[33] created by resource-allocation decision-making. However, from the analysis above it would seem likely that notions concerning which teaching methods are appropriate and acceptable will vary between subjects. In this respect, the different subject-departments may be considered as institutional sub-worlds each involving its own 'internalization of semantic fields structuring routine interpretation and conduct' (Berger and Luckmann 1967 : 158).

7   Mixed-ability: implementation and change

Gross, Giaquinta and Bernstein (1971) have criticized studies of educational innovation for their failure to pay adequate attention to the implementation stage. They argue that the success or failure of planned change can often be accounted for in terms of the resistance of organizational actors at this stage. At Beachside, however, the negotiable nature of the mixed-ability innovation allowed for the resolution of problems of implementation at the departmental level.[1] In this chapter, the implementation stage of the innovation will be examined at this level, as it affected the major academic subjects.[2]

In the first section, the planning for and anticipation of mixed-ability teaching by each department will be discussed, referring back to the perspectives and subject sub-culture differences outlined in the previous chapter. The second section will present a selection of transcripts and observation notes to demonstrate the range of different solutions to the problems of mixed-ability teaching both across and within departments, and to determine to what extent the various different classroom practices adopted in the mixed-ability context represent a change of pedagogy from those of the banded system. It is only possible to deal with a small sample of lessons in detail, although I have attempted to summarize the range of lessons observed in each subject.[3] I have also employed a focussing-down technique within this general exposition of teaching-methods; one subject-department is examined in greater detail than the rest, to demonstrate the variation of classroom practices within departments, and within this department the problems and classroom practices of one teacher are examined in order to highlight some aspects of the constraints which affect the strategies of the Beachside teachers. In the third section, the teachers' own evaluations of the innovation will be discussed briefly.

The implementation of the innovation will be examined not only in terms of the teachers' aspirations and intentions, but also analytically with regard to the extent of change in teaching methods involved. In this way, it may be possible to illuminate the extent to which the introduction of mixed-ability grouping embodies the kind of radical educational change suggested in the literature of de-streaming – in particular, the extent to which the introduction of mixed-ability brings about changes in pedagogy as suggested in the departmental reports discussed below.[4]

After the first vote in favour of mixed-ability, the headmaster was able, as he saw it, to go ahead with changes in the organizational structure of the school and to take other concomitant decisions relating to resources, finance, staffing, etc., which were his prerogative. Beyond this, however, 'professional practice' and tradition demanded that he left curricular matters and the organization of learning in the classroom to the individual departments and teachers. But the headmaster did ask each department to submit a report on the modifications that they felt would be necessary to implement the change and, if necessary, a revised outline-syllabus.[5] A summary account of these reports is offered below. However, it is important that the status of these documents be borne in mind. Although most departments had already begun to hold meetings to discuss plans for mixed-ability teaching, these reports were specifically requested by the headmaster. Not all the recommendations included in these reports were actually implemented (see pp. 199 and 207).

In contrast to the open parliamentary nature[6] of the formal decision to de-stream, the process of implementation did not involve any discussions of principle in meetings of the whole staff. This decision-making took place in various closed situations. The first-level implementational decisions, regarding syllabus and the organization of learning, were taken within subject-departments. In some cases, actual classroom practices and methods were discussed at this level – in Maths, for example – but for the majority of subjects, when it came down to the teacher having a mixed-ability lesson for the first time, the decision as to how he should organize the teaching and learning in his classroom was his. However, as indicated in chapter 7 (see pp. 179–81), this did not provide for total freedom in the choice of teaching-methods; there were a number of limitations and constraints on the range of possible practices. The nature of these constraints and limitations will be explored further later in this chapter.

The departmental reports

Without any guidance, most of these reports essentially addressed three main problems: methods, syllabus and assessment. Within each of these areas there was a considerable measure of agreement between departments, with some important exceptions. For instance, as regards *teaching-methods*, in almost every case the reports acknowledged that it would be necessary to introduce some form of individualized learning-programme. This is an extension of the notion, which often arose in the teachers' informal discussions about the innovation, that 'you cannot class-teach to mixed-ability'. It was felt that the wide range of abilities in a mixed-ability form would mean that, if the teacher spent much of his time doing traditional class-teaching, 'chalk and talk', the level of his 'pitch' would be unsuitable for a large proportion of the group. As a result the 'bright ones' would become bored because it was too slow, while it would be too fast for the 'slow ones'. Some means had to be devised to accommodate differences in the pupils' pace of learning. Although the range of ability in banded forms was also wide, it had been considered possible to 'aim at the middle' without creating any particular problems. For mixed-ability teaching, History, Geography, Technical Studies, Physics, Chemistry, Biology and Maths all suggested the introduction of some form of 'worksheet' method.[7] However, the French department dissented from this solution; their document reported:

> The most feasible approach seems to be the one adopted with existing band one forms, although the pace will necessarily be slower. The adoption of team teaching or the interchange of teachers between groups, with the reshuffling of groups for certain lessons each week, was not thought to be desirable or practical.

Thus, as might have been anticipated from the general tendency of the members of the French Department to espouse the *academic perspective* in opposition to mixed-ability in the innovation debates, and the strongly conservative view of teaching-methods evident in the subject culture of language teaching, the problems of mixed-ability teaching were not to be solved by a radical reorganization of teaching methods or of the syllabus in this subject.

However, in terms of the *ordering, organization and pacing of content-knowledge*, many other departments did see a necessity for changing their syllabuses 'to meet the needs of the first-year mixed-ability pupils'. In most cases, this involved devising an entirely new syllabus, or completely restructuring the previous first/second-band syllabuses. History, Physics, Geography, Maths and Biology recommended changes, considering that it would not be appropriate for a mixed-ability form to cover exactly the same ground either as the band 1 syllabus, which would again be too fast for the 'slow ones', or as the band 2 syllabus, which would be too slow for the 'fast ones'. Most of these departments recommended some form of 'basic' and 'extended' syllabus, the 'basic' which could be covered by all pupils and the 'extended' which would serve to 'stretch' the 'brighter child'. French, as noted above, retained the band 1 syllabus, although 'the pace will necessarily be slower'. This decision was clearly linked to the view of French, strongly held in the department, as a 'linear subject'.

The third issue discussed in the reports, *assessment*, proved to be the area of most disagreement between departments. History, Physics, Chemistry and Home Economics all recommended the abolition of absolute marking, in line with the notion that it would be inappropriate for pupils in a mixed-ability form to be marked against each other in competition. They argued that this would tend to dispirit and demoralize the 'slower ones' who saw their colleagues getting consistently better marks despite an equal amount of effort. But some staff argued that this was unrealistic: 'The kids always know who is the brightest and who is the slowest and it is ridiculous to try and hide it from them.' The Technical Studies department said in their report that:

> It is felt that it is better to be just rather than patronising with the pupil who gets lower grades. He will appreciate the justice of his grade himself in a direct and immediate fashion by comparing his work with his fellows.

In this connection, several departments also recommended that there should be a system of continuous assessment rather than examinations at the end of the year, for reasons similar to those stated above. With regard to marking and assessment, the Modern Languages department said that:

> Whatever was put on a pupil's work in the form of assessment of it there is no difficulty in keeping one's own records, and of having by the end of the year, or earlier, a good conception of each child's ability.

Overall, opinions on assessment did not appear to be related systematically to the different perspectives or to different subject cultures. However, the comment from the French department report, stressing the importance of assessment from the teacher's point of view, in order to obtain a 'good conception of each child's ability', is characteristic of the *academic perspective*. It should also be remembered, in relation to this, that French was to be 'set' in the second year.

The importance of the perspectives and the subject sub-cultures in making sense of the implementation process becomes clearer when actual classroom practices are considered.

As we have seen, many of the teachers were particularly concerned in the mixed-ability context with the problem of the different speed of working of pupils in the same classroom, and, related to this, with the feasibility of class-teaching a mixed-ability form. Differences in ability were often described in terms of speed of work and children were commonly referred to as 'fast ones' and 'slow ones'. For many of the departments, the solution to these problems was to introduce worksheets – in effect, to give greater control over the pacing and, to some extent, over the selection and organization of knowledge, to the pupil. To use Bernstein's (1971) terminology, the intention was to bring about a weakening of lesson *frames* – a term which 'refers to the degree of control teacher and pupil possess over the selection, organization and pacing of knowledge transmitted and received in the pedagogical relationship'. A strong frame is defined when it is the teacher who retains complete control over the transmission of knowledge in the pedagogical relationship. The introduction of worksheets can be viewed as being a weakening of frame, in that the individualization of learning that the use of worksheets is intended to achieve suggests an increase in the power of the pupil over what, when and how he receives knowledge. The actual extent of this weakening, however, presents problems. The concepts of classification and framing, although useful as descriptive categories, do lack specificity, and their use can all too easily lead to the reification of pedagogic and curricular processes. There are no operational definitions available for these terms. And as principles to describe and analyse the organization of curriculum knowledge, it is important that their meanings should be derived from the meanings and interactions held and entered into by teachers in their classroom practices. Pring (1975 : 70), in his critique of Bernstein's terms classification and framing, argues that:

So far there has been no empirical or social reality which he has applied himself to, or examined. He has simply provided a series of definitions leading to an undefined and ambiguous terminology.

While I do not dispute the basic thrust of Pring's criticisms, I would defend the usefulness of Bernstein's conceptual framework as a means to examine organizational or curricular changes in schools relative to the 'form' of schooling experienced by the pupil. It is important to note that, like the Beachside teachers, Bernstein (1971 : 58) comments in particular on the centrality of the relationship between the pacing of knowledge and pupils' learning.

It may well be that frame strength, as this refers to pacing, is a critical variable in the study of educability.

In the banded lessons, framing was clearly strong. In all those banded lessons I observed, except one,[8] it was the teacher who selected and who was responsible for ordering and arranging the subject-matter. Furthermore, none of the departments made any use of discovery methods or curriculum projects in the first three years. The teacher maintained strong control over the pacing of pupils' work-activities. All pupils were expected to learn at the same pace, lessons were 'aimed at the middle' and taught to the form as a single group. Teaching was for the most part didactic, with emphasis on the transmission of specific skills, and the behaviour of pupils was focussed on the 'chalk and talk' performance of the teacher. All teachers attempted to maintain explicit control over the pupils' talk, involvement and social relationships in lessons. The assessment of pupils was specific, grades or marks awarded for homework were given on a competitive norm-reference basis, as they were for the internal schools examinations, which were taken in all subjects at Christmas and at the end of the summer term. In the long term, each teacher was working towards the coverage of a particular amount of knowledge in each year. As has been noted (see chapter 6), in some subjects, all or part of the first three years of work was considered to be a necessary and important preparation for O-level.

Obviously, some of the elements of strong framing are maintained in the organizational rather than in the interactional framework of lessons and the syllabus, and were thus automatically changed by the introduction of mixed-ability grouping. Others, however, are embedded in the interaction of lessons and would not be changed simply by the reorganization of the form-groups.

In the organizational sense, the boundaries between pupils in terms of ability are broken down by the introduction of mixed-ability grouping. There is no immediately available social identity attached to pupils by virtue of allocation to a particular form, except for remedial pupils. However, as the previous chapters have shown, identities are also created and reinforced in the interaction between teacher and pupils. The move to mixed-ability does not preclude the creation of status differences *within* forms, especially if academic ability remains the major status-giving source in the classroom.

In the following section, I shall use the concept of framing to analyse and describe a sample of mixed-ability lessons: one lesson each in Geography, Maths, Biology, Chemistry, Physics and French and four in History. In each case, where relevant, the observations and comments on the lessons will be related back to the teachers' perspectives and subject sub-cultures discussed in the previous chapter.

Geography (15 mixed-ability lessons observed)

The Geography department had done a great deal to implement the recommendations of the report. A new first-year syllabus was devised independently by the staff of the department. No textbooks were used. The course was based upon aspects of the geography of the local area and community, and each topic was prepared by one member of the department. But a system of 'key' lessons that had been specifically mentioned in the departmental recommendations was not implemented.[9] For the second year, a commercial work-book and work-card system was introduced.[10] Those areas of the syllabus not covered by the work-book were prepared for the whole department by individual members.

There were seven staff who taught Geography and the variations in their organization of classroom learning were considerable. There was no standardization of methods. Thus, the lesson presented and discussed below cannot be said to be typical of the whole department; for example, this teacher tended to talk to the form as a whole much less than his colleagues. However, the description does provide an indication of how the work-books were used. Most of the comments focus on one particular group of boys in the form.[11]

Second-year Geography: lesson notes

The lesson has already begun when I arrive; the pupils are quiet and attentive. There is a short period of explanation by the teacher of work-tasks to be finished and new ones to be attempted, which work-book pages and sheets to complete. There is also some individual experiment work; pieces of sandstone and shale are given out. Movement around the room begins. The teacher circulates, checking progress and solving problems. Individual work goes on with a busy buzz of noise.

Desmond, Paul and Kevin seem to find it difficult to organize themselves and not get sidetracked. Desmond had not done the previous piece of work because he did not understand it, but had not said this when the teacher asked about people who did not understand. Paul has left his work-book at home. Kevin is confused about what work has to be done when asked about it by the teacher. Paul solves the mystery by explaining that Kevin was away for a previous part of the work. It did not seem to occur to Kevin as an explanation for him not knowing. (The typical bright middle-class articulate pupil can handle these situations much better?) The teacher leaves them; their talk has now moved on to a football match to be played at lunch time.

The teacher's problem here is that these boys are not working in the expected way; work is not done and not reported; he cannot deal with the problems which do not arise. Desmond was especially confused but incurs the teacher's disapproval by talking while the teacher goes over work with whole form.

The teacher explains that the work is to be done slowly, that if something is not understood, 'Don't take someone else's word for it, bring it out and ask me.'

Kevin and Desmond want to go out to see the teacher but are almost dissuaded by Paul who says that they have no need to. When they move to go anyway, each reinforcing the decision of the other, Paul says, 'I'm going too .' In a lesson like this with individual attention, Desmond and Kevin, and thus Paul, are brought into contact with the teacher who attempts to solve their work-problems. He spends 10 minutes with the small group of nine at the front trying to 'unconfuse' them, and bring them up to date in the work-book.

The book asks, 'How hard is shale?' and suggests scraping it with a knife. Paul, Desmond and Kevin seem unwilling to trust their own judgement and look for a solution in the book. Kevin tries scraping with his pen and then scissors but is still unsure. It is hard or soft; what is *hard*? 'What have you got, Dave? What have you got, Pete?' 'I'm going to put that it's fairly hard,' but is not entirely convinced without a group agreement on this. They all agree that 'it is hard' – but football at lunch time again becomes an issue – then back to answering questions. Now the book asks about the texture of particles scratched from the shale. The teacher arrives – 'Why are you doing that!' Kevin doesn't know why he is doing it and reads from the book. 'What does it feel like?' Again, very great uncertainty at own judgement – 'Like sand – mud – clay – pepper'. The teacher guides them back to the composition, and 'Now you've got to explain what you've discovered'. With support and reinforcement from the teacher, work for this group progresses much faster – and they appear to understand the terms 'porous' and 'impermeable'.

In the form as a whole, work is done individually but the pace is only flexible to a certain extent as material resources are used and the teacher introduces and de-briefs each topic in the work-book. He interacts with each pupil separately to check on progress and solve problems but uses the small-group teaching in order to 'catch-up' those who are fallen behind. But the concentration of the transcript on the one small group of boys does show how this technique may not be sensitive enough in picking up the unwilling or confused pupils, and also how without close monitoring of individual pupils, the pupils and teacher may end up talking at cross-purposes.

This teacher described his adaptation to mixed-ability as follows:

'I'm usually walking around and chatting, not a great change for my teaching method. I am very conscious of the time element. I am aware of a group of them moving fast. But the book this year allows people to go off in different directions. I try to encourage people to work together and help each other.'

In this lesson there is some weakening of frame, in that the behaviour of the pupils as a whole is not focussed on the teacher except on the occasional 'giving of directions'.

The introduction of the work-book allows some variations in the pacing and selection of knowledge by the pupils. 'The teacher arranges the context which the child is expected to rearrange and explore . . . within this arranged context, the child apparently has wide powers over what he selects, over how he structures and over the timescale of his activities' (Bernstein 1975 : 22). In fact, much of the selection and structuring is done by the work-books.

Much more of the learning in this context is socialized – between pupils ('What do you think, Dave?') and between pupils and teacher ('Why are you doing that!' 'What does it feel like?') – than was usual in banded classrooms. Indeed, much more of the pupils' learning is made available to monitoring by the teacher than is the case in class-taught lessons.

Ultimately, however, the teacher is still aware of the necessity of maintaining a 'manageable spread' in the differential progress of the pupils through the book, and the 'catching up' sessions are used to achieve this. The teacher still 'goes over' work with the whole form, but the transmission of knowledge appears much less central to this lesson than to the class-taught banded Geography lessons.

In line with their recommendations, the department did not use marks or grades to assess pupils' work, although some members of the department did report the end-of-year examination marks to their pupils.

In general terms, the observations of mixed-ability Geography lessons reinforced the comments made in the previous chapter about the range of opinion within the department on the value of the mixed-ability in-novation. To a great extent the degree of change in the classroom practices of the different teachers in the Geography department could be related back individually to their attitudes in favour of or against mixed-ability evident from my interviews with them. As noted previously, the differences which existed between the members of the department in their classroom methods were recognized by the head of department (see p. 186).

The Sciences (26 mixed-ability lessons observed)

In the case of the Sciences, Chemistry and Biology prepared their own worksheets for use with the first year, but without essentially redesigning the syllabus. One Chemistry teacher commented:

'The Chemistry Science course is too staid and academic for me; there's not enough entertainment or project work in the course and we've got kids who have scientific hobbies at home who are doing very badly in Science at school. And we haven't changed anything for mixed-ability really, it's more or less the same course as Band 1 had.'

And the head of Science explained:

'We just don't have the time to organize any sort of comprehensive reform of our syllabus.'

In relation to this, both these sciences failed to act upon their report recommendation.

In the Chemistry lessons I observed, the prepared worksheets were used only occasionally, and one member of the department was never observed to make use of them at all. For the most part the teachers continued with teacher-centred 'chalk and talk' methods, and, when they *were* used, the sheets became a guide to experiments to which the teacher referred. The head of department explained this in describing his teaching of one mixed-ability form:

'I'm doing something that I never thought I would do with this form and that's class-teaching; it goes against all the preconceived ideas of mixed-ability groups but I find with experiments like this that they can all understand and find their own level in their written work'.

First-year Chemistry: lesson notes
The teacher had intended to spend the first part of the lesson giving a test, but as several members of the form were at a school choir rehearsal, the substance of the lesson came first.
T 'O.K., so let's go round. What did we do last time when we were heating things?'
P1 [Untranscribable]
T 'What colour is copper to start with?'
P2 'Brown. Well, goldish brown.'
T 'Yeh! It's shiny; all metals are shiny; that's one of the things that makes them metals. It was a brown colour and you heated it and got this coating. Anything else happened, just to remind ourselves before we move on?'
P3 'It melted and . . .'
T '*Yes*, it did melt, when did it melt? Did it melt straight away?'
P4 'No, after a little while it was red hot first, then it started.'
T 'Yes, anything else happened?'
P5 [Untranscribable]
T 'Just copper . . . last time did we heat anything else?'

Chorus 'No!'

T 'Right, so working in your two's or on your own again, some people, because some people are away or because people are in the choir practice, will obviously have to be working on their own. Get out a bunsen burner and an asbestos mat and a pair of tongs.'

Two or three minutes pass while the pupils collect their apparatus and assemble it. The teacher then begins to pass out a worksheet.

T 'Once you get a worksheet read it through to remind yourself what you are doing . . . One thing you mustn't do – it won't do you any harm *now*, but it might later on – if you've got a pair of tongs like this chappie has here, instead of sort of playing with it and going like this and sticking it in your ear put it in the middle of the bench there and don't play with it. Sooner or later you'd play around with a thermometer or something and break it and cost you and me a great deal of money . . . Has everybody got one? . . . Here, give one to this chappie here.

Right, some of you have only just got hold of your worksheets I can see; the thing to do with these always is to remind yourselves what you were doing last time. This one is for, is going to last us about three or four weeks. There's an awful lot of work which we've got to do. This is one of them. Look towards me now; you can finish reading about that before you do the experiment, make sure you do that though . . . You've perhaps heard about this stuff [holding up a small bottle of chemical] and some of you may have seen your Junior School teachers using it . . . I was talking to Mr Baldwin from Iron Road and he was saying he does a fair bit of Science work with his people and its magnesium ribbon – you might possibly have seen it before; magnesium is a metal, the only thing that'll mean to you if you rub your finger along it, it can be seen to be shiny, and I did say before that something shiny is often a metal.'

The teacher talked for a further *five* minutes before the experiment was begun, the period of the experiment lasted for *five* minutes and then the pupils were called to attention again by the teacher.

T 'Right, stop, hush, turn your bunsen burners on to luminous, like that . . . right, there's no air on, the flame's luminous, it doesn't make any noise. And sit on your stools and look forward to me . . . Come on, Tracy, we're waiting for you . . . Now . . . all sorts of things have been said to me going round.'

The lesson continued in this fashion with two further experiments. In each case the metals were introduced by the teacher to the whole form and discussion of findings was also done in a class-teaching situation, although the teacher also discussed the experiments while they were in progress with small groups of pupils as he walked around the room. But in every case the interpretation of the experiment was discussed with the form as a whole.

T 'We are left with ashes — so we are. If you notice, actually if you look in
the air at the moment, if you look around the air at the moment you
see it's a bit foggy, it's not mist because mist is wet, isn't it? It's a bit
foggy, there's the dust, it's just the same as the ashes left on the end
of your pair of tongs, have a look and see . . . Now just for this once
we're going to do this exercise all together, because I'm going to
give you quite a few more to do now, if people finish one and write it
up properly they can have another one. Just for this once I want you
to fill in your table . . . I shall just clear a space on the board here, you
can do this on your own, but I'm just going to give some important
spellings, some important words . . . Right, well, let's put some
important words down . . . MAGNESIUM . . . RIBBON . . . Right, use
that when you are filling your table in . . . What else could we say. It
was very very hot for anybody here who knows what that means, it
was that hot, 2000 degrees centigrade . . . Right . . . You also saw
light given off, didn't you? I'll put that down for somebody who
wants some words to use, O.K., and it left you with white ash? . . .'
A period of writing followed.
T 'Right, if you've finished the write-up, come and get one of the test-
tubes . . . Right, one and one again, I'll give you some of this stuff,
don't touch this with your fingers . . . A straight line . . . Don't start
heating till I tell you to . . . Now before you start doing anything,
look this way, look at your worksheets . . . it tells you, "Put a
measure of one chemical in a test-tube. Make a note of the name and
what it looks like." So you'll forget the name if you don't note the
name, I'm going to have to tell you the name of this substance, we've
just done magnesium. This one's called Iodine. Now Iodine used to
be used by doctors as an antiseptic, does anybody know what
antiseptic means?'
P 'It keeps things clean.'
T 'Yes, it kills germs, doesn't it? And keeps things clean. Something like
that. It used to be used mixed with alcohol, actually, because Iodine
itself is a solid . . . Now I want you to heat that very gently. But you
will need something to hold the test-tube with, a test-tube holder.
Can you two please go round and give one of these to each person
with a test-tube. As soon as you get that you can gently heat the
Iodine using again a medium flame, let some air into the flame. And
once you've done that you can have the next one. I'll put the name of
Iodine here . . . Stop a minute, please, one thing I forgot to say very
important, when you heat something up don't point it at
everybody . . .
There was a further period of experiment with instructions being given to
the whole form.
T 'Don't make it too hot . . . Take it away from the flame now . . . That's
enough at the back there, you don't want it too hot . . . Turn the

> flame down now and just put it back in . . . but don't make it too
> hot.'

This was typical of most of the mixed-ability Chemistry lessons observed.
When used, the worksheets played a secondary role in the pupils'
relationship to the subject-matter. Invariably, the preparation of experiments and the de-briefing afterwards were done by the teacher to the whole
form. The pupils only worked on their own during the actual 'experiment-
ing', and the pace and timing of activities remained completely under the
teacher's control. The pupils' experiment work was begun and ended on
the teacher's command. His talk dominated the flow of the lesson and the
responsibility for the transmission of knowledge clearly remained with
him. Here the worksheet was used simply as a guide to experimental
procedures and a reminder of work done. But there were differences from
the banded lessons, particularly in the extent of pupils' participation in
experiments, and the head of Chemistry certainly felt that his department
had moved significantly away from traditional science-teaching methods.

As mentioned above, one of the Chemistry staff did not make use of
worksheets in any of the lessons observed. She explained that:

> 'When we were preparing for mixed-ability we produced lots of
> workcards and projects, but I haven't felt that they have been necessary. I
> feel that we can stretch the brighter kids by stimulating their minds in
> open-type lessons.'

The open-type lessons to which she referred followed essentially the same
pattern as that of the Physics lesson described below. The teacher would do
the experiment and then the pupils were asked questions.[12] This particular
teacher was also different from her colleagues in that she operated a system
of streaming *within* the classroom.

> 'They're organized here roughly, by the benches – the brighter ones at the
> back, the average ones on the middle bench and the slow ones on the front
> bench. I gave them a rough test at the beginning, and then I sometimes
> move them around. But they don't know this – I can keep some idea of
> the level at which I should be pitching my questions.'

In another sense it could be said that this was an attempt to create a more
individualized learning experience in a class-teaching situation. But overall
in Chemistry the introduction of worksheets did not in itself involve any
more than a marginal move towards the individualization of learning, and
the frame of lessons remained strong.

In Biology, worksheets were also used. Despite the fact that they
normally consisted only of detailed instructions for experiments,[13] rather

than substantive lesson material, in the Biology lessons observed it was apparent that the teachers spent much less of lesson-time in addressing the whole form than had been the case with banded forms. Most of the teacher's time was spent in talking with individual pupils and answering questions and problems.

> *First-year Biology: lesson notes*
> The pupils are given out their books as soon as the form is assembled.
> T 'Now then, in an orderly fashion I want you to go to the bench at the end and collect a worksheet, then one person from each group should collect a microscope, a slide and a mounted needle. And please be careful with the microscopes, they are very expensive to buy and we cannot replace them if they are broken. Before you begin your experiment you should read, CAREFULLY, through the worksheet. Now are there any questions? Right, off you go.'
> Almost the whole of the rest of the lesson is taken up with the experimental work by the children and then their attempts to interpret and make sense of what they observed. For the first part of the lesson the teacher was engaged in solving the technical problems created by the microscope, and the use of the slide and needle. Later, there was much discussion of the drawing of the cells and with some groups the description of the experiment. As pupils finished, some prepared slides were brought out to be looked at through viewers and drawn to compare with the human cells drawn first.
> With ten minutes of the lesson remaining some pupils were also finishing the second task, most of the others were just beginning this.
> P 'What shall I do now?'
> T 'You can sleep quietly for the last ten minutes.'

More than in either of the other sciences, the lesson format in Biology had changed for mixed-ability; the teachers talked much less to the form as a whole than they did under the banded system, and the pupils had much greater involvement in the substance of the lesson through experiment. The nature of these experiments tended to release the teacher, who could circulate and talk to small groups or individuals without being primarily concerned with the progress and safety of the form as a whole. Thus, the frame of the lesson appeared to be weakened considerably, and, as in the case of Geography, this method of organization of learning tended to give the teacher much greater opportunity to monitor the pupils' involvement with and understanding of lesson-material.

In Physics there was a state of affairs rather different from that among the two other sciences. From the time of the original vote to introduce mixed-ability in the summer of 1972 until the arrival of the first-year mixed-ability cohort in the autumn of 1973, there had been a complete turnover of staff and the department had its third head. None of the departmental report recommendations was implemented; there were no work-cards prepared and no revision of the syllabus. Indeed, there was little change either in methods or presentation of lessons for mixed-ability forms. There was much greater reliance on teacher-demonstrated experiments than in either of the other sciences, and this approach generally maintained a high degree of traditional teacher-talk in Physics lessons.

> 'We don't use a real mixed-ability course here, it is a version of the band 1 course which is a pity. But making a proper mixed-ability course that they could work through at their own pace would involve someone in the department in a great deal of time and effort. We could make use of the combined Science Course but the department don't seem to be keen on it.'
>
> (Physics teacher)

The following lesson may be regarded as highly typical of the mixed-ability Physics lessons observed.

First-year Physics: lesson notes
The form are sitting in rows at the dark-brown benches; the lesson begins with a recapitulation of the work done in a previous lesson.
T 'Who can tell me which of these two examples will exert the least pressure [a stiletto heel or an elephant's foot]?'
P1 'An elephant's foot.'
T 'Can anybody explain why?'
P2 'Because of the area of the surface.'
T 'Good boy.'
The teacher goes over the theory on the board explaining with an example how to work out pressure per square metre.
T 'If the weight is six kilos and the area is three square metres what is the pressure?'
The same few hands are raised as before.
T 'Yes?'
P3 'Two'
T 'Two what?... Yes?'
P2 'Two kilos per square metre.'
T 'Right.'
She now puts up a series of problems on the board to be worked out individually; the form work quietly; three boys are given individual help by the teacher.
T 'Anyone not finished put up your hand.'
Everyone looks around to see who has not finished; there are only a few

of the form without their hands up, predictably those who were also answering the questions; the teacher begins to organize some equipment that the lab. technician has placed on her desk.

T 'Anyone not finished put your hand up. [It is just a handful now, including those boys who had been 'helped'.] If you have finished read over what I've given you and sit quietly.'

She spends some more time with one of the boys who is having trouble.

T 'O.K., leave that now – you can finish them off at home; I want you to gather around the desk at the front.'

The teacher demonstrates a pressure experiment with water and asks questions.

T 'Why does the jet at the bottom go further from the rest?'

P1 'Because it is under greater pressure.'

T 'Good boy.'

Finally the experiment is to be 'written up'.

T 'I shall leave the conclusion for you to do for homework; I want you to explain what you think the experiment shows.'

After the lesson the teacher explained to me:

> 'They are a nice form to work with. I haven't really found any problems this year, although I have this fear that I am going way over the heads of some of them. I feel that if I tested them people like Graham Jones would not know anything. But it has not been too bad this year; I am not sure about what will happen next year. And I certainly would not want to teach Maths and French to a group like this.'

Without any teaching alternatives, except when equipment was available for pupils to do experiments, all the Physics lessons I observed approximated to this structure.

The teacher interacted individually with less than half the form and the majority of these interactions were by question and answer; the lesson was centred on the teacher's explanations and demonstrations. The pace was determined by the contents of the one lesson and a median pupil-speed. The 'knowledge' of the lesson was presented by the teacher in a traditional explanation-question-reinforcement format. Thus framing remained strong and there was little difference between the conduct of this lesson and the typical banded Physics lesson.

It is possible in the Sciences to account for the processes of implementation, to a great extent, in terms of the teachers' perspectives and their subject-identities. The head of Physics and the other Physics staff were against the introduction of mixed-ability and, as we have seen, they did little or nothing to change teaching methods to accommodate the new situation.[14] The Chemistry staff, however, were in favour of mixed-ability, at least in the first and second years, and made changes in the organization of lessons. Although these changes appeared to be superficial in terms of altering the locus of control over subject-knowledge, they did not involve a shift in the pedagogic basis of Chemistry teaching. In both cases, the teachers' view of the subject, as involving conceptual evolution and linear progression, was an important limiting factor in the degree of change.

It is not possible to account for the situation in Biology in the same way; although two of the three members of the Biology staff were in favour of mixed-ability, the head of department was decidedly against. Nevertheless, a shift in pedagogy was evident in the Biology lessons observed. It is certainly the case, though, that the Biology syllabus was less difficult to adapt to mixed-ability teaching than either Physics or Chemistry. It did not require a large financial outlay to introduce the more pupil-centred methods, whereas an equivalent redesigning in the other sciences would have been extremely costly. Neither did the changes in Biology involve the same safety hazards or problems of classroom organization as they would have done in Physics or Chemistry.

Perhaps most of all the departments, the Sciences were presented with considerable problems with the introduction of mixed-ability grouping, for any major changes in pedagogy and syllabus would also require the purchase of new equipment and materials. The department had considered the possibility of Schools Council Science but the cost of re-equipping proved prohibitive.

Languages (21 mixed-ability lessons observed)

Given the strong opposition to mixed-ability within the French department and the particular subject sub-culture identified with it, changes were not to be expected. Indeed, the lessons observed indicated little change in teaching methods from a typical band 1 lesson. As anticipated in the departmental report, lessons continued to be of a traditional book-based, teacher-centred variety, following much of the syllabus and pace of the previous band 1 first-years. It was clear from the recommendations in the departmental report and the head of department's comments, presented in the previous chapter, that no method other than traditional class-teaching was ever seriously considered.

> *First year French: lesson notes*
> The teacher is already in the classroom; she has had her previous lesson there. The first arrivals of the new form hesitate at the door when they see her.

T 'Come in.'

They enter and place their belongings – all are weighed down by briefcases and bags and books – but do not sit down. The form is in quickly; there are no stragglers, but two boys, seeming not to notice the others, do sit down.

T 'Some people seem to have forgotten their manners. [The two boys get quickly to their feet.] That's better. Bonjour mes élèves.'

Chorus 'Bonjour, Madame Oakes.'

T 'Asseyez-vous.'

The form sit waiting silently.

T 'We started last week to talk about endings, and how in French the endings of words that are adjectives change. Can someone tell me when they change?'

Half a dozen hands go up.

T 'Stephen.'

P 'For masculine and feminine . . .'

T 'And also for?'

P 'Plurals.'

T 'Good. Now let's try some examples on the board.'

Colours and other descriptive adjectives are used as examples, with the children putting their hands up to provide the correct endings, the answering is confined to about 10 of the form and the more difficult 'irregular' endings go to just two or three pupils, who thus answer a high proportion of the questions between them.[15]

T 'Now, let me see what I have in here. [She searches in the drawer of her desk and produces a paper bag.] Ceci c'est un sac de papier . . . What does "sac de papier" mean? [No answers.] Someone guess. [She repeats the sentence.]

P 'Paper bag.'

T 'That's right: "paper bag". [She repeats the sentence again.] Now, let's see what's inside. [She plunges inside and her hand comes out wearing a monkey glove puppet.] Celle-ci c'est Fifi.'

She repeats the sentence in English, moving the puppet with her fingers; the form is entranced. The monkey now disappears into the paper bag and emerges holding a small plastic banana.

T 'What is it?'

Hands up.

P2 'A banana.'

T 'And in French?'

P2 'Une banane.'

T 'Fifi likes bananas! Can anyone say any more about it? Paul, will you sit up straight, please.'

P1 'Elle est une petite banane.'

T 'Oui, très bien. Can anyone say any more about it? Remember what we have just been doing on the board.'

P3 'Elle sont . . .'
T 'Elle?'
P3 'Elle est.'
T 'That's it.'
P3 'Elle est une jaune banane.'
This is repeated with a series of fruits produced by the monkey from the paper bag; the questions again tend to be answered by the same group of pupils; only occasionally do other pupils put up their hands, but sometimes the teacher asks someone who has not volunteered.
T 'Allen, stop talking to your neighbour, please, that's very bad manners when I am talking. Now what is this, did we say?'
Allen 'Orange.'
T 'Just orange?'
Allen 'Petite orange.'
T 'Yes, but that wasn't what I meant. What goes before the word *in French*?' The boy looks blank.
T 'Who can help him out?'
P2 'Une orange.'
T 'Oui, une orange.'

The lesson follows a rigid question-and-answer pattern, the teacher supplying a model statement and persuading the children to grasp the principle by repeating similar statements. The pace of work is totally dominated by the teacher in the oral interchange with a minority of pupils in the whole form, the French that has been 'learned' within the lesson is that displayed by the competence of this minority. The lesson is centred entirely on the teacher, and the 'knowledge' of the lesson or 'that which is to be learned' is presented within the pattern of explanation-question-reinforcement. (Also, the teacher constructs her definition of control in the lesson so as to include not only behaviour, but also manners, attitude, concentration, and health – she made frequent references to sitting straight so as to take pressure off the spine, to keeping fingers out of mouths to avoid picking up germs, and so forth.)

In one sense, this lesson is highly untypical. The use of puppets was not a method employed by any other teachers observed. However, in another sense, it represents an almost stereotyped lesson format for mixed-ability French lessons. Pupils would be presented with some kind of stimulus and introduced to new or previously-covered grammatical rules, and new or previously-covered vocabulary. In other lessons a textbook or slides were used to provide these stimuli. There would then be some oral work usually of a question-and-answer type, and then written reinforcement through book exercises. Pace was always determined by the introduction of new rules by the teacher or through the book, and always involved the whole class at once; the pupils would start and finish new work at the same time. The frame in these language lessons remained very strong.

Mathematics (17 mixed-ability lessons observed)

In the Maths department a set of 'home-made' worksheets was used with the new first year based on work derived from the S.M.P. syllabus.

> *First-year Maths: lesson notes*
> The form arrives promptly and together and is quickly settled; exercise books have been given back; there is a general comparing of marks: 'I have got seven right, how many did you get?'
> *T* 'I want to go over the homework with you. [The tone is brusque but friendly.] When you are ready, George.'
> The teacher works entirely on the board. Everything is written down. She goes through the homework by question and answer, the answering being dominated by those who are most 'keen' to answer. Some members of the form who do not put their hands up regularly are peripheral to the central task-orientation. This question-and-answer session takes ten minutes; the teacher is precise and fast. Then exercise work is set.
> *T* 'I want you to go on and try exercise C. You may need the blocks that are on my desk; the answer book is also there.'
> The classwork is from work-cards of different colour with key-cards which give the answers. The teacher moves around the room for the whole of this time and speaks with individuals; this interaction appears to be half the time initiated by the pupils and half the time by her. By talking with pairs or groups of pupils she 'sees' all but seven members of the form. There is also a considerable amount of interaction among the pupils, most of it task-centred, comparing answers or giving help. The level of group noise is not too loud; the teacher issues one rebuke to the form as a whole. 'It's getting too noisy now, let's get down to some more work.' And once, to Paul and his friends at the back of the room: 'This is Maths, not football. You can talk about that at lunch time.'[16] This period of the lesson lasts fifteen minutes. With five minutes to go, everyone has finished the exercise and some have gone on to another work-card. The teacher calls a halt. The last five minutes are given to a mathematical quiz between the boys and girls.
> *T* 'What is 9 squared?'
> *T* 'How many degrees in a right angle?'
> *T* 'What's an equilateral triangle?'

The lesson is well-disciplined, but the teacher also allows considerable freedom of movement to the form; she is able to 'get round to see' almost all the pupils, although, given that this part of the lesson lasted for fifteen minutes, that would only allow for half a minute per pupil. The emphasis of the lesson switches from the teacher-centred question-and-answer format to that of individuals or groups working on the work-cards; the 'faster' ones move to the next work-card while the 'others' finish. In many respects, the work-card system of this kind combined with the teacher's explanation of tasks was not radically different from the traditional book-based banded Maths lesson observed. The work-cards do not attempt to introduce or explain new topics or concepts; they are essentially an adjunct to the teacher's 'teaching'. The teacher still carries most of the responsibility for ordering and explaining the knowledge-base of lessons. The work-cards cope with the different speeds at which pupils work through exercises, and with the elaboration of topics previously introduced by the teacher.

Unlike other departments, the Maths department did discuss teaching methods at its meetings. The head of department held strong views on methods and was always willing to discuss problems with, to observe and advise, or team-teach with, the members of his department. To a great extent, this produced a standard model for mixed-ability Maths lessons, of which the above example is typical.

In terms of changes in the framing of lessons, the use of these home-produced work-cards in Maths represented only a minimal reduction of the teachers' control over the organization and pacing of work. The work-card system did allow the 'faster' pupils to get on with new cards while the 'slower' ones were finishing, and beyond this, once the cards were exhausted, the teacher could set exercises from the S.M.P. book for the 'faster' pupil. But the setting of homework and getting through the first-year syllabus imposed important constraints upon the flexibility of pace in the classroom. Also, as in the case above, the teachers still considered it important and necessary to talk to the form as a whole to explain basic concepts or new work.

Marks, and getting the right answers, continued to be important in Maths lessons; in lessons observed, the teachers frequently 'collected in' homework marks by getting the pupils to call out how many they got right. Progress through exercises was frequently checked in terms of right answers. Typically:

> T 'Now, everyone's finished the green work-card 6, yes?'
> *Chorus* 'Yes.'
> T 'Right, who got them all right? [Hands go up.] One wrong. [More hands.] Two. [More hands.] Three. [More.] More than five. [Seven hands go up.] That's not very good, is it?'

The relative abilities of pupils were frequently paraded in this way, making each pupil's performance in relation to his classmates clear to himself and to others.

But paradoxically, despite its initial opposition to the extension of mixed-ability beyond the first year and general concern about the impact of the change upon 'standards', the Mathematics department eventually produced one of the most radical aspects of the whole innovation. Although Maths was initially 'set' in the second year, one mixed-ability group was created in order to experiment with mixed-ability teaching with a commercial work-card system.[17] At the end of the year the experiment was considered so successful that the whole of the next second-year cohort was taught Mathematics in mixed-ability groups in this way. The head of department explained:

> 'We are going mixed-ability in the second-year Maths because we are so pleased with the work-card group and how they are working, and they use the same cards at Windleigh School,[18] and it is going well there. It seems the sensible thing to do. Their motivation is good, they are meant to take two cards home for homework and some girls are taking eight or eleven. And when you go in you can't tell the difference between the "thick" and the "bright ones" because they are all working. And the bright ones can cover the same material on the cards as is involved in the first two years of the Grammar School Course.'[19]

The commercial system used was divided into three packs: a Main, a Supplementary, and a Preliminary pack. The Main pack of cards was arranged into topics which were subdivided. Pupils worked through the topics more or less as they chose; once they had finished one topic they selected which to do next from those left spare from the main pack. The topics were divided into 38 sections, with about 7 cards per section and there were 8 'starter' topics. But the system was not a programmed learning system. At the major decision-points, the pupil was referred to the teacher who had to consider the child's progress and, for example, decide whether he should continue to the next topic, or go back and re-do some cards, or go through some revision or preliminary work with the teacher. Thus, perhaps more than in any other subject, in the second year, when this system was introduced for the whole of the next cohort, control over the selection and pacing of curriculum knowledge had passed substantially from the teacher to the pupil. This is evident from the head of department's comments:

> 'Usually the very fastest children will finish all the topics after two terms, or sooner in exceptional cases, and these children are then guided through

the *number* book. The slowest children may not get through several topics by the end of the year, but throughout the year they are steered to the "core" topics to ensure these vital few will be covered. The content of the "core" of topics is decided by reference to the *letter* books which are used after the work-cards.'[20]

History (25 mixed-ability lessons observed)

The following observation notes and transcript materials are all taken from History lessons with mixed-ability forms; one transcript is presented from one lesson by each of the four members of the department. The History department provides an interesting case for examination, in that all of the four full-time members of the department were wholeheartedly in favour of mixed-ability, and had unanimously agreed to introduce home-made worksheets for mixed-ability teaching. However, the four transcripts presented below illustrated a range of different methods and forms of learning-organization covered by the notion of 'using worksheets'. It is clear that a commonly-agreed terminology was used to explain and describe a variety of different classroom practices. Sharp and Green (1976 : 175) discovered a similar situation with regard to the terminology of progressive primary education; they found that, 'If unprobed, the vocabulary [that teachers use to describe and justify their classroom practice] may legitimize a wide range of different personal categories used in their classroom practice.' This more detailed analysis of the implementation of mixed-ability in one department will also allow the exploration of some of the material constraints, as well as the ideological parameters, which impose limits upon the range of options available to the department, and to individual teachers, in the organization of learning in the classroom.

Second-year History: lesson notes. Mr Wheatley
The teacher arrives before the form and opens the book cupboard.
T 'Please give out these.'
He gives books to some of the boys as they come in; he also hands out the worksheets personally. Different members of the form are on different worksheets, and the teacher seems to be aware of the differences in individual progress.
T 'You've finished that one, haven't you?'
T 'I want to have a word with you in a minute, don't I?'
T 'Yes, you had done that.'
The form is quickly organized and quickly down to work. The teacher marks some books of those who have been 'first finishers'; he is standing over them at their desks; they get feedback from his questions and a

follow-up on their work. He asks questions which question their understanding of what they have written. Within the first twenty minutes of the lesson, the teacher has interacted individually with every pupil in the form. He is always moving around the room, answering questions, solving problems of organization and procedure, as well as difficulties in understanding.

T 'You read through that and see if you can find out and I'll be back in a minute.'

The teacher is checking too.

T 'How are you getting on, Robert?'

T 'Are you all right?'

T 'Which question are you on?'

He is monitoring the understanding of the pupils and their progress and learning-difficulties. He returns to the 'I'll be back in a minute' pupil. He asks more questions and the pupil explains to him. The teacher addresses a boy sitting on his own in the corner.

T 'Why are you sitting over there now, why don't you sit with them any more?' [Pointing to a group of boys on the other side of the room.]

P 'They're too noisy.'

The lesson ends with the collection of books and worksheets. The teacher has not once sat down at his desk during the lesson.

The teacher has organized the lesson to allow a considerable flexibility in the speed of coverage of material; three different worksheets are being used in the lesson; he interacts with pupils individually both at his own instigation and at theirs; and he seems to be aware of the progress of individuals. The worksheets are written in a form of 'discovery learning', so that the pupils must search for answers in the three textbooks that are available to them, but the teacher seems concerned with checking 'understanding' as well as coverage.

This way of organizing learning makes available to the teacher a great deal of the pupils' 'self'. Teacher-pupil interaction takes place on a one-to-one basis in a number of dimensions through the process of the lesson itself.

Learning here is also 'socialized'. The pupils are allowed to talk among themselves and there is a considerable amount of discussion about the worksheet questions.

'What does it mean when it says . . .'

'I can't find a bit about . . .'

'What did you put for B . . .', etc.

I shall discuss the role of the worksheet in the framing of the History lesson at the end of this section.

First-year History: lesson notes. Mr Foot

The teacher stands by the door as the form enters and sits down. He catches two boys as they come in to give out work-cards and books; when this is done and the form is sitting down, he signifies the formal commencement of the lesson.

T 'Right. [This is loud and sharp; there is total silence.] You should all have work-cards and books, I want you all to try to finish Section A today and I expect some of you will get on to question 2 or 3 in Section B; remember what I said last week about checking in more than one book before you answer. Off you go.'

The form begins to work in silence. The scratching of pens and turning of papers and pages are the only sounds. The teacher is sitting at his desk at the front of the room marking a pile of books. The silence continues for ten minutes; then a chair scrapes and someone goes to the front of the room; there is a quiet interchange and the teacher explains something; two of the girls at the back begin to talk.

T 'That isn't a sign for the rest of you to start talking', he barks.

The silence goes on for the rest of the lesson. Seven pupils go up to the teacher during this time and once he leans across to the boys in the front desks and points something out in their exercise books; there is one more rebuke to two boys.

T 'I don't think there's any need for you two to be talking to each other, is there?'

The form continues to work after the bell has rung, until the teacher interrupts.

T 'Will the boys who gave out the books and work-cards collect them in again. The rest of you pack your things away.'

T 'Off you go.'

Within certain limits – 'I expect everyone to finish Section A today' – each individual is left to work at his own pace, but there is no interaction between pupils, and very little between teacher and pupils. The nature of the organization of learning in the lesson does not encourage this. The teacher explained the rationale behind his organization of the lesson in this way:

> 'You can't have them chatting all the time, they never get any work done. I just establish a scene in which they can get on with their work and they get a lot done in that way.'

This, then, is the opposite extreme from 'chalk and talk' in the pedagogic role of the teacher. The teacher here has withdrawn from a transmission-role almost entirely and the pupils are left to interact individually with their worksheets. The worksheets in this lesson are used to establish solitary learning; the pupils are privatized from each other and the teacher. They have little opportunity in this learning-context to make the teacher aware of what they feel and think. Interaction is confined to a very narrow range of pupil activities, and little of the pupil's self is available to the teacher. He monitors their progress and production only indirectly in the marking of their books.

Second-year History : lesson notes. Mr Wright

The form comes into the hut without noise ; the teacher has arrived first. He has come from a free lesson and they have been on the other side of the school. The pupils do not sit down but stay standing behind their chairs, waiting and quiet. The teacher speaks to them quietly when everyone has arrived.

T 'Sit down.'

T 'Go immediately to the question you were on last week.'

T 'Put up your hands those who have got as far as question 4 – not yet up to question 4.'

The teacher makes no comment – he appears just to be collecting information ; the form is quickly at work. The teacher goes to the pupils to check their work, but he is approached only occasionally ; he has time to stand behind his desk at the front and look around the room. After twenty minutes, the teacher stops the individual work.

T 'Put your pens and pencils down for a minute.'

There follows a question-and-answer session for the remaining five or ten minutes of the lesson ; the teacher is going over the work already done, highlighting and elaborating some points and clarifying terms.

T 'What do they mean in the book by "emigration"?'

Hands up.

T 'Pauline.'

P 'When you leave your country and go to live in another one.'

T 'Right, and what is the word they use to describe someone who does this?'

Hands up.

T 'Henry.'

H 'Emi . . . emigrant.' He struggles over the word but makes it.

T 'That is good, emigrant, emigrant . . . and can anyone think of any countries that people from this country, from Britain, do emigrate to, today?'

About 20 hands.

T 'Sally.'

S 'Australia.'

T 'Right, anyone . . . June?'

J 'America.'

T 'Sometimes, not so much these days though, it's pretty full up now.'

The teacher shares the pupils' laughter at this.

T 'Another place, like Australia . . . Terry?'
T 'New Zealand.'
T 'Yes, that's it, New Zealand.'
The bell goes.
T 'O.K., before you pack away, it's your homework tonight?'
'It's not, sir,' two girls volunteer.
T 'No?'
The girls again 'Tomorrow.'
T 'O.K. then, I believe you, off you go.'

Here, part of the lesson is dominated by the worksheet, but there is also a period of 'class-teaching'. All of the History staff did spend time class-teaching, even Mr Wheatley and Mr Foot. But each transcript so far represents a lesson typical of the particular teacher, both in terms of lessons observed and from the teachers' own descriptions of their organization of learning. There are obviously similarities between Mr Wright's classroom and Mr Wheatley's, but there are two general points of difference. The first is that Mr Wright always made a point of doing some oral work in every lesson: 'I like to expose them to different stimuli; their worksheets and books is only one way.' But because of the number of different worksheets normally being done in his lesson, Mr Wheatley rarely addressed the form as a whole, and when he did so it was usually only in reference to general points of technique – 'Don't forget to check in all the books' – or administration – 'Does anyone else need a new book?', etc. The second difference is that in Mr Wright's and Mr Foot's lessons it was usual for the whole form to be on the same worksheet and to go on to a new worksheet all at the same time, thus making it possible for them to ask questions, or lecture to the form as a whole, knowing that everyone would be working on that topic. For example, Mr Wright found that he was able to ask the whole form, 'What do they mean in the book by "emigration"?', a word which appeared in question 4. Mr Wheatley, on the other hand, maintained up to three worksheets in use at any time in his lesson, and pupils were able to move from one worksheet to the next in their own time.

The fourth full-time member of the History department is Mr Card.[21] A long transcript is presented from one of his lessons, together with his own written description of the lesson and his comments on the transcript recorded sometime later.

First-year History: lesson notes. Mr Card
The teacher is five minutes late but the form is sitting quietly talking when he arrives – not working, but not misbehaving, either. The teacher quickly organizes the giving out of worksheets and textbooks; he then

gives back exercise books which he has been marking. He walks round the room and gives each one back personally with comments.

T 'Right, settle down, please . . . and some for you. [He is giving out books.] I didn't have a book from you . . .'

P1 'Mine's not here, either.'

P2 'I gave it in.'

T 'All right, see me later in the lesson . . . [To the whole form:] Very good, generally very good indeed.'

T 'Good [to an individual as the book is returned].'

T 'Very good.' [again]

T 'Not bad.' [again]

T 'Did I see your book?'

T 'Karrie, outstanding; if I read out all your work that was good I would read out every page.'

T [To the whole form:] 'As I was working through the books, most of your work is good, but what some of you are doing, in fact, is not really finishing off the question. Some of you are starting the question and then you, er . . . I don't know, you get to the end of the lesson half way through a question and you're coming back the next day and you've forgotten that you've got to do it. . .' [There follows a long explanation about the shortage of exercise books and how much they cost and the need to use every space.]

Mandy [Holding up her book] 'Shall I use this?'

T 'No, no, I don't mean a line like that, dear.'

P3 'I've got "See me".'

T 'Yes, I'll see you during the lesson . . . er [He looks at Barry and Michael] Could you give out the worksheets, please?'

Period of confusion.

T 'Right [noise dies away] . . . just start reading this worksheet . . . The one you finished off last week was the Saxon village, wasn't it? Saxon Village life. Now, what I want you to do is to finish off any question that you've got to do. I want you to finish that off at home, please. Don't start anything now on THAT worksheet, but if there's anything you can do, finish it. Yes, Steven?'

Steven 'I was drawing.'

T 'What were you drawing?'

Steven 'Saxon buildings.'

P4 'So was I.'

T 'From the book?'

Steven 'Yes.'

T 'I'll lend you a book.'

Desmond 'I need a book.'

T 'What do you mean?'

Desmond 'I've got to read the book, then write.'

T 'O.K., see me later.'

P5 'I'm doing Saxon buildings, too.'

T 'I'll lend you a book. Now then, about the Moot; the Witan Moot was not a man – some of you wrote, "They went to the Witan Moot and *HE* was a most important person." It was not a man. What was the Witan Moot? [Hands go up] The Witan Moot. [More hands] Yes, Nicholas?'

Nicholas 'The actual meeting.'

T 'Yes, the actual meeting of a number of men. Now which men? Do they go there to discuss Farmer Giles's cow or something like that, that the farmer next door said he owned or something? [One hand is up.] Klarisa.'

Klarisa 'The King's men.'

T 'Yes, yes, the King's men, the Lords, people like that. And they decide what? What might they decide? The Moot, this group of people who made up the Moot, what might they decide? [Hands up] Lennie?'

Lennie 'The new King.'

T 'Yes, who the new king would be if the king died and his son wasn't good enough. Michael?'

Michael 'Whether to make war or fight another country.'

T 'Yes, whether there would be war or peace, or something like that.'

Beryl 'Whether to have a new king or something. If one was bad they might choose another one.'

T 'Yes, right! important decisions. Whereas the Village Moot was just about the village, wasn't it? Just about the village. O.K., you must remember that . . . Now we can move on to the next worksheet. "The Spread of Religion in England." Now, have you all got that one? . . . slightly different from the worksheets you've done so far, inasmuch that you've got three sections. O.K. Two questions in Section A, you've got to answer both of them; and then in Section B, six questions on that, so you answer all them as well; and then we go on to Section C, if you make it in time, and you can do whatever you want of those. So, all Section A, all Section B, before you have a choice in Section C.'

Michael 'What's the difference between Section A and B?'

T 'Well, the only difference is in terms of time, because this is such a long theme we are doing, not just the Romans or the Saxons, but religion in the period from 450 A.D. right up to 1200, and we go through the Vikings and the Saxons and then the Normans, we go right through just talking about their religions.'

Beryl 'Do we have to LEARN the dates?'

T 'What do you mean LEARN the dates?'

Beryl 'Remember them.'

T 'What do you mean – roughly?'

Beryl 'Well, because it says from early Saxon times, 450 A.D.'

T 'Well, obviously if it's early Saxon times it helps to know what you're
talking about, doesn't it? It's all very rough, though, it's not exact
dates . . . Well, number one . . .'

The teacher now talks for the whole of the rest of the first half of the
double period, interspersing his monologue with occasional quick
questions. Most of the time is spent on the story of St Augustine, and the
Vikings.

T '. . . and now we are moving on to how it was – question 3
section B – how it was that the Church became very important in
people's lives, you see – it became important for the way people
lived; it taught them things, it helped the poor, helped the sick, it
was more or less the largest, most important part of the town or
village. O.K. Anyway, we will come on to that later . . . O.K., you
can start on section A then, section A, put the heading "The Spread
of Religion in England", leave yourself some space if you've got to
finish a question.'

There is a period of discussion with individual pupils. Three books
appear to be missing. The teacher leaves the form to get on while he goes
to look in the staffroom. Four minutes later he returns without the books.
The form has worked quietly while he was away. Most of the rest of the
lesson is given to the various 'see me' pupils and some initial problems
with the new worksheet.

Here is a lesson which is for the most part dominated by the teacher's talk
and by traditional class-teaching on the question-and-answer method; the
frame is rigid. The pupils are to finish the previous worksheet at the same
time, although they would have completed different amounts of it, and
there is some overlap by work 'to be done at home'. The following
comments represent the teacher's own analysis of the lesson written the
same evening.

Periods 7 and 8

Form sitting quietly when I arrived late. They went in alone and did not
stand when I entered (unusual for them).

No books given out – also unusual.

Exercise books to be distributed. Rest sat quietly while I did this. Made
a few comments; a bit more than I can with some forms who need books
immediately, but not as long as I would like to spend giving out books
and discussing work. Hence comments have to be general (finishing
work and filling up pages) when really need to be specific to a third of
form perhaps. Can give credit to few (e.g. Karrie: work excellent) but
careful not to always credit same people. A good effort by Desmond
shown as valid as good work by Steven, Richard, Beryl, etc. With band 1
and 2 lessons, I sometimes pick out pieces of work to read. Don't seem to

do it so much in mixed-ability; afraid of too often reading out same people's work, discouraging others. (Yet suspect I often read out only same few from band 1 or 2 forms.)

'Lesson proper'

Had to leave previous work-card; probably should have gone over it a bit before moving on, but forms often restless at doing 'same' work again. Some do not finish, but syllabus dictates time-scale for work-cards. Children do not like to leave things; switching from Saxon Village to Religion straight away. Yet kids adaptable; sooner carry on with work, I feel.

When discussing early religion, trying to bring out evil nature of Saxons, and bravery, foolishness of Augustine to go to Kent. Story/legend of how Augustine chosen (a teacher's hardy annual!). I wonder how many remember. Ask tomorrow. When discussing work, the continual problem of trying to involve everybody emerges. No matter how hard you try, some kids never answer. As they never like to, is it right to ask them? Simon answers because he knows; Richard because he is enthusiastic; Beryl and Barry because they like to get attention. Some occasionally answer (Mandy, Christine, Lennie, Colin, Klarisa, Nicholas, Judith) but a few never do unless asked (Judy, Sharon, Nicki, Paul, John). Should I 'involve' them by asking – what if they get it wrong? Is it better they sit there – Bernice rarely answers but her work is excellent – and so is Karrie's – and write when asked? Too often the same children answer, yet this also happens in band 1 and 2; perhaps you can allow half the form to write and half to discuss more often? As to religions, I could have used the blackboard more for names (Augustine, Ethelbert, Bertha, Pope Gregory) – (rarely use blackboard in first year) – and possibly get an example of a missionary today?

The dates 450–600 A.D.; 600–1200; very difficult – children rarely comprehend this sort of time scale. Perhaps a bit more help here by me rather than just saying about Romans, Saxons, Vikings, Normans?

When working a few of the boys made a bit of noise about the calendar dates, etc. They rarely talk – this is their way of talking in class. The girls worked quietly. Beryl asked questions (predictably), Claire gave a very good answer. Such an easy form to handle. I could sit there all lesson if I wanted. Do they act too quietly? They have enthusiasm, though, for things, and do take part in lots of activities. Got annoyed over my losing three books – justifiable – I would be cross with them if they lost theirs. They can do a great deal of good work but as today I sometimes wonder if they are demanding enough as a form.

This review by the teacher highlights some of the decision-making involved in the organization of learning in mixed-ability lessons, and also some of the 'management' constraints that the teacher is confronted with in this situation. He is committed to class-teaching to some extent, but is also aware of the difficulty of differential participation that this raises. When I discussed the lesson-transcript with him in an interview some time later, he commented:

> 'Well, one of my typical lessons, I suppose. I arrived late as I invariably do. A period of confusion which it always is at the beginning of my lessons, at least five minutes which is very bad. I realize I usually do this thing of giving out books and things. It is very difficult, isn't it? I mean it's fairly reasonable, I probably spoke a bit too much. I probably gave them too much information . . . probably the next lesson would have been slightly different because they would have been into it, perhaps the books wouldn't have had to be given out. They would have reached a different stage, wouldn't they? I mean, they are all kicking off at the same time, therefore you can talk to a class, can't you? When they're at different levels, that's when it's difficult . . . Probably next week I would have spent 10 minutes talking and then there would have been much more of them.'

This was a transition lesson when all the pupils are starting the new worksheet – 'they're all kicking off together'; it was not a time when 'they're at a different stage'.[22] Thus, class-teaching was deemed appropriate because all the pupils were on the same piece of work at the same time. This kind of thinking about the nature of the subject contributed to the feeling that mixed-ability was possible in History. Mr Wright explained:

> 'Unlike the Sciences it [History] does not involve conceptual learning. It's the sort of subject like other humanities which leads itself to a variety of learning situations . . . But so does Science, really, with all the super television materials.'

However, in History, as in Science, as we shall see, the innovation was implemented primarily in terms of the practical demands of the mixed-ability classroom, and various contextual constraints, rather than in terms of educational or social objectives.

The worksheet

For the first- and second-year mixed-ability forms, History was organized almost entirely round the series of worksheets designed by members of the department.[23] The worksheets were usually divided into sections – one or two basic sections which all pupils were expected to complete, and an extra optional section which was designed to cater for and 'extend' the 'faster' pupils after they had completed the basic sections (as was the case in the lesson-extract above).[24] In addition to the worksheets, each pupil would be provided with two or three textbooks.[25] The questions on the worksheets could be answered by reading from the textbooks and specific references were made in each question to the relevant pages in the books. The following example comes from a worksheet on 'Roman Towns'.

Section A

1. Copy in to your books the picture showing all the main parts of the Roman Town. Explain why the Roman Town was the size and shape you see above. Do you think it was a good idea to have straight streets and buildings in square blocks?
(Read page 63 'Living History'
page 31 'Roman Britain' (Sellman).)

Bernstein (1975 : 29) is highly critical of 'textbooks' and sees their use as epitomizing strong frames and strong classification, thus tacitly transmitting the ideology of the collection code. He argues that:

The textbook orders knowledge according to an explicit progression, it provides explicit criterion, it removes uncertainties and announces hierarchy.

Barnes (1976 : 317) argues that worksheets are more than anything else devices that teachers use to control what their pupils do, despite the fact that they are

often referred to in books as 'individual learning' or 'individualized instruction'. The name should not prevent us from understanding the sense in which the learning activities are 'individual'. Pupils work at their own pace; the fast worker can complete more calculations, fill more pages with writing, do an extra map or drawing. In no other sense is the work 'individual'; where there are options they are options for all.

While Barnes's comments do suggest that there is some weakening of framing over pacing inherent in the introduction of worksheets, he argues that in other respects framing remains strong. But even with regard to pacing, it is important to make the distinction between long-term and short-term control over the pacing of knowledge. Mixed-ability teaching based on worksheets often appears to give individual pupils more choice in the selection of questions and the speed of working on each worksheet, and sometimes between one worksheet and another, but in most cases it is the teacher who decides when one topic is to be discontinued and another 'begun', and the teacher who also controls the amount of knowledge to be 'got through' in the year. Many of the Beachside teachers maintained in interviews that 'teaching' in the conventional sense would be impossible in a situation where the pupils were given extensive control over the selection and pacing of their work.

The History worksheets were designed in a way very similar to those specifically criticized by Barnes (1976). Many questions merely demanded that pupils should 'rehearse' information which they had obtained from reading the relevant pages in the textbook provided. This demonstrates to the teacher that the pupil has achieved his set task. In the worksheet 'The Spread of Religion in England' which consisted of a total of 11 questions, questions 1, 3, 4, 7 and 8 all required the pupil to read and summarize or repeat information taken from the textbooks being used. As Barnes points out, 'It places little pressure on the pupils to make their learning explicit to themselves'. In addition, questions 10 and 11 were concerned with a similar exercise, but using a wider range of source-books, and numbers 5 and 6 were basically drawing exercises which could be copied from textbook illustrations. Only questions 2 and 9 appeared to call upon more creative skills on the pupils' part (many pupils did not get as far as question 9 or did not choose to do it).

Despite the introduction of worksheets, therefore, in History the social and intellectual hierarchy of teachers as the controllers, transmitters and producers of knowledge and pupils as the consumers remained basically intact.

The worksheet system continued to have the support of the full-time members of the History department, but the strengths and weaknesses of the sheets and the possibility of other methods were discussed. However, most alternatives to the use of worksheets tended only to objectify the constraints within which the teachers' views of mixed-ability teaching methods were set. Mr Card explained:

> 'I feel that what we have done is that we have reappraised as we've gone along, we haven't just done worksheets and left it. We've not only reappraised the worksheets at History meetings, we've also discussed how they've come across and how we can improve them. And certainly in the third year, there's been much more flexibility and we haven't necessarily used worksheets for all the topics. We've devised what we're going to do and talked over some ideas and we'll do it our own way and use whatever we want to use . . . but no one has had the time, or whatever, to sit down and actually plan and say, "We must use this and this, and we've got all these resources available." We could use drama, ideally, but is the room you're in suitable? You know, it's pathetic things like this. It seems pathetic on the surface but you've got the hassle of changing rooms and organizing timetable changes. You've only got the kids for a double lesson a week, and there's a certain amount of work we've got to get through. In the third year, for example, for them to take their exams and choose their options. So if I spend a month and say,

"Well, I'm going to scrap this and do a bit of drama and make it more interesting", which it probably would be – if all the kids muck up their exams and get low marks, where do I stand then? You know, you've always got this dilemma. On the one hand you're torn to do something, on the other you've got certain commitments to the school philosophy. It's a dilemma which is very difficult to solve, probably not solvable unless you say, well I'm going to damn the exams and we're going to go our own way.'

Here is a situation where, on the one hand, the teacher is confronted with what he perceives to be the demands and problems of mixed-ability teaching, and, on the other, the field of constraints within which he is obliged to operate, such as the practical difficulties of organizing alternative teaching-methods, the lack of time to organize and prepare resources, the limitations of time in terms of 'a certain amount of work to get through', and, closely linked to this, the demands of the parents and the pupils, which the school philosophy requires be met, that he should produce an acceptable level of academic excellence in terms of examination results.

In relation to their analysis of the organization of learning in the progressive primary classroom, Sharp and Green (1976 : 218) make the point:

We have tried to show how these practices are a function of the constraints both ideological and material which influence the practice of the individual teacher. Far from the stratification system being a mere product of interaction patterns at the micro-level, we have suggested that such interactions are socially structured by the wide context of which they are a part of whose major features they reflect and in turn reproduce.

Clearly, it is important to view mixed-ability in the same way. The previous chapter demonstrated now ideological constraints upon the practice of the individual teacher contributed to the emergence of certain views of forms of grouping and methods that are 'necessary' for effective teaching. In this case, the material and physical constraints are also apparent.

Apart from the four full-time members of the History department there was one part-time member, Mr Daniel, who did not find himself in sympathy with the department's approach to mixed-ability teaching. He explained:

'My understanding of mixed-ability teaching is not the same as the rest of the department, having worked in a middle school and having had groups working on different topics. There was no suggestion of a rotation system of different work-cards, so you can have low-ability groups and faster groups or mixed groups. There was no idea that we should move away from class-teaching, it's not mixed-ability, it's just class-teaching with a wide ability range . . . I don't like these worksheets.'

From his middle-school experience, Mr Daniel brought to bear on the mixed-ability classroom a different set of views of what was important and what was possible; he tended to find himself less constrained by the expectation of appropriate ways of working which clearly limited the practice of the other members of the department.

But even among the full-time History teachers there was a range of ways of organizing learning in the classroom subsumed within the notion of 'using worksheets'. The differences between the teachers can be explained in two dimensions, one relating to the extent of the control the teacher exerted over the organization and pacing of classroom knowledge, and the other relating to the extent of the teachers' control over the pupils' conditions of learning. The pupils experience conditions of learning ranging from *socialized* to *individualized*. The relationship between the two dimensions is shown in figure 10. Mr Foot is most easily placed, in that he operates rules of behaviour in the classroom which totally individualize the pupils' learning, and although he does not 'class-teach', there is a strict

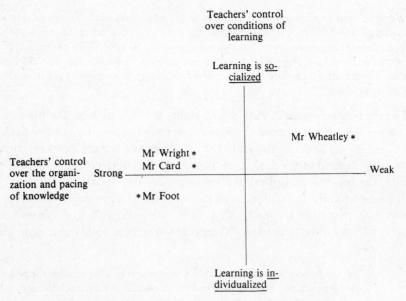

Figure. 10. Variations in the History teachers' use of worksheets

monitoring of speed of work. Mr Card and Mr Wright can be positioned together on the diagram. They 'class-teach' and monitor their pupils' speed of work quite closely, both of which factors have implications for the pupils' conditions of learning, and for the teachers' control over the pacing and organization of knowledge. However, Mr Card and Mr Wright do allow conversation and interaction between pupils when they are working through worksheets, thus allowing for socialized conditions of learning, at least during these phases of lessons. Mr Wheatley is different again. He does not 'class-teach', nor does he closely control the pupils' speed of work, and he allows the pupils to interact while working. Thus his control over the pacing and organization of knowledge is weak, and conditions of learning in his lessons are socialized.

The term 'using worksheets' thus explains and describes a variety of different classroom practices and ways of organizing learning, and therefore encompasses a range of different kinds of learning experience on the pupils' part.

English (23 mixed-ability lessons observed)

In several ways the English department is very difficult to deal with here. Because of their role in the vanguard of the change to mixed-ability and the amount of discussion and preparation that went on in the department before mixed-ability was accepted by the rest of the staff, a consideration of methods before and after the innovation is less realistic than in other departments.

> 'In English we have been preparing for this for several years, in fact, so we felt there was no need to change what we were doing then.'
> (English teacher)

English lessons, too, are less obviously concerned with the transmission of a subject knowledge. The English lessons observed varied more in format and style than any other subject, and therefore the presentation of a typical or representative lesson is more difficult.

It was apparent from lesson observation that English teachers addressed their forms as a whole less than teachers in any other subject did. Although each form would normally experience one oral lesson each week, most of the time the pupils were working on their own or in small groups. One period each week was devoted to reading individually, and usually one other was spent on writing. Each pupil was usually involved in writing a long story or project which would last several weeks, to which time could be devoted in lessons either by all the pupils as a group or when pupils had finished work individually and had time on their hands. The head of department's maxim was:

'I always make sure that they have twenty times more work to do than they can possibly finish.'

In group-work lessons, small groups of four or five pupils were involved in collaborative exercises – writing a play and producing a magazine, for example. In other lessons, the teacher might produce some stimulus for the form as a whole, such as a poem, a story, a film, a television programme or a piece of music, which the pupils were then to use as a basis for their own stories or poems. I also observed mixed-ability lessons involving discussions, the reading of a story by the teacher, the reading of a play by the whole form, and grammar work.

The policy of the department was clear and the approach of all the staff was fairly uniform. The techniques and rationale behind particular exercises and methods were frequently discussed at departmental meetings, and it was the only department to produce 'papers' for its members, on such topics as 'listening' and 'the English Syllabus'. In the latter document, written by the deputy head of department, it says:

> Professor M. A. K. Halliday opens an article entitled 'Linguistics and the teaching of English' with these words: 'There is probably no subject in the curriculum whose aims are so often formulated as are those of English language, yet they remain by and large ill-defined, controversial and obscure.' I would suggest one of the reasons for this is that English has little definite subject matter, as has Mathematics, Physics or History, for instance. In most subjects on the curriculum there is a body of knowledge which seems to lie out there, separate and distinct from the teacher and pupils, whereas in English we are frequently dealing with ways of apprehending the world. Reading *Macbeth* we struggle with notions of evil, greed, corruption, ambition, whereas reading a Graham Greene novel we are in the world of a loser, of a weak, disillusioned, frightened man. In other lessons children write about why they keep rabbits or describe a cold autumn day. As English teachers, the world – its people, books, music, poetry, newspapers – seems to be our stage and yet we long for coherence, surety, a sense that we are achieving something. Literature seems to offer a basis for much of our work. From the study of the novel can come comprehension exercises, personal writing, unstructured talk and formal discussions. I'm already stating the sorts of things that English teachers do.

Although, in comparison with most other curriculum subjects, English does lack a definite subject matter, the excerpt above also demonstrates the extent to which there is a body of knowledge which the teacher is concerned to transmit to his pupils. Apart from the skills upon which the department concentrates – reading, working, listening and talking – there is also a body of received knowledge, consisting of interpretations of literature, that the English teacher is concerned to impart to his pupils. The 'notions of evil, greed, corruption and ambition' in regard to *Macbeth* and 'the world of a loser, of a weak, disillusioned, frightened man' in regard to Graham Greene, are examples.

Also, despite the concentration upon individual work and production, the teacher still operates considerable control over the pacing of knowledge, such as it is; sets of books must be circulated between forms, stories must be finished ready for the next project, etc. However, the range of options available to pupils in terms of what, and, to some extent, how they write, read or say things, is wide. Compared with other subjects, then, the frame is weaker in many of its aspects.

Change in teaching-methods in relation to interpretations of the mixed-ability innovation

The links which exist between subject sub-cultures, teacher perspectives and adaptation to mixed-ability teaching should now be clearer. To a great extent behavioural changes at the classroom level can be related to support for the innovation during the period of discussion and debate, and lack of change can be related to opposition to the innovation and/or membership of an *academic* subject sub-culture. The teachers' actions in implementing the innovation may be understood in terms of their interpretation of it.

This may be illustrated by taking the continuum of 'perspectives' discussed in the previous chapter, and relating the modal positions on it to the overall degree of behavioural change in the implementation of mixed-ability (in the main curriculum subjects) during its first year (see figure 11). Obviously, the relative positions on the continuum would have to be changed over time; for example, the position of Mathematics would have to be changed in the light of the introduction of their commercial work-card system for second-year pupils in year 3 of the innovation.

As with the teachers' attitudes to mixed-ability, observed in the previous chapter, there are variations within, as well as between, subjects in the degree of change of method in the classroom, although the pattern of variation is not the same in each subject, as indicated in the lesson sample. Certain subjects were marked by different degrees of uniformity; Maths and French particularly, and the Sciences and English to a great extent also,

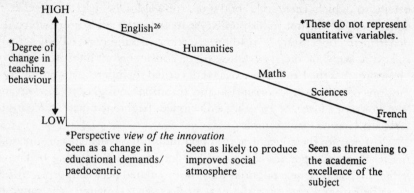

Figure 11. Change in teaching methods from those used with banded classes

tended to produce little variation in classroom method, but there was a great deal of variation in Geography and, to an extent, History. This pattern of scatter across the subjects is similar to that noted by Barnes (1976: 143) in relation to teachers' attitudes to written work and the position of different subjects on the continuum of methodology from transmission to interpretation modes.[27] He says:

It should be noted that teachers of Science and of Languages were not only nearest to the Transmission end of the scale but also were more homogeneous in their views than were teachers of any other subjects.[28] In effect specialism in a Science or in a Language seemed to place stronger constraints upon teachers than did specialism in other subjects. (The widest scatter was in Geography, which reminds me that it is an Arts subject in some universities and a Science subject in others.)

English teachers were firmly entrenched nearest to the interpretation end of the scale in Barnes's survey. Barnes goes on to make a further observation on the results of his survey, which is not unrelated to the findings of this study.

In both Science and Languages most teachers perceive themselves to have access to coherent and public bodies of knowledge which their pupils' everyday experience does not give them access to. Most English teachers do not believe themselves to hold a unique body of knowledge which is out of their pupils' reach, but see themselves as helping pupils to extend and refine the knowledge and skills they use in everyday life. Teachers of History, Geography and especially religious education are in a more ambiguous and intermediate position.

Barnes's findings, then, match very closely with the pattern of attitudes evident in the present study. And in general terms the distribution of support for the mixed-ability innovation and the willingness to change teaching methods here can be seen to be related to the subject-orientations discovered by Barnes.

Furthermore, it should be recognized that the *conditions of change* are not the same for each department, either conceptually or materially. The kind of conceptual leap involved in changing the way a subject is defined is clearly not of the same magnitude for all departments. As Eraut (forthcoming : 17) points out, what is viewed as an innovation in one context may well be considered as traditional practice in another.

Given a single institution there is a considerable variation. Differences in subject matter, differences in tradition, and differences in personnel all make it probable that many problems of teaching and learning will be specific rather than general.

But as Sharp and Green (1976) stress, it is necessary to view teachers' practices in the classroom, not as related simply to an ideological perspective, but also to the field of determinants in which that ideology is located. Thus, apart from the differences in conceptual problems, the expenditure of energy and the financial costs involved in changing are not the same for all departments. The Science departments were constrained to a much greater extent than History or English in these respects. It is important, therefore, that the relationship between teachers' classroom practices and the meanings attributed by them to the innovation should not be viewed simplistically or deterministically. When confronted with problems to solve in the organization of learning in the classroom, it is not necessarily the most committed innovators who provide the 'solutions', as the cases of Biology and Mathematics indicate.

Having taken into account the variations in the extent of change in classroom practice and the weakening of lesson-frames, I want to return briefly to consider those cases where there does appear to have been a weakening of frame through the introduction of the use of worksheets. However, even in these 'worksheet classrooms' the teacher in most cases still retains the major part of the responsibility for the pacing and organization of knowledge, flexibility for the pupils normally only existing between points in time specified by the teacher for 'covering' the work. In addition, the pupils' speed of working is monitored by the teacher even within these limits – 'I expect you to finish question 4 today', etc. And there is certainly little difference between the pupils' experience of 'learning' from transmission by teacher and from transmission by textbook; he still occupies a passive role as receiver. In most subjects, the worksheet method represents a 'socially-managed symbolic imagery' of mixed-ability teaching. It symbolizes a change in teaching method 'irrespective of the effects of such changes on the pupils' and teachers' constructions of school reality' (A. Hargreaves 1976 : 6).[29] Bernstein (1971 : 59) also highlights the possibility of 'a change in organizational style *without* there being any marked change in the education knowledge code'.

Certainly, inasmuch as *framing* represents a set of principles in the organization of knowledge, which are rooted in the meanings held by teachers and the interactions in which they are involved, it cannot be expected that the dominant pedagogy will be changed while the teachers' view of the classroom, definition of role, and attitudes to subject remain the same. As Trump (1967 : 23) argues:

> Obviously, if teachers continue to talk the same way, make the same types of assignments, question students in class in the usual manner, give similar kinds of tests, and so on, the results will be practically the same even though superficial changes occur in the educational setting and the enjoyment teachers get from the new approaches.

I shall return to the importance of the persistence of academic subject sub-cultures and particular kinds of pedagogy and classroom organization in the following chapters (see p. 267 and pp. 286–7).

The teachers' evaluation of mixed-ability

A clear restatement of the attitudes and commitments of the Beachside teachers to mixed-ability is to be found in their evaluation of mixed-ability teaching in practice during its first three years. The following comments, made in staff meetings and in interviews with me, clearly demonstrate that the issues discussed earlier in relation to the two major teacher-perspectives continue to dominate the categories of meaning which the teachers use to account for the innovation. The two major concerns reflected here are the improvement in 'social atmosphere' – that is to say, a general improvement in the state of teacher-pupil relationships in general, and control-relationships in particular – and worries about the impact of teaching in mixed-ability groups upon the levels of academic performance achieved. Both concerns are expressed in these comments made by the head of History in a staff meeting.

> 'Attitude to work reveals a great improvement for all groups. This is probably due to the worksheet method being used, rather than the mixture of ability, though it is an advantage to the teacher having a

smaller group of less well-motivated pupils in each form than used to exist in bands 2 and 3. The positive-minded tend to dominate the situation . . . In the attainment of the brightest pupils there has been no perceptible difference, for the average pupils their attainment is higher with mixed-ability; of the lowest ability a very few may be losing out in a mixed-ability form.'

But unlike many other evaluations, the head of History's remarks were concerned with the impact of mixed-ability grouping across the whole ability-range, rather than concentrating just upon 'the brighter ones'.

'We have had mixed-ability for some time in the sense that we do individual teaching. There has not been much difference in practicals but in theory work we have trouble in lessons to keep up the slower and stretch the brighter. But socially it's a very good thing: bands are trouble.'

(Head of department, Home Economics, Year 2, staff meeting)

'The standards are higher and the groups pleasanter, the brighter ones bring on the others.'

(Head of department, Games, Year 2, staff meeting)

'All groups have achieved the same level of ability.'

(Technical Studies teacher, Year 1, staff meeting)

'There is very little difference in attainment in the first year, although more reinforcement is needed for memory work.'

(Head of Chemistry, Year 1, staff meeting)

'In attainment the best appear to be less good, the worst probably not so bad in comparison with last year.'

(Head of department, Geography, Year 1, heads of department meeting)

'The ones who would have been on band 1 if we had one have attained as much as last year's band 1 classes.'

(Head of department, French, Year 1, staff meeting)

But in many evaluations, improvements in pupils' behaviour were to the fore.

The attitude to staff is much better.'

(Chemistry teacher, Year 2, interview)

'The main gain has been a much better social situation; you don't get the band 2, end-of-second-year/beginning-of-third-year "I-don't-want-to-know" group.'

(Technical Studies teacher, Year 3, interview)

'Music is a peculiar subject but mixed-ability is better to work with. There is an improvement in attitude to practical work and much greater involvement.'

(Head of department, Music, Year 2, staff meeting)

'Academic and artistic ability are not the same, so we have always had mixed-ability forms . . . so we have not had to make changes, but the social advantages have been obvious. It has created a better atmosphere in which to exchange ideas.'

(Head of department, Art, Year 2, staff meeting)

'The attitude of acceptance is very noticeable. Anti-social behaviour is still there, but it seems to spread less easily due to the mixture of pupils.'

(Physics teacher, Year 1, interview)

'This year more than last year, a very pleasant atmosphere. All can contribute to discussion and even the less able are willing to join in, in this set-up. I find them lively and co-operative.'

(Geography teacher, Year 2, interview)

'Economics is now mixed-ability for O-level/C.S.E. in the fourth year and we find things more pleasant.'

(Economics teacher, Year 2, staff meeting)

'You will never get good teaching when you have bad discipline and in this mixed-ability system we don't have bad discipline. The majority of children won't let the one or two be a nuisance.'

(Year tutor, Year 2, staff meeting)

The only note of reservation regarding the success of the innovation remains in the continuing concern of some staff 'that the brighter ones are not being stretched', but these qualms never threatened the continuance of the mixed-ability grouping during the period of the study.

It is clear that the idealist perspective was not to the fore in the teachers' evaluation of mixed-ability. Indeed, the idealist vocabulary of child-centred objectives for mixed-ability was not part of the commonly-accepted vocabulary of motives. (Discussion of these issues simply did not take place in the later staff meetings, and the expression of such views tended to be limited to statements made by particular members of staff.)

It would appear from these comments that the implementation of the innovation did not in itself produce resistance as suggested by Gross, Giaquinta and Bernstein (1970); indeed, as we have seen, in some cases, such as Maths, the result was quite the reverse. Overall, it may be seen from the chronology of the innovation that the proportion of 'resisters' among the staff remained the same as, or was reduced from, the level prior to the implementation. In part, this was facilitated by the open and undirected nature of the implementation, which allowed for the unproblematic accommodation of existing teaching practices for those teachers who did not interpret the innovation in terms of a radical reconstitution of educational practice. For these teachers the implementation would only have been problematic if the accommodation of existing practices had been made impossible. As we have seen, for most of the teachers the success of the innovation was seen in terms of the impact of the organizational change on the behaviour of the pupils, rather than a result of changes in teaching methods.[30]

Summary

Studies of educational innovation have failed, in general to take account either of the perspectives of the teachers who are involved, or the processes of social interaction through which the meanings of an innovation are exchanged and negotiated. Traditionally, studies of innovation have tended to recognize only objective definitions of change, and to ignore the social processes through which change is inter-subjectively created, defined, and sustained, and through which its meaning is collectively negotiated. However, in this and the previous chapter I have attempted to account for the negotiation of the meaning of the mixed-ability innovation among the teachers concerned.

In the absence of an agreed or imposed 'mandate' of change, the teachers at Beachside were free to attribute their own categories of meaning to the innovation. The minimum of ideological content to the innovation, apart from the concerns of the small minority of *idealist* teachers, allowed for the sublimation of a range of adherence and opposition. Furthermore, the absence of a mandate of change also meant that the teachers were not obliged to change their teaching methods. Indeed, in some respects constraints inherent in the culture and ethos of the school militated against drastic changes in the organization of learning in the classroom.

When the actor's interpretations, as well as external criteria of analysis, *are* taken into account in the consideration of changes in teaching methods, two different views of the nature of change become apparent. Many of the Beachside teachers felt that they *had* achieved a substantial change in teaching methods from those used in teaching banded classes, and in some subjects, in terms of some aspects of classroom organization, this was certainly true. However, analytically, there is little evidence of a shift away from a didactic pedagogy of transmission. But while this analysis concerned itself with change as *revolution*, consisting of an immediate and fundamental reconstruction of teaching methods, it is clear that the teachers' view of change is essentially *gradualist* and 'improving'. Indeed, when the system of constraints which impinge upon the teachers' practice is taken into consideration, the possibilities for revolutionary change in teaching methods are seen to be very limited. Both perspectives are useful, and indeed necessary, in the analysis of changes in teachers' practices. A model based entirely upon a conception of change-as-revolution, would certainly lack relevance and meaning as far as teachers are concerned.

Almost all available studies of ability-grouping in schools have concerned themselves exclusively with the measurable impact of form of grouping on achievement.[31] The research has been predominantly descriptive, with little attempt to *explain* changes in achievement and, as Dahllof (1971) suggests, the characteristics of the actual teaching-process, which may be regarded as an intervening variable, have been ignored. In this chapter I have attempted to indicate the importance of taking into account the actual teaching-process in understanding the introduction of mixed-ability grouping as an innovation. In the following chapter, I will examine and attempt to explain the impact of the actual teaching-process, in the mixed-ability context, on aspects of the pupils' experience of schooling. Using material from two case-study forms, the mixed-ability system will be compared with the banded system.

8   Mixed-ability and banding compared

This chapter will attempt to establish a comparison, as far as this is possible, between the case-study banded forms, described and analysed in chapters 2, 3 and 4, and two mixed-ability case-study forms. (To avoid repetition of similar material, most of the data presented in the body of the text will in fact refer to just one of these form groups, 2DY.) Any comparisons in natural situations are difficult to control and justify, and this is no exception. Indeed, there are a number of complicating factors which limit the range of possible comparisons, some of which derive from changes related to the introduction of mixed-ability itself and some of which derive from problems of the design of the study. First, in terms of the changes related to mixed-ability, the obvious point is that the comparison between banded and mixed-ability forms is a comparison between unlikes. By definition the make-up of the mixed-ability forms will be different in terms of social class composition, ability range, etc. In addition, there were a number of organizational and pedagogic adaptations accompanying the introduction of mixed-ability which produced differences in the pupils' experiences in the classroom, such as changes in the report system, introduction of worksheets and changes in syllabuses; to a great extent also, the mixed-ability forms dealt with here were taught by different teachers from those who taught the banded forms.[1] Secondly, in terms of the design of the study, there were a number of differences in the collection of data from the banded and from the mixed-ability forms. Although the methodology and techniques of data collection employed were almost the same, the career coverage of the two cohorts was different. As pointed out in the introduction, my field work began as the first mixed-ability cohort were in their first year; thus the period of full-time field work covered the first- and second-year career of the mixed-ability cohort, and the second- and third-year careers of the banded cohort, although *some* material of the mixed-ability cohort's third year was collected.

As indicated in chapter 2, the data from the first-year experiences of the

239

banded forms are extremely limited and mostly retrospective. As a result, the bulk of comparative material must necessarily be drawn from the second year of both cohorts.[2]

The methods of data collection for the mixed-ability forms were basically the same as those employed for the banded forms. Once again, classroom observation, sociometric questionnaires, and interviewing were used. During the two-year period of intensive field work I interviewed all but four of the original members of both mixed-ability case-study forms;[3] the pupils filled in eight questionnaires for me – five sociometric, one which asked about social life out of the school, one concerned with attitudes towards and 'involvement in school', and a Guess-Who-Test (see p. 297 n. 14). I also observed the forms in lessons in eight different subjects as well as in other structured and unstructured situations. Again, as with the banded forms, I was often able to attend pastoral periods and the form teachers made a point of keeping me up-to-date with events, like the break-up and make-up of friendships, hostility between groups in the forms, the academic attainments of the pupils, any 'trouble' they got into, and illnesses and absences. After several months of observation, as it became apparent that there were enormous similarities between the two mixed-ability forms, I began to concentrate more on one form, 1DY, and data from this form will be the prime source of comparison in this chapter. But, as in the banded cohort, I also observed all the other mixed-ability forms in the year at least twice and collected some data across the whole year-group.

Mixed-ability grouping

As demonstrated in the previous chapters, the majority of staff in favour of the introduction of mixed-ability supported it in the hope that it would bring about an improvement in social atmosphere, and, as we have seen from the teachers' own evaluation of the mixed-ability situation, this was achieved (see pp. 235–6). One aim in this chapter will be to investigate the behavioural differences between the banded and mixed-ability pupils. But a second motive for supporting mixed-ability grouping, clearly represented in the headmaster's view of comprehensive education, was that its introduction would bring about a greater degree of friendship and co-operation between pupils of different backgrounds, talents and abilities. Thus, the bases of friendship-choice and the extent of social mixing will also be compared between the two methods of grouping. Finally, de-streaming has also come to be regarded, mainly as a result of negative reasoning from the amount of research that has shown the deleterious influence of streaming, as a solution to the 'problems' of social selection and social inequality in schooling. Thus a school which introduces mixed-ability may come to be seen as moving towards a 'fairer' system of education. Yates (1966 : 130), for instance, argues in his review of research on ability-grouping that

> One of the reasons why research has not served to settle or even to diminish the controversies that centre around some grouping practices is because the differences of view involved are not entirely or even mainly about the measurable educational consequences of these practices. The sharpest conflicts would seem to be about the more far-reaching influences that grouping procedures . . . can exert on the structure of society as a whole, and on the distribution within it of privileges and opportunities.

Julienne Ford (1969 : 134) concluded from her study of social justice and comprehensive education that

> If we are to overcome the effects of early selection then we must abolish streaming in the comprehensive schools. For this form of selection has all the implications and all the consequences of segregation into separate schools.

There was a small number of the staff at Beachside who advocated mixed-ability on these grounds (see pp. 189–90), and they were among the prime movers in the introduction of mixed-ability. Thus, the processes of social selection and the social distribution of success and failure will also be compared between the two methods of grouping.

Making mixed-ability

The first-year cohort of 1973–4 was divided into twelve form-groups – ten parallel forms of mixed-ability,[4] and two remedial forms. Any school introducing mixed-ability for the first time is faced with the problem of how their mixed-ability groups should be created. A whole range of possible methods of allocation exists, including random selection, alphabetic selection, and testing. Beachside adopted a scheme using in effect the same procedure as was employed for the allocation of pupils to bands – based on primary-schoolteachers' recommendations. In this case, the primary-school recommendations were used to ensure an equitable distribution of ability in each form-group, so that they would be 'truly mixed-ability' and parallel. The primary-school headmasters were asked to identify five categories of pupils: the remedials, those considered to be in need of special teaching and/or a special environment, who were allocated to separate forms; the handful of 'exceptionally bright pupils', one or two

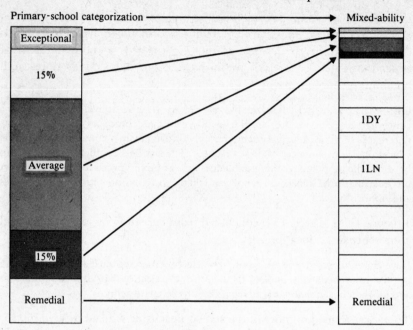

Figure 12. The allocation of pupils to mixed-ability form groups

of whom were allocated to each mixed-ability form; the remaining top 15 per cent of ability and bottom 15 per cent of ability; and the remaining pupils – approximately 50–55 per cent in the middle, the 'average'. Pupils from each of these categories were then allocated proportionally to each mixed-ability form (see figure 12).

Mixed-ability and pupil behaviour

The point made time and time again by the teachers in their evaluation of the mixed-ability system is that an anti-school sub-culture does not emerge. The anti-school groups in the band 2 forms produced considerable problems of control for almost all teachers, and a working atmosphere in lessons which most of the staff disliked. It was clear from observations, interviews, and questionnaire material concerning the mixed-ability forms in their first and second year that no such vociferous anti-school culture existed. That is not to say that there were no groups of pupils with anti-school attitudes; there were. Nor do I intend to suggest that there were no problems of misbehaviour in lessons; there were. But the size and in-

. fluence of the anti-school groups and the scale of their misbehaviour did not compare at all with the band 2 forms. Pupils in the mixed-ability forms were rarely disruptive.[5] One indication of the differences between the banded and mixed-ability cohorts in this respect is available from the comparison of the number of detentions given, although, as noted previously, official detention statistics represent only a partial reflection of 'punishable offences'.

Taking an equivalent period of $2\frac{1}{2}$ terms in the second year for both cohorts, the overall difference in the numbers of detentions received is considerable (see table 8.1). In total, the banded forms received almost three times as many detentions over the same period of time. And, as noted in the table, even in those mixed-ability forms where the number of detentions received is much higher than average, the majority can be traced to one or two individual pupils. In a similar way to the development of reputations for 'problem forms' in the banded context, in the mixed-ability grouping individuals tended to develop reputations as 'problem pupils'. However, when confronted with just one or two 'problem pupils' rather than with groups of such pupils most teachers found themselves able to

Table 8.1. *Comparison of detentions received by banded and mixed-ability forms over an equivalent period of their school careers*

	Banded forms			Mixed-ability forms		
Band 1	2CU	13	(11 times one boy)	2BA	3	(28 times two boys) (11 times one boy)
	2FT	2		2BC	31	
	2ST	9		2CD	0	
	2GD	2		2DE	15	
Band 2	2WX	39		2DY	3	(all Sam's)[6]
	2BH	19		2FG	5	
	2TA	108		2GH	5	
	2LF	31		2LN	0	
Band 3	2UD	8		2JK	0	
	2ED (R)	2		2KL	12(7.4)	
				2(R)	16[a]	
Total		243			90	
Overall	24.3 per form 0.85 per pupil			8.81 per form 0.30 per pupil		

[a] There was only one remedial form in the second year.

maintain control in the classroom. (I shall return to this point later.) It would be a distortion, however, simply to compare the 'improved' situation in the mixed-ability forms, with the band 2 'problem forms'. If the average number of detentions per pupil in the mixed-ability forms (excluding remedials) is compared with that for the band 1 forms, the average for the mixed-ability forms is very similar, 0.28 per pupil as against 0.24 per pupil. Indeed, this similarity in the number of detentions received reflects a number of similarities in social organization between the band 1 forms and the mixed-ability forms.

One of the notable similarities between the band 1 forms and the mixed-ability forms is that although both were dominated by pupils of a pro-school orientation, both also contained small groups, usually of boys, which could be described as incipient anti-school groups (see pp. 84–6). The incipient anti-school group in 2DY contained four boys:[7]

	Father's occupations	Social class
Paul	Roundsman	IV
Colin	Surveyor	I
Desmond	Van driver	IIIM
Kevin	Shopkeeper	II

These boys were noisy in lessons, and were often a 'nuisance' to staff. They tended to sit together at the back of the room talking whenever the teacher's attention was elsewhere or when the form was meant to be working individually. Their talk was invariably about football; they were all fanatical players and supporters. They organized a form game that took place at lunch time when the weather permitted, and gradually during the first year, football even came to take over the way they dressed. Their uniform jackets were replaced by track-suit tops, and school shoes by colourful training-boots; they each carried kit-bags for their books and 'equipment', adorned with the names and crests of their favourite teams. They usually spent the pastoral periods poring over football books and magazines, and exchanging programmes.

In the sociometric questionnaires, Paul and Colin reciprocated best-friend choices: they were the core of the group; there were occasions when one of the others, Desmond and Kevin, was out of favour. Paul and Colin had both attended Iron Road Primary school and were friends there. Desmond and Kevin had both attended North Beachside, and they too were friends already. None of the group was successful academically and they were generally poorly-perceived by their teachers. As the year wore on they also became less popular with their form mates. Steven, a pro-school boy in the form, said of them:

> 'They don't want to work, they just want to muck around and play games all day long – and they try to stop other people from working – it's showing off, really.'

One teacher described Paul in this way:

> 'He is often noisy in lessons, especially when he knows that the teacher will let him get away with it; his work is often left incomplete or not done at all; he does not pay attention and never answers questions voluntarily.'

Paul was mentioned 45 times in the Guess-Who-Test, but only 5 times in 'complimentary' categories. He was named 9 times as fitting the description, 'this person is immature and behaves in a silly way in lessons', 10 times for 'this one is a bully. He is always picking on others and annoying them', and 17 times for 'this person is badly behaved in lessons and is often being told off by the teachers'. Colin is mentioned 18 times in the Guess-Who-Test, including 9 times as 'badly behaved' and 4 times as 'amusing'.

This group of boys, even at an early stage in their secondary-school careers, demonstrated the embryonic characteristics of the anti-school pupils identified in previous chapters. They had little or no interest in their schoolwork and demonstrated a lack of identification with the norms and values of the school in their attitude to teachers and lessons. Their Maths teacher predicted that, 'That group is going to cause trouble higher up the school'. In questionnaires they wrote:

> *Colin* 'When a lesson is boring I play around.'
> 'History is my favourite lesson because you draw good pictures.'
> *Paul* 'I sit down and don't listen and mess around.'
> 'Teachers are horrible and too strict.'
> *Kevin* 'Games and woodwork are my favourite lessons.'
> *Desmond* 'When the teacher tells me my work is bad I don't mind.'
> 'Teachers are nuts.'

The group was recognized by the teachers and their classmates, and by themselves, as lacking many of the qualities valued by the school and which seem so necessary to success at school.

A further illustration of the attitudes of the group is afforded by the following extracts from interviews:

> *Kevin* 'We don't like French and Maths.'
> *S. B.* 'Why?'

Paul 'Well, French is boring 'cos you don't need it when you grow up.'

Colin 'Maths on Wednesday we have an hour and a half and it's so boring.'

Desmond 'We need it, though, don't we, really?'

S. B. 'What do you do when you get bored?'

Colin 'Go to sleep or we just talk about our cricket games but normally we get told off and we get lines and get moved.'

Paul 'Like in the Maths lesson we're always mucking around.'

Kevin 'I like it my last lesson on a Friday afternoon because I look forward to my weekend.'

Colin 'Mm! Football and cricket.'

Paul 'Yes, I do as well.'

S. B. 'What do you think of your teachers?'

Kevin 'Some are all right.'

Colin 'Oh, Mr Jones [Music], he's good fun, you can muck around with him and he takes a joke.'

Paul 'Not like Mrs Daly – you always have to say, "Yes, Mrs Daly", all the time, and you always have to go up to her instead of her coming down to us.'

S. B. 'What happens when you've got a new teacher?'

Desmond 'Well, you've got to try them out. In the first lesson we are good to see what they're like, and then we get bad over time, pushing and hitting and that!'

S. B. 'What do you think of the people in your form?'

Colin 'They're all right.'

Paul 'We don't get on very well with Richard.'

Kevin 'Oh, we do now.'

Paul 'June Smith, we don't get on with her . . . What I don't like about this school is when we first come to the school we're the naughty ones, so that they know we're the naughty group. So that if there's a load of noise, they always pick on us, don't they, the teachers in this school.'

Colin 'Like we've got split up now in Maths, in't we?'

Desmond 'Richard, Steve, Barry and Michael, they all go together.'

S. B. 'What are they like, then?'

Paul 'June Smith, she's troublemaker.'

Colin 'And us four, we're a group, and George, he acts out to be tough and he smokes but I don't think he is.'

Paul 'Karrie, Celia and Nicki, they're all copycats.'

Kevin 'Mothers' meeting kind of, they're always drawing on the back of their books.'

Colin 'Always making flashy pictures.'

S. B. 'What about your work?'

Desmond 'We're all about the same – well, Keith's untidy, but we're all about a quarter from the bottom.'

Paul 'But what I'm mainly good at is sport, in'it?'

S. B. 'What are you going to do when you leave school?'

Colin 'When I'm sixteen I am going to a P.E. college to be a Games Master.'

Paul 'I want to be a Policeman or join the Navy or something like that. But I'd love to be a milkman because I've been with the milkman for three years and I know everything about it and it's good and it's a lot of fun. But I know everyone laughs and says it's not a very good job. There's no career in it, is there?'

Colin 'My mum thinks I'm going to be a Chef but I don't say anything and I'm going to be a Sports Master. My dad was going to be a Sports Master.'

Desmond 'Well, I want to leave when I'm sixteen. I want to go in the Navy. You see the world and you have lots of fun and you've got money to go out with.'

Kevin 'Well, I don't really know, it depends what A-level I get.'

Paul 'There's one thing I'd love to be but I know I won't and that's a footballer.'

As with the anti-school groups in the banded forms, these boys tended to find most lessons 'boring' and they preferred 'mucking around'. It is also evident that they shared some antipathy towards other members of the forms who were 'brainy', especially the girls who were 'copycats'. But unlike the anti-school groups in the banded classroom, these boys were not alienated from all aspects of school; they were all particularly involved in sports and competed strongly to get in the football, cricket, basketball and athletics teams. Paul and Colin in particular represented the school in a number of sports in first-, second- and third-year teams. Another indication of the difference between these boys and the band 2 anti-school pupils is in a continued, if unenthusiastic, commitment to schoolwork. For instance, they reported an average of 40 minutes a night spent on homework, which, although the lowest in the form, would have placed them on a par with the pro-school boys in 2TA (see table 8.2). This high level of reported time spent on homework also occurred across the form in 2LN, the other case-study form.[8] The overall form average in 2LN was 45 minutes per night.

Furthermore, from interviews with form teachers it was clear that the continued commitment evident among incipient anti-school boys in 2DY was a general characteristic throughout the mixed-ability cohort. Anti-schoolness of the totally rejecting kind witnessed in the band 2 forms was limited to only two or three individual pupils in the mixed-ability groups.

During the second and third years the incipient anti-school group in 2DY, especially Paul, became involved with another boy in the form, George. George was the only boy in the form from Sortham primary

Table 8.2. *Average time reported per group spent on homework each night for all pupils in 2TA, 2CU and 2DY*

2TA	Time in minutes	2CU	Time in minutes	2DY	Time in minutes
Girls' groups			A 39		A 36
anti-school	0		B 48	Girls' groups	B 56
		Girls' groups	C 75	pro-school	C 45
Boys' groups		pro-school	D 30		D 67
anti-school	6		E 94		
Girls' groups				Boys' groups	E 54
ambivalent	22	Boys' groups	G 31	pro-school	F 48
		pro-school	H 49		
Boys' groups					
pro-school	40	Boys' incipient		Boys' incipient	
		anti-school		anti-school	
		group	26	group	G 40
		Isolate anti-			
		school	0		
Overall form		Overall form		Overall form	
average	16	average	47	average	43

school and in the first sociometric questionnaire completed by the form he received only one friendship choice, which came from Nicholas, another low-status boy. George was described by his form teacher as 'someone who tries to act tough, but he's not really'. He was always seeking to take advantage of teachers and was often 'naughty'. In the Guess-Who-Test he was mentioned eight times as being 'badly behaved in lessons and is always being told off and shouted at by members of staff'. While with 'strict' teachers he was quiet and attentive and would often volunteer answers to teachers' questions, but his homework was rarely done, and at the end of the year his examination position was 28th. His father was a toolmaker (IIIM).

He often sat alone in lessons during the first year, but as the year progressed he became more closely associated with Paul, Colin, Kevin, and Desmond. He made considerable efforts to ingratiate himself with the other boys in the form, though his 'toughness' tended to have the opposite effect. He may be described as a socially ineffective neglectee, of the type defined by Gronlund (1959: 175) as including those pupils who

did want to join in, but did not know how to do so. They were often noisy and rebellious, boastful and arrogant, sometimes delinquent and usually a nuisance in class. They had plenty of vitality and made ineffective and naïve attempts to overcome their insecurity and isolation.

This problem may have arisen, at least in part, from his having no friends from his primary school in the form.

The misbehaviour of these five boys, which developed during the second year, was most evident in the lessons of probationary teachers, who were least experienced in dealing effectively with problems of control and discipline. The boys found they could take advantage of these teachers in particular and they became more audacious in their misbehaviour as a result. Because of this, they began to be 'reported' to their form teacher and to the year tutor.[9] Some examples of their misbehaviour are evident in the observation notes below.

2DY lesson notes: Science
George and Paul are calling out from the back of the laboratory; they are changing the teacher's name and call out to her. There is no rebuke, she is ignoring them. Kevin shouts and the teacher stops her explanation at the front: 'That's enough; be quiet at the back.' Which makes absolutely no impression. The boys seem fully aware that the teacher has no idea how to cope with them. This creates a situation where the rest of the form feel free to talk when normally they wouldn't, but not more than occasional chatting. The teacher continues to talk over the noise from the back; she is attempting to teach the remaining two-thirds of the form. Paul and George are deliberately interrupting. 'I don't know how to use it.' 'I was away.' There is to be an experiment with batteries and light bulbs to make circuits. Richard volunteers to give out the batteries, but Paul grabs a whole handful and tries to link them all into one bulb. 'We are going to blow it up.' As the experiment gets under way, Paul and George are taking no part; they are still trying to blow up the bulb. Kevin and Desmond are completely unable to organize their circuit. George and Paul have begun to fight at the back of the room, on the floor, totally unnoticed – or ignored – by the teacher, Paul had put dust marks on George's new jacket. Now they are kicking one another.

2DY lesson notes: Science
Paul, George, Kevin and Richard are standing up at the back of the room. They are waving a football scarf in the air and singing football slogans.

2DY lesson notes: History
There is a lot of movement round the room while the groups do their own work. The teacher is still able to address the form quietly; there is an industrious atmosphere. Details and task descriptions have to be repeated for Desmond, Paul and Kevin. Nicholas, Norman and Sam are rebuked

for too much talking. The form are called to stand round the teacher's desk while she explains a diagram; some of the boys are pushing others forward, the teacher asks for the 'silly behaviour' to stop. It doesn't. Kevin, Paul, George and Colin are told to stay behind at break for pushing. They are kept behind at the end and given a 'talking to'.

I also asked 2DY's Geography teacher, in her probationary year, if I could come into her lesson with 2DY to observe, but she refused:

> 'Perhaps later when I have established myself with them. I am having some problems with some of them at the moment and I don't think that someone coming in to watch would help at all.'

I asked this teacher later in the term how she was getting on with 2DY:

> 'O.K., they're a nice group except for one or two silly beggars like Paul Collard. Colin Willis was away last week and he teamed up in the lesson with Sam.'[10]

The disruption being caused in 2DY's Science lessons continued during the term until a complaint was received from the parents of one of the girls. She had complained that it was impossible to do any work in the lesson because of all the noise and distraction caused by Paul and George and the others. Her father decided to ring the school and the year tutor took action. Paul and George and Colin were banned from sitting next to each other in any lesson for the rest of that term, and information to this effect was circulated to all their teachers.

2DY's Biology teacher also had a lot of problems with these boys, but finally with the support of the year tutor she was able to assert herself. She described her relationships with the form in this way.

> 'Of all the forms I take they are the one that has changed the most, from one I had most trouble with at the beginning to a form I have almost the least problem with. It was individuals, you know. Paul and Colin, and then Sam more recently. But they really have changed almost overnight and of course I have changed as well.'

As in the case of the band 2 anti-school pupils, Paul and George particularly had established by the second year presentations of self that made it necessary for them to reject and devalue schoolwork as unimportant. For them, academic failure was now a way of life, and their social status in the form now depended on this; being seen to work hard but remaining unsuccessful would have been damaging to their social identities. The pupil who is 'known' not to care about school-work has a vested interest in protecting this presentation of self, and efforts by the teacher to make him 'get on with some work' become a direct threat to that identity and the status derived from it. The incident quoted below was typical of Paul's attitude to work:

> *2DY lesson notes: Maths*
> Paul's inactivity has caught the attention of the teacher.
> *T* 'Paul, what's wrong with you, lad?'
> *P* 'I don't feel like doing any work now.'
> *T* 'Well, you have a break in 15 minutes to do nothing in. In a Maths lesson, unfortunately, you have to work. Unless you want to change them round.'
> *P* 'I don't want to do my work at break, either.'
> *T* 'Well, I don't particularly want to stay with you, but I will if you don't do some work now!'
> *P* 'Someone has nicked my long bit of paper.'

The form teacher said of Paul:

> 'He's so apathetic; he never has anything to do in the pastoral period, and when I ask him what he's got to do he says, "Only an old book to read". And he's so sneaky and underhand. He's always trying to wander over to Colin Willis, whom he is not allowed to be with, and he's always trying to mutter behind his case during registration.'

However, unlike the anti-school groups in the banded case-study forms, this group did not remain as a coherent entity throughout the second and third years. In the third year, the solidarity of the group began to break down. Paul especially became more active in his misbehaviour in lessons and became closer in friendship to George, while Desmond and Kevin and Colin, who were more moderate in their attitudes and behaviour, were gradually dropped.[11] Desmond in particular became a butt of George's bullying. The form teacher explained:

> 'It's interesting. I was thinking the other day about their "places" in the form, and Desmond is down. He's just utterly spineless. Barry is smaller than he is, but he doesn't get pushed around like Desmond. They respect Barry because he's got brains. But hardly a day goes by without George Hardy kicking or pushing him through the door.'

It was apparent that Kevin, Colin and Desmond were unwilling to follow Paul in the extremes of 'bad' behaviour he was demonstrating. But Paul and George alone were unable to sustain any potent challenge to good order in the classroom. Unlike those of the band 2 forms, the anti-school groupings in the mixed-ability forms were neither large enough nor coherent enough to dominate the ethos of any form. And as the year tutor explained:

> 'You know in a lesson anyone can cope with a naughty boy or even two; if you get three or four together and they're just grinning at each other and "topping" each other each time, you can't cope with that sort of thing.'

Thus, many of George's and Paul's acts of defiance were committed outside lesson time or outside the school context altogether.[12] For instance, it was said of George:

> 'His behaviour was never on the surface, it was always sly; he did damage to school property and things but never in a lesson, or anything like that, when the teacher's around.'
>
> (Form teacher)
>
> 'He came back to a school disco drunk already and took pictures from the wall and smashed them over his knee.'
>
> (Year tutor)
>
> 'And he was the one who made Desmond kick the door in, and things like this.'
>
> (Form teacher)

Paul and George also regularly attended league football matches in Pierton and 'bragged' to the other boys that they threw bottles in the crowd and 'beat up' opposition supporters.

However, even Paul maintained one link with the orthodox world of participation in pro-school oriented activities, through his interest in basketball.[13] This tended slightly to ameliorate the poor perception of him by his teachers, even though he was considered to have very little ability at the game.[14]

> 'Paul's saving grace is that he's keen on basketball. Mr Court takes him for that . . . He's not a regular player, he's a sort of reserve. He's not that good, actually.'
>
> (Form teacher)
>
> 'He hasn't really got the backbone ever to make a good basketball player. Because Mr Court demands the last inch of his players.'
>
> (Year tutor)
>
> 'He's not a Michael [a well-perceived, academically successful pro-school boy] who can work out moves and apply his brain – his feet just go and he hopes to be in the right place at the right time.'
>
> (Form teacher)

Further quantitative comparisons related to attitude and behaviour

Apart from the existence of this group of incipient anti-school pupils in DY (and a similar small group in LN), there are several other indicators which point to the similarity between the case-study mixed-ability forms and 2CU, the case-study band 1 form, and to the differences between these forms and 2TA, the case-study band 2 form. These are shown, for example, in terms of involvement in extra-curricular activities, school societies and clubs and teams. While in the band 2 form, 2TA, only 5 pupils reported participation in 8 extra-curricular activities, in the band 1 form, 2CU, 18 pupils reported participation in 36 activities. In the mixed-ability forms, 19 pupils in 2DY took part in 41 extra-curricular activities, and in 2LN 13 pupils reported participation in 23 such activities.

A similar pattern is evident when the numbers of pupils who reported 'liking' school are compared with the numbers of those 'disliking' it. In 2TA, 17 reported 'liking' school as against 16 'disliking'; in 2CU, 28 reported 'liking' and only 4 'disliking'. In the mixed-ability forms, 23 in 2DY reported 'liking' as against only 6 'disliking', while 25 in 2LN reported 'liking' as against 4 'disliking'. A further illustration of the 'improved' behaviour of the mixed-ability forms over the band 2 forms is obtained from the comparison of records of absence over equivalent periods of time, as shown in table 8.3. During the first year, as might be expected, the mixed-ability forms demonstrate a level of absence higher than that of the band 1 forms, but lower than that of the band 2 forms. In the second year the average rate of absence in the mixed-ability forms remains similar to the equivalent terms in the first year (see table 8.4). Indeed, the mixed-ability forms achieved a better attendance record than the band 1 forms in the spring term (although there was no repeat of the influenza epidemic which seriously increased absences in the banded cohort). The gap between the mixed-ability and the band 2 forms increased

Table 8.3. *Number of sessions absent per pupil per term during the first year*

	First term	Second term	Third term
Band 1 case-study form	7.53	9.45	8.10
Band 2 case-study form	6.66	7.70	9.47
Mixed-ability case-study form	7.74	8.44	9.44
Mixed-ability case-study form	11.17	7.59	9.83
All band 1 forms	6.23	7.54	7.29
All band 2 forms	7.67	10.55	9.82
All band 3 forms	10.24	11.71	10.91
All mixed-ability forms	9.52	10.18	9.14
All remedial forms	11.68	13.14	14.25

Table 8.4. *Number of sessions absent per pupil per term during the second year*

	First term	Second term	Third term
Band 1 case-study form	8.13	11.24	9.16
Band 2 case-study form	12.59	13.23	12.64
Mixed-ability case-study form	9.02	8.07	7.75
Mixed-ability case-study form	6.35	7.19	10.28
All band 1 forms	7.23	11.21	7.86
All band 2 forms	12.23	12.83	14.17
All band 3 forms	15.18	17.12	19.39
All mixed-ability forms	9.79	10.56	8.97
Remedial form	17.67	16.50	21.50

during the second year. However, the remedial form in the mixed-ability cohort has a worse attendance record in the second year than the band 3 forms.

Polarization and friendship-group structure

Despite the anti-school attitudes and behaviour of individual pupils in the mixed-ability forms, there is no evidence of the emergence of a coherent anti-school sub-culture. However, this should not be taken to mean that there were no processes of social separation taking place between differently-oriented groups. It is clear from both case-study forms that a process of polarization is an important factor in the evolution of the social structure of the pupils' friendships, especially among the boys. For instance in DY, the incipient anti-school group described above gradually became separated from the rest of the boys in the form, until it eventually disintegrated at the end of the third year. In the first two sociometric questionnaires completed by the pupils of DY, in the spring term and the summer term of their first year, Paul achieved star-status by being chosen six times as a friend. However, this appeared to be partly a reflection of his 'popularity' at this time rather than of actual friendship relations. By the time of the last questionnaire, administered in the summer term of the third year, he received only one friendship choice, that from George. However, although this separation off of the incipient anti-school group did take place, and although there was also a certain degree of antipathy between this group and the other boys in the form and most of the girls,

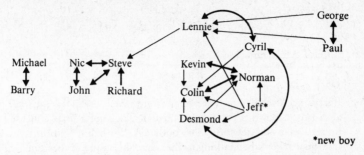

Figure 13. A sociogram of the friendship choices of 3DY boys: summer term, third year

there was never the same degree of mutual hostility as was evident between
the pro- and anti-school groups in 2TA. Throughout the first three years all
the boys, with the exception of George, and later Barry and Michael,[15]
played together regularly. Every lunch time when the weather was fine they
played football in the winter and cricket in the summer. When the weather
was too bad to use the playing fields, they played British Bulldog in the
playground. There was also a good deal of interaction among the members
of the form in pastoral periods and lessons. Once again, in this respect the
form was more like 2CU, the band 1 form.

The pattern of friendships that emerges at the end of three years in 3DY
is a familiar one. As far as the boys' peer-groupings are concerned, it is very
similar to the structure found in the band 1 form 2CU, and also to the
structure described by Lacey (1970) among top-stream grammar-school
boys. There were basically four identifiable friendship groups among the
boys in the form – two friendship pairs and two larger groups (see figure
13). The two friendship pairs were isolated from the rest of the boys, and
both – Paul and George, and Michael and Barry – were unpopular. The
characteristics which made Michael and Barry unpopular were exactly
opposite to those which made George and Paul disliked. Michael and Barry
were both totally uncompromising in their dedication to school and
schoolwork. They inevitably sat at the front of every lesson and would
dominate interaction with the teachers if allowed to do so. Their form
teacher said that they were competing against each other to see who did the
most work and got the most right answers or the better marks; even in the
third year they were still straining to answer teachers' questions when this
practice had long died out in the rest of the form. They showed little
interest in sport or any other 'social' activities that would have brought
them into contact with the other boys. Their attitude to and involvement in
work are illustrated in the following extracts from the lesson notes.

In History
Michael 'Are we doing the Normans next, sir?'
Teacher 'Yes.'
Michael 'Oh – fantastic!'

In Geography
Barry and Michael are working through the work-book; they are pages
ahead of the rest of the form, as usual. They are a little confused about
how to answer a question. The book asks for a description of limestone
but the teacher when talking to them had mentioned limestone landscape.
Michael felt that the teacher was just explaining to them about limestone
but Barry seems sure that he wanted them to write about the landscape as
well.
Michael 'You only have to write about the rocks, really.'
Barry 'You've got to do what the teacher says.'
Michael is convinced and they begin to describe a limestone landscape.

From the fifth sociometric questionnaire Barry receives 11 'rejection
choices' and Michael receives 8.

At each extreme, then – the pro-school extreme (Barry and Michael) and
the anti-school extreme (George and Paul) – the boys are isolated and
unpopular. As was the case in the band 1 form and among the grammar
school boys in Lacey's study, inflexibility of attitude results in social
rejection.

The rest of the boys are divided into two clear sub-groups, one composed
of the four most academically successful boys in the form (apart from
Michael and Barry), and the other of the least academically successful (apart
from George and Paul). There are no anti-school groups among the girls in
DY, incipient or otherwise. As in 2CU, it is only among the boys that any
anti-schoolness is evident. But this was not the case for all the mixed-ability
forms. In the other case-study form, LN, there was a group of incipient
anti-school girls (see pp. 258–9 below), although no groups of girls
emerged within this mixed-ability cohort as 'problems' in the way the
group A network did in 2TA. All the pupils who established any sort of
widely-known reputation as 'problem pupils' in this cohort were boys.

Mixed-ability and social control

It would appear that in general terms, as far as this cohort is concerned, the
emergence of a vociferous anti-school sub-culture among the pupils is
prevented by the mixed-ability grouping. One very important factor in this
appears to stem from the increased possibilities for teachers' social control

of pupils, particularly for the monitoring and manipulation of pupils' social relations. This increased social control does not, however, completely account for why more of the unsuccessful pupils in mixed-ability forms did not become behaviour problems. It is likely that this involves several factors acting in relation, including the distribution across the year-group of pupils with different educational standards; the absence of structurally determined labels of relative status; the reduced possibility of the domination of the ethos of a particular form by anti-school pupils; and the control of social relationships.[16]

The importance of this control was made explicit by two of the pastoral year tutors:

'You've got your individuals in mixed-ability but they're not supported, they're isolated. And from the beginning we've worked on that principle. Whenever we see a spot of bother discipline-wise, we split them up. We have a talk with all the staff together, and say who thinks they could make anything of this lad because he's going wrong. And if we see two hanging together.'

(Year tutor 1)

'As a year tutor my reasons for voting for mixed-ability were not educational but social. I had the same kids being referred to me week after week from the banded system and I had very little I could do with them, and I voted for mixed-ability to solve my own problems. It would give me elbow room. I can move them around and break up the problem groups and hopefully get some of the kids off the path to a sticky end.'

(Year tutor 2)

Thus, the pastoral staff, in co-operation with form tutors, were actually able to inhibit the development of anti-school peer-groups by moving 'key' personnel into other forms. Unlike the banding situation, this did not involve movement between one problem form and another. There was therefore a much reduced possibility of the emergence of a coherent anti-school ethos within any one form.

These kinds of movement had an impact upon the social fabric of both DY and LN. In both forms, pupils were moved in and out.[17] In DY, Sam was the first to move. He had been moved into the form from a remedial group at the end of the second year, in line with the school policy of re-integrating the remedial pupils into the ordinary mixed-ability forms. However, he was moved out during the third year when it seemed that he was becoming 'involved' with Paul and George. At the end of the third year, both Paul and George were also moved.

'Paul's been moved into Mr Court's form. And I think if Mr Court can keep him interested in basketball that might be his saving grace. George went happily off to 4LN. I think he liked the fact that he was going to have a male form teacher. We haven't got anyone else who is in any way anti-school.'

(Form teacher, beginning of fourth year)

As this comment illustrates, it was also possible in the mixed-ability context for constructive motives to be put forward for moving pupils. In the banded context, movement within bands was invariably accounted for negatively. Speaking of LN, the year tutor said:

'Antonia was moved because her mother more or less asked for her to be moved, because she was very much under the influence of Dolores Smith in that form, who is a very strong personality. Not only did she lead four or five of them in very nasty aggressive behaviour, banging heads and biting arms. . . but. . .I was already very angry with them and I told them all, "I shall split you up". . . They'd done this housebreaking the night before and had been found smoking somebody's cigarettes in an unoccupied furnished house.'

As well as effectively breaking up incipient anti-school groups, this movement of 'trouble makers' strengthened the view that 'problems' were caused by individual pupils rather than that there were 'problem' forms. The manifestations of misbehaviour – disruption, vandalism, etc. – were regarded by the pastoral staff in terms of the influence of particular 'ringleaders' or 'rotten elements', and 'problems' were dealt with on this basis.

'In fact, Dolores Smith came back after about a week, and cried, and said she couldn't find any friends in her new form, and I thought, Good, because I don't want them going your way. Now she's all right, actually, and she has in fact corrupted one or two others. . . Altogether, she is a bad influence.'

(Year tutor)

The very small proportion of incipient anti-school pupils in each form prevented the emergence of a dominant anti-school value-system in any one form or group of forms. Furthermore, the dispersal of inchoate anti-school groupings precluded the possibility of the development of a coherent anti-school sub-culture at this stage. Cohen (1955 : 43) makes the point in his study of delinquent boys that a group-being is necessary if a sub-culture is to develop.

It is the hallmark of sub-cultural delinquency that it is acquired and practised in groups rather than independently contrived by the individual as a solution to his private problems.

That is to say, a crucially necessary condition for the development of a sub-culture is the existence of a group of people facing the same problems of adjustment. Mixed-ability grouping would seem to provide conditions, through the possibility of moving pupils and splitting up social groups, which are unfavourable to the formation and definition of sub-cultural groups. In Cohen's terms, the splitting up of 'troublemakers' would inhibit the process of 'joint acceptance and elaboration of exploratory gestures'.

However, it is also true that the mixed-ability grouping, unlike the banded system, does not provide the teacher with pre-existing typifications of pupils based upon their structural identities (except for remedial pupils). The teachers are now in a position where they must 'make' rather than 'take' the identities of pupils. Even so, there are clearly a number of categories which are commonly used and understood by the teachers which, while they are free of structural connotations, do effectively locate and identify pupils in a fairly exact way.[18] 'Brighter', 'faster', 'slow', 'thick', 'average', 'dull' and 'problem' are a few examples. However, in a mixed-ability context the teacher does not find that such information is available to him prior to his contact with the pupils, except in the case of certain individuals. He must fit pupils into these categories by gathering information in his interaction with them (see pp. 271–2).

Mixed-ability and social development

One of the features of the impact of the mixed-ability innovation that is difficult to characterize in any sociological sense is the apparent inhibition of the pupils' social development. Many teachers felt that the experience of being in mixed-ability form-groups tended to slow down the pupils' social maturation;[19] the pupils' period of childhood appeared to be extended and the onset of adolescence retarded in the mixed-ability as compared with the banded forms.

One indication of the difference between the two cohorts in this respect comes from the social system of friendships among the girls in the case-study form DY, particularly the status of two girls, Mandy and Christine, a friendship pairing which occurred in every one of the five sociometric questionnaires. Mandy and Christine were described by the other girls in the form at the end of the first year as 'always talking about their boyfriends'.[20] They were evidently socially more sophisticated than the other girls in the form and shared a serious out-of-school interest in dancing. They attended lessons two nights each week.

In the first sociometric questionnaire administered in the first year, both girls exchanged friendship choices with a third girl, Beryl. But during the first year, as Mandy and Christine showed an increasing interest in boyfriends and out-of-school social life, Beryl steadily became hostile towards them and they to her. In contrast to these girls' interests, Beryl said in an interview:

> 'I don't like boys, they are bullies . . . I like to go to discos but not very often. You never know who is going to be there, and they go on late. I usually go to bed at half-past eight, but you can't go home early because people make fun.'

Beryl was typical of the girls in DY, while Mandy and Christine were exceptions. The difference between Mandy and Christine and the rest was that they had already begun seriously to enter the world of the teenager. They had already made the transition from childhood to adolescence, which still awaited the others. This transition gave them a different view of the world and a different set of values and interests. Their social horizons extended to encompass Pierton, the large seaside resort along the coast from Beachside, as a place to 'go out' to; they went to local discothèques and had boyfriends. The other girls rarely 'went out' except with their parents. They still inhabited the world of 'playing' with friends and going to bed at 8.30.

During the first year, the sociometric status of Mandy and Christine declined considerably. They received six choices between them from the first questionnaire, apart from their own exchange of choices, but only one other choice in the summer-term questionnaire, and no other choices at all in the questionnaire in the first term of the second year.[21] Thus, while in the banded forms the most socially mature and sophisticated girls attracted most friendship choices (Miriam and Daphne, for example), in 2DY the reverse was true, these girls being of low sociometric status.[22]

A further indicator of the difference in terms of social development between the mixed-ability and the banded forms comes from their reported out-of-school commitments. Sixteen pupils in 2DY reported membership of 18 different clubs or groups outside school.

Girl Guides	5
Scouts	2
Red Cross	1
Dancing classes	2
Sea Cadets	2
N.T.C.	2
Crusaders	2
Choirs	2
Boys Clubs	1

This compares with only two pupils in 2TA who mentioned 3 clubs or groups, and seven pupils in 2CU who mentioned 9 clubs or groups, at a similar point in their school careers. Furthermore, in response to questions about spare time and leisure activities, eight members of 2DY actually mentioned 'playing' as a description of what they had done the previous evening. This is not a category of meaning that derives from the world of adolescence, but from that of childhood. It was only mentioned once in either 2TA or 2CU in their responses to these questions.

Mixed-ability grouping and social mixing

Although it did not emerge as an important issue in the mixed-ability debate at Beachside, social mixing was clearly a major factor in the headmaster's conception of comprehensive education (see chapter 1), and is a factor that often occurs as a stated advantage to be gained from mixed-ability grouping in the literature on mixed-ability (cf. C. M. Morrison 1976). It thus deserves attention. Most of the research available to date comparing streamed and mixed-ability groups shows no differences between groups on this basis (cf. Deitrich 1964, Johannesson 1962, Ross et al. 1972).

Given the method of allocation of pupils to their mixed-ability forms at Beachside, each form-group was composed of a cross-section of pupils with very different histories of academic achievement and social backgrounds. (Other methods of allocation – for instance, random or alphabetic allocation – can accidentally produce homogeneous groups.) The social class composition of the two case-study forms is shown in table 8.5. With this greater diversity and balance of social class backgrounds and levels of achievement (in comparison with the bands) the possibilities for social interaction and social mixing between pupils are increased on two levels. First, the mixed-ability classroom provides a context in which pupils of different achieved-abilities and social backgrounds can hear and

Table 8.5. *Distribution of social classes across the case-study forms DY and LN*

	I	II	IIIN	IIIM	IV	V	Unclass.	Total
DY	3	8	3	12	2	1	–	29
LN	1	6	4	13	3	–	1	28

see each other engaged in schoolwork. The second level is the translation of these possibilities into actual friendship choices. This level of social mixing can be plotted through the friendship choices made by pupils in sociometric questionnaires.

In order to compare the extent of social mixing within the banded and the mixed-ability forms, Procter and Loomis's (1951) Index of In-group Preference will again be employed. As explained in chapter 3, the index enables a comparison to be made between populations on the basis of the ratio of choices for members of any in-group in each population to choices for members of any out-group. Social mixing, as opposed to 'consciousness of kind', is indicated by In-group Preference (I.P.) values of less than unity.

The I.P. values obtained from the sociometric choices made by each of the case-study forms, banded and mixed-ability, are presented in tables 8.6 and 8.7, taking both social class and levels of academic achievement as in-group/out-group indicators. A dichotomy between non-manual and manual occupations is used as the basis for the social class groups, and the top-half and bottom-half positions in the school examinations are used as the basis for the academic-achievement groups.

In the banded cohort the tendency was observed for pupils to make most of their friendship choices within their form-groups, and very few choices outside their own band. Although the opportunities for children from different social classes to mix was not negligible in the banded forms, these more homogeneous social units tended to foster a 'consciousness of kind', both in terms of social class and achieved-ability; from tables 8.6 and 8.7 it may be seen that there is evidence of in-group preference in both dimensions.

In CU, the band 1 form, social class is a consistently divisive factor among both boys and girls (see pp. 80, 94, and 99). The I.P. values are greater than unity in all cases except two in the three questionnaires completed. But there is an overall decline in values through the second and third years. The in-group preference by levels of achievement is less clear-cut. There is only one I.P. value greater than unity in the first questionnaire, and two greater than unity in each of the second and third questionnaires. In other words, among the bottom groups of boys and the bottom groups of girls there are I.P. values of greater than unity in two out of the three questionnaires.

In TA, the band 2 form, a reverse of the band 1 pattern is apparent. Achievement is the divisive factor. In all cases except one, the I.P. values remain greater than unity over the three questionnaires. In the case of social class, there are only three instances of I.P. values greater than one in the

Table 8.6. *Comparison of social class In-group Preference values for the banded and mixed-ability forms*

(The I.P. values are presented so that questionnaires completed at the same point of pupils' careers may be easily compared.)

Timing of questionnaires in pupils' school careers	DY				LN				TA				CU			
	Boys		Girls		Boys		Girls		Boys		Girls		Boys		Girls	
	Working-class	Middle-class	Working-class	Middle-class	Working-class	Middle-class	Working-class	Middle-class	Working-class	Middle-class	Working-class	Middle-class	Working-class	Middle-class	Working-class	Middle-class
1st year	0.82	0.70	0.49	0.58	1.75	1.96	4.00	16.50	–	–	–	–	–	–	–	–
1st year	0.67	0.57	0.91	0.70	–	–	–	–	–	–	–	–	–	–	–	–
2nd year	1.38	1.71	0.38	0.18	–	–	–	–	0.84	0.00	1.06	2.5	5.00	5.25	0.81	2.17
2nd year	1.05	2.13	0.57	0.36	5.50	1.75	1.86	35.75	0.85	0.00	0.58	0.75	3.75	0.92	2.17	1.43
3rd year	1.14	3.73	1.13	1.20	–	–	–	–	1.49	0.00	0.95	0.00	1.5	2.29	1.38	1.58

Table 8.7. *Comparison of academic achievement In-group Preference values for the banded and mixed-ability forms*

(The I.P. values are presented so that questionnaires completed at the same point of the pupils' careers may be easily compared.)

Timing of questionnaires in pupils' school careers	DY				LN				TA				CU			
	Boys		Girls		Boys		Girls		Boys		Girls		Boys		Girls	
	Top	Bottom	Top	Bottom	Top	Bottom	Top	Bottom	Top	Bottom	Top	Bottom	Top	Bottom	Top	Bottom
1st year	1.40	2.23	0.94	0.44	3.75	0.86	1.71	1.96	–	–	–	–	–	–	–	–
1st year	1.80	2.04	1.50	–	–	–	–	–	–	–	–	–	–	–	–	–
2nd year	1.80	2.81	0.44	0.91	–	–	–	–	1.69	0.41	2.92	1.11	0.8	0.91	0.6	1.1
2nd year	8.75	4.26	0.94	0.68	3.73	2.17	3.75	2.77	1.13	2.64	1.97	2.83	0.86	1.27	1.67	0.7
3rd year	4.67	16.00	8.10	0.00	–	–	–	–	2.27	2.22	2.50	2.31	0.57	1.09	0.42	1.0

three questionnaires, and never more than once in the same category. In general terms, then, in the socially homogeneous band 2 context, achievement is the major factor of 'consciousness of kind' between pupils. In the more socially heterogeneous band 1 context, social class is the major factor of 'consciousness of kind'. In comparison with Ford's (1969) findings, which did not take into account the sexual polarization of friendship choice in the co-educational classroom, the extent of social class in-group preference is much less in the banded forms at Beachside than in either of the streamed comprehensives she investigated.[23]

If it is true that the pupils in the mixed-ability forms do not mix only with children of their own social class and level of achieved-ability, as many of the arguments in support of mixed-ability grouping suggest, I.P. values of less than unity, or at least closer to unity than those found in the banded forms, should be expected. But, as can be seen from the tables, this is not the case. Although in DY the I.P. values for social class start out at less than unity, the middle-class and working-class group values are greater than unity, for both boys and girls, by the end of the third year. In fact, in the case of the boys in-group preference by social class emerges even earlier. In LN, the social class I.P. values are all greater than one even in the first questionnaire. Among the girls, the I.P. values for social class are higher than any recorded in the banded forms (with one exception). In the case of I.P. values for choice between pupils of similar levels of achievement, there is a clear difference in pattern between boys and girls in DY. Among the boys there are I.P. values of greater than unity in all the questionnaires, but this occurs in only two instances among the girls. In DY, in-group preferences in terms of achievement are established among both boys and girls by the third year, in LN in the first year.

Overall, there are 29 instances of in-group preference out of 48 cases in the banded forms (60.42 per cent), and 35 instances of in-group preference out of 56 cases in the mixed-ability forms (62.5 per cent).[24]

In both mixed-ability forms, the increase in I.P. values over time may be considered in relation to the increasing element of setting in the pupils' timetables in the second and third years, and the concomitant increase in the importance of academic achievement as the point of separation into O-level and C.S.E. courses comes closer.

However, while it is apparent that the increase in face-to-face interaction between pupils of different social classes and achieved-abilities does not bring about any increase in social mixing in terms of friendship choice, it is evident from observation of DY and from interviews with pupils that there is less antagonism between pupils of different levels of achievement than there was between the different bands, and none of the intractable negative stereotypes of the kind that developed between the bands.

This may be evidence for the greater tolerance that some advocates of heterogeneous grouping hoped for, but, to reiterate the conclusion drawn by Ford (1969 : 82), these figures offer little support for those who 'put their faith in comprehensive reorganization as a means of destroying class barriers in interpersonal relations'.[25]

Mixed-ability and social equality

If the teachers' perspectives, identified in chapter 8, are considered in relation to the teachers' evaluations of the mixed-ability system in practice (see pp. 234–7), it is clear that in terms of the *academic* and *disciplinary* perspectives the innovation was a 'success'. Yet in terms of the third perspective, the *idealist*, the egalitarian goals stressed by some of the teachers in the mixed-ability debate appear to have been abandoned as criteria of evaluation.[26] Indeed, these goals became subsumed by the concern evident in all subject-departments for the maintenance of academic standards.

This section will explore the fate of the idealist perspective, to demonstrate the countervailing importance of ability differentiation in the teachers' perceptions of and teaching of mixed-ability forms. To this end, the mixed-ability case-study forms will be compared with the banded forms along a number of dimensions.

Even in those departments where support for the egalitarian goals had been strongest during the early stages of the debate, the teachers became involved in establishing academic rather than egalitarian justifications for the innovation. For example, as noted earlier, the head of English, despite a continued personal support for social equality, collected and carefully analysed and compared with the results of previous years the O-level and C.S.E. results achieved by the first mixed-ability fifth-year cohort. He then presented these figures at a staff meeting to demonstrate the 'success' of mixed-ability English.[27] In History, too, despite a commitment in the departmental report on mixed-ability to abandon examinations, a multiple-choice examination paper was set at the end of the first mixed-ability year 'to check attainment and progress'.[28] Once again, the results were used to demonstrate the success of mixed-ability grouping.

The climate of concern for the progress of the brighter child and the maintenance of academic standards, evident in the mixed-ability debates, became important to all teachers seeking to establish the credibility of their methods of work. Giving emphasis to the categorization of types of pupil served, in its turn, to ensure that academic competition would be a fundamental aspect of the mixed-ability classroom, as it had been in the banded. This continuity in the teachers' and pupils' conceptualizations of the classroom, from the banded to the mixed-ability context, was identified by the head of English, who said in an interview:

> 'I think we are still living in the era when it was banded. And the school is still dominated, I think, by banded thinking and by competition between pupils. And I think most kids, when you talk to them, and most of the staff, think that kids have to measure themselves against each other. And think in terms of whether they are better at Geography than somebody else. And I suppose, the main motivation for work and study in this school is examinations, external O-levels and A-levels. That seems the basic driving force of the school. It seems a pity.'

Certainly, the continued importance of academic achievement was evident in the teachers' classroom practices. The practices of mixed-ability teaching that were implemented at Beachside corresponded, as we have seen, to the teachers' sense of the possible, and were constrained by it. The teachers' perceptions of parental concern were clearly a major consideration in the selection of appropriate teaching strategies (see pp. 186–7 and p. 227), whereas the imperatives of mixed-ability theorists (such as Tucker 1971, Elliot 1976, and Kelly 1974) remained essentially irrelevant. As indicated previously (see p. 186), the Beachside innovation was one of mixed-ability grouping rather than mixed-ability teaching. With the exception of the head of English, even those teachers who had been concerned with the egalitarian possibilities of mixed-ability considered that these possibilities had been accomplished in the organizational creation of mixed-ability groups, rather than in the process and practice of mixed-ability teaching.

The world of the mixed-ability classroom as it appeared to the teachers demanded first and foremost a resolution of the practical problems involved in maintaining certain academic standards. The achievement of a new social order was not a prime concern. Changes in teaching-methods were, for the most part, adaptational responses to the practical problems of teaching 'a wide range of abilities'. In consequence, the language employed to distinguish significant pupil types was not changed from that evident in the organization and teaching of the banded lesson. Indeed, there were several factors at the classroom level, apart from the general climate of concern for the brighter child, which reinforced the need to stress differences in academic achievement.

First, several departments introduced teaching-methods, as we have seen, which were intended to increase the individualization of learning. While there were limitations on the extent of this individualization, the practice of differentiating between pupils in the classroom, particularly in terms of the coverage of the syllabus, became a natural consequence of these teaching methods. Second, the pupils themselves were particularly concerned about their achievements relative to those of their peers, probably in consequence of previous experiences of schooling, and, in some cases, parental interest and concern. Pupils put considerable pressure on their teachers to give them actual numerical marks for tests and examinations, a pressure to which many teachers yielded despite the policy of not giving marks, as contained in the recommendations of several departmental reports on the preparations for mixed-ability. Third, the 'setting' introduced in the second and third years (in Maths, French, and then Sciences) objectively separated pupils who were considered to be of higher or lower ability. There were two sets for Maths and the Sciences and three for French.[29]

The immediacy of these concerns was also reflected in the teachers' perceptions and constructs of the mixed-ability classroom. Teachers tended to view mixed-ability groups in terms of a threefold, normal distribution of ability – bright, average and dull – reinforced in some cases by knowledge of the system of allocation of pupils to forms.

From lesson observations it was apparent that the use of ability-identities as an interactional shorthand sometimes also involved a physical separation of pupils in the classroom (see also p. 205); for example:

> 'I have been taking out some of my first year round the table at the front, to do extra punctuation work.'
>
> (English teacher)
>
> 'I have the slower ones at the front of the form so that they are near to the board.'
>
> (English teacher)

In effect, the teachers saw and interacted with the mixed-ability pupils in terms of the classification of ability upon which the banding system was based. Sharp and Green (1976 : 140) noted a similar process in primary school classrooms.

As the children enter the class, the teacher attempts to develop working categories for her relationship with them. These categories have implications for their likely success, failure and difficulties and so on.

Apart from becoming formalized in the structuring of classroom activities, in some cases these differentiations also become institutionalized through the structure of the syllabus. For example, in Music:

> 'The first year all learn the recorder, split into groups by musical ability, whenever this is possible on the timetable.'
>
> (Music teacher)

Indeed, it was evident from my interviews with staff that the problems of organizing learning for a greater diversity of pupils, together with the pressure to maintain academic standards, *increased* rather than reduced the concern they had for their pupils' relative levels of achievement (see also p. 235). Consequently, there is no evidence to suggest that in the organization and conduct of mixed-ability lessons the criteria of status and social worth based on academic success, which were fundamental to the banding system, were joined or replaced by other criteria of evaluation.

Despite the fact that the system of school reports had changed to give greater emphasis to effort as against achievement, and although there were fewer school examinations and a reduction in the number of subjects using grades or marks, the actual learning milieu changed little. 'The social and psychological and material environment in which the students and teachers work together' (Parlett and Hamilton 1972:11) was dominated by essentially the same ethos of practice and academic production as was evident in the banding system.

One clear indication of the prime role played by achievement criteria in the teachers' separation and ranking of pupils in the classroom is available through the use, once again, of the Kelly construct method.[30] Although it involves the comparison between construct systems elicited from different teachers, the similarity between the constructs elicited from the teachers of the banded forms (presented in chapters 3 and 4) and the teachers of the mixed-ability forms is clear.[31] All of those teachers who co-operated in producing sets of personal constructs derived from the mixed-ability forms included an 'ability' construct,[32] and in each case the correlations between the rank-orders based on these sets of constructs and the forms' examination positions were statistically significant.[33] Taking two examples of these construct systems, as before, for the case-study form 2DY, the constructs elicited from the Mathematics and History teachers were as follows, in order of priority:

Maths teacher's constructs	History teacher's constructs
Bright – poor	Enthusiastic – unenthusiastic
Works together – works alone	Well organized – disorganized
Tries hard – lazy	Makes an effort – does not make an effort
Self-sufficient – very poor	Articulate – lacking in oral ability
	Enjoys work – does not enjoy work
	Gregarious – quiet
	More able – less able[34]

The rank-order positions derived from these construct systems, cross-tabulated with examination positions, are shown in table 8.8. It may be noted that there are only eleven discrepant cases between construct rank positions and examination positions in the History teacher's construct system and only ten in that of the Mathematics teacher.

Thus, in the mixed-ability context, as in the banded, there is a close relationship between the pupils' academic performance and their rank-order position in the teachers' perceptions. And as with the banded forms many of the exceptions to the pattern of covariation between the teachers' perceptions of pupils and their level of academic achievement can be explained in terms of variations in attitude and behaviour. Indeed, all of those pupils who appeared in the top ten construct rank positions of either teacher were notably well-behaved in lessons and positively-oriented to school.[35]

The importance of academic achievement in the teachers' perceptions of pupils was tested further by eliminating the 'ability' constructs from the calculation of the rankings. In both cases, the level of correlation between

Table 8.8. *Cross-tabulation of construct rank-order positions and examination positions: 2DY*

Mathematics teacher's constructs				History teacher's constructs			
	Examination positions				Examination positions		
Construct rank positions	1–10	11–17	18–27	Construct rank positions	1–10	11–17	18–27
1–10	8	1	1	1–10	6	3	1
11–17	1	3	3	11–17	2	3	1
18–27	1	3	6	18–27	1	1	8

$r_s = 0.071$ signif. at 0.001 level. $r_s = 0.64$ signif. at 0.001 level.
The correlation between the two sets of construct rankings is also significant at the 0.01 level, $r_s = 0.59$.

the construct rank positions and the examination positions remained significant at the 0.001 level.[36]

The pupils themselves were made aware of their relative status in the classroom, in part at least, through the *cues* given by the teachers in the normal interactional routine of the mixed-ability lesson. Most straightforwardly, cueing takes place in the reading out of examination results, or through comments made when the teacher returns homework, or when the form is divided up, or through the choice of the same people to answer questions. As one girl in 2DY commented, 'She always asks *them*.' But cueing is also embodied in other ways in the interactional flow of lessons. For example:

> *History: lesson notes*
> *Nicholas* 'In question two . . .' The teacher interrupts.
> *Teacher* 'Haven't you done that yet?'
> *Nicholas* 'No, I'm on it.'
> *Teacher* 'You haven't finished it, you're pretty slow, aren't you?'

The teacher tells this pupil and the rest of the form that he is working too slowly, that he has failed to achieve the teacher's standard of an adequate speed of working. This indicates to other pupils on question two that they are also slow.

Cues are often a part of the teacher's control over the organization of learning in the classroom.

> 'Put your hands up those of you who have started section C on the work-card.'
> (History teacher)

> 'Put your hands up those of you who have finished work-card B2.'
> (Maths teacher)
> 'Put your hands on your head when you have done all of question 2.'
> (Maths teacher)
> 'Put up your hands if you have done or are on question 4.'
> (History teacher)
> 'Anyone still writing?'
> (English teacher)

This cueing may also occur in the flippant remark that is intended to embarrass or rebuke:

> 'Come on, Edwards, speed it up a bit, – see if you can get a three speed gear box.'
> (Maths teacher)

Or comparisons may actually be made between pupils by setting the performance of some as a target for others:

> 'Put up your hands. . . We have five people who have finished. . . I will give you two minutes to finish.'
>
> (Geography teacher)

Once internalized by the pupils, this awareness of relative ability may be used and reinforced by the teacher in his management of the classroom:

> 'If you want to read the part of Green you have to be a good fast reader because if you're a slow reader we will be hanging about for you, it's a big part. Put up your hands then if you want to read Green.'
>
> (English teacher)

The teacher here is relying on the self-images of the pupils, their knowledge of their teacher's perception of them and their ability relative to other pupils in the form. The pupils who raised their hands, and those who did not, acknowledged their awareness of their relative abilities and reinforced the status differentials pertinent to that form.[37]

In competitive aspects of the classroom process, the teachers do not take account of the unequal resources of pupils:[38]

the teacher perspective transforms competition between individuals with markedly different resources relevant to the competitive process, into a competition of equals.

> (Lacey, 1976 : 83)

It is in this way that differences between pupils in terms of social class culture, linguistic ability, motivation, support and encouragement from parents, etc., become relevant in terms of differential performance, and thence are translated into a differential allocation of rewards and status.

In a similar detailed analysis of informal primary school classrooms, Sharp and Green (1976) were able to demonstrate the emergence of a stratification among the pupils resulting from the classroom management strategies operated by the teachers. The threefold system of social stratification identified by Sharp and Green in the primary teachers' view of the classroom – a few very bright pupils, a few maladjusted or problem children, and the majority of normal children – is essentially similar to the Beachside teachers' view of the mixed-ability classroom.

Thus, at Beachside, the mixed-ability system is organized as a competitive order. The identification and development of talent remains inherent in the teachers' conception of their task and role. This clearly involves the 'sponsorship' of 'talented' pupils, who are accorded special

Table 8.9. *Covariation of exam position and social class:*
1DY

Exam. positions	Middle-class	Working-class
1–10	10	–
11–20	3	7
21–9	1	8
Total	14	15

Table 8.10. *Covariation of exam position and social class:*
1LN

Exam. positions	Middle-class	Working-class	Unclassified
1–10	7	3	–
11–20	3	6	1
21–8	1	7	–
Totals	11	16	1

provision both within the mixed-ability classroom and in the 'setting' of high-status subjects. Indeed, the mixed-ability form-group appears to reproduce a microcosm of the banding system, with the processes of differentiation and polarization taking place *within* each form-group.

The impact of these processes is most apparent in the covariation between social class and academic achievement. In both case-study forms, the top positions in examinations are dominated by pupils from middle-class backgrounds (see tables 8.9 and 8.10), and there is little change in the pattern in DY by the end of the third year (see table 8.11).[39] Those changes that have taken place may be related to the alterations in the friendship structure and the process of polarization taking place within the form – that is, the emergence of sub-cultural differences between the pupils. Colin, George, Desmond and Paul, who belonged to the incipient anti-school group, occupy the bottom four places, while Kevin is 24th. June, the least successful girl, is 23rd. The only dramatic change of position from the first to the third year is that of a girl, Nicola, who rose from 27th to 14th. She was uniformly identified by her form-males as 'always poor at work' in the first year,[40] but her membership of a group of successful, pro-school, middle-class girls may not be unrelated to her improvement.

Table 8.11. *Covariation of exam position and social class: 3DY*

Exam. positions	Middle-class	Working-class
1–10	9	1
11–20	3	7
21–30	2	8
Totals	14	16

(There is a correlation between the first-year and third-year examination positions significant at the 0.001 level; $r_s = 0.82$.)

Compared with the figures for the banded forms, these results indicate the way in which mixed-ability grouping can effectively reduce the number of success-role experiences available to working-class pupils. Previously, the band 2 and 3 forms, which were mostly populated by working-class pupils, had provided a context in which at least some working-class pupils could be 'top of the form' and achieve good marks relative to their immediate peers. The distribution of middle-class pupils across the whole cohort creates a situation where it is possible for them to dominate the formal success roles and statuses in the classroom, both major and minor.

This change in the distribution of experience of success-roles may have contributed to the considerable reduction in the 'problem' of over-aspiration with regard to option choices made at the end of the third year. In contrast to the banded forms, especially the band 2 forms, the incidence of pupils making 'inappropriate' choices was small.

Option choice and option allocation

The option-choice procedure through which the choices made by the first mixed-ability cohort were processed was not exactly the same as that described earlier for the banded forms. Some changes were introduced into the mechanics of the system. In particular, the form teacher was given prime responsibility for the negotiation of a set of choices between the pupils and the subject teachers, – in the first instance. But once total numbers were collected, the senior master and the year tutor still had the responsibility for overcoming discontinuities. The senior master described the option-allocation process for the first mixed-ability cohort in the following way:

'It's much the same, the same problems. There are 41 wanting to do Rural Science and only 24 places. 50 wanting to do Human Studies and there's only going to be one group. Too many for Geology, but only three for Latin.

'It seems that the traditional subjects are going down and C.S.E.s are becoming more attractive. We thought that mixed-ability would make them go for O-levels, but no. The C.S.E. syllabi are more interesting and O-level seems to have lost its aura.

'I'm still counselling some individuals but the parents have been very good. We had two meetings and most have come up, although we had to send for some. And some still want to move their kids or are insisting that they do O-levels. It's the professional parents and those who don't know anything about it who tend to dig their heels in!'

As indicated by the senior master, the choice-problems in this cohort were primarily problems related to the capacity of particular courses. While some redirection and counselling was necessary for certain oversubscribed courses, the rate of reallocation of choices which were made to an 'inappropriate level' was small compared with that of the bands. While the senior master explained this by suggesting that the C.S.E. courses were more interesting and that the 'O-level seems to have lost its aura', in fact only one department, Music, had introduced a new C.S.E. course for the mixed-ability cohort.

The relatively small number of 'inappropriate' choices in this cohort is certainly evident in 3DY's options.[41] The proportions of courses initially chosen by the pupils were O-level 63 per cent (113), O/C.S.E. 6 per cent (11) and C.S.E. 31 per cent (56). If these choices are considered in relation to the pupils' positions in the option examinations, among those pupils in the top 10 rank-order positions only 2 C.S.E. and 2 O/C.S.E. courses were chosen. In the bottom 10 positions 40 C.S.E. and 5 O/C.S.E. courses were chosen, but only 15 O-levels (see table 8.12). Furthermore, of the

Table 8.12. *3DY: option courses chosen initially by pupils, cross-tabulated with third-year examination performance*

Third-year examination positions	O-level	O/C.S.E.	C.S.E.	Totals
1–10	56(93%)	2(3.5%)	2(3.5%)	60(100%)
11–20	42(70%)	4(6.6%)	14(23%)	60(100%)
21–30	15(25%)	5(8%)	40(66%)	60(100%)
	113	11	56	

Table 8.13. *3DY: initial option choices made for practical and 'new' subject courses, related to third-year examination performance*

Third-year exami-nation positions	Courses chosen	
	Practical courses[a]	'New' courses[b]
1–10	5	–
11–20	7	–
21–30	11	9

[a]Needlecraft, Technical Drawing, Technical Studies, Art, Home Economics and Rural Studies.
[b]Home Studies, Human Studies, Modern Applications of Science.

40 C.S.E.s chosen by the pupils in the last 10 positions, 26 were chosen between Kevin, Colin, Desmond, Paul and George, the boys identified earlier as belonging to an incipient anti-school friendship group.

A closer examination of the distribution of courses chosen reveals further sub-divisions within the form along the same dimensions noted in the earlier analysis of option choice in the banded context. Taking the top, middle, and bottom 10 examination positions once again, the pupils in the bottom 10 positions chose 11 practical and 9 'new' courses; the pupils in the middle 10 positions chose 7 practical courses and no 'new' courses; and the pupils in the top 10 positions chose 5 practical courses and no 'new' courses (see table 8.13). Once the allocation of pupils to courses was completed, the pattern remained essentially the same, except for a slight realignment among the low-achievers away from O-levels to C.S.E. (see table 8.14). Among the low-achievers there was a reduction of 4 in the number of O-levels taken, as against those chosen, and an increase of 5 in the number of C.S.E.s taken as against those chosen. Kevin, Colin, Desmond, Paul and George ended up taking only 3 O-level courses between them, out of 30 option choices. There was also a slight increase in the numbers of 'new' courses taken by the low-achievement group (see table 8.15). Compared with the banded cohort, the proportion of O-level choices reallocated in 3DY is very similar to that of the band 1 forms, but considerably lower than that of the band 2 forms (see table 8.16). This cannot be explained simply in terms of there being more pupils accepted to do O-levels in this mixed-ability cohort compared with the banded cohort.

Table 8.14. *3DY: option courses taken by pupils, cross-tabulated with third-year examination performance*

Third-year exami-nation positions	Courses taken		
	O-level	O/C.S.E.	C.S.E.
1–10	55	2	3
11–20	40	6	14
21–30	11	4	45
	106(59%)	12(6.6%)	62(34.4%)

Table 8.15. *3DY: option courses taken by pupils in practical and 'new' subjects, related to third-year examination performance*

Third-year examination positions	Courses taken	
	Practical courses	'New' courses
1–10	5	–
11–20	7	–
21–30	12	10

Table 8.16. *Rejections from O-level courses as a percentage of all choices made for O-level*

Band 1 forms	5.6%
Band 2 forms	32.14%
3DY	6.2%

Indeed, the number of O-level courses taken per pupil is smaller in the mixed-ability cohort – 2.20 per pupil as against 2.78 per pupil in the banded cohort. Although it was not possible to collect the choice and allocation figures for the whole mixed-ability cohort,[42] which would have provided a direct and rigorous comparison between the banded and mixed-ability cohorts, it was clear from the interviews with the senior master that the pattern of choices in 3DY was typical of the whole cohort. Very few pupils were seen as overaspiring, compared with the banded cohort, even though the proportions of O-level and C.S.E. courses available remained the same.

From these figures, then, it appears that the mixed-ability situation, compared with banding, provides a much more 'effective' basis for the socialization of appropriate aspirations for this important choice point. To a great extent it also provides a solution to the warming-up/cooling-out problems evident in the banded system. It is certainly possible that the continuous comparison between peers in the mixed-ability classroom, and the change in the distribution of success roles that mixed-ability grouping brings about, are responsible for producing these more 'realistic' choices.[43]

In two major respects, in terms of the pupils' behaviour and the management of pupils' aspirations, mixed-ability grouping appears to produce important changes from the banding system. Social control and the socialization of pupils are effectively 'improved' in the mixed-ability context. And yet in other ways, in terms of the organization of friendships and the social distribution of success and failure in particular, mixed-ability produces little change from the banded situation. The friendship structures of the mixed-ability forms are divided up on the basis of differences in social class and academic achievement, reproducing the social cleavages evident in the banded cohort, and the processes of academic selection continue to ensure that middle-class pupils are over-represented among those chosen for high-status positions.[44]

Despite some necessary adaptations, the operating assumptions held by the teachers about the organization of their subjects, syllabuses, teaching methods and assessment of pupils were not in themselves basically changed by the introduction of mixed-ability grouping. Quite clearly, as in the bands, the pupils are perceived and evaluated by their teachers in terms of a competitive and hierarchical system of achieved-ability, which is transmitted to the pupils in the teachers' pedagogy and talk. Although it is inappropriate directly to compare the processes of a total structure, the banding system, with a single mixed-ability form, it does appear that the stratification of pupils produced through the bands is condensed and reproduced within each mixed-ability form-group. And through the allocation of pupils to options, the processes of the separation and ranking of pupils in the classroom can be directly related to the distribution of initial life-chances in the occupation market. However, this chapter must be viewed primarily as exploratory rather than conclusive. It became apparent towards the end of the final field work stage of the research that certain 'effects' brought about by the mixed-ability grouping might not be explicable without longer-term and more intensive observation and analysis of teacher-pupil interaction in the mixed-ability classroom. The orientation of the analysis of the mixed-ability context has been towards the examination of the innovation process and the implementation of the innovation, rather than a study of classroom interaction *per se*. Classroom observation was not employed to obtain data on the details of teacher–pupil interaction or differences in the nature of that interaction from one pupil to another.[45] Furthermore, in evaluating the wider relevance of the findings of this chapter, it should also be taken into account that the particular cohort referred to here is the first mixed-ability year-group to go through the school, and mixed-ability teaching and syllabuses were being attempted for the first time by most of the staff. Thus, the possibility of a classic 'Hawthorne effect' cannot be ruled out.[46] Finally, the sample basis for the comparison of the mixed-ability forms with the banded forms is extremely restricted, especially as it was not possible to examine the option choice and option allocation ratios quantitatively across the mixed-ability cohort. Generalizations drawn from specific points of comparison must therefore be regarded as tentative.

Clearly, there is a great deal more to be done in the way of sociological investigation into mixed-ability grouping and the teaching of mixed-ability groups,[47] especially with regard to the ways in which teachers perceive pupils differently, interact with them differently, and convey to them different conceptions of personal worth. There is also a need to consider the sociological implications of the differentiation of the curriculum within the mixed-ability classroom and the ways in which this differentiation might affect the pupils' experience of schooling and access to high-status courses. But one point that does emerge clearly from this examination of mixed-ability is that research into educational innovation cannot be divorced from the consideration of teachers' definitions and constructs, and the social and organizational determinants which they perceive to be constraints upon their practice. The importance of the teachers' commitments and interpretations in relation to the implementation of the mixed-ability innovation will be discussed more fully in the final chapter.

9   Conclusions

As with most case-study research based on a methodology of participant observation, the outcomes of this study do not lend themselves to conclusions in terms of one or two carefully-tested hypotheses, but rather to a set of inter-related propositions. Indeed, I did not enter into my field work with specific hypotheses to test or a rigidly predetermined research design. But I did have general issues in mind and a theoretical framework which directed my attention to certain events in the field. It quickly became apparent which issues would be theoretically important, but I would certainly not claim to have exhausted all possible aspects of the exploration of the field or even of my own data. Once propositions began to emerge from the analysis of data, I made efforts to search for negative or qualifying, as well as supporting, instances, although the organization of the study over a long period of time did not always make this easy, or as extensive as I would have wished.

Streaming and selection in the comprehensive school

The examination of the careers of the banded pupils at Beachside clearly replicates the findings of other studies of streaming in secondary education – that is, 'that differentiation and polarization occurred as the pupils moved through the school' (Lacey 1970 : 187). Also, as found elsewhere, the anti-school and pro-school sub-cultures which emerged from these processes were linked to a social class differentiation (see figure 14). It is apparent from the analysis and description of the banding system that there is little evidence of the aims and objectives of any of the ideological models of comprehensive education (discussed in chapter 1) being achieved to any significant degree at Beachside. For instance, comprehensive schooling at Beachside failed, in terms of the meritocratic model, to provide a greater equality of opportunity or a 'fairer' system than the selective bipartite system it replaced; it still involved the selection and

280

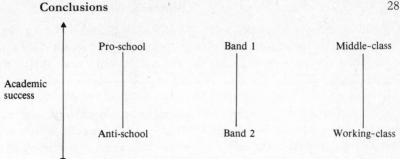

Figure 14. Pro-school and anti-school sub-cultures, and social class differentiation (adapted from Lacey 1970 : 187)

separation of pupils at their point of entry into the secondary sector.[1] The allocation to bands also entailed a separation of school-career experiences for pupils; differences in the pupils' experiences of schooling began at once in the first year, and may be viewed in the long term as being related directly to the distribution of occupational opportunity and future life-chances.

The experiential differences between the band 1 (predominantly middle-class) forms, and the band 2 and band 3 (predominantly working-class) forms include curricular differences, syllabus differences, pedagogical differences, and relational differences.

There were curricular differences in the first three years, in that band 1 pupils were introduced to a second language in the third year but band 2 and band 3 pupils were not, and in the cohort examined the band 3 forms dropped all language work at the end of the second year. But curricular differences were of greatest importance in the fourth and fifth years through the choice of, and allocation to, options. It is clear that the access of band 2 pupils to 'higher status' subject careers and examination courses was limited. But in order to account for this difference between the bands it is necessary to refer to other differences which emerged during the first three years.

Syllabus differences in the first three years can, as noted earlier (chapter 6), have a considerable impact upon the range of possible option choices available to pupils at the end of the third year. This was apparent, in one way or another, in almost all subjects. For instance, in Mathematics, French, Chemistry and Music, syllabus differences between the bands were institutionalized. In Mathematics, band 1 and band 2 forms followed a different course using different text books (S.M.P. numbered books and S.M.P. lettered books). In Music, band 2 forms were not taught major scales, and in Chemistry they were not introduced to atomic structure. In

French, different text-books were used for each band (*Le Français d' aujourd' hui, De Jour en Jour*, and *On y va* respectively), and the ultimate aims of the subject differed considerably for 'the academically more gifted', for 'the average child', and for the 'less able child'.[2]

In these and other subjects, there were also informal syllabus differences operating. These informal differences tended to be related to the teachers' expectations of the abilities, the individual level, and speeds of development of the pupils from the different bands. This gave rise to differences in content, differences in bias, and differences in the time allocated to particular topics. 'Topics' covered by band 1 were left out or treated differently in the band 2 syllabus, and certain 'topics' were taken more slowly, which often meant that band 2 and band 3 forms did not cover the whole syllabus.[3]

These kinds of syllabus differences were closely related to pedagogical differences; the 'pacing' and 'presentation' of knowledge in the different bands obviously had an impact on the coverage of the syllabus. Band 2 forms and band 3 forms tended to be taught differently from each other, and both were taught differently from band 1 forms. As we have seen in chapter 2, discussion was far more commonly used in band 1, and more boardwork and exercises were used in band 2. The teachers spent much longer talking in band 1 lessons and mentioned that they less often felt the need to reiterate basic principles.

These pedagogical differences in turn connected with the sort of relationship that exists between a teacher and pupils – that is, to relational differences. Some teachers found it necessary to modify their teaching-methods in band 2 lessons because of behavioural problems stemming from difficulties of control. In band 2 forms the relationship between teachers and pupils tended to be set within a regulative rather than an instructional context.

Furthermore, the teachers believed the band 1 and band 2 pupils to be different from each other, a fact which is apparent in the band stereotypes. Implicit in these stereotypes, and clearly evident from the teachers' constructs of the classroom, is the moral evaluation of pupils. Generally, the staff considered band 1 pupils to be more like themselves; their relationships with these pupils were as consociates and with band 2 pupils as contemporaries.[4]

Thus, generally in band 2 lessons over several years of secondary schooling, the pupils' relationships with their teachers tended to be strained and often hostile. It also became apparent that teachers were most concerned with what they perceived as the negative characteristics of band

2 pupils, and their perceptions were linked with expectations that they had of appropriate behaviour. Band 2 pupils were often seen to lack those qualities which were considered by teachers as desirable and appropriate to school, whereas most band 1 pupils appeared to be seen as possessing these qualities. The 'negative' aspects of the band 2 pupil emerged whenever a teacher compared band 1 and band 2 pupils.

These differences in the experience of schooling between bands gave rise to separate and different physical and intellectual environments for the pupils. Furthermore, these differences became institutionalized into a separated and hierarchically-organized curriculum by the end of the third year, through the allocation of pupils to both subject-options and examination-options. Thus in the examination of the school careers of the banded pupils, it is possible to establish links between the internal mechanisms of schooling at Beachside and the access of pupils to different positions in the occupational hierarchy.

It is difficult, clearly, to argue whether or not working-class pupils are 'better off' in a comprehensive school than in either a secondary modern or a grammar school. One is presented with the problem of equating moral and philosophical judgements with sociological evidence and analysis. It was possible to examine the covariation of test-scores and band allocation, but this proved to be generally inconclusive. However, it is apparent that while going some way towards solving the gross social problems and social inequalities which were a characteristic of the bipartite system, the streamed comprehensive school does produce an unstable, polarized social structure amongst its pupils, which in turn gives rise to considerable teaching and control problems for teachers.

As far as 'social engineering' is concerned, Beachside does ensure that children from different social classes enter and share the same building, excepting of course those who do not participate in the state sector. However, it is clear from the high levels of intra-band choices recorded in chapter 2, that banding itself inhibits the extent of social mixing in the school and even within the banded forms there was a tendency towards in-group choice among pupils from the same socio-economic backgrounds.

As far as the egalitarian ideology of comprehensive education is concerned, the initial selection for, and separation of, pupils through banding is totally opposed to the basic tenets of this ideology.

These findings suggest, then, that as far as the streamed comprehensive school is concerned (and streaming still takes place in the great majority of all comprehensive schools) the claims[5] of the advocates of comprehensive schooling are exaggerated, or irrelevant. Obviously, changes have taken place as a result of bringing all children into one school, but the form and principles of the previous bipartite system of education remain embedded within the comprehensive school. As in the bipartite schools, the comprehensive school pupil learns early on what kinds of position he can expect to achieve in the occupation market.

Mixed-ability innovation and change

The abandonment of streaming and the introduction of mixed-ability grouping present an increased possibility for the reform of conventional interpretations of comprehensive schooling. Ideologically, at least, the entire educational nexus – curriculum, teaching methods, text-books, school organization, and organization of the teaching profession – comes into question. However, from the evidence of this study, the ending of physically-separated experiences of schooling must not be naïvely taken as an indication of the end of selection and differential socialization through schooling. In Beachside, and in many other schools which have begun to introduce some mixed-ability, the end of the third year still marks a point of the separation of routes, environments and experiences for pupils. Mixed-ability teaching comes to an end in almost all subjects at this time, if it has not already petered out lower down the school – as we have seen, setting still introduces an element of early sponsorship into some subjects, particularly Mathematics and Languages. But apart from any obvious 'selective mechanisms' there are continuous selective processes within the mixed-ability classroom which must not be neglected. While school values are still essentially concerned with competition and the primacy of academic success, the mixed-ability system continues to feed its pupils more or less 'efficiently' into examination courses of different status and different negotiable value further up in the school. In the mixed-ability context it is apparent that it is the teacher who is the prime agent of selection. His relationship with the pupils in the classroom is fundamentally concerned with the separation and ranking of them according to perceived academic ability, and the allocation of status. This contributes to their development of self-image and a sense of worth – which may be inevitable in a competitive system.

One important point to be drawn from this is that it is misleading to look at comprehensive education or mixed-ability (or a common curriculum and a common examination for that matter), in the short run at least, as solutions to externally-imposed 'problems', or as effective (or adequate) techniques for political social engineering. The rhetoric of comprehensive education is concerned with equality of opportunity, but this is not the same thing as saying that comprehensive schools are being set up and run to achieve this aim. While structural justifications for ascribed status in the school may be becoming less evident, 'subtle modes of ascription continue to operate which have resulted in little change in the underlying structure of opportunity' (Sharp and Green 1976 : 225).

Perhaps the most striking aspect of the analysis of the mixed-ability forms in this study is the absence of dramatic change. Certainly, to use Bernstein's terms, there is no apparent shift in the education knowledge code.[6] The reasons for this absence of change become clearer when these observations are referred back to the analysis of the innovation from the point of view of the staff.

It is clear that much of the institutional support that mixed-ability receives at Beachside is a function of its greater effectiveness for social control.[7] Issues relating to social control have emerged at several points in the study. Problems of discipline and the behaviour of pupils were major concerns of the Beachside teachers.

Social control was certainly an aspect of the teachers' evaluation of pupils in the continuous processes of differentiation in the classroom. The teachers' perceptions of pupils were clearly and decisively influenced by the pupils' behaviour in the classroom. Especially in the context of banding, classroom behaviour was shown often to be of greater importance than academic performance in the ranking of pupils. In addition, as we saw, particular behavioural traits became identified in the minds of teachers and, to an extent, in the minds of the pupils, too, as indicators of being 'anti-school'. Although teachers' immediate self-interest in the interactional aspects of pupils' behaviour is undeniable, the stress placed upon social control in the social relations of the classroom may also be considered in terms of the pupils' internalization of authority relations.[8]

The vast majority of teachers were either in favour of mixed-ability, in the hope that its introduction might eliminate discipline problems in the classroom and improve the 'social atmosphere' of the school, or they were opposed to its introduction because they feared it would reduce the level of academic excellence in their subject. Those teachers who were ideologically committed to a mixed-ability system represented only a handful of the total staff group. But even among these ardent adherents justifications for the mixed-ability system were sought in terms of the maintenance or improvement of academic standards. The 'problem of the brighter child' was uppermost in the thinking of those teachers who hoped for a solution to disciplinary troubles as the basis of their support for mixed-ability and in their anticipation of mixed-ability teaching. In part, at least, the absence of radical changes in classroom methods, in the implementation of mixed-ability, may be linked to the lack of ideological commitment to the innovation by the teachers, although organizational and social constraints, as well as the teachers' 'residual' attitudes, played their part in this.[9]

As an educational concept, mixed-ability resides essentially, not in the grouping of pupils in a certain way, but in the way in which teachers play out their roles in the classroom, the teaching methods they use, and the way that they 'see' and organize their interaction with pupils. Berger and Luckmann (1967 : 92) suggest that

the realization of the drama depends upon the reiterated performance of prescribed roles by living actors. The actors embody the roles and actualise the drama by presenting it on a given stage. Neither drama nor institution exist empirically apart from the recurrent realization.

Mixed-ability is unlikely to involve radical changes in schooling while the 'organizing notions' embodied in the teachers' attitudes and views of the classroom remain essentially unchanged. It is apparent that most of the teachers continue both to believe in, and to think in terms of, 'types' of children. Indeed, as noted in the preface, the categorizing of children according to different needs in the classroom may be a pragmatic response to the practical problems of both teaching and learning in diverse groups of pupils, especially where the maintenance of high levels of academic achievement continues to be a major concern for teachers. But it is also clear from the teachers' own comments that the constraint of 'getting good examination results' is a major organizing principle in the selection of classroom methods, the ordering of syllabus knowledge, and the hierarchization of the curriculum. The community and institutional pressures on the staff at Beachside do define the teacher's primary function as 'producer'. I am not trying to say here that the institutional and societal constraints to produce examination passes necessarily prevent the Beachside teachers from acting in ways that accord with their own sense of what is important and valuable in education. For the most part, that is not true. But these systematic constraints do provide a vocabulary of motives which can be set against the arguments for change. And certainly, 'the institutional framework and the norms of the profession create pedagogic expectations that are impossible to ignore' (Eraut, forthcoming). But it is also evident that most teachers are actually committed to particular traditional conceptions and practices which they carry over into the mixed-ability classroom. In common with Esland (1971 : 72), I would suggest that educational opportunity is conditioned from the ideologies and classroom practices of teachers. Through their pedagogy and subject presentation, they are making critical, albeit 'taken for granted', decisions about the future of their pupils.

The abandonment of streaming does not necessarily change either those aspects of the socially-defined limits of 'good practice' or the ideologies of teaching within school, which relate to the organization of classroom knowledge, to teaching methods and to conceptions of ability which are fundamental to the process of differentiation.

It is worth while relating this argument back to the theoretical approach to the understanding of the innovation, outlined in chapter 8. The innovation was portrayed and analysed as a subjective cultural process with 'reference to the different meanings and significance which it has for the individuals who experience it' (Esland 1971 : 105). The application of this approach was an attempt to move away from the conception of innovation as an objective and reified structural entity. I hope to have demonstrated that the process of the innovation, and of its implementation, should be considered in terms of the 'embedded' social constructs of the actors involved and that in its inception, definition and social maintenance, this process does not necessarily give rise to a fixed or collectively-adhered-to reality.

In the past, innovations in education *have* normally been apprehended and studied as abstract and fixed social realities, and research has tended to neglect the social context of innovation, and the processes of interpretation and understanding on the part of the actors involved in doing the changing. From the present study it is clear that a teacher's response to a proposed innovation and later his implementation of it, if it is accepted, are heavily dependent upon his commitment to professional and organizational norm reference-groups, particularly his subject department and subject sub-culture community, and upon the limitations of perceived constraints upon his practice, in terms both of collectively-held definitions of good practice, and of the demands upon him as a 'producer' – that is, his perception of the demands made of him by super-ordinates within the school, his pupils and parents as clients, and the public community to achieve certain 'standards' or numbers of examination passes among the pupils he teaches.

Thus it quickly becomes apparent that an 'outsider's' view of de-streaming, taken from the 'literature', is inappropriate to the understanding of the innovation at Beachside. While it is clear that the organizational features of the school are important in contributing to the pupils' experience of schooling, and that the constraints upon teachers' practices must also be recognized in understanding the fate of innovations in British schools, the ideologies and commitments of the teacher must not be neglected in examining and accounting for the absence of change within schools. Certainly, the objectives which lead teachers to formulate their priorities must be accounted for if we wish to be able to understand and analyse classroom interaction,[10] and if there is to be any realistic dialogue between the sociologist of education and teachers.

In analysing educational innovations there is a tendency to overlook the fact that the reform of the education system also involves the reform of the educators. And as Hoare (1965) points out, this is a political task. If the introduction of mixed-ability grouping is viewed in this way, it would be unrealistic to expect any automatic or immediate changes in the social distribution of school success and failure. Indeed, as Bernstein (1965 : 308) points out:

Democratization of the means of education together with the internalizing of the achievement ethic by members of the working-class strata, may lead to an individualizing of failure, to a loss of self-respect which in turn modifies an individual's attitude both to his group and to the demands made upon him by his society.

Mixed-ability and comprehensive ideologies

Despite the narrowness of the examination of the practice of mixed-ability teaching and grouping achieved here, certain issues do emerge which can again be usefully referred back to the models of comprehensive education discussed earlier. In terms of the grouping of pupils and the organization of the curriculum, at least in some subjects, the introduction of mixed-ability obviously represents the sort of change in the internal structure of the school advocated by egalitarian comprehensivists. It also provides greatly increased possibilities for the achievement of the aims of social mixing and social tolerance advocated by the social-engineering supporters of comprehensive education, and the aims of greater equality of opportunity advocated by the meritocratic supporters. However, as we have seen, little of the innovation debate at Beachside was couched in these terms. And, as noted in the previous section, the 'organizing notions' in the teachers' working assumptions about the mixed-ability classroom tend to perpetuate a view of the classroom predicated upon the 'typing' and differentiation of pupils according to the single criterion of achieved-ability. Furthermore, when the physical separation of pupils does take place, through setting and then through the formation of O-level and C.S.E. classes in the fourth and fifth years, in the case-study form at least, the middle-class pupils are over-represented in top sets and O-level courses. In addition, the mixed-ability grouping creates, in effect a situation where many fewer working-class pupils have the opportunity to experience major success roles[11] in the classroom, because of the tendency of middle-class children to dominate the top positions in examinations and tests. This may also go a long way to account for the almost exact 'fit' between option choices and option allocations in the case-study form at the end of the third year, recorded in chapter 8. In the context of banding it was possible for pupils in bands 2 and 3 to be top of the form and still be regarded by their teachers as 'not up to much academically', thus creating a mismatch between warming-up and cooling-out experiences, and producing in some cases what were regarded as 'inappropriate' option choices – that is, over-aspiration. This did not occur in the mixed-ability forms. Thus, it would seem that so long as schooling continues to be seen by teachers as a stage of preparation for what succeeds it, and achieved ability is the single, and narrowly-defined, criterion for success in school, then the pupils' experience of education will inevitably be one of competition within a rigid hierarchy of rewards and esteem.

Schools are not autonomous and neutral institutions, and education is not simply a universal good, as much of the rhetoric surrounding comprehensive education and mixed-ability grouping appears to assume. The evidence of this study of the practice of comprehensive schooling suggests that, rather than being a profound egalitarian change in our education system, as is often suggested by 'utopian romantic idealists'[12] in educational literature, mixed-ability grouping in fact represents a new ideology of implementation[13] in the British school, which replaces more traditional ideologies whose legitimacy has been called into question. At the ideological level, the *Black Paper*[14] writers present mixed-ability grouping as a fundamental challenge to existing educational practices and values, and yet this study suggests that such challenges are by no means a necessary part of introducing mixed-ability groups. Indeed, continuity of traditional practices may be all too easily achieved. If this is true of comprehensive schools generally, then, in Turner's (1960) terms, even the comprehensive school which introduces mixed-ability is 'securing a system of sponsorship mobility behind a context mask' (Woods 1976 : 146). From this perspective the 'comprehensive debate', the publicly-rehearsed ad-vocacy of and opposition to comprehensive education, may be seen to be totally divorced from the realities of comprehensive schooling. If

Beachside is at all typical, then in terms of teachers' practices, comprehensive schools do not represent a socialist alternative to the 'selective' system. Indeed, when viewed in relation to current practice in the comprehensive school the 'comprehensive debate' appears merely to be a form of ideological in-fighting between the conservative, the rationalizing and the democratic schools of thought in British education.[15]

Notes

1 Comprehensive education: theory and practice

1 These two versions of comprehensive education as social engineering may be compared with the Beachside headmaster's views.

2 As I have tried to illustrate in this chapter, there is no single philosophy of comprehensive education but several. An important weakness in Ford's study, as noted by Holly (1972), is that she does not appear to be aware of the distinct and often conflicting views which have been involved in the push for comprehensive reorganization.

3 49 out of a total staff of 87 completed the questionnaire. However, the members of the P.E., Craft, Art and Home Economics departments were not asked to complete the questionnaire.

4 In terms of staffing, Beachside is very much a second-stage comprehensive. By the time this study was begun, that is, the school was well established as a comprehensive, with few vestiges of the secondary modern era remaining. However, of those teachers who had taught before coming to Beachside, the single largest group (39 per cent) had taught previously in secondary modern schools, with those who had taught in comprehensive schools (35 per cent) the second-largest group.

Table N1. *Teachers' professional experience previous to Beachside*

Secondary modern	Comprehensive	Grammar or Technical	Public or Private	Others	Total
18(39%)	16(35%)	6(13%)	5(1%)	1(2%)	46

5 This represents an 85 per cent sample of the first, second, fourth and fifth-year cohorts in the academic year 1973–4.

6 Unfortunately, the reader will find that the pastoral work of the school is poorly represented in the body of the book. Most of the counselling and guidance work of the pastoral staff, in dealing with pupils' problems, was naturally carried out in private in the year tutors' rooms. Consequently, in the material that does refer to pastoral care the more public problems of discipline in the school are over-represented.

7 This notion of 'the preferred view' comes from the work-in-progress of A. J. Bailey, Education Area, University of Sussex.

8 There was one experiment in integration in the academic year 1974–5 when three members of staff – from the English, Geography and History departments – were

permitted to organize an integrated studies course for three first-year forms. This course was run again the following year with the 'rump' first year but disappeared altogether when the middle-school reorganization in Beachside was complete and no more 11-year-old first years entered the secondary school. The headmaster was not in favour of subject integration, he said in an interview (1975).

> I'm not a committed integrated curriculum man. I think there's a lot of advantages in having a clear structure within which people work. But I can certainly see the possibility that a tide of integrated curriculum will roll through here. We didn't like what we saw on the integrated studies that was going on. We didn't think much of the standards.

And commenting on the experiment that he did allow he said

> the real problem about it is that you've got three people there who wanted to do it. They're excellent teachers, and so you can say almost *however* they're teaching, it'll come out all right.

But these comments demonstrate the importance of 'standards' in the headmaster's thinking on innovation at Beachside.

9 This was done by a vote of staff. The result was taken by a show of hands and was not recorded.
10 See note 8, above.

2 Banding, identity and experience

1 I am using the term career here as outlined by Hughes (1937), to refer to both an objective historical process and a subjective experience.
2 That is to say, a system of streaming where each form-group was identified separately in an academic hierarchy in relation to every other form-group.
3 Although some band 3 forms in some years did present particular problems.
4 The band 3 forms were also smaller than forms in bands 1 or 2, and were taught by specialist members of the remedial department for a large proportion of their timetable.
5 It must be borne in mind that these figures only represent 'trouble' that has been 'processed'. Punishments carried out independently by teachers are not recorded here. And as with all official statistics there are unknown factors which may have contributed to the differences between groups. For instance, it may be that similar offences manifested both in band 1 and band 2 lessons were punished more harshly in band 2 because of policies of 'stamping out trouble' or 'not letting them go too far' operated by particular teachers.
6 See N. Flanders (1970), *Analyzing Teaching Behavior*.
7 I found that this was generally true of staff throughout the school; during the three-year field work period, only three teachers were reluctant to allow me to 'sit in' on their lessons. In each case, they were young probationary teachers who were finding problems in controlling the forms I had asked to observe.
8 These similarities are borne out in the quantitative measures presented later.
9 The notion of a 'strict' teacher was a category used extensively at Beachside by teachers and pupils, especially by the pupils. It normally referred to the particular ability of certain teachers to control and monitor the behaviour of the forms they taught in such a way as to reduce disruption and misbehaviour to an absolute minimum.
10 See the lesson notes and transcripts presented on pp. 61–4.
11 All responses that could not be straightforwardly fitted into the Registrar General's classifications – e.g. 'engineer', 'he works at Smith's Factory' – were consigned to the

Unclassified category, as were the responses 'deceased', 'unemployed', 'I haven't got a father', etc.

12 The distribution of social class across the whole cohort is presented in table N2.

Table N2. *Distribution of social classes across the second-year cohort, 1973–4*

	I	II	IIIN	Total non-manual	IIIM	IV	V	Total manual	Unclass.
2CU	5	10	5	20	12	–	–	12	–
2GD	4	8	5	17	12	–	–	12	4
2ST	–	2	3	5	14	3	–	17	8
2FT	2	6	10	18	11	2	–	13	3
Band 1	11	26	23	40	49	5	0	54	15
2LF	–	4	1	5	13	6	1	20	8
2BH	2	2	6	10	12	4	–	16	8
2WX	1	2	4	7	15	5	1	21	3
2TA	2	3	2	7	15	8	3	26	–
Band 2	5	11	13	29	55	23	5	83	19
2UD	–	2	4	6	6	5	–	11	4
2MA	2	2	–	4	5	4	–	9	2
Band 3	2	4	4	10	11	9	–	20	6

The questionnaire on which this table is based was not completed by nine pupils in the cohort. The relationship between banding and social class is significant $r^2 = 20$ d.f. $= 2$ p $< .001$.

13 I.Q. testing was abandoned by the Local Authority in 1972.
14 See pp. 179–81.
15 See J. Floud and A. H. Halsey (1957), 'Social class, intelligence tests and selection for secondary schools'.
16 Once established, the existence of band stereotypes has very important ramifications for the school careers of pupils.
17 Michael Innes was the only pupil in 2TA to be promoted to band 1 after the first term.
18 Within the mixed-ability cohorts, the same process of primary school recommendation was used to allocate pupils to ensure a reasonable distribution of abilities in each form. The subject teachers were unaware of the primary school recommendations in regard to individual pupils; assessments thus had to be 'made' rather than 'taken'.
19 This stereotyping may be considered and examined in another sense via the teachers' linguistic behaviour. The member's management of problems in any organization may

be 'seen in the devices he uses to make them consistent, repetitive, normal and natural. By means of his linguistic behaviours the actor selects things which through meaning become social objects. That is they have potential for action when they are named, counted, assessed and ordered' (Manning 1971 : 224).

In this case the relevant lexicon of concepts and usages is that which refers to categories of pupils. Apart from the band labels, categories in normal use, applied to particular populations, were: 'remedial', 'bright', 'fast', 'slow', 'thick', 'dumb', 'less able', 'academic', 'less academic', 'problem', 'anti-school', 'pro-school', and 'average'. All of these categories appear to be concerned either with imputed academic ability or behavioural characteristics – that is, the same contours of relevance that are evident in all other aspects of the teacher-pupil relationship.

20 The emergence of these stereotypes of bandness is important to the school careers of these pupils in several ways, as we shall see in the following chapters, but especially in the development of form reputations within the school, and as a label of capability with which the pupils must negotiate in making their option choices for examination courses at the end of the third year (see chapter 6).

21 In addition, the inferior status of the band 2 and band 3 forms is both reflected in and exacerbated by the allocation of teacher-resources (see pp. 17 and 18).

22 Tony Talston.

23 The differences in adaptation of the different groups of pupils to the pressures and problems of schooling could be related to Merton's (1968) typology of modes of adaptation: conformity; innovation; ritualism; retreatism; and rebellion.

24 This, of course, relates to the amount given. Teachers did not expect band 2 pupils to do as much as band 1 pupils, but the difference was not of the magnitude of 3 : 1.

25 These figures may be compared with the times reported by the second-year grammar school pupils in Lacey's (1970) study, p. 68.

Table N3. *Estimated length of time spent on homework (after Lacey)*

Form	Estimated average time spent each night after streaming: second year	
2E	2 hours	0 mins
2A	1 hour	45 mins
2B	1 hour	18 mins
2C	1 hour	7 mins

26 This was Tony Talston, see p. 88.

27 This was Peter Masters, see p. 87.

28 The teacher in a 2CU Geography lesson, for instance, said, 'Perhaps you might also see what you can find out about the life of Captain Cook and we will spend a little while talking about it at the beginning of next week's lesson.'

29 When other problems emerge, the reaction of staff can be seen to be different from their reaction to the band 2 forms (see pp. 101–2).

30 Similar processes have been observed in American studies of academic stratification.

For example, Wilson (1963) found in a study of 14 elementary schools in Berkeley, California, that the normalization of diverging standards by teachers crystallized different levels of scholastic achievement. Teachers were seen to adapt their norms of success and their concepts of excellence to the composition of their student bodies. And in a review of a number of other similar studies, Passow (1966 : 100) concluded: 'Teachers accept much less from low income children. The normalization of lower standards of performance in the less favoured socio-economic group provides the same kind of circular reinforcement for the group that normalization of past performance does for the individual student.'

31 This was done by the collection of sociometric data.
32 The role of social class bias in the informal relations between the pupils will be returned to in chapter 3.

3 Two case-studies of banded forms

1 See Meyann (1979) for an account of this among groups of girls in a middle school.
2 The use of the number of sociometric choices received by individuals as a measure of 'popularity' obviously presents some difficulties, and this should be regarded merely as a general indication of liking. Jennings (1950) equates high-choice status with leadership and it is common to consider the number of choices an individual receives to be an indication of that person's popularity. I am not unaware of, or unsympathetic to, Northway's (1967) warning against the transference of choices from the subject who makes the choice to the object of that choice: she rejects the assumption that the more choices an individual receives the better off he is, as a false value typical of a consumer society.
3 Unlike Ronny's, their quietness was not defined as a 'problem' by their teachers.
4 It was never quite clear to me exactly what he had done.
5 Technically speaking, not an isolate.
6 I made use of a modification of one of Kelly's (1955 : 23) elicitation routines in order to collect the data for the construction of the tables presented in the text. Kelly himself makes the point that 'the procedure can be varied in a great many ways'.
I presented teachers with cards with the names of pupils from one form in groups of three, and I asked the question, 'In what way are two of these pupils the same and one different?' From this, by going through all the pupils in the form, one or both ends of 'bi-polar' constructs were noted. Sometimes both ends emerged from one set of three pupils. For example: 'John is very quiet, whereas Paul and Ian are very noisy.'
Sometimes the 'other end' was obtained from a different set. When the whole form was completed I went over the constructs with the teacher, checking the meaning of those that were not clear, comparing them with each other, and sometimes asking for the 'other end' of an unfinished pair. The next stage was to ask the teacher: 'If you were going to be taking over a new form and had the opportunity to talk with the person who had been their teacher up until that time, which of these constructs would be most important to know from him?' etc., etc. This ranks the constructs in order of importance.
I then asked: 'At which end of these constructs do you think a pupil should be in order to be successful at school?' and on the basis of these 'ends' and with the teacher's help each of the constructs was put into the form of a four-point scale. So that, for instance, bright – dull, became bright – tends to be bright – tends to be dull – dull. Finally, I asked the teacher to go through the list of pupils in the class and give a score for each pupil on each construct.
In most cases the elicitation routine progressed smoothly and the teachers were very co-

operative, and willing to accept the form of the procedure. The number of tables of scores I finally obtained was, however, small because of the length of time it took to go through the procedure – usually about an hour. Obviously, this kind of use of Kelly's elicitation routine must be seen for what it is, a crudely simplified way of collecting, presenting and analysing the teachers' views of pupils. However, in this context, I would argue, taken in relation to other sources of data, it does provide a useful and acceptable shorthand method for illustrating teachers' perceptions.

In Kelly's view (1955 : 107), if you want to discover how another person thinks, you must try to understand his construct systems.

'Man looks at his world through transparent patterns or templets which he creates and attempts to fit over the realities of which the world is composed. . . Let us give the name constructs to these patterns that are tried on for size. They are ways of construing the world.'

Bannister and Fransella (1971 : 18), two of the main exponents of Kelly's work in Britain, make the point that:

'Kelly is . . . asserting that we cannot construct an interpretation-free reality directly. We can only make assumptions about what reality is and then proceed to find out how useful or useless those assumptions are.'

And they note that 'It is the user of the theory who has to supply a content of which the theory might make sense.' In this case, teachers' assumptions about pupils in the classroom are the content with which we are concerned.

7 As it turned out, this affected the social structure of 3TA only marginally.

8 Indeed, the rate of repetition of individual choices is almost the same for both forms, as can be seen from the two sociometric questionnaires administered during the second year: in 2CU 68 per cent of choices made in the first questionnaire were repeated in the second; in 2TA 67 per cent of choices made in the first questionnaire were repeated in the second.

9 A third questionnaire was also administered to the pupils of 3TA at this time.

10 This insularity is demonstrated also in the small proportion of choices made *between* the identified friendship groups.

Table N4. *Choices made between friendship groups as a percentage of all choices*

	2CU			2TA		
	1st	2nd	3rd	1st	2nd	3rd
		questionnaire			questionnaire	
Total choices made inside the form	86	76	84	84	83	97
Number outside identified friendship groups	7	8	7	4	1	5
Percentage	8%	9%	8%	5%	1%	5%

11 Using the formula:
$$\text{I.P. value} = \frac{\text{Number of in-group choices} \times \text{Number of pupils in the out-group}}{\text{Number of out-group choices} \times \text{Number of pupils in the in-group}}$$

12 In a previous study by the author (Ball 1973), *The Study of Friendship Groups in a Multi-*

Racial Comprehensive School, social and economic status striations *were* found to be an important part of the pupils' thinking about the social structure of their form-groups.

13 It should be borne in mind that some of the sociometric questionnaires were administered farther from the July and December examination periods than were others. The time that has elapsed between the previous examination period and the administration of the questionnaires may be a factor in making academic achievement a more or less important factor in the making of friendship choices.

14 The Guess-Who-Test is a means of isolating and evaluating an individual's reputation within his social group, originated by Hartshorne *et al.* (1930). The test involves presenting the pupils with a series of character vignettes on a questionnaire – for example:

This person is very quiet. He/she is usually alone and is not much involved with other people in the class.

This person is very intelligent. He/she always does well in exams and can always answer questions in class.

The pupils are then asked to write underneath each description the name of the person or persons in class who best fit that description.

15 Except Talston.

16 Tawy's father offered him £ 1 for every mark over 50 per cent that he achieved in these examinations.

17 All the forms were asked if they would like to organize some activity to collect money for charity. 2TA did not in the second year, but they did in the third.

18 See Lacey (1970), chapter five.

19 See Becker (1952), 'Social class variations in the teacher – pupil relationship'.

20 There was also a significant level of association between these grid positions and the rank-order positions in the third-year examinations, both at the .01 level. Although the level of significance is less, the congruence remains clear. Science grid $r_s = 0.53$, English grid $r_s = 0.49$. The association between the rank-orders from the second-year and third-year examinations is also significant, at the .001 level, $r_s = 0.61$.

21 Several pupils in both forms kept diaries for me. I provided them with small notebooks which they then filled in day by day and returned to me when they were full. All pupils were painstaking and conscientious in keeping up entries.

22 I was able to interview all of the new arrivals during the third year.

23 This particular formulation is derived from a paper by P. Yates, 'The school as a culture', given at a Saturday School on *Social Reality and Socialization: The Pupils' Perception of Schooling* at the University of Sussex Centre for Continuing Education, 22 October 1977.

4 Adolescents, social life and school life

1 In using this all-embracing term I do not intend to give support to Coleman's (1961) notion of the emergence of a classless culture of youth, separated from the dominant adult culture. On the contrary, the following analysis suggests that the bifurcation of the pupil body in school extends to activities out of school as well. As Murdock and McCron (1976 : 10) argue, the social life of adolescents is marked by 'the continuing centrality of class inequalities in structuring both life styles and life chances'.

2 The questionnaires were both administered on a Friday; thus, the evening referred to is a Thursday.

3 Social life activities involved membership of a group or attendance at a communal meeting place.

4 Obviously, the evidence based on one arbitrarily chosen evening must be regarded as only a tentative indication of normal patterns of activity, but the picture which emerged from these questionnaire responses was reinforced by the diaries which several pupils in 2TA and 2CU completed for me.

5 Eight pupils in all, three in 2TA and five in 2CU, kept diaries for me.

6 I am sure, however, that some of the pupils in 2TA did revise.

7 These entries may represent the participation of these girls in what McRobbie and Gerber (1976 : 220) call 'the culture of the bedroom' :
   'Teeny-bopper culture can easily be accommodated, for ten- to fifteen-year-old girls, in the home, requiring only a bedroom and a record player and permission to invite friends.'

8 In general terms, the point made by Lacey (1970), Sugarman (1957), and Murdock and McCron (1976) must be made again here, that the polarization and differentiation of the school culture are also evident in the adolescent sub-culture.
   Contact out of school between pupils who were anti-school and pupils who were pro-school was rare. They were normally involved in different kinds of activities and in different locations. For instance, several members of 3CU belonged to a church youth club in Beachside, but none of the pupils in 3TA did. Talston of 3TA sometimes visited this club, but Veronica explained to me that 'he always comes here on his own, he never brings his "friends".'

9 Lacey (1970 : 21) represents this in the following diagram, which illustrates the developing discreteness of roles and disjunction between the world of the school and the adolescent peer-group.

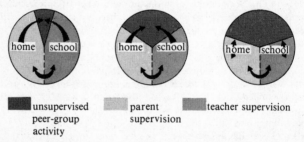

10 Indeed, some manifestations of sub-cultural 'style' were against the school rules on uniform.

11 See also Birksted (1976).

12 For the term 'delinquescent', see Hargreaves (1967).

13 As Murdock and McCron (1976 : 17) write :
   'Rather than replacing class-based cultures, the new teenage leisure culture [is] . . . being laid over the top, setting up an increasingly complicated interaction between the two.'

14 In some cases, this led to a desire to 'get exams' alongside a continued alienation from the normative order of the school.

15 See Hargreaves (1967 : 80).

16 These may be relevant as micro-systems of sub-cultural allegiance within the classification described in the subsequent paragraphs on p. 120.

17 Lambert argues that different schools would manifest different dominant informal systems among the pupils.

18 I took up this issue in a questionnaire completed for me by five fifth-year forms. I asked,

'What do you want to get out of school now?' Of the 95 replies, 52 (62 per cent) mentioned *only* instrumental ends, and a further 13 (14 per cent) mentioned instrumental ends with others. The other ends included, for instance, 'a good education', 'friends', 'to learn to get on with people' and 'I expect to learn things which will be helpful to me.' Of the remainder, only 8 (8 per cent) mentioned only non-utilitarian ends, and 15 (16 per cent) replied 'nothing'. Most of the utilitarian responses linked 'getting good exam results' with 'getting a good job'.

5 Subject-option choice: the selection of knowledge and the management of pupils

1 Some pupils, because of their age, can leave at Easter in their fifth year and therefore not take any examinations unless they want to.

2 These choices are negative in the sense that the pupils choose them because they have to fill up their timetable, not because they have any commitment to the subject.

3 It is important to note that in the year following the one dealt with here the option-allocation system was revamped to increase the amount of counselling received by pupils. The negotiation of options for individual pupils was given over to a much greater extent to form tutors. This meant that the pupils received much more guidance in making their original choices, and often received support from their form tutor in pressing for acceptance of choices.

4 These were among comments written by teachers on lists of pupils who had chosen their subject; they were repeated many times.

5 These are courses which are designed within the school and moderated by the C.S.E. regional examination board.

6 Similarly, Cicourel and Kitsuse (1963) found in their study of Lakeshore High School that assignment to college or non-college courses was mostly dependent upon the interpretations of a student's ability and aptitude by admissions personnel.

7 This clearly diverges from the equality-of-opportunity ideology of comprehensive education.

8 The term 'familial resources' is intended here in the sense used by Lacey (1970 : 125–6):
    '1.Psychological. In addition to the pupils' I.Q., this variable includes the emotional resources of the family unit.
    2. Social. Includes all the resources which stem from the social position of the family unit. Indicative of this variable are occupation and income.
    3. Cultural. Includes the parents' ability to understand and manipulate an "academic" or "school" culture. An important indicator of this is the educational background.'

9 The 'make up' of a teaching group – that is, which pupils are accepted – will also, as we have seen, go a long way towards deciding what sorts of teaching difficulties the teacher is going to face.

10 These 'new' subjects offered at Mode III C.S.E., mainly under the auspices of the Human Studies department, were part of the school policy of ensuring that every pupil in the fourth year would be involved in a full programme of examination courses. This was a deliberate attempt to move away from the pejorative status division, which still exists in many schools called comprehensive, between those pupils who are taking examination courses and non-examination pupils.

11 This represents a clear example of 'cooling out' in terms of Goffman's (1952 : 452) original usage. He wrote
    'An attempt is made to define the situation for the mark in a way that makes it easy for him to accept the inevitable and quietly go home.'

12 In Woods's (1976) terms the over- and under-aspiring pupils are both 'system disruptive'.

13 Clark (1960) argues that this forces the pupils to confront themselves and also serves to detach the school and the staff from the emotional aspects of 'cooling out' work.

14 The account remains at the level of 'because of' rather than 'in order to' statements.

15 Committee of the Secondary Schools Examinations Council Report (1943) on Curriculum and Examinations in Secondary Schools (Norwood), London, H.M.S.O.

16 Where once these differences in clientele and curricula were embodied in the grammar school, technical school and secondary modern school differentiation, a similar division of capabilities is now used to differentiate between the pupils in bands 1, 2 and 3, and the courses appropriate for them.

17 At Beachside, entry into A-level courses required at least a B grade in the equivalent O-level.

18 For example, the options handbook said of Human Studies (Citizenship):

> It is a preparation for young people to understand the society in which they will soon be playing an adult role. The topics studied include the family, personal health and Health Services. Sometimes it includes half-a-day a week in experience of community service. For example, meals on wheels, hospital work, helping in nursery school.

Similarly for Home Studies:

> We aim to prepare the pupils for the practical aspects of home management and to provide an opportunity for all pupils to have an understanding of practical knowledge essential to young adults in today's society.

The Careers Master also taught a Mode III C.S.E.:

> My C.S.E. is Chemistry for Living, I think a lot of these other subjects would say the same really, it is not for qualifications. I think we can't live today in this technological age without knowing a lot of Chemistry, a housewife needs to know more than the husband does, but I see it as my job to make them into good husbands and good wives or good employees.

19 It is important to qualify this statement so that it does not suggest an absolute increase in the closeness of the connection between qualifications obtained at school and occupations attained afterwards. Recent research by the Oxford Mobility Study Group (cf. Goldthorpe and Llewellyn 1977) indicates that although the link between education and occupational attainment is increased, with a high level of direct entry into social classes I and II (on the Hope-Goldthorpe classification), the significance of social mobility through work-life movements is not diminished.

20 The differences between the courses and subjects in terms of the knowledge involved and relationships between them may be represented diagramatically (see p. 301).

21 Hollingshead (1961 : 217) noted that
'In 1941, the class I's and class II's concentrated on the college preparatory (64 per cent) and ignored the commercial course. Fifty-one per cent of the class III's were in the general, 27 per cent in the college preparatory, and 21 per cent in the commercial course. The class IV's entered the general (58 per cent) and the commercial courses (33 per cent) and avoided the college preparatory; only 9 per cent were in it. The pattern for the class V's was similar to the class IV's, except that 38 per cent were in the commercial and 4 per cent in the college preparatory course. . . this condition undoubtedly is related to the values associated by students and teachers with the college preparatory course in contrast to the general and commercial courses.'

22 A further aspect of difference apparent in the choices made by the pupils in these two classes is a difference in subject-popularity between boys and girls. This is a difference both across and between the bands.

Theoretical and academic school-based
knowledge. Non-vocational qualifications
may be viewed by the pupils as vocational
in the sense of 'getting a good job'.

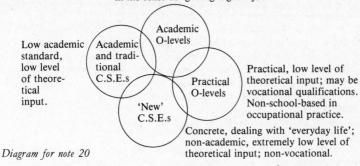

Low academic
standard,
low level
of theore-
tical
input.

Academic
and tradi-
tional
C.S.E.s

Academic
O-levels

'New'
C.S.E.s

Practical
O-levels

Practical, low level of
theoretical input; may be
vocational qualifications.
Non-school-based in
occupational practice.

Concrete, dealing with 'everyday life';
non-academic, extremely low level of
theoretical input; non-vocational.

Diagram for note 20

For example, overall in the Sciences (for both classes) boys chose 51 Science courses (18 in 3TA and 33 in 3CU) and girls chose only 21 Science courses (20 in 3CU and only 1 in 3TA). However, this trend was reversed in the case of Biology: 10 girls chose it, but only 6 boys.

These differences between the sexes in certain subjects were apparent throughout this year-cohort. For example, in the choices made for O-level courses presented in table N5, girls are over-represented in French and Music, and boys in Chemistry and Physics, but History, Geography and R.K. are not dominated by one sex or the other. These curricular differences between boys and girls also reflect the findings of the D.E.S. Education Survey 21 (G.B. D.E.S., 1975). In a sample of 488 secondary schools an exactly similar pattern of differences was found.

Table N5. *Sex and subject choice, showing the
numbers of boys and girls choosing O-level courses*

	Boys	Girls	Total
French	21(30%)	50(70%)	71(100%)
Chemistry	29(71%)	12(29%)	41(100%)
Music	7(27%)	19(73%)	26(100%)
History	38(49%)	40(51%)	78(100%)
Geography	27(50%)	27(50%)	54(100%)
Physics O(N)	19(76%)	6(24%)	25(100%)
R. K.	15(42%)	21(58%)	36(100%)

23 The importance of these being first-job destinations must not be underestimated, especially in the light of recent social mobility studies (cf. Goldthorpe and Llewellyn 1977) which indicate both the continuing contribution of intra-generational work-life mobility and the occurrence of counter-mobility ('that is of work-life movement which has the effect of returning an individual back to his class of origin, following some initial shift away on his entry into employment, and which thus serves to promote intergenerational stability') in the case of men from the 'service' and 'cadet' classes in the occupational hierarchy.

24 These destinations were obtained from the Local Youth Employment Service and totalled 105 pupils; 8 others were on the books of the service but their job destinations were unknown. A further 88 pupils stayed on into the sixth form from this particular cohort, leaving 68 pupils (25 per cent), who had been on the books of the school in this cohort at some time during 1973–4, unaccounted for.

25 Parsons (1959 : 315) makes a similar point:
    'it should be kept in mind that secondary school is the principal springboard from which lower-status persons will enter the labour force, whereas those achieving higher status will continue their formal education in college, and some of them beyond.'

26 Although of course other extraneous factors, such as age, play a part in the differences between the groups. Aspirations may also be important.

27 See chapter 2.

28 This accounts for all but one of the sixth-form leavers in this cohort.

29 Woods (1976 : 142) argues that
    'Institutional channelling creates its own effects, and in association with (the) group perspectives that form within the channels and the development of teachers' typifications, brings about a crystallization of opportunities at a very early stage.'

30 Young (1971b : 24) makes the point that
    'Education is . . . a selection and organization from the available knowledge at a particular time which involves conscious and unconscious choices. It would seem that it is, or should be, the central task of the sociology of education to relate the principles of selection and organization that underlie curricula to their institutional and interactional setting in schools and classrooms and to the wider social structure.'
    In one sense this analysis of option-choices fulfills Young's imperative. For here is a point in the pupils' school careers at which the processes of selection and the stratification of the curriculum and the management of knowledge are closely related.

31 The execution of the analysis through both a selection perspective and a management of knowledge perspective has been particularly fruitful here. The use of one approach to the exclusion of the other would surely have detracted from the insights provided by their contribution.

32 This was certainly the case in relation to the introduction of mixed-ability at Beachside.

33 See Lacey (1976).

34 This is important both for the stereotyping of band 2 and 3 pupils and the departmental concern with pass-rates.

35 The national figures for all maintained schools for 1972–5 are shown in table N6.

Table N6. *Percentage passes at G.C.E. O-Level, Summer Examinations*

Years	Boys	Entries	Girls	Entries	Total
1972	58.3	1,205,002	63.3	1,099,865	60.7
1973	58.6	1,215,844	63.0	1,163,146	60.7
1974	58.2	1,225,243	60.7	1,222,077	59.5
1975	58.1	1,322,229	60.8	1,269,017	59.1

Source: *Statistics of Education, 1975*, Vol. 2: *School Leavers C.S.E. and G.C.E.*, H.M.S.O.

36 This is equivalent to an O-level pass.
37 Benn and Simon (1972) reported that the 'open' sixth form had been adopted by 68 per cent of all comprehensive schools by 1968.
38 Both upper and lower sixth form and A-level and non-A-level pupils were organized into mixed tutor-groups and then taught separately by course and year.

6 Mixed-ability: innovation and debate

1 Certainly related to this is the fact that neither the headmaster nor the teachers attempted, during this period, to highlight the innovation or present the school as a 'showpiece'. As far as the parents were concerned the teachers maintained a 'low profile' for the innovation.
2 A term used by Smith and Keith (1971); see below, p. 166.
3 There were only two public-relations exercises concerning the introduction of mixed-ability. One involved the headmaster visiting each of the feeder schools to address parents whose children would be moving to the secondary school. The second, in year three of the innovation, was a school association (P.T.A.) meeting to discuss mixed-ability.
4 The head of the English department in particular was identified with this position, as we shall see.
5 Parallels do exist between Cambire and Beachside even though the levels at which the comparison is made are different. Whereas the 'bureau' was the agent of change at Cambire, at Beachside the initiative for change emerged from the teachers. At Cambire the changes in teaching methods were imposed upon the staff of the school, and it was expected that *their* behaviour would change. At Beachside the change was imposed upon the pupils and it was expected that their behaviour would be different from that of previous cohorts.
6 Because of the lack of specificity of the innovation, considered as a cultural process, I felt that it would be inappropriate to designate the innovation in a particular genre or category, as is done in some of the literature of educational innovation (cf. Dalin (1970), Goodlad (unpublished), Holmes (1973) and Marklund (1972)). Marklund (1972: 278), for example, suggests a categorization of innovations in terms of their 'level' within the structure of the school. He describes three 'levels' of innovation:
    'Level I: the external structure of the school, above all in respect to the grades, stages and divisions into different courses of study.
    Level II: timetables and syllabi, with aims and content of subjects or groups of subjects.
    Level III: teachers' instructional methods, the pupils' way of working, educational materials, study materials and forms of evaluation.'
    The innovation at Beachside was posited at level I, but it would be false and unrealistic to divorce that conceptually from the implications at levels II and III.
7 See House (1974).
8 This participative decision-making was the headmaster's idea. He felt that the commitment of the teachers would be lacking if they could not identify themselves with the decision.
9 Jackson (1968: 148–55) questions the commonly-made assumption that a teacher's primary concern is the pupils' learning. He suggests that the immediate concerns of teachers are more likely to be how to survive and how to maximize personal satisfactions.

10 Following Becker's (1961) quasi-statistical analysis, the frequency and distribution of statements related to the three teacher-perspectives were as follows:

Table N7. *Statements of perspective*

	Academic	Disciplinarian	Idealist	Total
Volunteered	14	16	9	39
In response to direct questioning	12	14	4	30
	26	30	13	69

11 Nevertheless, there is a clash of paradigms in English teaching between the 'grammar' and 'creative writing' schools of thought which tend to reflect attitudes of traditionalism and progressivism, respectively, toward educational issues in general.

12 A similar division of attitudes among subject departments towards the grouping of pupils was found by Richardson (1973 : 87–90) in her study of Nailsea School. As at Beachside, streaming, setting and mixed-ability tended to be discussed in terms of the extent to which particular forms of grouping were necessary for the effective teaching of different subjects.

13 However, as we shall see later, the Mathematics department did change its position and extend mixed-ability into the second year in year 3 of the innovation.

14 This may be contrasted with the approach outlined by the heads of the English and History departments, who were both strong advocates of mixed-ability.

> English is only important in relation to people; it is their responses and reactions which are the important things in lessons.
>
> The subject-material is basically a means towards the understanding of their own situation.

15 A similar configuration of opposition to mixed-ability grouping was indicated in an Inner London Education Authority Inspectors' Report (1976) on the introduction of mixed-ability in six comprehensive schools.

16 Dalin (1973 : 230) makes the point that

> 'only in a very few cases is consensus the basis for innovation in education and . . . conflicts are a natural consequence of conflicting values and vested interests.'

17 At this time, though, Mathematics moved over to mixed-ability grouping in the second year.

18 Mathematics was an exception, as described below, p. 214.

19 This is an aspect of selection not dissimilar from the academic ideology of the grammar school.

20 See Esland (1971) for a discussion of paradigms and educational practice.

21 That is, discovery methods as in the Schools Council Integrated Science Project.

22 Mode III C.S.E. courses are an exception.

23 Bailey (1976 : 25) goes on to argue that, in terms of the 'logical conceptual structures or activities and performances connected with a subject', it is subjects such as Mathematics, Sciences, History, Geography, English-language work and foreign languages that are appropriate for pupils to study in mixed-ability groups, because 'they are all areas in which *individuals* have to acquire complex and formalized systems of thought and understanding' (p. 28). Whereas in other activities, necessarily taking place in groups, such as Physical games like football and hockey, the playing of music and drama

activities, 'there are satisfactions to be thwarted and frustrated if the ability and information mix is too diverse. The teaching and organizational problems of the teacher increase proportionately to the degree of mix' (Bailey 1976 : 28).

24 In an early interview (see p. 170) the headmaster suggested that the teachers' expectations were the important factor in the behaviour and performance of band 2 pupils. In a later interview, however, he attributed the improvement to the dilution effect of disbanding groups of 'problem' pupils, thus suggesting that the 'problem' behaviour was an inherent quality of particular pupils rather than an outcome of their experiences of failure.

25 Isolation – that is, one teacher per class behind closed doors – is commonly referred to as autonomy. But the use of the term autonomy introduces a misleading element of complete freedom into the teaching-situation which ignores the constraints upon the teachers' practice at the institutional level and beyond.

26 This did vary from department to department, however. The English and Mathematics departments in particular spent time in departmental meetings discussing 'ways of teaching', but there was little discussion of the specific problems of teaching mixed-ability groups; and certainly no provision of in-service courses related to mixed-ability teaching was made. Indeed, the situation in the school, in this regard, was not unlike that discussed by Gross, Giaquinta and Bernstein (1971 : 160) at Cambire:
'Our field observations revealed that teachers received little help within or outside their classrooms as they attempted to implement the innovation and that there was little communication between teachers and administrators about the problems to which the teachers were exposed during this period.'

27 There is a tendency in some recent literature in the sociology of education to portray teachers as unconsciously constrained and unaware of the pressures that shape and limit their practice; this is a false and patronizing over-generalization.

28 This comment was made at the time of Tameside Council's refusal to implement comprehensive reorganization.

29 It may be seen that both attitudes and experiences of practice are represented here.

30 Thus, essentially the same issues were being raised in year 3 of the innovation as in year 1 and in the preparation stage.

31 This analysis may also suggest that similar variations in interpretation may arise even when changes are externally promoted – for example, curriculum projects or comprehensive reorganization itself.

32 The G.C.E. and C.S.E. results of the first mixed-ability cohort were not available within the time-period of this study but will, I hope, be dealt with in future.

33 Kollas (1973 : 34) uses the term 'proximal frames' to refer to decisions made at the institutional level which operate directly on the teaching process. The frame factors involved are: (1) personal frames, i.e. decisions regarding the selection of teachers and students; (2) organizational frames, i.e. decisions regarding group-size, formal grouping procedures of students (allocation to forms), examination practices, etc.; (3) time frames, i.e. decisions regarding the available time for instruction and its allocation; (4) content frames, i.e. decisions regarding subject-matter, sequencing of contents, textbooks, etc.; and (5) physical frames, i.e. decisions regarding the physical environment for teaching. However, in this context the headmaster, as is normal, left the content-frame decisions to be taken at departmental level.

7 Mixed-ability: implementation and change

1 Each department was required to submit a written report to the headmaster.
2 Geography, Chemistry, Biology, Physics, Maths, French, History and English.

3 This small sample is obviously unsatisfactory in many ways, but the limitations of space make it impossible to present a sample that would be satisfactory. There are several dimensions of variation that could be taken into account within each subject that render any serious attempt at sampling impossible, for instance: (1) the teacher. Departments varied in size from 2 to 11. However, the variation between the teachers in one department is explored to some extent by the presentation of descriptions of all the members of the History department teaching mixed-ability groups. (2) Types of lesson. Obviously, most teachers do not organize their lessons in the same way every time. There are a number of factors, related to the syllabus, type of work set, aims and objectives of lessons and administrative expedience, which may produce pedagogic and organizational variations. Giving back homework, discussions, preparing for examinations, having a test, being disruptive, being punished, starting a new topic, finishing a topic, etc., would be some of many possible examples. (3) The experience of previous lessons. The behaviour of the class or the teacher or the standard of work produced or demanded in previous lessons may have had its impact on the conduct of the lesson being observed. However, none of the descriptions presented below is of an isolated or uncharacteristic instance. In all cases, they are examples selected from a number of teachers observed in that subject and a number of lessons observed, of that teacher.

4 The changes implied here are changes in teaching methods towards more individualized learning. In particular, I shall examine changes in the control over the pacing of knowledge as a crucial aspect of this individualization.

5 All departments were required to lodge a full syllabus with the headmaster's office.

6 See Smith and Keith (1971).

7 For a discussion of the use of worksheets in History, see p. 224.

8 This was a band 1 English lesson in which a small group of girls were able to convince the teacher of the necessity of doing a lesson on 'parts of speech', because, they said, their parents were dismayed that the grammar in their English essays was so poor.

9 The Geography department report on mixed-ability teaching proposed that
> All first-year Geography should be taught a 'key lesson' which could be given in the Hall, once a week. It will then be possible to co-ordinate a complex programme of study and also use the full potential of the staff.

10 Farleigh Rice (1973), *Patterns in Geography, Book One,* London, Longman.

11 This group of boys will in fact feature in some detail in the following chapter.

12 Once again, this practice is related to the 'problem' of stretching the brighter child.

13 They were similar in this respect to the Chemistry worksheets.

14 The Physics department, however, also suffered staffing problems during the period of the innovation. There were four different heads of department between the preparatory year and the end of year 3 of the innovation, and a complete turnover of all other staff. This certainly appeared to affect the morale of the department.

15 A similar questioning strategy was apparent in the French lessons observed in a previous participant observation study by the author (Ball 1973).

16 This group of boys is discussed in some detail in chapter 8.

17 *School Mathematics Project Cards* (1973), Cambridge, Cambridge University Press.

18 A nearby comprehensive school which had been visited by the head of Mathematics in order to observe the use of S.M.P. work-cards before their introduction at Beachside.

19 This was an *ad hoc* term used by the Mathematics department to refer to the S.M.P. *Number* book course.

20 Here, then, is a clear example of syllabus differentiation within the mixed-ability classroom. Pupils are actually 'guided' to cover a different course on an individual basis. Although they share the classroom in a physical sense, they do not share the same learning experiences.

21 There was one part-time member of the department, Mr Daniel, who is mentioned later.

22 It is interesting to note that in the Humanities subjects it was usual when organizing learning in the classroom to regard ability differences between pupils in terms of speed of working rather than in terms of ability to grasp concepts or perform certain tasks, as was the case in Mathematics, Languages and the Sciences.

23 Except for a few topics, such as the Norman Invasion, which were left to be dealt with in other ways by the teachers individually.

24 Not all the worksheets were divided up in this way and some of those which were were divided on the basis of topics rather than in relation to the pupils' abilities.

25 J. Liversidge (1958), *Roman Britain*, London, Longman; R. Mitchell and G. Middleton (1967), *Living History, Book One*, Edinburgh, Holmes McDougall; R. R. Sellman (1959), *Roman Britain,* London, Methuen; and R. J. Unstead (1961), *Looking at History, Book Two: The Middle Ages*, London, A. and C. Black.

26 Strictly, in a pre- and post-innovation comparison, English would not be in this position in relation to other subjects; the time-scale of change in the English department was much longer. Syllabus and methods had been under discussion for several years prior to the innovation.

27 The terms 'transmission mode' and 'interpretation mode' refer to different forms of the organization of language in the classroom. In the first case, Barnes (1976) suggests that language is like a speaking tube; the teacher sends knowledge down and the child receives it or fails to receive it. The pupils' speech and writing function to test their reception. Learning is a process of accumulation and memorization. In the interpretation mode, however, language is a means of helping the pupil to think more effectively. Knowledge has to be made by each person for himself, rather than being a concrete world of reality that is transmitted from the teacher to the pupil.

28 Mathematics was not included in this study.

29 For example, several first-year History worksheets contained questions in the optional sections, designed to cater for the 'faster' pupils, which suggested that the pupils build models. One question suggested building a model of a section of Hadrian's Wall, another suggested a Viking longship. However, only one teacher, who taught part-time in the History department, actually allowed and encouraged pupils to attempt to build these models. As the end of the year this teacher was criticized by the head of History for not 'getting through the work'. His form was reported to have completed fewer worksheets than any of the others.

30 The immediate concern of the teachers in their classroom practices, in terms of problems of control and management, may also be relevant in their selection of 'appropriate' methods for mixed-ability. Certainly, it was evident that in most cases the decision about methods was subordinate to the demands of content, of conceptual development (especially in Mathematics and the Sciences), and of syllabus coverage.

31 The headmaster had suggested in my first interview with him that mixed-ability grouping would serve to obviate the development of different expectations among the teachers, and thus prevent the emergence of anti-school behaviour. But later he argued that the improved behaviour record of the mixed-ability pupils compared with the banded pupils stemmed from the dispersal of 'problem pupils'.

8 Mixed-ability and banding compared

1 As may be seen from table 1.2, p. 17, the greatest proportion of mixed-ability teaching was done by the youngest, least experienced teachers. Mixed-ability teaching was considered 'easier' because it involved the younger children and did not present great problems of control, and yet many teachers also recognized that mixed-ability teaching,

teaching to a wide range of ability, presented great difficulties to the less experienced staff, and demanded skills which they were the least likely to possess.

2 Other problems arose from the fact that the data collection for the two cohorts, the mixed-ability and the banded, was contiguous. There was no opportunity to reconsider the data-collection methods for the mixed-ability groups in the light of the analysis of the banded groups. If this had been possible there would undoubtedly have been a number of changes in the way in which data were collected from the mixed-ability form which would have increased the range of comparability.

3 The four I did not interview were all girls who were reluctant to talk to me, and indeed rarely spoke in lessons.

4 This ten-form entry involved a reallocation of resources to support the innovation. Class sizes were reduced to an average of 29 in the mixed-ability forms. The headmaster felt that this smaller class size would ease the problems of teaching to heterogeneous groups. The average mixed-ability class size was increased slightly in the second year by the absorption of the pupils from one of the remedial forms.

5 I intend a distinction here between disruption and misbehaviour.

6 Sam was a pupil, mentioned later in this chapter, who was moved into 2DY from a remedial form, and who was involved with 'the bunch', a gang based in the upper school. In lesson time he was also sometimes involved in misbehaviour with the four boys described below as being 'incipient anti-school.' These detentions were received for truancy with boys from 'the bunch' and as the first person in 2DY to receive a school detention Sam's social status among the boys in the form was considerably enhanced.

7 Similar groups were identifiable in most, but not all, of the other mixed-ability forms. But not all such groups were boys' groups.

8 As noted earlier, these times are considerably lower than the times reported by the grammar school pupils in Lacey's (1970) study.

9 This process of 'reporting' often occurred when inexperienced teachers found it impossible to assert themselves over particular pupils. As a result these pupils would be drawn into an institutionalized system of rebuke and punishment, as distinct from their informal punishments given by class teachers. This reporting, and the subsequent dissemination and storing of information in the pastoral system, effectively 'labelled' the miscreants as 'problems'.

10 For Sam, see n. 6 above, and p. 257.

11 Both Kevin and Colin were of middle-class background.

12 George and Paul reported spending time together outside school during the third year going to discothéques, football matches, cafés, etc.

13 He was eventually transferred, at the end of the third year, into the form of Mr Court, the basketball coach.

14 This may be an example of the halo effect; neither the year tutor nor the form teacher ever saw Paul playing basketball, but they may have discussed him with Mr Court.

15 This is explained below, p. 256.

16 Previous findings concerning the 'unsuccessful' pupil in heterogeneous ability-groups are conflicting. Passow, Goldberg and Tannenbaum (1967) found that slower pupils tended to have higher opinions of their own ability when taught in homogeneous groups, but that when taught together with brighter children their self-opinion 'slumped', although their academic standards rose considerably. Barker-Lunn (1969:275) found that 'more boys of below average ability in streamed schools had a "good self-image" compared with a comparable group of boys in non-streamed schools, presumably because, although they are likely to be in the lower ability stream, some could still be top or do the best work in their class'. However, one must take care not to assume too readily that 'self-image' reflects the attitude to school, values and behaviour

in lessons. The only report of mixed-ability in an English secondary context so far available, the Banbury Study (1975 : 12), found that 'less able children are more content with their situation in heterogeneous grouping.' This would appear to be borne out in the present study.

17 As noted in chapter 2, in the banded cohort during the first two years 40 pupils had been moved from one form to another. In the mixed-ability cohort over an equivalent period only 30 pupils were moved, and that includes those integrated from the remedial forms. By the end of the third year the number of movements in the mixed-ability cohort was still only 44.

18 Fuchs (1968) explains this process in a U.S. ghetto school.

19 This was also related to improved discipline by the teachers.

20 This was mentioned in a group discussion I had with seven of the girls in the form.

21 In the sociometric questionnaire administered at the end of the third year, both girls received friendship choices from Paul and George, but did not reciprocate.

22 This happened on a much larger scale in 2LN, with a clear separation between the girls of low social maturity and the others.

23 Although there is no coherent pattern of differences between the sexes in the banded context, taking the sexes together to calculate I.P. values does affect the overall picture. In several classes a high I.P. value or a low I.P. value among the girls (or boys) had the effect of outweighing an opposite value among the boys (or girls).

24 Admittedly, this is an extremely crude way of comparing the banded context with mixed-ability, because it ignores the closeness of values to unity.

25 Ford (1969 : 82).

26 See the remarks made by the head of English on this subject, p. 176.

27 The figures quoted are presented in table N8. The head of English had the problem initially of comparing the fully mixed-ability cohort with previous cohorts which had been denuded by pupils leaving at fifteen before the raising of the school leaving age. To cope with this he asked his teachers to estimate the likely achievement of pupils who had left at the end of the fourth year. Thus, in 1973 39.1 per cent obtained O-level or grade 1 C.S.E., in 1974 43 per cent, in 1975 36.99 per cent and in 1976 39.3 per cent. Over three years the percentage pass-rates for the mixed-ability cohorts compares favourably with the first cohort taught in separated O-level and C.S.E. sets.

Table N8. *Comparison of O-level and C.S.E. examination attainment for banded and mixed-ability cohorts*

	C.S.E. (percentage of leavers)				O-level (percentage of leavers)		
Grade	1973	1974	1975	Grade	1973	1974	1975
[a] 1	9.8	13.6	10.7	A(1–2)	2.8	0.9	1.2
2	15.5	11.4	15.5	B(3–4)	11.8	10.1	12.1
3	18.4	16.7	24.5	C(5–6)	14.7	18.4	12.9 [a]
4	13.9	16.7	15.5	D(7)	4.5	3.9	1.7
5	2.4	3.5	3.0	E(8)	2.9	2.2	0.8
U	0.8	1.3	2.1	U(9)	2.4	1.3	0.0

[a]Counts as O-level pass.

28 This was a multiple-choice examination based on worksheet topics covered by all forms during the first year.

29 2DY were 'set' as follows, with three sets for French and two for Maths.

French Set A	Social class	Maths Set 1	Social class
Bernice[a]	II	John	II
Steve[a]	I	Barry	IIIN
Diane[a]	II	Richard	IIIM
Carole[a]	II	Cyril	V
Alice	IIIM	Michael	II
Yvette[a]	IIIN	Steve	I
Richard[a]	IIIM	Nicholas	II
John[a]	II	Mandy	II
Mandy[a]	II	Carole	II
Michael[a]	II	Sylvia	unknown
Margaret	IIIM	Christine	IIIM
Sylvia[a]	unknown	Yvette	IIIN
		Diane	II
		Bernice	II
		Judy	IV

[a]Also in Maths set 1

French Set B	Social class	Mahts Set 2	Social class
Barry	IIIN	Norman	IIIM
Paul	IV	George	IIIM
Cyril	V	Colin	I
Desmond	IIIM	Kevin	II
Nicholas	II	Desmond	IIIM
Sharon	I	Lennie	IIIM
Christine	IIIM	Margaret	IIIM
Celia	IIIM	June	IIIM
Judy	IV	Jennifer	IIIM
		Celia	IIIM
		Sharon	I
		Nichola	IIIM
		Alice	IIIM
		Paul	IV

French Set C	Social class
Lennie	IIIM
Sam	IV
Colin	I
June	IIIM
Jennifer	IIIM
Norman	IIIM
George	IIIM
Kevin	II
Nichola	IIIM

As would be expected from the analysis so far (a) the top sets are dominated by those pupils who were successful in the end of year exams, (b) the top sets are dominated by pupils from middle-class family backgrounds (9 out of 12 in French Set A and 11 out of 15 in Maths Set 1), and (c) there is a considerable overlap of personnel between the sets at the top and the bottom. Only 2 pupils in French Set A are not in Maths Set 1, none of the pupils in French Set C are in Maths Set 1.

30 See pp. 72–4.

31 As we have seen already in this chapter, academic achievement also became important in the divisions which existed among the pupils themselves.

32 Other sets of constructs from 2DY and 2LN teachers were:

2DY English teacher	2DY Science teacher
Concentrates–easily distracted	Well-behaved–troublesome
Tries–does not try	Forthcoming–quiet
Answers in class–quiet	Likeable–unpleasant
Hardworking–lazy	Works hard–lazy
Keen–unwilling	Bright–hopeless[a]
Neat–untidy	Open–underhand
Produces good work–does not produce good work[a]	
Exceptional–not exceptional[a]	
Organized–disorganized	

2LN Languages teacher	2LN Geography teacher
Strong–weak[a]	Mature–immature
Self-assured–shy	Polite–cheeky
Hardworking–lazy	Successful–unsuccessful[a]
Conscientious–not conscientious	Tries hard–never works
Fits in the class–does not fit in the class	Conscientious–happy-go-lucky
Sense of humour–dull	Interested–uninterested
Intelligent–tries hard	
Quiet–noisy	

[a]Denotes ability constructs.

33 Two sets of constructs were elicited from 2LN teachers and the cross-tabulation of construct positions with examination positions is shown in table N9.

Table N9. *Teacher perceptions and pupil achievement*

	Languages teacher				Geography teacher		
	Construct rank positions				Construct rank positions		
Examination positions	1–10	11–20	21–8	Examination positions	1–10	11–20	21–8
1–10	7	2	1	1–10	6	3	1
11–20	2	4	4	11–20	4	3	3
21–8	1	4	3	21–8	—	4	4

$r_s = 0.44$ significant at the 0.01 level. $r_s = 0.53$ significant at the 0.001 level.

34 It is interesting to note that while both teachers introduce an ability construct, this construct is rated first in importance by the Mathematics teacher and last in importance by the History teacher. Referring back to the construct systems produced in the banded forms, 2TA's Geography teacher rated her ability construct 7th of 10, 2CU's English teacher 6th of 7, and 2CU's Science teacher 1st of 7. 2TA's English teacher did not produce an ability construct. These differences may be related to the relative importance of the *academic* perspective in the different departments.

35 With the exception of Paul, in the Mathematics teacher's ranking, all the members of the incipient anti-school group, identified previously, come into the bottom ten positions of the construct rankings.

36 In the case of the History teacher's rankings, the congruence was greater than when the ability construct was included.

37 Silberman (1969) makes the point that a teacher's utterances, although addressed to individual pupils, are heard by all, and have the effect of influencing the perceptions of, and interaction with, those individuals by their peers. Almost all of the teacher's talk in the classroom is public. But cues are not only related to the 'ability' dimension of teachers' perceptions of the pupils; the 'behaviour' dimension is also referred to. Typically, for example:

> We're waiting for the same old people, we are not carrying on until you are all absolutely quiet – we are still waiting for those pupils who keep us waiting every lesson.

38 That is, socio-psycho-cultural resources. See Lacey (1970), chapter 6.

39 There were no formal examinations during the second year, although some teachers did institute their own informal end-of-year or mid-year 'tests'.

40 In the Guess-Who-Test.

41 3LN's form teacher mislaid his examination lists, as did serveral other teachers, so I was only able to recover four complete sets of examination lists. The year tutor had mislaid the option-choice sheets compiled from the original choices made by the pupils, so I was only able to compare achievement, choice and allocation in 3DY whose option choices I had collected independently. I did raise the possibility of collecting the other forms' choices retrospectively but the year tutor felt, probably quite rightly, that this might create resentment among those pupils who had been rejected from courses they chose. This phenomenon of lost information was not unusual at Beachside; record-keeping was not given great importance and was generally haphazard. Perhaps paradoxically, the retention of records of the kind mentioned above was even more haphazard in the mixed-ability context, partly because of the devolution of the option allocation procedure and partly because of the reduction in the *formal* importance given to the numerical assessment of pupils' work.

42 See note 41, above.

43 These choices are 'realistic' as far as the teachers are concerned, in terms of the complex relationship between the pupils' established achieved-ability status and the teachers' estimation of likely success. This was explored in chapter 5 in relation to banded pupils.

44 This is apparent if the tables (8.9 and 8.14) which demonstrate the relationship between social class and examination achievement, and examination achievement and option allocation, are considered together. But in the absence of testing as basis for the allocation of pupils to mixed-ability forms it is impossible to compare choice of and allocation to courses directly between the mixed-ability and banded cohorts. Thus, it is impossible to estimate the extent to which the mixed-ability grouping allows for a greater flexibility of access to high-status courses than did the banded system.

45 My observation of lessons was primarily ethnographic rather than quantitatively based on interaction or category analysis. If it had been possible in the time available for field

work, the use of both types of observation would have proved worth while.

46 The term 'Hawthorne effect' is taken from the work of Roethlisberger and Dickson (1939) at the Hawthorne Electric plant in the United States. In an attempt to explore the relationship 'between the conditions of work and the incidence of fatigue and monotony among employees' (p. 3), Roethlisberger and Dickson found a greater experimental effect deriving from their involvement with employees than from the manipulation of experimental variables. The changes in employee work-behaviour appeared to stem from a response to the novelty of being studied and a concern to co-operate with the researchers in making the experiments 'successful'. It may be that the teachers stimulated a similar experimental effect among the pupils in the first mixed-ability cohort. There were indications from the teachers' comments about the cohort which followed the one discussed here, that the improvement in their behaviour relative to the banded forms was not so marked.

47 A fruitful line of future research into mixed-ability teaching would be an interaction analysis based on the observation techniques developed by Nash (1973) and the recording and analysis of linguistic interaction between teacher and pupils. Through this kind of micro-analysis, combining ethnographic and social-psychological techniques, it would be possible to explore the ways in which pupils experience the same classroom in different ways. In particular, this would require examination of quantitative and qualitative differences in the interaction contacts between the teacher and individual pupils, but also exploration of the ways in which the curriculum as a classroom process is socially constructed, and portrayed differently, for individual pupils or groups of pupils in the same classroom.

9 Conclusions

1 The design of the study does not provide for any indication of the marginal quantitative changes in the distribution of opportunity that may be produced by comprehensive reorganization.

2 From the Modern Language syllabus (January 1974):
TERMINAL AIMS
(1) *For the academically more gifted.*
  (a) To be able to understand and speak the language with some degree of facility. Understanding of the spoken language will always be arrived at more easily than production of the language.
  (b) To read the language sufficiently well to be able to understand the principal points to be found in a lengthy passage, and to understand perfectly such a passage if the use is made of a dictionary.
  (c) To write simple French* with confidence and accuracy (*or German or Spanish).
  (d) To become interested in the way of life, customs, culture and attitudes of the people of the country concerned.
  (e) To have opened to them new areas of learning in such a way that their general cultural education is fostered.
(2) *For the average child.*
  (a) To be able to conduct a simple conversation in the foreign language.
  (b) To understand the gist of a newspaper article, poster or short story within the limits of the pupil's experience.
  (c) To be able to exchange letters with a correspondent, involving simple writing in the foreign language.

(d) To become interested in the way of life, customs, culture and attitudes of the people of the country concerned.

(e) To have opened to them new areas of learnings in such a way that their general cultural education is fostered.

(3) *For the less able child (2-year course in French).*

(a) To be able to understand very simple spoken French and to give an intelligible reply, which may consist of only one or two words.

(b) To understand written French that one might see on notices in France.

(c) As item (d) above.

(d) As item (e) above.

3 Keddie (1971) demonstrates the way in which teachers may orient topics differently to 'suit' different groups of children in the context of a policy of common curriculum. Thus, the content *per se* may be the same, but it may be 'handled' very differently.

4 For Schutz (1972) the terms 'contemporaries' and 'consociates' stand for different forms of social relationship. While the consociate is experienced as a fellow man, as being in some way 'like me', the contemporary appears as more or less anonymous, as representative of a type, exhibiting certain characteristics, rather than as a unique individual. Contemporaries are experienced in the form of a they-relation, consociates in the form of a we-relation.

5 As discussed on pp. 6–10.

6 It is probably only changes that are actually related to the organization and transmission of knowledge and its evaluation, and to the definition of what counts as knowledge, that Bernstein (1971) sees as bringing about a shift in the *education knowledge code* and that will bring about any greater degree of social equality in education. But having said that, it is essential to note Bernstein's important point that change of code involves fundamental changes in classification and framing and, therefore, changes in the distribution of power and principles of control. It is no wonder that deeply felt resistances are called out by issues relating to change in educational codes. In terms of teachers' practices in the classroom, the organization of learning, etc., the introduction of mixed-ability classes at Beachside involved only a slight weakening of the framing of educational knowledge and no weakening at all in its classification. There were certainly no changes in the distribution of power or in the principles of control, nor in the teachers' view of the classroom, their attitudes to their subjects, their definitions of what counts as successful performance, nor in their task-role.

7 Sharp and Green (1976) provide a similar view of progressive primary education.

8 Certainly, discipline in the classroom can ensure a superficial peace and order which can allow teachers to proceed. However, the predominance of the issues of discipline and control in the social relations of the classroom has broader implications. Durkheim (1961 : 148) argues that 'In reality . . . the nature and function of school discipline is something altogether different . . . It is the morality of the classroom . . . Discipline . . . is essentially an instrument of moral education.' But, he warns, 'Too often . . . people conceive of school discipline so as to preclude endowing it with such an important moral function' (1961 : 148–9). In essence, according to Durkheim, the teacher is 'society's agent, the critical link in cultural transmission' (1961 : xiii), and fundamentally concerned with the initiation of pupils into the accepted ways of life of the adult community; 'It is by respecting the school rules that the child learns to respect rules in general, that he develops the habit of self-control and restraint simply because he should control and restrain himself' (1961 : 149). This socializing role is an aspect of schooling which has been neglected since Durkheim until more recently Althusser (1971) and Bowles and Gintis (1976) have reasserted its importance.

9 Barker-Lunn (1969 : 56) makes a similar point in relation to de-streaming in the primary school.

10 Unfortunately, much of the work done in the analysis of classroom transactions, especially 'interaction analysis' (cf. Flanders 1970), neglects the ideologies and objectives of the teachers as contributions to the understanding of classroom processes.

11 That is, 'best pupil' or 'top of the form' or 'top in exams'.

12 Term used by Sharp and Green (1976 : 227).

13 See Hopper (1971b : 97).

14 Most recently Cox and Boyson (1975).

15 Terms used by Hoare (1965).

Bibliography

Althusser, L. (1971). *Lenin and Philosophy and other Essays*, London, New Left Books.

Armstrong, M., and Young, M. (1964). *A New Look at Comprehensive Schools*, Fabian Research Series 237, London, Fabian Society.

Bailey, C. (1976). 'Mixed-ability teaching and the defence of subjects', *Cambridge Journal of Education*, vol. 6, no. 1/2, pp. 24–31.

Ball, S. J. (1973). *The Study of Friendship Groups in a Multi-racial Comprehensive School: Research and Methodology*. Unpublished M.A. Dissertation, University of Sussex.

Banbury School (1975). *The School as a Centre of Enquiry*, Banbury, Publansco.

Banks, O. (1955). *Parity and Prestige in English Secondary Education*, London, Routledge and Kegan Paul.

(1974). *Sociology of Education: An Inaugural Lecture*, Leicester, Leicester University Press.

Bannister, D. (1970). 'Science through the looking glass', in D. Bannister (ed.), *Perspectives in Personal Construct Theory*, London, Academic Press.

Bannister, D., and Fransella, F. (1971). *Inquiring Man*, Harmondsworth, Penguin Books.

Bantock, G. H. (1975). 'Progressivism and the content of education', in C. B. Cox and R. Boyson (eds.), *The Fight for Education: Black Paper 1975*, London, Dent.

Barker-Lunn, J. (1969). *Streaming in the Primary School*, Slough, National Foundation for Educational Research.

Barnes, D. (1976). *From Communication to Curriculum*, Harmondsworth, Penguin Books.

Becker, H. S. (1952). 'Social class variations in the teacher-pupil relationship', *Journal of Education Sociology*, vol. 35, no. 4, pp. 451–65.

(1963). *The Outsiders*, New York, Free Press of Glencoe.

Becker, H. S., Geer, B., Hughes, E. C., and Strauss, A. L. (1961). *Boys in White: Student Culture in Medical School*, Chicago, University of Chicago Press.

Bellaby, P. (1977). *The Sociology of Comprehensive Schooling*, London, Methuen.

Benn, C., and Simon, B. (1972). *Half Way There*, 2nd edn, Harmondsworth, Penguin Books.

Berger, P. L., and Luckmann, T. (1967). *The Social Construction of Reality: A Treatise in the Sociology of Knowledge*, London, Allen Lane.

Bernbaum, G. (1973). 'Countesthorpe College, Leicester, United Kingdom', in *Case Studies of Educational Innovation, III: At the School Level*, Centre for Educational Research and Innovation, Paris, O.E.C.D.

Bernstein, B. (1965). 'Social class and linguistic development: a theory of social learning', in A. H. Halsey, J. Floud and C. A. Anderson (eds.), *Education, Economy and Society*, London, Collier-Macmillan.

(1971). 'On the classification and framing of educational knowledge', in M. F. D. Young (ed.), *Knowledge and Control*, London, Collier-Macmillan.

(1975). 'Class and pedagogies: visible and invisible', *Educational Studies*, vol. no. 1, March.

316

Bernstein, B., Elvin, H. L., and Peters, R. S. (1966). 'Ritual in education', *Philosophical Transactions of the Royal Society of London*, B, vol. 251, no. 772, pp. 429–36.

Birksted, I. (1976). 'School performance: viewed from the boys', *Sociological Review*, vol. 24, no. 1, pp. 63–77.

Bourdieu, P. (1971). 'Systems of thought and systems of education', in M. F. D. Young (ed.), *Knowledge and Control*, London, Collier-Macmillan.

Bowles, S. (1972). 'Unequal education and the reproduction of the social division of labour', in M. Carnoy (ed.), *Schooling in a Corporate Society: The Political Economy of Education in America*, New York, McKay.

Bowles, S., and Gintis, H. (1976). *Schooling in Capitalist America*, London, Routledge and Kegan Paul.

Bronfenbrenner, U. (1971). *Two Worlds of Childhood*, London, Allen and Unwin.

Burgess, T. (1973). *Home and School*, London, Allen Lane.

Central Advisory Council for Education (England) (1963). *Half Our Future*, London, H.M.S.O.

(1967). *Children and their Primary Schools*, 2 vols., London, H.M.S.O.

Chancellor, V. E. (1967). *Medieval and Tudor Britain*, Harmondsworth, Penguin Books.

Chitty, C. (1969). 'Non-streaming in comprehensives', *Comprehensive Education*, no. 12, pp. 2–8.

Cicourel, A. V., and Kitsuse, J. I. (1963). *The Educational Decision-Makers*, New York, Bobbs-Merrill.

Clark, B. R. (1960). *The Open Door College: A Case. Study*, New York, McGraw-Hill.

Cohen, A. K. (1955). *Delinquent Boys: The Culture of the Gang*, Glencoe, Illinois, The Free Press.

Cohen, L. (1974). 'Labelling and alienation in a British secondary school', *Educational Research*, vol. 26, February, pp. 100–8.

Cohen, S. (1972). *Folk Devils and Moral Panics: The Creation of Mods and Rockers*, London, MacGibbon and Kee.

Coleman, J. S. (1961). *The Adolescent Society: The Social Life of the Teenager and its Impact on Education*, New York, Free Press of Glencoe.

(1966). *Equality of Educational Opportunity*, Washington, D.C., U.S. Government Printing Office.

Cox, C. B., and Boyson, R. (1975). *The Fight for Education: Black Paper 1975*, London, Dent.

Crosland, A. (1956). *The Future of Socialism*, London, Cape.

Cuddihy, R. (ed.) (1966). *Red Papers*, Islander Publications, n.p.

Dahllof, U. S. (1971). *Ability Grouping: Content, Validity and Curriculum Process Analysis*, New York, Teachers College Press, Columbia University.

Dalin, P. (1970). *The Process of Innovation in Education* (Technical Report), Paris, C.E.R.I./O.E.C.D.

(1973). *Case Studies in Educational Innovation, IV: Strategies for Innovation on Education*, Paris, C.E.R.I./O.E.C.D.

Daunt, P. E. (1975). *Comprehensive Values*, London, Heinemann.

Davies, B. (1977). *Social Control and Education*, London, Methuen.

Davies, R. P. (1975). *Mixed-ability Grouping: Possibilities and Experiences in the Secondary School*, London, Temple Smith.

Deitrich, F. R. (1964). 'Comparison of sociometric patterns of sixth grade pupils in two school systems: ability grouping compared with heterogeneous grouping', *Journal of Educational Research*, no. 57, pp. 507–12.

Delamont, S. (1976). *Interaction in the Classroom,* London, Methuen.

Douglas, J. D. (1971).*Understanding Everyday Life: Toward the Reconstruction of Sociological Knowledge*, London, Routledge and Kegan Paul.

Douglas, J. W. B. (1964). *The Home and the School: A Study of Ability and Attainment in the Primary School*, London, MacGibbon and Kee.

Downes, D. (1966). *The Delinquent Solution: A Study in Sub-cultural Theory*, London, Routledge and Kegan Paul.

Durkheim, E. (1961). *Moral Education*, New York, Free Press of Glencoe.

Elliot, J. (1976). 'The problems and dilemmas of mixed-ability teaching and the issue of teacher accountability', *Cambridge Journal of Education*, vol. 6, no. 1/2, pp. 3–14.

Englemann, S., and Bereiter, C. (1966). *Teaching Disadvantaged Children in the Preschool*, Englewood Cliffs, New Jersey, Prentice-Hall.

Esland, G. (1972). *Open University Educational Studies, Second-level Course (School and Society), Unit 12: Innovation in the School*, Milton Keynes, Open University Press.

(1971). 'Teaching and learning as the organization of knowledge', in M.F.D. Young (ed.), *Knowledge and Control*, London, Collier-Macmillan.

Etzioni, A. (1961). *A Comparative Analysis of Complex Organizations,* Glencoe, Illinois, Free Press.

Evetts, J. (1973). *The Sociology of Educational Ideas*, London, Routledge and Kegan Paul.

Farleigh Rice, W. (1973). *Patterns in Geography, Book One*, London, Longman.

Flanders, N. A. (1970). *Analyzing Teaching Behavior,* Reading, Mass., Addison-Wesley.

Floud, J., and Halsey, A. H. (1957). 'Social class, intelligence tests and selection for secondary schools', *British Journal of Sociology*, vol. 8, no. 1, pp. 33–9.

Ford, J. (1969). *Social Class and the Comprehensive School*, London, Routledge and Kegan Paul.

Ford, J., Young, D., and Box, S. (1967). 'Functional autonomy, role distance and social class', *British Journal of Sociology*, vol. 18, no. 4, pp. 370–81.

Frankenberg, R. (1963). 'Taking the blame or passing the buck'. Paper presented to the B.S.A., Aberdeen, 4 September.

Fuchs, E. (1968). 'How teachers learn to help children fail', in *Transactions*, September, pp. 45–9.

Furlong, V. (1976). 'Interaction sets in the classroom: towards a study of pupil knowledge', in M. Stubbs and S. Delamont (eds.), *Explorations in Classroom Observation*, London, John Wiley and Sons.

G. B. Department of Education and Science (1965). *Circular 10/65: The Organization of Secondary Education.*

(1975). *Education Survey* 21, London, H.M.S.O.

Goffman, E. (1952). 'On cooling the mark out', *Psychiatry*, vol. XV, November, pp. 451–63.

(1968). *Asylums*, Harmondsworth, Penguin Books.

Goldberg, M., Passow, A. H., and Justman, J. (1966). *The Effects of Ability Grouping*, New York, Teachers College Press, Columbia University.

Goldthorpe, J., and Llewellyn, C. (1977). 'Class mobility in modern Britain: three theses examined', *Sociology*, vol. 11, no. 2, May, pp. 257–87.

Goodlad, J. I. (unpublished). *Educational Change: A Strategy for Study and Action.*

Goodson, I. (1975). 'The teachers' curriculum and the new reformation', *The Journal of Curriculum Studies*, vol. 7, no. 2, pp. 160–9.

Gronlund, N. E. (1959). *Sociometry in the Classroom*, New York, Harper and Row.

Gross, N., Giaquinta, J. A., and Bernstein, M. (1971). *Implementing Organizational Innovations: A Sociological Analysis of Planned Educational Change*, New York, Harper and Row.

Hallworth, H. J. (1953). 'Sociometric relations among grammar school boys and girls', *Sociometry*, vol. XVI, no. 1, pp. 39–70.

Halsey, A. H. (1972). *Educational Priority*, vol. I, London, H.M.S.O.
   (1974). 'Education and social mobility in Britain since World War II'. Paper given at the O.E.C.D. Directorate for Social Affairs, Manpower and Education, Inequality and Life Chances, held in Paris, 6–10 January.

Halsey, A. H., Floud, J., and Anderson, C. A. (1961). *Education, Economy and Society*, London, Collier-Macmillan.

Halsey, A. H., Floud, J., and Martin, F. M. (1956). *Social Class and Educational Opportunity*, London, Heinemann.

Hargreaves, A. (1976). 'Progressivism and pupil autonomy'. Paper given at a working party funded by the S.S.R.C. on Classroom Decision-Making, University of Keele, September.

Hargreaves, D. (1967). *Social Relations in a Secondary School*, London, Routledge and Kegan Paul.
   (1972). *Interpersonal Relations and Education*, London, Routledge and Kegan Paul.
   (1977). 'The process of typification in classroom interaction: models and methods', *British Journal of Educational Psychology*, vol. 47, no. 3, pp. 274–84.

Hartshorne, H., *et al.* (1930). *Studies in the Nature of Character*, vol. III: *Studies in the Organization of Character*, New York, Macmillan.

Hayes, K. (1976). 'Which subjects can be taught in mixed-ability classes? Teachers' views', *Cambridge Journal of Education*, vol. 6, no. 1/2, pp. 32–8.

Hoare, Q. (1965). 'Education – programmes and men', *New Left Review*, no. 32 (July-August), pp. 40–52.

Hollingshead, A. B. (1961). *Elmstown's Youth*, New York, Science Editions.

Holly, D. (1972). *Society, Schools and Humanity: The Changing World of Secondary Education*, London, Paladin.

Holmes, B. (1973). 'Leicestershire, United Kingdom', in *Case Studies of Educational Innovation, II: At the Regional Level*, Paris, C.E.R.I./O.E.C.D.

Hopper, E. (ed.) (1971a). *Readings in the Theory of Education Systems*, London, Hutchinson University Library.

Hopper, E. (1971b). 'The classification of education systems' in Hopper 1971a.

House, E. R. (1974). *The Politics of Educational Innovation*, Berkeley, California, McCutchan.

Hughes, E. C. (1937). 'Institutional office and the person', *American Journal of Sociology*, no. 43, pp. 404–13.

Inner London Education Authority (1976). *Mixed-Ability Grouping: Report of an I.L.E.A. Inspectorate Survey*, London, I.L.E.A.

Jackson, B., and Marsden, D. (1962). *Education and the Working Class*, Harmondsworth, Penguin Books.

Jackson, P. (1968). *Life in Classrooms*, New York, Holt, Rinehart and Winston.

Jencks, C., *et al.* (1972). *Inequality: A Reassessment of the Effect of the Family and Schooling in America*, New York, Basic Books.

Jennings, H. H. (1948). *Sociometry in Group Relations*, Washington, D.C., American Council of Education.
   (1950). *Leadership and Isolation: A Study of Personality in Interpersonal Relationships*, 2nd edn, London, Longmans.

Johannesson, I. (1962). 'School differentiation and the social adjustment of the pupils', *Educational Research*, no. 4, pp. 133–9.

Keddie, N. (1971). 'Classroom knowledge', in M. F. D. Young (ed.), *Knowledge and Control*, London, Collier-Macmillan.

Kelly, A. V. (1974). *Teaching Mixed-Ability Classes: An Individualised Approach*, London, Harper and Row.

Kelly, G. A. (1955). *The Psychology of Personal Constructs*, vol. I, New York, Norton.

King, R. A. (1973). *School Organization and Pupil Inovlvement*, London, Routledge and Kegan Paul.

Kollas, D. (1973). *On Educational Scientific Research*, Pedagogiska Institutionen, Lunds Universitet, Fack, 220 07, Lund 7, Sweden.

Lacey, C. (1970). *Hightown Grammar*, Manchester University Press.

(1974). 'Destreaming in a "pressured" academic environment', in J. Eggleston (ed.), *Contemporary Research in the Sociology of Education,* London, Methuen.

(1976). 'A review of the methodology of Hightown Grammar', in M.D. Shipman (ed.), *The Organization and Impact of Social Research,* London, Routledge and Kegan Paul.

(1977). *The Socialization of Teachers*, London, Methuen.

Lacey, C., Horton, M., and Hoad, P. (1973). *Tutorial Schools Research Project.* vol. I: *Teacher Socialization: The Post-Graduate Training Year,* London, S.S.R.C.

Lambert, R., Bullock, R., and Millham, S. (1973). 'The informal social system', in R. Brown (ed.), *Knowledge, Education and Cultural Change,* London, Tavistock.

Lawton, D. (1977). *Education and Social Justice*, London, Sage.

Liversidge, J. (1958). *Roman Britain*, London, Longman.

Lupton, T. (1963). *On the Shop Floor: Two Studies of Workshop Organization and Output*, Oxford, Pergamon Press.

Maddock, J. (1977). 'Academic stratification and the sustaining of identity types', *Sociological Review*, vol. 25, no. 3, August, pp. 575–84.

Manning, P. K. (1971). 'Talking and becoming: a view of organizational socialization', in J. D. Douglas (ed.), *Understanding Everyday Life: Toward the Reconstruction of Sociological Knowledge,* London, Routledge and Kegan Paul.

Marklund, S. (1972). *The New Role of the Teacher in Swedish Innovative Schools,* Paris, C.E.R.I./O.E.C.D.

Marsden, D. (1971). *Politicians, Equality and Comprehensives*, T. 411, London, Fabian Society.

McLeish, J. (1970). *Students' Attitudes and College Environments*, Cambridge, Institute of Education.

McRobbie, A., and Gerber, J. (1976). 'Girls and sub-cultures: an exploration', in S. Hall and T., Jefferson, *Resistance through Rituals*, London, Hutchinson.

Medlicott, P. (1974). 'Streaming and the comprehensive school', *New Society*, 14 November, no. 162, pp. 414–17.

Merton, R. K. (1968). *Social Theory and Social Structure*, rev. edn, Glencoe, Illinois, Free Press.

Meyann, B. (1979). 'School girls' peer groups', in P. E. Woods (ed.), *Pupil Strategies*, London, Croom Helm.

Ministry of Social Security (1967). *Circumstances of Families*, London, H.M.S.O.

Monks, T. G. (1968). *Comprehensive Education in England and Wales: A Survey of Schools and their Organization*, Slough, N.F.E.R.

Monks, T. G. (ed.) (1970). *Comprehensive Education in Action*, Slough, N.F.E.R.

Morrison, A., and MacIntyre, D. (1971). *Schools and Socialization*, Harmondsworth, Penguin Books.

Morrison, C. M. (1976). 'Ability grouping and mixed-ability grouping in secondary schools', *Educational Issues, Review No. 1*, Edinburgh, The Scottish Council for Research in Education.

Murdock, G., and McCron, R. (1976). 'Youth and class: the career of a confusion', in G. Mungham and G. Pearson (eds.), *Working Class Youth Culture*, London, Routledge and Kegan Paul.

Murdock, G., and Phelps, G. (1973). *Mass Media and the Secondary School*, London, Macmillan.

Nash, R. (1973). *Classrooms Observed*, London, Routledge and Kegan Paul.

National Association of Schoolmasters (1964). *The Comprehensive School: An Appraisal from Within*, London, N.A.S.

National Foundation for Educational Research (1966). 'Research into Comprehensiveness in Education. Joint Statement by Groups I and II', 8 July.

Neave, G. (1975). *How They Fared: The Impact of the Comprehensive School upon the University*, London, Routledge and Kegan Paul.

Newbold, D. (1977). *Ability Grouping – The Banbury Enquiry*, Slough, N.F.E.R. Publishing Co.

Newcomb, T. M. (1947). 'Autistic hostility and social reality', *Human Relations*, vol. I, no. 1, pp. 67–86.

Northway, M. L. (1944). 'A study of the personality patterns of children least acceptable to their age mates', *Sociometry*, no. 7, February, pp. 10–25.

   (1967). *A Primer in Sociometry*, 2nd edn, University of Toronto Press.

Parkinson, M. (1970). *The Labour Party and the Organization of Secondary Education 1918–1965*, London, Routledge and Kegan Paul.

Parlett, M., and Hamilton, D. (1972). *Evaluation as Illumination: A New Approach to the Study of Innovatory Programmes*, University of Edinburgh, Centre for Research in Educational Sciences.

Parsons, T. (1959). 'The school class as a social system: some of its functions in American society', *Harvard Educational Review*, XXIX (Fall), pp. 297–318.

Passow, A. H. (ed.) (1963). *Education in Deprived Areas*, New York, Teachers College, Columbia University.

   (1966). 'Diminishing teacher prejudice', in R. D. Strom (ed.), *The Inner-City Classroom: Teacher Behaviors*, Columbus, Ohio, Charles L. Merril Books.

Passow, A. H., Goldberg, M., and Tannenbaum, A. J. (1967). *Education and the Disadvantaged*, New York, Holt, Rinehart and Winston.

Pedley, R. (1969). *The Comprehensive School*, Harmondsworth, Penguin Books.

Pring, R. (1975). 'Bernstein's classification and framing of knowledge', *Scottish Educational Studies*, vol. 7 (Nov.), pp. 67–74.

Pritchett, R., and Middleton, G. (1967). *Living History, Book One*, Edinburgh, Holmes McDougall.

Procter, C. H., and Loomis, C. P. (1951). 'Analysis of sociometric data', in M. Jahoda, M. Deutsch, and S. Cook (eds.), *Research Methods in Social Relations*, New York, Dryden.

Reynolds, D. (1976). 'When pupils and teachers refuse a truce: the secondary school and the creation of delinquency', in G. Mungham and G. Pearson (eds.), *Working Class Youth Culture*, London, Routledge and Kegan Paul.

Richardson, E. (1973). *The Teacher, the School and the Task of Management*, London, Heinemann.

Ridge, J. M. (ed.) (1974). *Mobility in Britain Reconsidered*, Oxford Studies in Social Mobility, Oxford, Clarendon Press.

Robbins Report (1963). *Higher Education: Report of the Committee Appointed by the Prime Minister under the Chairmanship of Lord Robbins 1961–63*, London, H.M.S.O.

Roethlisberger, F. J., and Dickson, W. J. (1939). *Management and the Worker*, Cambridge, Mass., Harvard University Press.

Ross, J. M., *et al.* (1972). *A Critical Appraisal of Comprehensive Education*, London, N.F.E.R.

Schools Council (1970). *Sixth Form Pupils and their Teachers*, vol. I, London, Schools Council, Books for Schools.

Schur, E. M. (1971). *Labelling Deviant Behavior*, New York, Harper and Row.

Schutz, A. (1972). *The Phenomenology of the Social World*, London, Heinemann.

Sellman, R. R. (1959). *Roman Britain,* London, Methuen.

Sharp, R., and Green, A. (1976). *Education and Social Control*, London, Routledge and Kegan Paul.

Shipman, M. (1971). 'Curriculum for inequality', in R. Hopper (ed.), *Curriculum: Context, Design and Development*, Edinburgh, Oliver and Boyd.

Silberman, M. L. (1969). 'Behavioural expression of teachers' attitudes towards elementary school students', *Journal of Educational Psychology*, vol. 60, no. 5, pp. 402–7.

Silverman, D. (1970). *The Theory of Organizations*, London, Heinemann.

Simpson, I. H., and Simpson, R. L. (1969). 'Women and bureacracy in the semi-professions', in A. Etzioni (ed.), *The Semi-Professions and their Organization*, London, Collier-Macmillan.

Smith, L., and Geoffrey, W. (1968). *The Complexities of an Urban Classroom: An Analysis Toward a General Theory of Teaching*, New York, Holt, Rinehart and Winston.

Smith, L., and Keith, P. M. (1971). *Anatomy of Educational Innovation: An Organizational Analysis of an Elementary School*, New York, Wiley.

Sugarman, B. (1957). 'Involvement in youth culture, academic achievement and conformity in school', *British Journal of Sociology*, vol. 18, no. 2, pp. 151–64.

(1966). 'Social class and values as related to achievement and conduct in school', *Sociological Review*, vol. 14, no. 3, pp. 287–301.

Taylor, P. H. (1971). 'Are colleges of education ready to change?', *Higher Education Review*, vol. 3, no. 2, 1971, pp. 46–52.

Trump, J. L. (1967). International Conference on 'The Changed Role of Teachers Required by Educational Innovations'.

Tucker, M. (1971). 'Relationships in the unstreamed school', *Ideas*, no. 21, December, pp. 15–17.

Turner, R. (1960). 'Sponsored and contest mobility and the school system', *American Sociological Review*, vol. 25, no. 5.

Unstead, R. J. (1961). *Looking at History, Book Two: The Middle Ages,* London, A. and C. Black.

Vaizey, J., and Debeauvais, M. (1961). 'Economic aspects of educational development', in A. H. Halsey, J. Floud, and C. A. Anderson (eds.), *Education, Economy and Society*, London, Collier-Macmillan.

Waller, W. (1961). *The Sociology of Teaching*, New York, Russell (original edn 1932).

Ward, J. P. (1976). *Social Reality for the Adolescent Girl*, Faculty of Education, University College of Swansea.

Warnes, T. (1975). 'French', in R. P. Davies (ed.), *Mixed-ability Grouping*, London, Temple Smith.

Webb, J. (1962). 'The sociology of the school', *British Journal of Sociology*, vol. 13, no. 3, pp. 264–72.

Wedge, P., and Prosser, H. (1973). *Born to Fail*, London, Arrow Books, for the National Children's Bureau.

Willis, P. (1977). *Learning to Labour*, London, Saxon House.

Wilson, A. (1963). 'Social stratification and academic achievement', in H. Passow (ed.), *Education in Deprived Areas*, New York, Teachers College, Columbia University.

Wolcott, H. (1967). *A Kwakiult Village and School*, New York, Holt, Rinehart and Winston.

Woodrow, D. (1973). 'Mixed-ability grouping in Mathematics', *Mathematical Education for Teaching*, April, pp. 47–52.

Woods, P. (1976). 'The myth of subject choice', *British Journal of Sociology*, vol. 27, no. 2 (June), pp. 130–49.

Woods, P. E. (1977). 'Teaching for survival', in P. E. Woods and M. Hammersley, *School Experience*, London, Croom-Helm.

Yates, A. J. (1966). *Grouping in Schools*, London, John Wiley.

Yinger, J. M. (1960). 'Contra-culture and sub-culture', *American Sociological Review*, vol. 25, no. 5, October, pp. 625–35.

Young, M. F. D. (ed.) (1971a). *Knowledge and Control*, London, Collier-Macmillan.

Young, M. F. D. (1971b). 'An approach to the study of curricula as socially organized knowledge' in Young 1971a.

Index

Absence: in bands, 42–4; in mixed-ability, 253–4
Academic orientation, 16, 18, 45–6, 119, 266–8
Academic perspective, 173–5
Althusser, L., 314
Anti-school sub-culture, 68, 71, 72, 76, 86, 94, 101, 116–17, 256–7, 258, 285
Armstrong, M., and Young, M., 7

Bailey, C., 183, 304–5
Ball, S. J., 306
Banbury School, 309
Banding: and academic differentiation, 46–9, 281–3; and attitude to school, 38–9, 43, 44, 65, 68; and curriculum differentiation, 129, 281–2; and discipline, 23, 25, 28, 41–2, 137, 172–3; and examination attainment, 157–2; and friendship choice, 49–52, 283; movement between bands, 34–6; and polarization, 48, 51–2, 69–70, 71, 77, 93–4, 109, 116, 119–21; and social class, 31–4, 79–80, 93–4, 99, 103–7; stereotypes, 29–30, 36–40, 128; and subject choice, 128–32, 141–4; teaching methods, 198, 281–2
Banks, O., 9
Bannister, D., and Fransella, F., 74, 296
Bantock, G. H., 7
Barker-Lunn, J., 308–9, 315
Barnes, D., 225, 226, 232–3, 307
Beachside Comprehensive: ethos, 15–20; history of, 13–20; school roll, 14; staffing, 14, 15
Beachside community, 14, 110

Becker, H. S., 175, 297, 304
Behaviour and performance, 74–5, 88, 90, 97–8, 269–70
Bellaby, P., 4
Benn, C., and Simon, B., 2, 4, 8, 16, 18, 303
Bernbaum, G., 9
Bernstein, B., 19, 20, 72, 197, 225, 234, 285, 288, 314
Birksted, I., 118, 298
Bowles, S., and Gintis, H., 314
Boyfriends, 56, 65, 69, 82, 83, 100–1, 106, 113, 259–60
Brighter child, the, 174, 178–80, 182, 190, 234–5
Bronfenbrenner, U., 116
Bullying, 64, 66, 89, 251
Burgess, T., 156

Cicourel, A., and Kitsuse, J., 122, 299
Circular 10/65, 2, 5, 11
Clark, B., 300
Clubs and extra-curricular activities, 15, 16, 43–4, 56, 57, 63, 81, 86, 252, 253, 260–1
Cohen, A., 49, 68, 258–9
Cohen, S., 38
Coleman, J. S., 115, 118, 297
Comprehensive education: and equality, 31, 152, 176, 280–4; ideologies of, 2, 6–10, 12–13, 23, 280–1, 288–90; and mixed-ability, 170, 176; and social mixing, 7–8, 261–6
Constraints, 18–19, 179–85, 186–8, 286–7
Cox, C. B., and Boyson, R., 315

Creative Design department, 124–5
C.S.E. examinations, 17, 122, 138–9,
  139–48, 159–60, 275–8; Mode III,
  20, 127, 155, 276

Dahllof, U., 238
Dalin, P., 303, 304
Daunt, P., 3, 5, 6, 9
Deitrich, F. R., 261
D.E.S., 122, 301
Detentions, 24, 25, 41, 54–5, 61, 70, 89,
  127, 243–4
Disciplinary perspective, 172–3, 175–6,
  235–6
Domestic Science department, 127
Douglas, J. W. B., 31, 156
Dress, 65–6, 113–14, 115–16, 244
Durkheim, E., 314

Elliot, J., 189, 190, 267
English department, 27, 28, 73, 95–6,
  229–31; exam results, 191, 266; Head
  of department, role in innovation, 170,
  176–7, 190–1
Eraut, M., 233, 286
Esland, G., 140, 164, 304, 185, 286–7
Etzioni, A., 120, 121
Examination achievement, 18–19, 46, 71,
  102–3, 131–3

Feeder primary schools, 30, 51, 244, 249
Flanders, N., 25, 315
Ford, J., xvii, 6, 10, 32, 33, 50, 80, 241,
  265, 266, 309
Framing, 197–8, 225, 231, 233–4
Frankenberg, R., xi, xvi
Fuchs, E., 309
Furlong, V. J., 57

G.C.E. examinations: O-level, 17,
  139–48, 150, 159, 275–8; A-level, 17,
  150–2, 160–2
Geography, 73, 188, 199–201, 255
Gluckham, M., xi, xvi
Goffman, E., 299
Goldthorpe, J., and Llewellyn, C., 300,
  301
Goodlad, J. I., 303
Gronlund, N. E., 53, 248
Gross, N., Giaquinta, J. A., and Berns-
  tein, M., 164, 165, 193, 236, 305

Guess-Who-Tests, 81, 86, 87–8, 115,
  240, 245, 248

Halsey, A. H., 148, 150, 153
Halsey, A. H., and Floud, J., 31
Halsey, A. H., Floud, J., and Martin, F.
  M., 156
Hargreaves, A., 234
Hargreaves, D., xv, xvi, 48, 50, 71, 74,
  114, 116, 119
Hartshorne, H., *et al.*, 297
Headmaster: role in innovation, 169–71;
  views of comprehensive education, 12
History department, 59, 215–29, 249,
  255, 271
Hoare, Q., 6, 9, 315
Holmes, B., 303
Homework, 44–5, 70, 111, 114, 247–8
Hopper, E., 136, 137, 152, 315
House, E., 303
Human Studies, 20, 133–4, 138–9, 300

Idealist perspective, 176–7, 189–91,
  236–7, 266–7
Innovation: debate on, 172–7; implementation of, 167–72, 193–8; natural
  history of, 167–72; theory, 163–7,
  191–2, 237–8, 284–8

Jackson, B., and Marsden, B., 156
Jackson, P., 303
Jennings, H. H., 53, 295
Job destinations, 144–53
Johannesson, I., 261

Keddie, N., xvi, 39, 72, 314
Kelly, A. V., 267
Kelly, G., 72, 295–6
King, R. A., 44, 153
Kollas, D., 305

Lacey, C., xv, xvi, xvii, xviii, 16, 18, 19,
  48, 50, 52, 68, 69, 71, 72, 100, 101,
  109, 114, 116, 119, 121, 148, 156,
  183–5, 255–6, 272, 280, 281, 294,
  297, 298, 299, 302, 308, 312
Lambert, R., Bullock, R., and Millham,
  S., 121
Languages department, 130, 177–9,
  179–80, 188, 209–12
Lawton, D., 4

L.E.A., opposition to mixed-ability, 10–11, 165
Lupton, T., xi, xvi

McLeish, J., 183
McRobbie, A., and Gerber, J., 298
Maddock, J., 39
Marklund, S., 303
Marsden, D., 6, 9, 21
Mathematics department, 35, 41–2, 88, 129, 134, 177–9, 212–15, 251; SMP, 183, 214–5, 281, 306
Meyann, B., 295
Mixed-ability: and attitudes to school, 253; and curriculum differentiation, 215, 267–9; and discipline, 172–3, 234–6, 240, 242–54; evaluation of, 234–7; and examination attainment, 175, 275–8, 309; and friendship choice, 240, 261–6; and polarization, 254–6; and social class, 273–4, 288–9; and social control, 256–9, 285; and social development, 259–61
Monks, T., 3
Morrison, A., and MacIntyre, D., 156
Morrison, C. M., 261
Murdock, G., and McCron, R., 297, 298
Murdock, G., and Phelps, G., 50, 81, 106, 113, 114
Music department, 129, 269

Nash, R., xvi, 313
National Association of Schoolmasters, 4, 7
Neave, G., 161, 162
Newcomb, T. M., 52
Northway, M. L., 63, 295

Option choice: allocation to courses, 141–4, 276–7; and banding, 128–30, 134–5, 136–7, 140–1; and examination results, 132–4, 159–60, 275; and life chances, 144–53; and mixed-ability, 274–8; Mode III C.S.E.s, 127–8, 129, 133–4, 138–9, 276, 299; negotiation, 126–38; procedures, 123–6, 274–5; rejection, 125, 127–8, 277–8; and role of parents, 153–7; and subject status, 138–41

Parents, 60, 64, 84, 87, 104, 122, 131, 136, 153–7, 250, 258, 275
Park, R. E., xvi
Parkinson, M., 4
Parlett, M., and Hamilton, D., 269
Passow, A. H., 295
Passow, A. H., Goldberg, M., and Tannenbaum, A. J., 308
Pastoral care, 15, 16, 26, 64, 256–9
Perspectives, definition of, 175
Pons, V., xi
Pop-media, 56, 66–7, 81, 93, 112–15, 116, 118, 120
Pring, R., 197
Procter, C. H., and Loomis, C. P., 79, 262
Pro-school sub-culture, 68, 71, 94, 107, 116

Remedial classes, 23, 42, 241–2
Richardson, E., 304
Roethlisberger, F. J., and Dickson, W. J., 313
Ross, J. M., *et al.*, 261

Science department, 95, 181–2, 201–9, 249; Biology, 28, 205–7; Chemistry, 29, 101, 130–2, 202–5; Physics, 130–2, 207–9
School Governors, 11, 19
Schur, E., 314
Schutz, A., 47
Sentence Completion Questionnaires, 58, 62–3, 83, 87, 245
Shipman, M., 140
Silberman, M. L., 312
Silverman, D., xvii, 163
Sixth Form: A-levels, 17, 160–2; open policy, 160, 162; and sex differentiation, 158, 160; and social class, 161–2
Smith, M. L., and Keith, P. M., 164, 165, 166, 303, 306
Social class, 14, 31, 52, 108, 117–18, 273–4, 280–4, 297, 310; and academic achievement, 103–7, 157–60, 272–4; and banding, 31–4, 103–5, 158; and friendship choice, 79–80, 93–4, 99–100, 262–6; and mixed-ability, 261–6
Sociometry, 49, 53, 54, 100, 244–60; popularity, 66–7, 82, 92, 99, 115, 244,

260, 295; rejection, 58, 63, 78–9, 85, 88, 95, 256

Subject departments: opposition between, 177–91; reports on preparation for mixed-ability, 194–8; variations in, 186–9

Subject sub-cultures, 182–7, 196, 231, 287

Sugarman, B., 113, 298

Teachers: experience, 15, 102, 249–50; perceptions of pupils, 36–40, 71–6, 76–7, 95–8, 268–71; relations with pupils, 23–4, 282–3

Test scores: and banding, 30; and social class, 31, 32–4

Timetabling, 17, 23

Trump, J. L., 234

Tucker, M., 267

Turner, R., 289

Vaizey, J., and Debeauvais, M., 7

Waller, W., 64

Ward, J. P., 100

Warnes, T., 180

Weber, M., xvi

Wilson, A., 295

Woodrow, D., 180

Woods, P. E., 13, 35, 122, 124, 132, 136, 152, 153–4, 156, 289, 300, 302

Worksheets, 195, 197, 199–200, 202–5, 206–7, 215, 216, 217, 219, 220, 224–9, 233

Young, M. F. D., 140, 302